SATURN:

The King Maker

MRIDULA TRIVEDI

T. P. TRIVEDI

MOTILAL BANARSIDASS
INTERNATIONAL
DELHI

Reprint Edition: Delhi, 2023
First Edition: Delhi, 2017

ISBN : 978-81-19196-61-6

Also available at
MOTILAL BANARSIDASS INTERNATIONAL
H. O. : 41 U.A. Bungalow Road, (Back Lane) Jawahar Nagar, Delhi - 110 007
4261/3 (basement), Ansari Road, Darya Ganj, New Delhi - 110 002
203 Royapettah High Road, Mylapore, Chennai - 600 004
12/1A, 2nd Floor, Bankim Chatterjee Street, Kolkata - 700 073
Stockist : Motilal Books, Ashok Rajpath, Near Kali Mandir, Patna - 800 004

Printed in India
MOTILAL BANARSIDASS INTERNATIONAL

I am glad that Mr. Abhishek Jain, the Publisher of Motilal Banarsidass International, Delhi has agreed to carry forward the legacy of my parents Late Sh. T.P. Trivedi and Smt. Mridual Trivedi. Being the Legal Heir I have granted the rights to print/publish and distribute all the titles earlier published with the parent company

I wish him great success.

Vishal Trivedi

February, 2023

Preface

ग्रहराज्यं प्रयच्छन्ति, ग्रहराज्यं हरन्ति च ।
ग्रहेस्तु व्यापितं सर्वं, जगदेतच्चराचरम् ।।

"Planets can make one a king and snatch away kingdom from any kind and make him a pauper. Planets are omnipresent and exert influence on everything-animate or inanimate."

Saturn's character is enigmatic and contradictory. On the one hand it ruthlessly ruins the native, while on the other hand, if favourable, it catapults him to the status of a king.

The book **Saturn : The King Maker** unravels the King-Maker role of Saturn as well as timing events accurately. The book attempts to present in the first chapter a multidimensional analysis of Saturn as the proper background against which later, the King-Maker role is developed. We have provided a complete delineation of this mysterious planet in the very first chapter entitled **Saturn : Multidimensional Analysis.**

The second chapter named as **Saturn and Spectrum** deals with all physical spiritual and influential properties of Saturn due to unfounded fears, Saturn has been known as the 'Taskmaster', the 'Grim Reaper', 'Father Time', the 'Disciplinarian', the 'Planet of Old Age' and the 'Great Malefic', misleading and are nurtured by narrow mindedness. Saturn is distinguished by being the 6th planet from the Sun, the 2nd largest planet in our solar system, and particularly by the system of three rings surrounding it making it the most spectacular of the planets.

The third chapter provides a detailed description of **Saturn's Placement in the Twelve Houses,** which is necessary to be familiar with the various dimensions that confer several optional nomenclature and appropriate results of the placement of Saturn in various houses.

The fourth chapter deals with **Saturn in Twelve Signs and Aspect of Planets.** The enigmatic Saturn renders a variety of results when placed in different signs or rashis. The impact of Saturn in the various signs is carefully studied and described. Signs play a prominent role in making accurate predictions about the placement of Saturn in a particular sign. Similarly, the aspects of various planets on Saturn or Saturn's aspects over other planets may change the results to an amazing extent. A malefic Saturn may become a benefic, if placed in a suitable and appropriate sign under the aspect of friendly planet or a benefic like Jupiter or Venus.

The fifth chapter unravels the **Different Positions of Mysterious Saturn.** It goes without saying that a purified mind is the essential condition in developing spiritual quest, in reprogramming life by accepting right kind of values and it is here that Saturn's role as a purifying or cleansing crucible is to be understood. The chapter narrates, among other things, Saturn in both Ascendant and Retrograde profiles, giving a treatment to Saturn posited in kendra to the Ascendant as well as a brief discussion on the position of Saturn in all the 12 houses, as many as 26 states of the mysterious Saturn are described. The book ends with a note on the various mantras, Vedic, Pauranik and Tantrik with relevant tips on metal and stones beneficial, as well as articles that should be donated to appease Saturn.

The sixth chapter is named as **The Transiting Saturn:**

The Determinant of Marriage, which determines the marriage of a native since it is the transiting Saturn which brings about this transition of human bondage when it aspects the natal Saturn. There are so many proven principles about the transit of Saturn, which can determine the time of marriage accurately and exactly.

The seventh chapter deals with **Nadi Principles About Saturn's Transit,** which is the soul of this book. The study of this chapter in depth can make one extremely expert in predicting events very accurately, as far as timing of events is concerned. We have explained the Nadi Principles of Transiting Saturn in the most simple way of traditional astrology.

The eighth chapter deals with the crux of the theme and is titled as **Saturn : The Great Timer.** We have observed that Saturn has a great prominence in the birth charts of many celebrities, statesmen and industrialists. It was this insight that triggered further research. The chapter contains detailed event-by-event analysis of the lives of great personalities such as Sheikh Mujibur Rehman, Albert Einstein, Adolf Hitler, Swami Vivekanand, etc. This chapter is very well timed in the series of chapters and is titled **Saturn : The Great Timer.** It contains 12 rules with regards to predicting the exact spell of time interspersed with examples to explain the rules propounded.

The ninth chapter of this great research work titled as **Saturn : The King Maker** deals with the most marvelous and amazing role of Saturn in elevating one to the position of king, Head of the Country, State or industries. Saturn, if well fortified in any birth chart, makes the native an Emperor, the King or the Head of the country or State. Strong well placed and Yoga forming Saturn makes one Prime Minister, Chief Minister or Cabinet Minister. Number of industrialists also have powerful Saturn in the 10th house. Saturn's prominent position in the horoscope with regard to the 10th house can bestow unaccountable success and prosperity to the native with regard to the aspect of his professional position.

On the contrary, adversely disposed Saturn brings miseries, loss of power and fall from a high position. This is dealt in the tenth chapter titled as **Saturn in the 10th House : Fall From Power.**

A majority of astrologers hold that if Saturn is well placed in the 10th house it elevates the individual to dizzy heights and thereafter causes a steep downfall. In the backdrop of this, the present study attempts to marshal data to prove that if Saturn of the 10th house is well associated or aspected by benefics, the downfall does not take place.

The eleventh chapter is titled as **The Sun-Saturn Relationship Regarding Marriage,** which sheds light on the obstructive role played by the Sun and Saturn in setting up a marriage. The fact that if the Sun and Saturn happen to be associated in the 7th house, this association will not let the marriage happen in explained in 9 different combinations of the planets in different houses, by means of actual real life examples.

The twelfth chapter captioned as **Misogamous Role of the Sun and Saturn** which brings out the implications of the conjunction of the Sun and Saturn in the backdrop of the Sun's combination with other planets with a perspective to what such combination spells in regard to matters other than marriage.

The thirteenth chapter is named as **Saturn Jupiter Nexus: An Exposition,** which probes into the questions like (1) whether Jupiter in the 5th house gives daughters,

(2) fifteen salient features about the relationship between Jupiter and Saturn, one of which categorically holds that the combination of Jupiter and Saturn in the 5th house will give no male child or male children will not survive. Other fourteen observations go to establish well reasoned findings with the help of 18 case studies from actual life.

The fourteenth chapter focuses on **Birth in the Sun's Dasa: Elevation in Saturn's Dasa** with special treatment to Elevation in Saturn's Dasha. It is very important to understand the relationship between the Sun's constellation and Saturn's dasha prior to the analysis and interpretation of the horoscope. With special attraction of events from the horoscopes of such political heavyweights as Jyoti Basu, Bala Saheb Thackery, Ram Vilas Paswan, Abraham Lincoln and Indira Gandhi.

This vast research oriented work on the complicated role of the most misunderstood planet, Saturn, could be completed only owing to most valuable, true inspiration and heartfelt blessings provided to me by Trailokya Mohini Tripur Sundari, who was in true sense driving the chariot of knowledge and inspiration every moment. This work has been brought out in such a magnified, unique and intellectual manner only due to the great enlightenment provided to me by the Goddess Tripur Sundari, who has been with me around the clock and kept on guiding me in each and every sentence of this exhaustive research work titled as **Saturn: The King Maker.** Thus and therefore every breath of my life is indebted to the Goddess of Heaven Trailokya Mohini Tripur Sundari in each and every birth.

We are thankful to Mr. Rajeev Prakash Jain, M/s. Motilal Banarsi Dass, Delhi for bringing out the book in such a nice get-up and wide access associated with his name and image.

We also thanks to Mr. Rohit Misra for his unstinted help in preparing the manuscripts in presentable form. Thanks are also due to Dr. Chandrashekhar Vyas, the Director Institute of Professional Studies and Research, Lucknow for his editing support. We are indebted to Mr. Rajesh Tyagi and Mr. Sadashiv Tiwari, whose real cooperation and hard work has made this work on Saturn, the best treatise in the history of astrological writings on the subject of Saturn so far.

We hasten to add that the matter given in our books **"Saturn : The King Maker"** and **"Saturn : The Manager of Events (Marriage, Vocation, Health etc.)"** was published by the publisher M/s. UBS Publishers, Delhi earlier. This all matter was covered in four books named as **Saturn : The King Maker; Re-understanding Saturn; Secrets of Saturn** & **Saturn : Maladies and Remedies.** These books are now being published by M/s MLBD due to certain technical and personal reasons with different titles *i.e.* **Saturn : The King Maker** and **Saturn : The Manager of Events (Marriage, Vocation, Health etc.).**

Lastly we thank our vast readership whose queries and expectations are first and foremost in our minds that have enables us to pen through more than 100 books on making astrology, which is a humane and spiritual science a need and passion of the household.

'Mridul Vatika', 24 Mahanagar Extn.   **Mridula Trivedi**
Opp. E-40, Corporation Quarters,   **T. P. Trivedi**
Pili Colony, Lucknow-06 Tel: 2326625

Vijayadashmi, 11.10.2016

Contents

Contents

About the Book
Saturn: The King Maker

Book **'Saturn: The King Maker'** unravels the king maker role of Saturn in addition to Saturn's significance in timing various vital events of life. **'Saturn: The King maker'**, an unparallel work on the mystiques of Saturn so far, contains 14 chapters. First two chapters deal with the introduction of Saturn as a member of the solar system and its astrological connotations. Much dreaded ruthlessness of Saturn is only a one sided picture and a fuller understanding of this Graha requires systemic study. Various information regarding Saturn, its significations, and occupations & diseases etc under Saturn's control are vividly discussed. Saturn in Puranic contexts makes an interesting reading.

Next two chapters describe in detail Saturn's placement in twelve houses and twelve signs. Introducing various dimensions of different houses of birth chart we proceed discussing the appropriate results of Saturn's position in different bhavas at the time of birth. The enigmatic Saturn renders modified results when placed in different signs or Rashis. The impact of Saturn in various signs is carefully studied. How the aspect of various planets on Saturn, and vice versa, change the results to amazing extent and how the malefic Saturn becomes benefic are the subject matter of these two important chapters.

The fifth chapter unravels the **'Different positions of Mysterious Saturn'** which narrates Saturn in Ascendant and Retrograde profiles as well as brief discussion on the positions of Saturn in 12 houses: as many as 26 states of Saturn are described.

Next three chapters deal broadly with the transit of Saturn. The 6th chapter discusses about proven principles about transit of Saturn which can determine the time of marriage, accurately and exactly. The 7th chapter deals with the 'Nadi principles about Saturn's transit'; expertise in which can make one predict precisely the timing of events. And the 8th chapter 'Saturn the Great Timer' contains detail event-by-event analysis of lives of great personalities and contains various rules with regard to predicting the exact spell of time interspersed with examples to explain the rules propounded.

The chapter on **'Saturn: The King Maker'** deals with crux of the theme, the most marvelous and amazing role of Saturn in elevating one to the position of King, minister, head of the state or of the industries. On the contrary, adverse disposition of Saturn brings fall from power, miseries and losses which is the point of discussion in the chapter Saturn in the 10th house: Fall from power.

Next 4 chapters shed light on the relationship of Saturn with other planets such as Sun and Jupiter which play an important role in deciding events related to marriage, progeny and profession. Thus, in totality, the book demystifies the commonly held view about Saturn's enigmatic character and describes at length its constructive role in molding the basic pattern of life. It is a must read to gain comprehensive knowledge about Saturn and to remove the myths about its malfeasance.

1 SATURN
Multidimensional Analysis

The whole creation is a mystery beyond knowledge acquired through the senses. Since the primeval beginning of consciousness, the eternal melody of Mahamaya's glory has been all pervading. The Divine Mother's will to disseminate One into Many has been creating and annihilating the entire cosmos. The mystery of the universe, which is informed with a wonderful self-discipline, and is yet indescribable and unfathomable has always been agitating the human intellect. Man has been wonder-struck by the motion and influence of the stars and planets which illumine both heaven and earth. Practical Astrology is the wide ranging outcome of the equational research about the influence of the planets or the Grahas, on the one hand, and human inquisitiveness on the other.

Astrology is replete with wonderful description of the nine planets or the Navagrahas. The Graha which is well known for its profound mysteriousness is Shani or Saturn, the deadly, evil-generating progeny of the Sun. In the common man's mind the very name of Shani is a symbol of terror, fearsome behaviour, and unavoidable, gruesome tragedies.

But this notorious ruthlessness of Saturn is a one sided and imperfect picture. A fuller delineation of this Graha requires a thorough and systemic study. The conceptual formulations of astrologers regarding its origin and the range and scope of its influence should be reassessed in the light of the latest modern research.

Saturn : Initial Introduction

Kalyan Varma has described Saturn's appearance by way of sign-depiction :

पिंगो निम्नविलोचनः कृशतनुः दीर्घः शिरालोऽलसः
कृष्णांगः पवनात्मकोऽतिपिशुनः स्नाय्वाततो निर्घृणः ।
मूर्खः स्थूलनखद्विजोतिमलिनो रुक्षोऽशुचिस्तामसः
रौद्रः क्रोधपरो जरापरिणतः कृष्णाम्बरो भास्करिः ।।

that is, "Saturn is the Planet with yellow eyes, downcast glance, a thin body, tall figure is hairy, lethargic, black complexioned, wind-dominated, gossip-loving, strong nerved, ruthless, dull-witted, with thick nails and teeth, shabbily attired, lustreless, profane, of low qualities, bad tempered, old inspiring lowly environment, dressed in black and fearsome".

It is the slowest moving among the nine planets that is why it is called Shanishchar or Shanaischar [Shanaih (slowly) + Chara (moves)]. It has been addressed variously in different contexts—Shanishchara, Chhayasoonu (Shadow-born), Sauri (Sunborn), Taranitanaya (Sun's offspring), Suryasuvan (Son of the Sun), Asit (Non-white), Pangu (Lame), Neelkaya (blue-bodied), Cruel, Krishang (thin limbed), Kapilaksh (yellow-eyed), Yamagraj (Yama's elder brother) and Kona etc. While in English it is Saturn, in Urdu and Persian it is called Judul or Kodvan. It is orignally counted among the evil planets. Although it is established as "Daas" (slave) amongst planets yet astrologers and scientists have accepted it as the most beautiful planet in the heavens.

Sequentially the sixth planet in our solar system, it looks very attractive with its rings. Innumerable tiny stars surround it in a circular expanse. These stars appear as a glowing ring or circle around it. No other planet has such beautifying features. From the earth it appears of a deep blue colour. It has a radius of 1,42,60,00,000 kms.

It is slightly smaller than Jupiter in size, having a gravitational force ninety five times greater than that of the earth. It is situated at a distance of 88,60,00,000 miles from the Sun and 89,00,00,000 miles from the earth. It takes 29 years to complete one revolution round the Sun, and stays in one Rashi for about 2.5 years. It is supposed to have ten moons. A period of 38 days elapses between its setting and rising again. After which it moves with normal speed for 135 days and with a retrograde motion for 105 days. Moving retrograde it sets in the west.

Origin of the Gotra :

Shani is born of Chhaya (shadow), the wife of the resplendent Sun god. It is also praised as *"Kaashyapeyam Mahaddyutim"* because it is acknowledged as belonging to the lineage of the sage Kashyap. One school believes that the Kaashyapeya yagya which was performed under the supervision of the great sage Kashyap is connected with Shani's birth.

Colour :

From the point of view of colour or complexion, Shani is not very attractive. Because of its dim glow, being the smallest and most distant member of the planetary family according to an ancient belief, it appears of an ash grey colour. Because of this deep grey blue tint bordering on black, it gives a fearsome and unattractive impression. That is why substances like coal, iron, black cloth and mustard oil etc are prescribed for *"Daan"* (giving away or donation) to appease it.

Situation :

Astrologers have declared its permanent abode in the west. With repect to India, Saurashtra, that is Gujarat and Kathiyawar, are its dominion. Generally mysteriously hidden valleys, caves, deserts, mountains, ruined houses, coal mines, dirty smelly places, cremation grounds, grave yards, church compounds or cemeteries, barren and infertile lands etc. are known to be under its domination.

Mount :

The mount of an individual or planet is according to its shape and nature. Saturn has also selected its mount suited to its fearsome, arid and lowly (*taamsik*) characteristics. It is known to travel mounted on a Vulture, a bird which is a symbol of lethargy, gluttony, selfishness, insensitivity, ire, violence, physical strength, fondness for flesh, farsightedness and lowly nature. All these characteristics are fully reflected in Shani.

Influence :

When Saturn is located in the west during the course of its movement, it influences the western hemisphere with its direct rays. Saurashtra in India is situated in that direction. All animate beings and inanimate matter feel the changes internally as well as externally caused by the disturbance of its rays. Besides, Saturn inspires and influences the very nature of the area belonging to the Rashi (sign) through which it happens to be passing. This influence extends to all overt and covert beings, humans, vegetation, produce of the earth, environment, atmosphere, creatures other than humans, even atoms present in any form in the cosmos. Right from the watery depths of the oceans to the limitless expanse of the space all are affected by Saturn's potent rays. Its strongest influence is perceived on the sensitive mental structure of the homosapiens.

Shape and Nature :

Learned astrologers have defined and described Saturn's external and inherent characteristics variously. Acharya Varah-mihir has dedicated one chapter to Saturn's description in his famous work "Brihatsamhita". According to him:

मन्दोऽलसः कपिलदृक् कृशदीर्घगात्रः ।
स्थूलद्विजः परुषरोमकचोऽनिलात्मा ।।

that is, Saturn is a planet which is dull-witted, lazy, yellow-eyed, thin and tall bodied, ugly toothed, wind dominated in nature and rough-haired. The dard complexioned Saturn has inherited his incendiary power from his sire–the Sun–and he, therefore, chars people with the fire of terrible miseries. He influences the nervous system, old clothes, iron, winter season, soury taste and filthy places.

Mantreshwar has expressed his thoughts in the following words :

पंगुर्निम्नविलोचनः कृशतनुर्दीर्घः शिरालोऽलसः ।
कृष्णांगः पवनात्मकोऽतिपिशुनः स्नाय्वात्मको निर्घृणः ।।

This shloka or couplet is also attributed to Kalyan Varma. "Lameness" has been added to other characteristics. Saturn's influence extends to sense of touch, sesame seeds, death, abode of people of low status, air etc. Mantreshwar has underlined the tamsik nature (negative & harmful qualities) of Saturn. According to Daivagya Mahadeva :

क्रियास्वपटुः कातराक्षः कृशदीर्घांगो बृहद्दन्तो
रूक्षतनूरुहो वातात्मा कठिनवाक् निन्द्यो मन्दः ।

6   *Saturn : The King Maker*

Lack of expertise, fearful eyes, notoriety, harsh language etc. are his special attributes.

Acharya Dhundhiraj has underlined qualities like evil spiritedness, abundance of matted locks and wicked deeds.

श्यामलोऽतिमलिनश्च शिरालः सालसश्च जटिलः कृशदीर्घः ।
स्थूलदंतनखपिंगलनेत्रोऽयुक् शनिः खलतानिलकोपः ।।

According to the Astrologer Vaidyanath, Saturn's complexion is dark like *Doorva* (a kind of grass). His temperament is dominated by phlegm as well as wind. He rises from the West. Saturn is fourfooted, fond of roaming in forests and on mountains, bitter-natured and sharp sighted. His deity is Brahma and gem is blue sapphire. From the Ganga to the Himalayas is his domain. The terrible power of Saturn is manifested in Libra-Capricorn-Aquarius signs, the house of wife, the hemisphere south of equator, Dreshkan birth chart, in own house, Saturday, own period, the end period of a Rashi, dark fortnight and retrograde placement. He specially influences people of low castes. He is defeated by the Sun, but overpowers Mars. In the words of Vaidyanath :

काठिन्यरोमावयवः कृशात्मा दूर्वासितांगः कफमारुतात्मा ।
पीनद्विजश्चारुपिशंगदृष्टिः सौरिस्तमोबुद्धिरतोऽलसः स्यात ।।

Saturn's characteristics accepted by Jaideva are—old age, bird like appearance, significator of land, mixed parentage and thick lips.

शनिः कृशः श्यामलदीर्घदेहोऽलसोऽनिलात्मा कपिलेक्षणश्च ।
पृथुद्विजः स्थूलनखौष्ठकेशः शठः शिरौजाः पिशुनः स्वभावात् ।।

Jaideva has also mentioned his veins being full of glowing energy ("*Tej*").

According to Acharya Punjraj Saturn is stupid, lazy, thin, dark and dirty-bodied, argumentative, strong-nerved, yellow-eyed, dominated by wind and bile and with ugly nails, teeth and hair.

मूर्खोऽलसः कृष्णतनुः कृशांगः स्यात् स्नायुसारो मलिनोऽतिदीर्घः ।
क्रोधी जरत् पिंगदृशोऽर्कसूनुः सपैत्त्ररूवायुः पृथुरोमदन्तः ।।

Punjraj has also found worth mentioning the powerfulness of Saturn in the absence of Sun : 'रविजस्तथाऽन्ते'.

In the opinion of Sage Parashar Saturn belongs to "*Shudra Varna*", is dependent on darkness and powerful at twilight hours. He dominates rough matter and things and unfortunate persons. In his words :

शनिः शूद्रः तमः बली ज्ञेयो दिनशेषे दुर्भगाद् सूर्यपुत्रकः ।
नीरसान् सूर्यपुत्रश्च गृहेषु मन्दो वृद्धोऽस्ति ।।

In another shloka Parashar has described Shani as a coarse-haired Brahmin : 'खररोमकचो द्विजः'.

The famous astrologer Acharya Gunakar has described Saturn's attributes as follows :

दुःखं दिनेशात्मजः । दुःखदायकः प्रेष्यः सहस्त्रांशुजः ।
भास्करिः कृष्णदेहः धातुः स्नायुः । वसतिः क्षित्युत्करः ।
वस्त्रं स्फाटितं । लोहधातुः शिशिरर्तुः क्षाररुचिः ।

Wherein besides the characteristics enumerated earlier Saturn's dominance over service and soury tastes has been stressed.

Apart from these oriental masters of astrology among the western thinkers who have pondered deeply on Saturn's characteristics the names of Lily and Alan Leo are in the forefront. Many a time they differ from the Indian schools of thought.

William Lily believes that Saturn is located in an orbit further than Jupiter's orbit. It is a lustreless, ash grey planet. While going retrograde and direct it stays immobile for five days.

Alan Leo maintains that Saturn dominates Capricorn and Aquarius signs of the zodiac. In Libra it is exalted. The point on which the influence of Sun ceases is the one from where Saturn's area of influence begins. That is why Saturn is also called Seemagraha (the planet on the fringe). Saturn torments the universe with miseries and misfortunes.

Acharya Varahmihir has thrown light on the good and evil attributes of Saturn in the 21st shloka of the 10th chapter of "Brihat Samhita" :

वैदूर्यकान्तिविमलः शुभकृत्प्रजानां वाणातसीकुसुमवर्णनिभश्च शस्तः।
यं चापि वर्णमुपगच्छति तत्सवर्णान् सूर्यात्मजः क्षपयतीति मुनिप्रवादः।।

That is, Saturn proves to be beneficial to persons when it possesses a beautiful blue tint that of flower of Alasi. But acquiring other hues it afflicts people according to the colour.

Saturn-dominated individual : At a Glance

Generally each individual's life is directly or indirectly influenced by the activity of Shani. But it predominates in certain birth charts. In other words it can be called the chief planet of that birth chart. Such a person is then called "Shani Pradhan Jataka" or Saturn-dominated individual.

According to Lily, a Saturn-dominated individual can be classified as per his physical characteristics. Such a person is of medium built, has a dull and dusky complexion, black and narrow eyes, doleful glance, high forehead, black, coarse and curly hair, large ears, downward tilted eyebrows, small chin and full nose and lips. The body is dryness prone. The face is clouded with worries or sorrows. Shoulders are broad but uneven, stomach is pulled-in, and knees and feet are shaped awkwardly. The gait appears to be that of someone intoxicated. When Shani is situated in the east then roughness is somewhat less, but when it is in the west then hair is sparse, and thinness and darkness are more pronounced.

"Shara"-lessness in Saturn gives extreme slimness while with excess of "Shara" the physique is fleshy. A southward "Shara" makes for a stout but agile body. Northerly "Shara" renders the body hirsute and plump. A stable Saturn gives average fullness to the body. When it is direct it makes for an ill proportioned and thin body.

When Saturn is favourably placed in the birth chart, enhancing auspiciousness, the individual's life, personality and conduct are comparatively disciplined. He believes in speaking only after considering all pros and cons, and that too in very few words. His behaviour is systematic. He likes expressing his logical, deep and well thought-out opinions on all important issues. But Saturn-dominated individuals have to put in unnecessary and unexpected hard-work. Always being involved in some or the other business is their destiny. They take initiative in contributing freely to social and personal interaction.

On the other hand, if Saturn is unfavourably influencing the birth chart the individual's life is full of chaos. Such persons pick-up enmity with others without any rhyme or reason. They are constantly consumed by greed and jealousy. They do not find anybody worth trusting in the whole world. Their conversation and life style make them appear as afflicted with unbearable problems. They are paranoid because of their inferiority complex. They depend on lying, idleness, miserliness and deceitful behaviour. They lack respect for womenfolk and treat them as mere objects of lust. These frustrated individuals earn unpopularity because of their masochist disposition. They stick to their reasonable or firm opinions to the extent of absurdity. These malicious individuals do not forget to take revenge even after long gaps of time. Crookedness is their policy. They mock religion, culture and traditions. Even in everyday transactions they disregard accepted mores and use foul language. Conning other people all the time, these individuals are also gluttons.

Alan Leo, a western thinker, has depicted the positive side of the above noted features. According to him the excessive calm, sobriety and thoughtfulness of these natives cause misleading and false notions to become current about them. In their appearance, temperament and thinking a lasting imprint of maturity is perceptible. Extreme self confidence results in an uncommon cleverness in them. Such a native does not accept anybody's superiority easily. Some people may called their ability to deal with and please different persons in different ways, cunningness. They are alert, thrifty and narrow minded. They feel relaxed only when maintaining a certain aloofness from others. They do not believe in excessive and outward expression of joy. They are always making lots of plans because of their farsighted and ambitious nature. A knack of distinguishing between reality and illusion is a speciality of such natives.

The views of Mr. H.N. Katve :

Noted astrologer Mr. H.N. Katve has been long admired for his books of thoughtful research. After a critical study of various schools of thought he has ascertained the internal and external characteristics of the Saturn-dominated natives, both when Saturn is placed favourably and unfavourably in the birth chart.

According to him when Saturn is favourably placed in the birth chart of the individual, his personal, familial and social attributes are enhanced. Such individuals plan and actively participate in programmes of social and economic change which would contribute to public welfare. They have self confidence without being over arrogant. They are interested in deep study of difficult subjects. Book publishing, spread of knowledge, helping others, detachment, love of justice, self respect, hard work, discipline, founding of institutions, following own decisions, stubborn persistence and bearing a grudge are the characteristics which become manifest. Such natives excel in knowledge of subjects which are supernatural or metaphysical. They wish well for their country and the entire world. They diligently fulfil their work and ceaselessly follow their goal against all odds, without caring for public opinion, if they are convinced of the rightness of their beliefs. That is why people take their advice and suggestions very seriously and confer rights on them. Because of their secretive nature the love or intention of such natives is not known easily. They have few friends. They are interested in legal intricacies and political activeness. Such a placement of Saturn also causes Dattak Yoga or chances of adoption.

When Saturn is unfavourably placed in the birth chart, the native manifests unexpected and unbecoming tendencies. Jealousy, over spending, harsh speech, addiction to vices, lustfulness, unrestrained behaviour, licentious conduct, laziness, lack of activeness, untrustworthiness, arrogance, dishonesty, disloyalty, misappropriation of others' wealth are the symptoms which predominate. Profession in medicine suits them. If they gain power and position they prove extremely cruel, wicked and unbridled rulers. Obviously the adverse influence of Saturn overcomes and frustrates the entire personality.

Saturn in Puranic contexts :

Numerous references are available in ancient Indian texts explicating the unique and multifarious characteristics of Saturn or Shanideva. These references enunciate directly and symbolically the might of this planet. To fully reveal the character of Saturn a perusal of these ancient texts is absolutely necessary. They delineate how, right from Incarnations of God to mighty emperors were affected by Saturn's potent energy.

1) The Birth Lore :

When Parabrahama created 'Aadidevtrayi' (the primal Divine Trinity of Brahama, Vishnu and Shiva), it was Lord Shiva who took the heavier responsibility of annihilation of the creation. Controlling and disciplining each living being in the creation according to its conduct was a difficult task. To help him in this stupendous work he brought into being associate Ganas. About this time itself Chhaya gave birth to the nine sons of Bhaskara, the Sun God. Among these nine sons, Shani and Yama displayed amazingly fearsome potentiality, therefore, Shiva the Destroyer accepted them in his ministration. He bestowed on Shani the authority to punish according to Karma or conduct. Yama was appointed for Death. This ancient account furnishes several deep hints concerning Shani's activities as well as underlines the importance of worshipping Shiva in placating Shani.

2) Saturn and Sun :

Saturn tops the list of Surya's nine sons in fierceness. The dark complexioned Yamuna is Saturn's sister and Yama, the controller of death is his younger brother. Saturn's harshness is also caused by his strange family. According to ancient myths Surya, the Sun God, allocated a separate 'loka' to each of his progeny on attaining maturity. But

Saturn, who was by nature evil and greedy, was not satisfied with reigning over only one Loka. He made a plan to invade all the other Lokas. Surya was extremely pained by this maldesign of Saturn. But his sane counsel had no effect on Saturn's evil intention. Eventually Surya appealed to Lord Shiva. Ever ready to deliver his devotee from fear Lord Shiva appeared and warned the impudent Saturn. When Saturn ignored him a battle ensued between the two. Saturn vanquished all the Ganas of Lord Shiva along with Nandy and Veerbhadra with his amazing valour. On seeing the destruction of his army Shiva was outraged and he opened his third eye. Saturn also targeted him with his eye's deadly vision. The whole of Saturn 'Loka' was engulfed in an unparalleled light born of the two mighty sights. An enraged Shiva then struck Saturn with his trident. Saturn could not withstand its blow and fell unconscious. Seeing his son in this state, Surya was overcome with grief. He prayed Shiva to spare Shani's life. Easy to please Shiva eliminated all the troubles of Saturn. After this Saturn accepted Shiva's omnipotence and sought forgiveness from him. Impressed by the fighting skill of valiant Saturn Lord Shiva admitted him in his service and appointed him the executor of punishment.

3) Saturn and Harishchandra :

A scion of Raghukul, King Harishchandra is ever remembered for his truthfulness and generosity. He always enjoyed the blessings of devine powers. Despite this he could not escape Saturn's devastating influence.

To test Harishchandra's truthfulness, Indra, the king of Deities, called on Sage Vishwamitra, who sought Saturn's co-operation to harass Harishchandra with endless troubles. Harishchandra was known the worldover for his popularity. Yet his life was assailed with terrible tragedies because of

Shani's adverseness. His kingdom was lost. He had to sell his son, his wife and even himself to pay the amount of Dakshina. He suffered under the influence of Shani's seven and a half year's period of ordeal. Transformed as a snake Shani bit Rohit, the son of king Harishchandra. When Shaivya, the king's wife, went to cremate Rohit's corpse, Harishchandra who was working as a Chandal's servant at the cremation ground asked her to pay the tax for cremation. When Shaivya tried to tear a portion of her *Sari* to pay the tax Vishwamitra and Shani appeared. It was the climax of Harishchandra's trial. Vishwamitra restored his kingdom. When the king came to know of Saturn's predominant role in his tragic predicament, he cursed Shani that those individuals who abided by religious laws and had a pious conduct, shall not be affected by Saturn's evil influence. This episode highlights the trouble-causing role of Saturn.

4) Saturn and Nala :

Nala was an emperor unsurpassed in valour, wealth, fame, piety and looking after the welfare of his subjects. His younger brother Pushkara, too, tread in his footsteps Nala's wife empress Damyanti could bewitch the three Lokas with her beauty. She had married Nala after choosing him in a Swayamvara from amongst a galaxy of kings and deities.

Although Saturn himself was not present as a suitor of Damyanti at the Swayamvara, he could not tolerate the defeat of other deities. He started his evil designs to destroy the happy conjugal life of Nala and Damyanti as well as their prosperous kingdom.

Saturn influenced Nala's younger brother Pushkara's good sense so that he challenged Nala to a game of dice. Ill starred Nala played despite a premonition of defeat,

Pushkara won all his wealth with his gambling tricks. Nala was forced to relinquish his kingdom and leave for the woods with his wife in a state of utter helplessness and penury. He faced tremendous hardship there. Ill luck doggedly followed him. In a moment of utter dejection he even forsook his beloved wife. Leaving her asleep he escaped.

Somehow Damyanti reached her paternal home. All this while Nala had to serve in a stable as a horse-keeper. Damyanti came to know of the cause of her predicament from the learned men of her father's kingdom. The astrologers told her that all the tragedies were caused by Saturn's evil eye on Nala. Damyanti started the prescribed treatment to placate Saturn. She also worshipped Lord Hanuman with single minded devotion. The evil influence of Saturn started to wane. Gradually Nala and Damyanti regained their lost glory.

5) Saturn and Lord Rama :

The whole world is familiar with the ideal life history of *Maryada Purushottam Shri Rama*. Saturn caused terrible upheavals in his blameless life. His stay in the forests and all the other subsequent happenings were doings of Saturn, it is believed.

6) Saturn and Pippalad Muni :

This ancient lore explains the reason of Saturn's slow movement. Pippalad Muni lost his father when he was only a child. Saturn had tormented his father terribly when he was passing his life as a sage on the banks of the river Yamuna. He died of ceaseless attacks of poverty and disease. Pippalad's mother regarded Saturn as the sole cause of her husband's death.

When Pipplad came of age he came to know of these

facts from his mother. He was terribly angry with Saturn, the killer of his father, and started looking for him. All of a sudden he saw Saturn on a Peepal tree. He aimed his *Brahmadanda*, which he had acquired through the power of his penance, at Shani. The *Brahmadanda* followed and tortured Saturn throughout the three Lokas. Finally it broke both his legs. Anguished Saturn prayed to Lord Shiva fervently. Shiva appeared and enlightened the sage that Saturn was only following the laws of creation. It is not possible to overcome the movement of Time, so Saturn was not to be blamed for Pippalad's father's death.

Pippalad forgave Saturn. He said that reciting of this story and worshipping Pippaleshwar Lord Shiva would help avoid troubles caused by Saturn.

Because of his legs being broken by *Brahmadanda* Shani's natural speed was hindered and he came to be known as the slow mover.

7) **Saturn and Shri Hanuman :**

The happenings delineated in this ancient lore speak of not only Saturn and Shri Hanuman but also of the tragic fate of Ravana, the king of Rakshasas.

The entire cosmos trembled in the face of Ravana's invincible might. He was well versed in all the Veda-Vedangas, was an unparalled warrior, owner of unlimited wealth and conqeuror of the three Lokas. He was also an expert of all the overt and occult disciplines of knowledge, of astrology, limitless power of spirituality and fine application of Tantra. Ravana could suspend the motion of constellations and planets. But even he had to suffer punishment for having slighted Saturn.

Considering Saturn and Mahakal, the greatest impediments in his quest for immortality, Ravana invaded

Shani-loka. Both Saturn and Mahakal put up a tremendous defensive fight but Ravana had the boon from Brahma that, except man, monkey, and bear, he would not be vanquished by anybody else. He badly wounded Saturn with the trident given to him by Lord Shiva, and tying with Brahmapasha, hanged him upside down in Lanka's prison house. Mahakal was also imprisoned and kept immobile near Saturn. Both of them, who were co-operators in the operations of creation invoked their master Lord Shiva, who appeared before them and told them that even they were not free from the laws of Brahma. He assured them that after some time they would be freed on the arrival of Shri Hanuman.

When Hanuman set Lanka to fire, he was surprised to see that despite burning, the city was not turning black. Then he noticed the hanging Saturn who was lamenting his bad luck. He introduced himself to Hanuman and told him how Ravana had nailed his might with his power of Yoga. If he were freed, he would turn the golden Lanka to ashes. When Hanuman freed Saturn he cast his evil eye on Lanka which instantly became black as ash. Then he requested Hanuman how he could repay him. Hanuman told him that he should not torment his devotees in future. Likewise Hanuman also freed Mahakal.

Later on Ravana had to suffer the retaliatory anger of Shani. He was destroyed with all his family.

8) Saturn and Pandavas :

Shani extended his influence to afflict Pandavas who were happily reigning in their kingdom. Shani perverted Draupadi's mind and made her use harsh words for Duryodhana. This led to the game of dice, resulting in loss of everything. Later during their stay in the forest, when Bheema had the auspicious of Lord Hanuman, then only the evil influence of Saturn was removed by him and Pandavas won the war.

9) Saturn's downcast glance :

The secret of Saturn's downcast glance and cruelty is hidden in the curse given by his wife. Saturn was deeply devoted to Lord Krishna right from his childhood. Day and night he worshipped Krishna. When Saturn reached maturity his father Surya married him to the strong charactered, and accomplished daughter of Chitraratha. Once having had her ritual bath after the menstruation period, she went to Saturn, desiring a son. But Saturn was engrossed in meditation. He did not even look up to her. Her desire was unfulfilled. She was hurt and cursed him that in future his eyes would always remain downcast and whomsoever he would look at, would be destroyed. Although she was repentant later on when her anger subsided, yet the curse had taken effect. Since then Saturn's glance became downcast forever.

10) Saturn and Dasharatha :

Astrologers opine that if Saturn crosses the constellation Rohini, it causes "Rohini Shakat Bhedan Yoga", which results in a terrible famine for twelve years, that ends in Pralaya or total destruction. When King Dasharatha of the *Ikshavaku* dynasty was ruling, this Yoga was going to take place. At the advice of sages to prevent Saturn from causing this catastrophe, he reached the Nakshatra-loka, mounted on his chariot. When Saturn did not relent even after verbal persuasion Dasharatha attacked him. Saturn was impressed by his valour and devotion to duty. He offered to grant him a boon. Dasharatha asked him never to do "Shakat Bhedan" when the Sun and other planets were present. Saturn consented.

Afterwards a grateful Dasharatha praised Saturn with beautiful verses. Pleased, Saturn offered to grant him one more boon. Dasharatha asked that he should not torment anyone without reason. Granting the boon, Saturn said that if he was placed in the first, fourth or eighth house in a birth chart, he could afflict the Jataka with deadly troubles. Bit if the individual native worshipped Saturn's idol and recited the verses composed by Dasharatha in praise of Saturn, then he would not torment him. On the contrary he would protect such native.

Significance of Ancient Myths :

It is a special feature of Indian culture that it is steeped in a unique system of symbols. Puranic tales establish symbolic truth. Tales referring to Saturn throw an interesting light on his shape and disposition.

The impact of Saturn's cruel glance is well known. The native afflicted with it gets involved in a series of mishaps. According to Acharya Shatrughna Lal Shukla, "physical problems, paucity of funds, loss of prestige, impediments in work, running away, exile, imprisonment, poverty, confusion, danger from enemies etc. are several painful situations which confront a native. Such a Saturn afflicted individual can be called a chronic patient of misfortune. Even when the beneficial effect of other planets lends support, Saturn's evil effect has to be borne" (Bhartiya Tantra Vidya, p. 369). In terms of a modern interpretation, it can be said that Saturn is the responsible guard of the eternal law of the Almighty who is omnipresent, invisible yet present in each particle of the creation.

Saturn's Significations :

According to planetary system each Graha or Planet

rules over certain things, instincts, results, areas and activities. Before one predicts the effects of a planet a thorough knowledge of the planet's range of influence is essential.

Although every astrologer has dwelt upon this aspect of the planets, yet the poet Kalidasa in his "Uttara Kalamrita" has given a detailed account of "Karakatva". In this context five of his shlokas are quotable :

जाड्यादिप्रतिबन्धकाश्वगजचर्मार्यप्रमाणानि संक्लेशो
व्याधिविरोधदुःखमरणस्त्रीसौख्यदासीखराः ।। 1 ।।

चण्डाला विकृताङ्घ्रिनो वनचरा वीभत्सदानेश्वरा,
आयुर्दायनपुंसकान्त्यजखगास्त्रेधाग्निदासक्रियाः ।
आचारेतररिक्तपौरुषमृषावादित्वदीर्घानिला
वृद्धस्नायुदिनान्तवीर्यशिशिरत्वत्यन्तकोपश्रमाः ।। 2 ।।

कुक्षित्रोदिकुंडगोलकजनिर्मलिन्यवस्त्रं   गृहं
तादृग्वस्तुमनोविचारखलमैत्रीकृष्णपापानि च ।
क्रौर्यं भस्म च नीलधान्यमणिलोहौदार्यसंवत्सराः ।
शूद्रो विट्पितृकारकोऽन्यकुलविद्यासंग्रहः पंगुता ।। 3 ।।

तीक्ष्णं कम्बलवस्त्रपश्चिममुखे संजीवनोपायका-
ऽधोदृष्टी कृषिजीवनायुधगृहजातिर्बहिःस्थानकाः ।
ईशान्यप्रियनागलोकपतने   संग्रामसंचारिता
शल्यं सीसकदुष्टविक्रमतुरुष्का जीर्णतैलेऽपि च ।। 4 ।।

दारुब्राह्मणतामसे   च विषभूसंचारकाठिन्यके
भीतिर्दीर्घनिषादवैकृतशिरोजाः सर्वराज्यं भयम् ।
छागाधा महिषादयो रतिरतो वस्त्रादिशृंगारताः
मृत्यूपासकसारमेहरणाः कठिन्यचित्तं शनेः ।। 5 ।।

According to the points mentioned in the above shlokas,

Shani is the ruling planet of the following—Stupidity, hindrance, imprisonment, horse, elephant, income, proof, troubles, disease, opposition, sorrow, death, female, company, ass, 'chandal', physical handicap, wild creatures, repulsiveness, generosity, longevity, impotence, low-born, bird, ghost, fire, slave, conduct, manliness, loss, lying, wood, air, old, nerves, evening, semen, winter season, extremely foul temper, hard labour, illeginimate, offspring, slovenliness, home, filthy clothes, impious thoughts, friendship with the wicked, heinous sin, cruelty, ashes, black colour (dark complexion), grains, iron, large heartedness, year, shudra, vaishya, father, knowledge about other families, lameness, sharpness, blanket, west direction, means of livelihood, downcast gaze, farming, weapons, caste, foreign lands, battle in Naagloka, debate, staying elsewhere than home, surgery, lead, daredevil courage, the Turks, old oil, brahmin, evil nature, strong veins, kingdom, male goat, sexual intercourse, cloth, make-up, death worship, dog, deer, hard-heartedness, worshipper of Yama, rule by common people, fearsome face, representative of father, height, etc.

Apart from Kalidass, Kalyan Varma, Gunakar, Vaidyanath, Parashar, Vyankat Sharma, Mantreshwar, Vaidyaranya and William Lily have reflected upon Saturn's Karakatva. Their references are important enough to be mentioned.

According to Kalyan Varma :

त्रपुसीसकाललोहककुधान्यमृतबन्धभृतकानाम् ।
नीचस्त्रीपण्यकदासवृद्धजनदीक्षाप्रभुः सौरिः ।।

that is, Saturn is significator of tin, lead, iron, light grains, pall bearers of the dead, buying and selling of low status women, slaves, the old, and initation rites.

Mantreshwar has added a few more items in the list of Saturn's significators. He says :

तैलक्रयी भृतकनीचकिरातकायस्काराश्च
दन्तिकरताश्च पिकाः शनौ स्युः।
बौद्धाहितुण्डिकखराजवृकोष्ट्रसर्प-
ध्वांतादयो मकरमत्कुणकृम्युलूकाः।।

वातश्लेष्मविकारपादविहतिं चापत्तितन्द्राश्रमान्
भ्रान्तिं कुक्षिरुगन्तरुष्णभृतकध्वंसं च पार्श्वाहतिम्।
भार्यापुत्रविपत्तिमंगविहतिं हृत्तापमर्कात्मजो
वृक्षाश्मक्षतिमाह कश्मलगणैः पीडां पिशाचादिभिः।।

that is, merchant of oil, slave, low person, wild creature, iron smith, elephant, cuckoo, snake-charmer, a Buddhist, ass, male-goat, wolf, camel, snake, crow, mosquito, bed bugs, owl, wind and cough dominated problems, disease of legs, labour, confusion, pain in ribs, lack of servants, troubles on wife or children, heart disease, injury from tree or stone, being possessed by spirits etc. fall under the control of Saturn.

Gunakara also considers Saturn to be the significator of slaves. The opinion of learned Vaidyaranya is also not different, hence it need not be quoted separately, while Vaidyanath maintains that :

आयुर्जीवनमृत्युकारणविपत्संपत्प्रदाता शनिः।
दारिद्र्यदोषजनिकर्मपिशाचचौरैः
क्लेशं करोति रविजः सह सन्धिरोगैः।।

the causes of longevity or death, wealth, troubles, poverty, haunting by ghosts, disease of the joints and terrible ordeals are signified by Saturn.

The sage Parashar has added a few more points to the aforesaid range of significations from his own experience. He says :

आयुष्यं जीवनोपायं दुःखशोकमहद्भयम् ।
सर्वक्षयं च मरणं मन्देनैव विनिर्दिशेत् ।।

महिषायगजतैलवस्त्रशृंगारप्रयाणसर्वराज्यदावार्युधगृहयुद्धसंचार-
शूद्रनीलमणिविघ्नकेशशल्यशूलरोगदासदासीजनायुष्यकारकः शनिः ।

Wood, weapons, family feuds (or civil war), blue gems are also dominated by Saturn.

William Lily maintains two standpoints while considering Shani's governance. One is occupation and the other is disease. The following occupations are governed by Shani— begging, clowning, cultivation or farming, leather making, manual labour at night time, mining, dealing in tin, pottery making, broom making, plumbing, brick making, cookery, chimney sweeping, digging, horse or cart driving, dealing in coal, horticulture, candle making, cattle keeping and manufacturing black fabric. As far as diseases are concerned the following fall under Shani's control—dental problems, problems in the right ear, fever due to heat, depression, tuberculosis, jaundice, migrane, hypochondria, shivering, madness, arthritis, haemorrhage, fractures, cramps and dropsy.

Besides the above noted matters, others that can be included as falling under Shani's control are banking, lending money, factories and laws and rules governing them, geology, Muslim law, partnership, printing and pressing factory, brokership, insurance companies, medicine, agricultural education, laws governing land belonging to the state, Roman laws, archaeology, neurology, 'Hathayog', high court, judiciary, municipal corporations, district councils, legislature, underworld activities, villainy, penal code, foreign secrets, orthopaedic diseases, kidney and liver diseases, venereal diseases, malodorous perspiration etc.

Occupations related to Saturn

Generally occupation is indicated by the tenth house. The lord of mavamansh occupied by the 10th lord plays the chief role in deciding the 'individuals' occupation. The planet in the 10th house, its lord and the planets aspecting the 10th house - together they determine the kind of occupation. The subject of determining the occupation in itself is very wide and large, therefore we propose to bring out a separate volume on it. Here, it would suffice to say that in case Saturn happens to be the determining planet then the following occupations are indicated :

1. Service

2. Leather related occupation, such as manufacturing of shoes, chappals, purses, bags, etc.

3. Any occupation dealing with iron, such as steel factory or manufacturing iron utensils. Even stainless steel comes under Saturn's purview.

4. All types of oil related occupation such as production or sale of oil.

5. Carpentry or furniture making is indicated by Saturn. However, the wood is signified by Sun.

6. The legal profession, advocates, judges, law officers or lower ranking workers in the legal profession.

7. Tea leaves, coffee etc. are indicated by Saturn.

8. Typing, or occupations related to it *i.e.* clerical work. Woollen garments or knitting and weaving of blankets, carpets, rugs etc. lie also in Saturn's domain.

9. Beggary or related work, if malefic and debiliated Saturn indicates occupation.

10. Brokership, domestic help's job, sweeper's job, cobbler, executioner, butcher, employee in a jail, undertaker, cremater of dead bodies.

11. Agriculture is also indicated by Saturn. Hence the native may be a farmer or peasant, if Saturn represents profession.

12. Glass factory or coal mine or manufacturing of glass items also fall under Saturn's domain.

13. Saturn also controls real estate business, or selling of plots of land for building construction.

14. Saturn may also make one a gambler. Other speculation based occupations such as lottery, betting etc. are also Saturn inspired.

15. Occupations related to oil seeds.

16. Mining and engineering.

17. If Saturn is fully strong and benevolent or yogakaraka, influences the 10th house, or such potent Saturn is the chief determinant of occupation, then the native may be a king or prosperous, brave, glorious and skilled politician or statesman like a king.

18. Saturn also controls occupations of cobbler, potter, gardner, labourer, especially labourer in a mine, washerman, hair dresser, plumber, mason, painter, sweeper, beggar, broker, coolie, shephard, tonga or rickshaw driver, watchman, conductor etc.

It is noteworthy at this point that several occupations, businesses and services are the means of livelihood in modern times. Apart from the occupations listed above, there are many others which are controlled by Saturn. But the nature of a particular work itself clarifies as to which particular planet is in charge. Each planet indicates more than a hundred occupations. Hence it is essential to consider other factors also. For instance, if Saturn is in the 10th house along with Venus, or in the sign of Venus and Mercury is influencing the 10th house, then the native would be a lawyer. If Libra and Aquarius signs also are included in the combination, then the native would be a Judge or Magistrate. Thus not Saturn alone but many other planets and signs in combination also indicate a particular occupation. The occupations listed above are primarily indicated and determined by Saturn. If Saturn is strong and beneficent then the native may be a king or king-like. If it is debilitated and malefic, then beggary would be his lot. The final conclusion about occupation should be arrived at only after thoroughly analysing all other factors along with Saturn.

Areas and Subjects controlled by Saturn

Age, death, strugglefull life, fame, lean or sick physique, buffalo, horse, ass, goat, black and woollen clothes, bone, veins, hair, muscles, coal, oil seed, hot flavour, injury, wounds, thief, dacoit, hurdles, impdiements, sorrow, pain, agony, suffering, old age, darkness, gambling, wool, iron, glass, storms and tempests, western direction, earth, prison, stupidity or imbecility, elephant, leather, opposition, chandal (one who works at the place of cremation), physical handicap, wild animals, repulsive or impotent person, birds, ghosts, slaves, evil conduct, telling lies, loss, wood, air, nerves, evening, hard labour, illegitimate children, illegitimate income, filthiness, impious thoughts, unclean clothes, bad company, sin, cruelty, ashes, black colour, iron, shudra, lameness, blanket, sharpness, agriculture, weapons, abode of the snakes, war. controversy, exile, adventure, crooked person, old oil, mean temperament, poison, landscape, fear, defect, state or kingdom, worship of death, dog, deer, hard heartedness, democracy, fearsome looks, trade of low women, greed, inequality, slaves, destruction, poverty, sesame, urad (black gram), black grains, livelihood–they are all determined, affected or controlled by Saturn.

Blacksmith, snake charmer, wolf, camel, snake, crow, mosquito, bed bug, owl, disease of the legs, lethargy, pain in ribs, injury from tree or stone, work with tin or in mines, labour at night, working in a stable or cowshed with horses or cattle, shaping bricks in a klin (the bricks or the klin itself fall under the domain of Mars) - these are also determined by Saturn. While studying these, along with care, knowledge gained through experience should be used. Location and effects of other planets should also be considered otherwise the prediction may not be correct.

Saturn indicated diseases

All chronic diseases, weakness of nerves, arthritis, spondylitis, typhoid, asthma, tuberculosis, liver enlargement, kidney problems, kidney stones, wind induced diseases, deafness, lameness or diseases of the legs, hair and teeth problems, constipation, impotence, intestinal problems, body ache, weakness, right ear problems, jaundice, fever with shivering, body cramps, fractures, physical weakness, paralysis, madness, and mental depression are the diseases controlled by Saturn. It also plays an important role in the calculation of age at death.

The above noted points would help in defining the results indicated by Saturn. For the prediction of Saturn related results a thorough knowledge of these things is imperative and, therefore, useful.

Conclusion

Summing up, Saturn is widely known for his multifarious favourable and unfavourable positions among the nine planets. Individuals are terrified by the mere mention of Saturn's ferocity. King Dasharath underlined Saturn's destructive capacity in the following words :

ब्रह्मा शक्रो हरिश्चैव ऋषयः सप्ततारकाः ।
राज्यभ्रष्टाः पतन्त्येते त्वया दृष्ट्याऽवलोकिताः ।।
देशाश्च नगरग्रामा द्वीपाश्चैव तथा दुमाः ।
त्वया विलोकिताः सर्वे विनश्यन्ति समूलतः ।।
प्रसादं कुरु हे सौरे! वरदो भव भास्करे ।।

that is, even Brahma, Indra, Vishnu and Saptarishi, are dispossessed when you (Saturn) gaze at them. Countries, cities, villages, islands, vegetation all are completely destroyed by your gaze. Therefore, O Saturn, the offspring of the Sun God, be pleased and grant us auspicious boons.

Thus, a through consideration of Shani's origin and the range of his influence proves that in his nature and disposition, this planet is unparalled. The ancient lores and accounts concerning Saturn also reinforce the indubitable all-tormenting power of this mighty planet.

●

2 Saturn and Spectrum

Because of unfounded fears, Saturn has been known as the 'Taskmaster', the 'Grim Reaper', 'Father Time', the 'Disciplinarian', the 'Planet of Old Age' and the 'Great Malefic', misleading and are nurtured by narrow mindedness.

Saturn is distinguished by being the 6th planet from the Sun, the 2nd largest planet in our solar system, and particularly by the system of three rings surrounding it making it the most spectacular of the planets. It takes Saturn 29 years, 167 days, and 5 hours, in earth time, to complete one revolution around the Sun. To the ancient Greeks Saturn was known as Cronus, holding the cycle of necessity and eternity in one hand and the symbol of death in the other. The planet Saturn signifies silent meditation in Kabalistic literature. It corresponds to the auricular attributes of the 'Grand Man' and therefore represents the senses of hearing and listening within the constitution of humanity. In order to meditate there must be silence, hence, listening and hearing. Meditation is but the listening of the mind to the inspiration of the soul.

Saturn has three rings around it at an angle of 27°. These transparent rings are seen when the signs Taurus, Gemini and Aquarius are occupied by Saturn. The edges of the rings are seen when Saturn occupies Leo and Aquarius. It has 10 satellites. The largest satellite, Titan, has an atmosphere of methane and ammonia gas. Saturn and the rings possess atmosphere of methane, ammonia, helium, etc.

Since energy carried by photons or light particles varies inversely with the 4th power of the wavelength, violet rays reflected by Saturn to the earth are more powerful than the light rays of the other nine planets of the solar system. Violet colour has a wavelength much smaller than the other components of visible light.

The magnetic field of Saturn is more than 1000 times that of the earth. Unlike Jupiter it has no radiation belt. The energy of violet radiation is more than the energy of red radiation. Saturn's position in the palm: the middle finger and the mount below it.

Saturn is the ruler of constellations viz., *Pushya*, in Cancer, *Anuradha* in Scorpio and *Uttara bhadrapada* in Pisces. The colours of the light reflected by constellations in Libra, Capricorn and Aquarius are indigo, violet and violet respectively. According to the relative distance between the Sun and planets, the planets are prescribed ownership signs. The colour of the light reflected by constellations under Capricorn and Aquarius also is akin to that of Saturn.

The ancient seers allotted Leo to the Sun as own house and *Moolatrikona*. They took the Sun as the king of Gods and Saturn as the king of devils. So to challenge the Sun, Saturn was allotted Aquarius as its own house and *Moolatrikona*.

But from a scientific point of view we find the light of Aquarius stars and Saturn resemble. Natural malefic are assigned *Moolatrikona* signs in anti clockwise direction from Cancer and natural benefics are allotted *Moolatrikona* signs in clockwise direction from Leo.

On March 21, the Sun enters *Ashwini* constellation in Aries, a fiery sign. Duration of the day period and intensity of light and heat increase thereafter in the northern hemisphere. So Aries is the exaltation sign of the Sun. Libra is its debilitation sign. Thus Libra is its exaltation sign and Aries is its debilitation sign.

The 12 signs have different colours of the light of the constellations of the respective signs. The planets are accordingly allotted own house and *Moolatrikona* houses depending upon their light spectrum.

The colour of Libra is indigo and is allotted to Venus, having indigo colour of its own. Venus is a friend of Saturn. The symbol of Libra is a pair of scales. The sign Libra stands for social justice and peace, tranquillity, equality harmony between material and spiritual affairs.

In Libra there are three stars, of which, *Chitta* stands for material prosperity, selfish nature, unsocial activity and is sexual; *Swati* stands for *Japa, niyama, asana, pranayama, pratyahara, dhyana, dharana, Samadhi,* jealous/temperament, good economic and revolutionary nature.

All the qualities of these stars tally with the nature of Saturn. So Saturn is allotted Libra as exaltation and Aries as debilitation signs. The object of Saturn is to give trouble, some material prosperity and through trouble to open the spiritual *eye* of the individual for self realisation. Saturn is *Yogakaraka* for Libra ascendant and *badhakipati* for Aries ascendant.

Of the seven *lokas* described in the Vedic scriptures, Saturn owns the *Bhuva* (preta loka). Of the seven *chakras* in the body Saturn owns the sahasrara.

The various parts of the body produce a spectrum of colours in the spectrometer. Accordingly the brain emits violet owned by Saturn. Any disharmony and disorder due to deficit or excess of violet radiation in relation to the

other radiations of the body can cause serious brain and
nervous trouble. In *Ayurveda*, Saturn is assigned *Vata* nature
on account of its powerful violet radiation emitted from
the human head and by the planet itself.

In addition to its big size, Saturn has rings around it at
an angle of 27°. It reflects 42% of the light falling on it.
The speciality of Saturn is that it reflects all powerful
radiations like X-rays, ultraviolet rays, etc. Due to excessive
reflection its inner surface is cool. No radiation belt like
that of Jupiter has been discovered around Saturn. Presence
of organic gas vapours led scientists to believe that existence
of life is possible on Saturn. The American probe gave
encouraging evidence about the possibility of existence of
life in Saturn.

Friends and Foes of Saturn: Saturn signifies over
thinking, delay, chronic nature, imaginative and cautious
action, silence, reserved nature, patience, perseverance,
preservation, sincerity, faithfulness, envy, jealousy,
untruthfulness, laziness, unscrupulousness, dishonesty,
dissatisfaction, elderly look, the old and philosophical, the
poor and down trodden, neglected things, broken goods,
mines, geology, old age, gambling, no peace, no joy, no
satisfaction, no harmony, public faith, teeth, nails, ears,
hidden side of the body, connective tissues, fibrous tissues,
isolated in mode of thinking, sensitivity to shame, failure in
enjoyment, betrayal in love and affection, etc.

Saturn signifies these indications in the following
manner in relation to houses:

1. As the lord of the star of the occupant of the house.

2. As the occupant of the house.

3. As the lord of the star owner of the house.

4. As the owner of the house.

5. As a planet aspected by the above significators.

Aspect: Like the other planets, Saturn aspects the 7th house and also has special aspects- the 3rd house and the 10th house aspects. Due to its powerful violet radiation ruling over the *Sahasrara Chakra*, Saturn is taken as the *karaka* for longevity. The 8th house indicates longevity. The 8th from the 8th is the 3rd house and the 3rd from the 8th is the 10th. So Saturn governing longevity has the 3rd house and the 10th house aspects in addition to the 7th aspect.

Saturn's aspect is bad because of its destructive violet rays radiation. But the aspect of Jupiter (the 7th, the 5th, the 9th) is good due to its (blue or yellow) colour radiation. So unlike Jupiter, Saturn's position in a house is good but the aspect is taken as harmful. For this reason when Saturn is placed in malefic houses like the 3rd, the 6th, the 11th, it produces very good results. But in the case of Jupiter the aspect is very good and its position in a house is not harmful. For the same reason Jupiter and Saturn, when they aspect each other, produce very good results. But in the case of the Sun and Mars having their spectrum on the opposite side of the violet are inimical to each other. Therefore, their mutual aspect is very bad.

Saturn and Venus are good friends; their aspect to each other is good. But from the marriage point of view it leads to delay, trouble and frustration. This is because Venus signifies sexual and material enjoyment. Saturn signifies spiritual enjoyment and eternal truth.

Saturn stands for material destruction and spiritual upheaval. It teaches eternal truth through sorrow and suffering.

Saturn is a *yogakaraka* for Taurus and Libra ascendant being the 9th and the 10th lord and the 4th and 5th lord respectively. Saturn is a *yogabhangakari* for Aries, Gemini and Leo lagnas. Saturn creates sorrow, suffering, deep discontentment, enmity with a view to teach the person the real truth of life. In the zodiac Saturn owns two houses consecutively. If one house indicates the bad, the other indicates the good. This is so only in the case of Saturn.

As a result we find that in the life history of great persons' spiritual, material and political fields, Saturn plays a dominant role more than any other planet, for them, failure is a pillar of strength.

Without benefic Saturn connected with the ascendant nobody can become a trustworthy leader of the masses. Similar is the case of saints and sanyasins. The real intention of Saturn is to teach the truth. The greatness of a person is related to how benefic Saturn is for the horoscope. The more a person suffers the more he learns. This is the speciality of Saturn's influence.

In the *Dasa* and *Antara* of Saturn and Venus one gives the result of the other irrespective of any connection between them in the horoscope. Saturn and Venus are natural friends.

Saturn is a malefic from the material point of view. But Saturn is a super benefic from the spiritual point of view. Its objective is to give *Moksha*. So when Saturn is a *Maraka* Saturn takes the life superseding other planets. Saturn teaches truth. It hesitates to give material prosperity without first giving sorrow, suffering, pain and trouble. Through ups and downs of life it teaches lessons. No other planet is benevolent like Saturn. Without benefic Saturn no great personality has ever existed either in the material or spiritual field. Either as a benefic or malefic or *maraka*, no other planet can match Saturn.

This is a fact, not an exaggeration of the benefic rewarding results of Saturn. We attempt to prove this truth in our book entitled "Saturn : The King Maker". So far as the relationship between Venus and Saturn is concerned, it is truly mysterious. Uttara Kalamrita mentions, if Saturn and Venus are well placed in a birth chart both are enatted or both occupy their own signs there will be great destruction, and downfall of the native. The native will lose his empire and there will be steep fall from power. This finding of Uttara Kalamrita has been repeatedly tested. However, if either Saturn or Venus is not placed in own sign or in the sign of exaltation, the dasha bhukti of Venus and Saturn and vice versa will be quite rewarding, progressing and promising.

Biologically speaking, Saturn rules the bone structure and its process of hardening. It rules formation of the 'stones' which sometimes plague our bodies and also the ageing process which confronts us all. Saturn also rules the skin, the teeth, the spleen, the medullary portion of the adrenal gland and, of course, the organs responsible for our hearing. We discuss the effects of the placement of Saturn in various signs as below:

In Aries, Saturn takes on the colouring of Mars which is the exact opposite of Saturn. Persons who have Saturn in Aries have great ambitions, defiance, selfishness, obstinate modesty and endurance.

In Taurus, Saturn is quite comfortable as in all Earthy signs. It is coloured with Venus the ruler of Taurus, and this gives a mixture which manifests itself in perseverance, economy, the unge to acquire personal possessions or property and self control in love relations and jealousy. This gives a tendency of over confidence in addition to making criticism of others. Such persons suffer in emotional matters, because they never feel emotionally very close to anybody.

Saturn's influence takes on the flavour of Mercury when it is in Gemini and the result is a blend of the two powers. A man with this combination would have a zeal for study, logical thinking, pre-occupation with difficult problems a tendency to view life seriously and would be shrewd and cunning. Ambition is the driving force behind activity. Lack of communication would hinder the positive attributes of the Gemini-Saturn combination.

When Saturn is in Cancer, ruled by the Moon, it is not very comfortable, but much depends on the native and how he or she responds to the positive vibrations of the planet. This position is manifested in a controlled emotional life and love of independence. There is sometimes a strained contact with the members of the family because of aggravating circumstances that usually develop and the mind is given to self pity. This is an undesirable position for timely marriage; married life is also questionable. The native seeks mental energy and inspiration through the emotions of love with opposite sex. He or she believes in switching over at early or long intervals because persons with Saturn in Cancer get saturated soon.

When Saturn is in Leo, we have another contrasting combination. The Sun is said to be the enemy of Saturn. The Sun is the giver of life and Saturn takes it away. The positive attributes of this combination are loyalty, simplicity, reliability. Negatively, Saturn in Leo means inhibitions in regard to social life and children, and rebellion against formalities.

Saturn in Virgo endows the native with a thirst for knowledge and usually a specialised skill. Mercury is also the ruler of Virgo but the effects are much different from those of Gemini. This position of Saturn will give rise to meticulous nature and make the bearer serious, correct, thorough, and critical. Negatively speaking this combination would mean a person with little ability to comprehend and a nagging, pedantic disposition.

Saturn is exalted in the sign of Libra and again is combined with a Venus ruled sign. This position endows the native with a strong sense of duty, conscientiousness, soberness and reliability. In negative manifestations, it stands for inhibitions in love and personal relationships with other people.

When Saturn is in Scorpio we have a combination of forces, that produce the necessary qualities to delve deeply into research be it matters of investigation, medicine or occult subjects. If a native with Saturn in Scorpio has no outlet in one of the foregoing subjects, it can cause a person to be jealous, revengeful, or dictatorial. There seems to be an untiring struggle for power and recognition.

Jupiter's influence flavours Saturn in Sagittarius and natives with this placement have a strong sense of justice, engage in philosophical research and have an affinity for the legal profession. In the negative sense, Saturn in Sagittarius could produce a lack of understanding, hypocrisy, distrust, an egotistical nature, miserliness, and wastefulness.

Saturn is in its own elements when it is in Capricorn which is commonly known as home rule. It produces a strong will, diplomacy, a slow but sure advancement in life, economy, and industry. On the other hand, one-sidedness, partially, stinginess, and a cold nature could influence the life in such a way as to cause much worry and anxiety.

The combination of Saturn in Aquarius produces unusual qualities when the colour of Uranus is added. A harmonious association of planning, the realization of ideals, and practical creativeness will enhance the life of the native. Too much eccentricity and extravagance can lead to disappointments. A native's plans and ambitions often do not have enough practical foundation to be realised. A fanatical concentration upon unusual aims can lead to much heartache for the person with this combination.

Saturn in Pisces brings the mysterious influence of other planets. Like Scorpio, there is the ability to conduct research. The native sometimes has wired and out of the ordinary objectives and these objectives many times occur without recognition on the part of the native. Timidity and loneliness are often characteristics. Negatively, objectives could be obtained by deception or extra legal means.

Saturn gives best results in Pisces and Sagittarius. These are the general results of placement of Saturn in various signs. We have explained the verses of various classical works in our another treatise "Saturn : The King Maker".

To find out the exact influence of Saturn on a particular nativity one must examine the results of Saturn with regard to the house, sign, constellation and position in the birth chart. In addition to this, conjunction, aspect or exchange if any, we will discuss about the rule of Saturn in determining one's occupation, marriage and health in subsequent chapters.

3 Saturn's Placement in the Twelve Houses

Every birth chart is divided in twelve houses. These houses are calculated on the basis of the twelve Rashis (signs of the Zodiac), right from Aries to Pisces. The first house is based on the sign that is in ascendance in the East at the time of birth. Since the sequence of Rashis or signs is unchangeable, the first house is marked by the ascending sign at birth time. The next eleven houses are decided according to the sequence of the rest of the signs.

Besides the numerical names like the '1st house' or '7th house', all houses are also known by names denoting their special qualities. Each house signifies certain facts and truths, therefore, the matters to be considered under them also bestow names to these houses. Before analysing the effect of Saturn's placement in the twelve houses it is necessary to be familiar with the various subjects that confer this optional nomenclature.

The optional or alternative nomenclature is as follows:-

3.1 Twelve Houses - Optional/Alternative Nomenclature :

1. First house : Tanu (body), Udaya (rising), Aadya (initial), Janma (birth), Hora (hours).

2. Second house : Vak (speech), Mukti (deliverance), Arth (finance), Netra (eyes), Dhana (wealth), Swa (self), Kutumb (family).

3. Third house : Vikram (valour), Sahodara (sibling),

Veerya (semen), Dhairya (patience), Bhratri (brother), Karna (ears).

4. Fourth house : Paataal (the nether world), Kshiti (earth), Mattri (mother), Vidya (earth/knowledge), Yan (vehicle), Geha (house), Sukha (comfort), Bandhu (relative), Purushartha (Chatushtaya (the four aims - righteousness, money, sex and salvation).

5. Fifth house : Dhee (intelligence), Deva (Deity), Raaj (rule/region), Pitri (father), Panchak (group of five), Santan/Suta (children/son).

6. Sixth house : Vyaadhi (disease), Ripu (enemy), Anga (limbs), Shastra (weapon), Bhaya (danger), Kshati (harm/loss), Rina (loan).

7. Seventh house : Kaam (sex libido), Kalatra (wife), Sampatti (wealth), Yatra (journey/travel), Dyuta (gambling), Bhoga (enjoyment), Jaayaa (daughter), Jaamitra (son-in-law), Asta (setting/decline), Mada (drinks), Madan (sex/libido).

8. Eighth house : Aaya (age/life span), Randhra (orifice-hole), Rana (battle), Mrityu (death), Vinaasha (destruction).

9. Ninth house : Dharma (pious conduct - spiritual duty), Guru (teacher), Shubha (auspicious), Tapa (penance), Nava (new), Bhaagya (destiny).

10. Tenth house : Vyaapaar (trade), Aajeevika (livelihood), Gyaan (knowledge), Raajkarma (serving the state/kingship), Aaspada (generating), Pitri (father).

11. Eleventh house : Upaantya (last but one), Bhava (world), Aaya (income), Laabha (profit).

12. Twelfth house : Vyaya (expenditure), Antya (end/last), Bhog (indulgence), Moksha (salvation).

Subjects/Matters to be considered under house

Each house indicates effects or results according to its characteristic limitations, placement of Rashis, location of Grahas and other astrological influences. An acquaintance with the relevant matters of each house is, therefore, desirable.

1. First House :

According to Jataka Parijata :

शरीरवर्णाकृतिलक्षणानि   यशोगुणस्थानसुखासुखानि।
प्रवासतेजोबलदुर्बलानि फलानि लग्नस्य वदन्ति सन्तः।।

that is, physique, complexion, figure, physical peculiarities, fame, qualities, location, suffering, happiness, stay outside home/town, power, efforts, courage, weakness, disability, worries, anxiety and determination are issues decided according to the lagna or first house. Lagna is the head of a birth chart.

The importance of a strong lagna is, therefore, paramount to the interpretation of a birth chart. Sun is the significator of the first house.

2. Second House :

Jupiter or Brihaspati is the significator/ruling planet of the second house. Mars or Mangal is rendered ineffectual when positioned in this house.

वित्तं नेत्रं मुखं विद्या, वाक्कुटुम्बाशनानि च।
द्वितीयस्थानजन्यानि क्रमाज्ज्योतिर्विदो विदुः।।

This house has to be considered in deciding matters concerning money, right eye, face, family affairs, friendship, eatables, liquids, right limbs, common sense, buying and selling and speech.

3. Third House :

The ruling significator planet of this house is Mangal or Mars.

ज्येष्ठानुजस्थितिपराक्रमसाहसानि कंठस्वरश्रुतिवराभरणांशुकानि ।
धैर्यं च वीर्यबलमूलफलाशनानि वक्ष्ये तृतीयभवनात् क्रमशोऽखिलानि ।।

सहोदराणामथ किंकराणां पराक्रमाणामुपजीविनां च ।
विचारणा जातकशास्त्रविद्भिस्तृतीयभावे नियमेन वाच्या ।।

तृतीयराशेः सहजाभिवृद्धिं भक्ष्यं मलं चापि पुनश्च कर्णम् ।
सहोदराणां क्रमशस्तु सख्यं भुक्तौ विशेषादपि मूलकादीन् ।।

As per the shloka, this house determines matters concerning sibling (elder or younger), patience, courage, semen, valour, bones, throat, ears, clothes, servants, fruits and tubars, medicine, hearing ability, ornaments, food and enjoyment etc.

4. Fourth House :

The Karaka Graha or significator of this house are Moon and Mercury (Chandra, Budha). But Mercury located in the fourth house is ineffectual. Jatak Parijata says :

वदन्ति विद्याजननीसुखानि सुगन्धगोबन्धुमनोगुणानि ।
महीपयानक्षितिमन्दिराणि चतुर्थभावप्रभवानि तज्ज्ञाः ।।

that is, the matters to be considered under this house are education, mother, happiness, fragrance, cow, relatives, mind, kingdom, vehicle, land, house, comforts of house, and arrogance, born of learning.

5. Fifth House :

This house, which denotes begetting of otherwise of sons, is ruled by Jupiter or Brihaspati, though placed in this house Jupiter loses its influence.

पुत्रादेवमहीपपुत्रपितृधीपुण्यानि संचिन्तयेद् ।
यात्रामस्तसुतस्वकर्मभवनैर्दूराटनं रिष्फतः ।।

Devotion to Gods, sons, intelligence, pious deeds, secret consultations, favours from the king/state, brain, power, meditation about the Supreme Being or Brahma, heart, stomach, analytical/logical skill, ready wits, and according to one school of thought, matters related to father are decided according to this house.

6. Sixth House :

This is the house of enemies. Significators are Mars (Mangal) and Saturn (Shani). Venus (Shukra) placed in this house becomes ineffectual.

रोगारिव्यसनक्षतानि   वसुधापुत्रारितिश्चिन्तयेद् ।
उक्तं रोगकरं तदेव रिपुगे जीवे जितारिर्भवेत् ।।

This house decides matters regarding enemies, loans, disease, loss, hurdles, thieves, wounds/injury, maternal uncle and aunt, food delicacies, enjoyment, entertainment, stomach ailments etc.

7. Seventh House :

Venus or Shukra rules over this house which is concerned with wife or spouse. Saturn located in this house is rendered powerless.

यात्रापुत्रकलत्रसौख्यमखिलं संचिन्तयेत्सप्तमा-
दुक्तं पुत्रसुखागमफलं र्सर्व च यत्तद्धदेत् ।।

रणांगणं चापि वणिक्क्रियाश्च जायाविचारागमनप्रयाणम् ।
शास्त्रप्रवीणैर्हिं विचारणीयं कलत्रभावे किल सर्वमेतत् ।।

युवतिपदादुद्वाहं   भार्यापतिसूपदधिगुडक्षीरम् ।
आगमनं सरिदाप्तिं मूत्राशयं च नष्टधनम् ।।

According to this shloka, wife, husband, travel, nephew, marriage, knowledge or learning, acquiring positions of power or status, trade, regaining lost wealth, genitals, milk, curds, sweets, brother's son, field of struggle, knowledge of scriptures of Shaastras, water resources, are matters determined according to this house.

8. Eighth House :

This death denoting house is ruled by Shani or Saturn.

आयुर्दायमनिष्टहेतुमुदयव्योमायुरीशार्कजै-
रक्तं तत्सकलं तथापि निधनप्राप्तिं प्रवक्ष्ये पुनः ।।

Life-span, death, causes of death, place of death, food, promotion, demotion, victory, defeat, sensual power and genitals related matters are decided according to this house.

9. Ninth House :

This house denoting religious piety is ruled by Sun and Jupiter.

भाग्यप्रभावगुरुधर्मतपःशुभानि-
संचिन्तयेन्नवमदेवपुरोहिताभ्याम् ।।

This house is considered in deciding matters regarding leadership quality, wealth, religious conduct, religion, penance and abdication, favour/grace of Guru (mentor/ teacher), journey of sacred places, destiny, diseases caused by bile and wind, grand children, thighs, law, and sudden happenings.

10. Tenth House :

This house is concerned with actions. Jupiter, Sun,

Mercury and Saturn are its ruling planets.

आज्ञामानविभूणानि वसनव्यापारनिद्राकृषि-
प्रव्रज्यागमकर्मजीवनयशोविज्ञानविद्याः क्रमात् ।।

Order/command, state power, honour, dress and ornaments, sleep, trade, means of livelihood, agriculture, and impression, gaining of position, travel abroad, right conduct, science, prestige due to learning, examination results, ambition of high positions, knees, life styles, father etc. are considered according to this house.

11. Eleventh House :

This house of income is ruled by Jupiter (Brihaspati).

लाभस्थानेन लग्नादखिलधनचयप्राप्तिमिच्छन्ति सर्वे
लाभस्थानोपयातः सकलबलयुतः खेचरो वित्तदः स्यात् ।
भानुश्चेज्ज्ञातिवर्गादतिधनमुडुपो मातृवर्गेण भौमः
स्वोत्थाच्चान्द्रिर्यदीष्टप्रभुविबुधसुहृन्मातुलैर्वित्तमेति ।।

Various sources of income and wealth, alround profits or gains, elder brother/sister, friend, elephant, horse, left ear, ear-ornaments, friendliness are considered according to this house.

12. Twelfth House :

Twelfth house or house of expenditure is ruled by Saturn.

लग्नादन्त्यतदीशभानुतनयैर्दूराटनं   दुर्गतिं
दातृत्वं शयनादिसौख्यविभवं वित्तक्षयं चिन्तयेत् ।।

Long journey, deep breath, torture, pain, adverse circumstances, donations, bed-related comforts, expenditure (well spent money or ill spent money), various comforts and enjoyments, travel, suffering in the hell, left eye, imprisonment, penalisation by the king or decline etc. are matters considered under this house.

From this detailed description of subject matters deliberated under the twelve houses, we move on to the multidimensional effect of Saturn's presence in these houses, which, described at length by astrologers, is as follows :

3.2 Saturn in the First House

According to Vaidyanath :

दुर्नासिकोवृद्धकलत्ररोगी मन्दे विलग्नोपगतेऽङ्गहीनः ।
महीपतुल्यः सुगुणाभिरामो जातः स्वतुंगोपगते चिरायुः ।।

that is, Saturn when placed in the individual's lagna (first house) adversely affects the nose making its shape or nature a cause of worry. His wife is old-looking, that is, her appearance and mentality are those of the old. The individual suffers from illness or diseases; some part of his body has a defect or blemish. But if Saturn also happens to own this house (Swagrihi) or is called (Uchchastha) then the individual is endowed with an appearance, qualities, honours and prosperity worthy of a king. He also has a long life.

Sage Vashishtha has condemned Saturn placed in the lagna or first house, calling such a one destructive and a cause of unbearable miseries.

Acharya has given a detailed description of the effects of Saturn's location in the first house :

कंडूतिपूर्णांगकफप्रवृत्तिर्लग्ने शनौ स्यात् सततं नराणाम् ।
हीनाधिकांगत्वमधःप्रदेशे कर्णान्तरे वातगदः सदैव ।।

लग्ने मंदेऽथवा दृष्टे कृशदेहश्च दुःखितः ।
मूर्खश्च मदनाचारो भिन्नवर्णस्तनौ भवेत् ।।

लोहादिभिः शिरःपीडा आत्मचिन्ता निरन्तरम् ।
तुलाकोदंडमीनानां लग्नसंस्थे शनैश्चरे ।।

करोति भूपतिं जातमन्यराशौ गतायुषम् ।
प्रकृत्या स भवेद् वृद्धो मान्यः सर्वजनेषु च ।।

that is, first house-placed Saturn makes an individual phlegmatic. He suffers from skin diseases like scabies. His lower body has some defect or deformity. He suffers from chronic ear-ache because of wind induced illness and has a lean figure. Such an individual is stupid, lustful, unhappy and shabby. He is afflicted with head-ache due to some injury or disease. The individual is self centred or self concerned. His life-span is also relatively short.

These negative results differ with the change of sign in the first house. When the sign in the first house is Tula (Libra), Dhanu (Saggitarius) or Meen (Pisces) then the native is rich and prosperous in every respect like a king. He enjoys a long life. Saturn situated in these signs gives profusely positive results. It is a widely held view that when a mature planet like Saturn or Brihaspati (Jupiter) is located in the first house (Lagna), the individual has a mature mind. He receives approval or support from people. Dividing results given by Saturn into two parts according to the signs, Harivansh says :

स्वोच्चे जीवगृहे स्वालयस्थः शनिश्चेत् लग्ने कोणे भूपतुल्यं मनुष्यम् ।
कुर्याच्छेषे संस्थितो रोगयुक्तं दीनं हीनं दुःखभावं दरिद्रम् ।।

that is, Saturn placed in the first house under Tula (Libra), Dhanu (Saggitarius), Makar (Capricorn), Kumbha (Aquarius) and Meen (Pisces) makes the individual enjoy like an emperor. Under any other sign Saturn makes the individual sickly, unhappy and lacking in resources. According to Bhrigusutra :

दृष्ट्यैव रिपुनाशकः तनुस्थाने शनिर्यस्य धनी पूर्णतृषान्वितः
स्थूलदेहः विषदृष्टिः वातपित्तदेहः। उच्चे पुरग्रामाधिपः
धनधान्यसमृद्धिः। स्वर्क्षे पितृधनवान्। वाहनेशः कर्मेशो
भाग्यक्षेत्रे बहुभाग्यं महाराजयोगः। चन्द्रमसा दृष्टे परान्नभुक्।
शुभदृष्टे निवृत्तिः।

that is, if Saturn is located in the first house or lagna, the individual can subdue enemies merely by looking at them. He is prosperous, greedy, stout and sharp eyed. His constitution is dominated by wind and bile. Exalted Saturn makes the individual head of the village or city. Saturn under Capricorn or Aquarius gives lots of wealth through inheritance. Saturn being the lord of 9th or 10th house occupies its own sign then it makes 'Raajyog', that is a combination causing king like status of power and prosperity. Aspected by the Moon, it makes the individual depend on others for livelihood.

In the opinion of Kashinath, Saturn placed in the first house makes the individual chronically ill throughout life. Such a native is ugly, miserly, sinful, wicked and crooked.

लग्ने शनौ सदा रोगी कुरूपः कृपणो नरः।
कुशीलः पापबुद्धिश्च शठश्च भवति ध्रुवम्।।

It has been stated in 'Vrihadyavan Jataka', while enumerating the special effects of Saturn occupying the first house,that if it is situated in its exaltation sign, its own house or in Mooltrikona, it confers on the individual headship of a nation or province. But placed in the other sign Saturn causes illness, difficulties and poverty.

प्रसूतिकाले नलिनीशसूनौ स्वोच्चत्रिकोणर्क्षगते विलग्ने।
कुर्यान्नरं देशपुराधिनाथं शेषर्क्षसंस्थे सरुजं दरिद्रम्।।

The ill effects of a debilitated or weak Saturn have been described in such works as 'Jatak Paarijaat' and 'Gadaavali'. According to these works, in that case the individual suffers from poverty, diseases, of the joints and is haunted by evil spirits. He undergoes punishment for wrong deeds. His wealth is stolen. The diseases afflicting him may be of the following nature— respiratory problems, body-aches, pain in the sides, venereal diseases, heart problems, depression, joint problems, trembling and disease caused due to wind (Vaat).

According to Jeevanath Daivagya :

यदा मन्दे लग्नं गतवति धनैरेव लसितो
विषादी वादेन प्रबलरिपुहा तोषरहितः।
सदा व्यग्रश्चंडः शनिरिव तदा पश्यति नरः
परोत्कर्षासह्यः कृशतनुरयं व्याधिगणतः।।

that is, the individual is prosperous but unhappy because of controversies, destroyer of enemies yet dissatisfied, anxious, evileyed, full of short comings, sick and jealous of others' progress.

The learned Jaideva has proved that in certain Signs Saturn is beneficial. He opines that when Saturn is situated in Dhanu (Saggitarius), Meen (Pisces), Kumbha (Aquarius) and Tula (Libra) Sign, it confers learning, prosperity and a comely physique. In other Signs it causes poverty, heart diseases, unclean body, sickliness, lethargy and passion.

Varahmihir, the ace astrologer, holds :

अदृष्टार्थो रोगी मदनवशगोऽत्यंतमलिनः
शिशुत्वे पीडार्त्तः सवितृसुतलग्नेत्यलसवाक्।
गुरुः स्वर्क्षोच्चस्थे नृपतिसदृशो ग्रामपुरपः
सुविद्वांश्चारुवंगो दिनकरसमोऽयत्र कथितः।।

that is, Swagrihi (located in his own house), exalted or Saggitarius/Pisces/Capricorn/Aquarius/Libra placed Saturn always gives beneficial results. Such an individual is good looking, a leading person of ability, who is first among the learned men and prosperous like a king. Placed elsewhere Saturn makes the individual sickly, sex-crazy, poor, doer of mean acts or of a low vocation in life.

According to Mana Sagara, when situated in Capricorn or Aquarius, Saturn makes the individual a slayer of enemies. In other singns it is negative and the affected individual is lean and thin, sparse-haried, sex-crazy, with a low, disrespectful profession, wicked and lethargic.

सततमल्पगतिर्मंदपीड़ितस्तपनजे   तनुगे   खलु   चाधमः।
भवति हीनकचः कृशविग्रहो जितरिपुर्निजसद्मनि मानवः।।

Similar effects of Saturn have been delineated by Dhundhiraj, Kalyan Varma, Mantreshwar and Mahesh. They do not show any novelty in their description.

Abdurrahim Khankhana considers Saturn in the first house or Ascendant as absolutely inauspicious. He maintains that :

ताले यदि स्याज्जहलो वदअक्लश्च लागरो मनुजः।
शठ कंवुरं वेदिलः वाममतिपूर्णः प्रभुर्भवति।।

that is, the individual is ruthless, ugly, weak, stupid, wicked, crooked and possessor of ill gotten wealth. This shloka is also attributed to other astrologers.

'Hillajataka' and Parashara hold that Saturn in the ascendant causes diseases of the head, opposition from brother/relatives, heat and boils etc.

Jageshwar adds further to Saturn induced results :

यदा मन्दतो वह्निखेटा विलग्ने,
नरं दन्तुरं दन्तरोगान् प्रकुर्युः ।
काष्ठपाषाणजैश्चापि धातैः सलोहैः
सदा दुःखितो वायुरोगैर्भवेत् सः ।।

शनिर्यस्य शीर्षे बलं चाधिकारं
तथा सौष्ठवं कुत्र लभ्यं च तस्मात् ।
स्वयं मत्सरी क्रूरदृष्टिः सकोपः
स्त्रिया संजितः स्त्रीप्रधानो भवेद् वा ।।

that is, large teeth, dental diseases, wind-induced ailments, lack of power and authority, disproportionate body, cruel, jealous nature, domination by women and pain due to injury (from wood, stone or iron) are the ill-effects of Saturn.

A novel elucidation is provided by Narain Bhatta who maintains :

धनेनातिपूर्णोऽतितृष्णो विवादी तनुस्थेऽर्कजे स्थूलदृष्टिर्नरः स्यात् ।
विषं दृष्टिजं तद्विकृत्व्याधिबाधाः स्वयं पीडितो मत्सरावेश एव ।।

that is, the individual remains greedy despite being rich. His hunger for wealth is never satiated. His viewpoint lacks depth. He has an argumentative disposition. Like Saturn his glance is retrograde, wicked and destructive. He constantly suffers from attacks of jealousy, illness and worries.

Gopal Ratnakar has added lack of sons, displeasure of king or authority and evil friendship to the results of Saturn's placement in the Ascendant.

Aryagrantha maintains that lethargy in movement, hair loss, physical debility and friendship with enemies are the chief results of Saturn being in the first house.

Western researchers in the field of occult science have also discussed effects of Saturn from several angles. In their opinion Saturn, placed in the first house, makes the individual suffer from unexpected troubles throughout life. He is neutral, determined, persuasive, shy, alone and a man of words. By fair means or foul, he follows his own interests. He possesses untraditional and unusual kind of thoughts regarding religion, along with greed, suffering and cheating others. If Saturn is in a benefic combination, then destiny soon shows its effect. The initial period of life is spent in facing problems and troubles, but continuous and untiring efforts ultimately bring high achievements. When Saturn is in malefic combination, the individual becomes controversial, dependent on others, engaged in petty matters, unhappy, scared, non-trusting, wicked, greedy, jealous, restless and afraid of people. Never forgetting a wrong done to him, he seeks revenge even after long. For various reasons he never attains popularity. His life is afflicted deeply with troubles, suffering, obstacles, helplessness and dejection. There is always a risk of his suffering from cold induced diseases and falling from high altitudes. In the signs of Scorpio, Leo, Cancer and Libra it gives constipation, blood impurities, blood pressure, indigestion and diseases of bladder respectively.

Saturn in the firey signs results in simplicity, trustworthiness, and friendliness along with controversy, resentment, intrigue, and boldness in the native. In the earthy signs Saturn gives lethargy, narrow mindedness, revengefulness, wickedness, suspicion, cunningness, competence in discussions, selfishness, laboriousness, greed, miserliness, restlessness, unnecessary caution and anger. In the airy signs Saturn causes thoughtfulness, practicality, orderly economy, reverence for gods, truthfulness, lack of deceit, faith, sentimentality, determination, patience, diligence, activeness, fondness for edifying company along with self seeking, pride and obstinacy. In the signs of Pisces, Cancer and Scorpio, the effect are somewhat unsavoury. In the firey signs dissatisfaction is added to dexterity. Saturn in the earthy signs makes the individual stupid, thoughtless, fond of stories, suspicious, miserly and dependent on others' wealth.

Saturn is an unique and distant planet in the solar system. Its position affects the results caused by it. Loneliness, lethargy, mysteriousness and indifference are its innate symptoms.

According to Sri H.N. Katve, an individual with Saturn in Aries, Leo, Saggitarius, Cancer, Scorpio or Pisces signs earns his livelihood from service in some office. He attains promotion only after struggling with his superiors. He is very possessive in life. Mostly he gets daughters. The later half of the life is comparatively more prosperous. Saturn in Aries-Leo or Saggitarius causes abnormal physique, defective eyes, arrogant voice and helpful nature in the individual.

Saturn in Gemini causes conditions for a second marriage, childlessness and education in law or medicine. The first half of life is full of struggle but the second half is full of name and fame.

In the signs of Cancer, Scorpio and Pisces, Saturn gives a combination of sweet voice, gentle behaviour, logicalness, fondness for power and a comfortable life. Saturn placed in Taurus, Virgo, Libra, Capricorn or Aquarius makes one highly ambitious in career. One also achieves top positions. Usually people who prefer service are influenced by such a Saturn. Their marital life is full of discord. Indications of second marriage, arrogance, impractically and sickness of life partner are present. The individual loses either parent at an early age. He keeps contact with low standard persons. School education remains incomplete due to earning his livelihood. Partnership proves lucky. Inheritance causes disputes. The individual is good at negative roles. Relations with parents are not cordial. Their fortune or destiny does not help him in his progress. Activeness despite struggle, cultural integrity, vanity, revenge, unattained ambitions, detachment and innate cunningness are the results of such a Saturn. Independent business from the 26th year onwards and rise in fortunes from the 36th year onwards is certain. Till the 56th year life is carefree. But the 25th, 27th, 31st and 32nd years are unpleasant.

Saturn occupying the 1st house and afflicted by Venus gives different results. No marriage or marital discord, death of the spouse, debauchery, loss of either son or wealth, occupational problems or mishaps and lots of daughters are the consequences of such a combination. Saturn in the first house and afflicted by Mars indicates untimely or unexpected death, accident, imprisonment, false accusations and lack of money.

In Aries, Leo and Saggitarius, Saturn gives freedom from disease; in Cancer, Scorpio and Pisces, it gives chronic illness, cough, cold, constipation, insanity and urinary diseases, in Gemini, Libra, Aquarius it gives wind induced illness; and in Taurus, Virgo, Capricorn, syphilis, and cough diseases are the probabilities.

If we analyse from the standpoint of nature or disposition, we find that generally Saturn in the first house damages the influence of one's personality. In Aries, Cancer, Scorpio, Saggitarius and Pisces it lets an individual's personality traits and specialities become manifest only after a long acquaintance. In other signs, it makes the individual full of villainy. In Virgo, Capricorn, Aquarius and Taurus signs, the individual happens to be cunning, deceptively sober, given to lying, garrulous or loquacious and extremely given to fulfilling self interest.

3.3 Saturn in the Second House

In this context the opinion of Narain Bhatta deserves to be quoted primarily. He says :

सुखापेक्षया वर्जितोऽसौ कुटुम्बात्
कुटुम्बे शनौ वस्तु किं किं न भुङ्क्ते ।
समं वक्ति मित्रेण तिक्तं वचोऽपि
प्रसक्तिं विना लोहकं को लभेत ।।

which means that Saturn in the 2nd house gives separation from home and family. The individual undertakes journeys to far off places in search of happiness and prosperity. His fortunes rise away from ancestral home. Rude behaviour without any reason, indiscreet, argumentative and meaningless speech is his speciality. The individual earns wealth through business in iron.

Vaidyanath criticises Saturn placed in this house of wealth :

असत्यवादी चपलोऽटनोऽधनः
शनौ कुटुम्बोपगते तु वंचकः ।

that is, the individual tells lies, and is constantly away from home. He is without money, fickle and an expert in befooling others.

Vashishtha and Parashar maintain that the cause of the suffering of such an individual is loss of wealth.

Garg analyses this in somewhat greater detail :

काष्ठांगाराल्लोहधनः कुकार्याद् धनसंचयः ।
नीचविद्यानुरक्तश्च नीचकार्येषु तत्परः ।।
धने मन्दे धनैर्हीनो निष्ठुरो दुःखितो भवेत् ।
मित्रसौम्यैर्युते दृष्टे धर्मसत्यदयान्वितः ।।
मृतवत्साभगिन्यादि गर्भस्त्रावादिकं वदेत् ।
प्रतिवेश्मादि बालादि विपत्तिरपि कथ्यते ।।

The individual earns money from the trade of wood, coal or iron. He begets huge wealth through wrongful acts and means. He acquires learning in fields usually not considered good. His wealth, happiness, home, children and gentle emotions diminish and suffer. These unhappy consequences can be reduced if some friendly and auspicious planet aspects it or conjoins with it.

According to Bhrigusutra, Saturn placed in the 2nd house, the house of money or wealth makes the individual poor. He suffers from eye problems. There is probability of two marriages. The individual can be the manager of some religious place or institution. There is a shortage of agricultural land. Saturn combined with a malefic planet shows betrayal or befooling of women. The individual makes money by exploiting women.

Kashinath holds Saturn placed in 2nd house responsible for lack of money and good qualities as well as for wind, bile, cough induced and bone related diseases.

धने मंदे धनैर्दीनो वातपित्तकफातुरः ।
देहास्थिपित्तरोगश्च गुणैः स्वल्पोऽपि जायते ।।

The descriptions of Dhundhiraj and Vrihad Yavan Jataka are similar :

अन्यालयस्थो व्यसनाभिभूतो धनोज्झितः स्यान्मनुजश्च पश्चात् ।
देशान्तरे वाहनराजमानो धनाभिधाने धवनेऽर्कसूनौ ।।

The first half of the individual's life is spent in residing in others' house, with troubles and contempt from relatives. He has no younger brother. In the later half, the individual acquires comfort and happiness away from ancestral or paternal home. He also gets state favour.

Mantreshvar, Kalyan Varma and Mahesh have declared unanimously held results in this context. According to them, such an individual is not good to look at. He is of an unjust disposition, and is impractical. The later half of his life is better than the first half.

In Jageshwar's opinion :

धने पंगुना विद्यमाने सुखं किं कुटुम्बात् तथा क्लेशमाहुर्जनानाम् ।
न भोक्ता न वक्ता वदेन् निष्ठुरं वै धनं लोहजातं न शत्रोर्भयं स्यात् ।।

that is, the individual is neglected by family and society and is bereft of means of comforts. He is not adept at conversing, on the contrary he often says unpleasant things. He is afraid of enemies. Trading in iron suits him.

The conclusions of Aryagrantha are slightly different. According to it :

धननिकेतन वर्तिनि भानुजे भवति वाक्यसुहासधनान्वितः ।
चपललोचनसंचयने रतो भवति चौर्यपरो नियतं सदा ।।

the individual is soft spoken, rich, quick eyed, holder of money and user of wrongful means.

Jeevnath has proved that the effects of Saturn placed in this house of wealth are even sharper.

कुटुम्बत्यक्तोऽपि प्रभवति कुटुम्बे यदि शनौ
विदेशे संगच्छन् किमिति नहि भुंक्ते प्रियतमम् ।
सदा मिष्टं मित्रैरपि सह सदा तिक्तवचने
प्रवक्ति स्वार्थं ना सपदि परिगृह्णाति च शरम् ।।

The individual can enjoy comfort only when he is away from ancestral home and family. Even with friends he behaves like enemies. He is always trying to serve self interest and adopts even violent means to fulfil this end.

The only thing added to the above by Gopal Ratnakar is a 'break in studies'.

Acharya Gunakar and Varahmihir have specially mentioned state's displeasure on the individual's wealth.

According to Khankhana :

यावागो बदहालः कोतोदतश्च गुस्वरो जोहलः।
जरखाने यदि मनुजो नाढ्यः परदेशगश्चापि।।

which means that he spends his life in low and undesirable circumstances, in distant places and in constant deprivations. Indiscreet anger abounds in him.

Western astrologers have done some serious thinking in this regard. According to them debility or otherwise of Saturn affects its infleunce or results. When Saturn is surrounded by benefics, it results in prosperity through various sources of wealth. Business in antiques, shares, public welfare, financing give of favourable results. Saturn in Libra creates conditions for ancestral property, farsightedness, discretion, investment in some big business, thriftiness, wealth and honour. But if it is devoid of strength it results in financial loss, business failure, poverty and constant but fruitless hard work.

Astrologer Katve maintains that Saturn is the significator of permanent wealth and ancestral wealth both. Aspects by Saturn leads to suffering but presence of Saturn is beneficial. When it is placed in the house of wealth it is responsible for acquiring ancestral property. The individual also succeeds in his efforts for additional financial gains.

Even getting back money which has been lost is probable. The birth of such an individual can create the 'Yoga' or condition for death in the family. Signs such as ordinary service, little success in self controlled business, being reticent, popular and learned are also indicated. One special factor is that such individuals cannot earn prosperity under the patronage of their father.

Saturn placed in Taurus, Virgo or Capricorn indicates one marriage, troublesome youth, fondness for travelling, authorship of educational, inspiring and interesting writing, keeping one's words, stubbornness, firmness of thought, indifference towards clothes, food and dwelling, and social activeness.

In the signs of Aries, Gemini, Saggitarius, or Leo, Saturn paves the way for two marriages, lots of children, fickleness, prosperity, prestige, impracticality, change in opinion, fondness for food, constant discontent, soft spokenness, efficiency or expertness in serving self interest, investment in real estate, charity, quarrelsome marital life and high ambition. Saturn in Cancer, Scorpio, Pisces also gives almost similar results.

In the signs of Libra or Aquarius, Saturn results in little education, small number of children, two marriages, loss of wealth and self seeking attitude.

By and large astrologers have discussed the inauspicious effects in detail. Specially staying away from home for livelihood, two marriages and matters relating to ancestral property are stressed. If such individuals trade in stone, sand, lime, metals, iron, coal, wood or other materials obtained from the earth, they have good gains.

3.4 Saturn in the Third House

Placement of Saturn in the 3rd house indicates some unique results. Jeevanath has dealt with them in detail, as follows :

यदा भ्रातुः स्थानं गतवति शनौ जन्मसमये
धनानां व्यापारान्नहि परमहर्षो जनिमताम् ।
भवेद् भाग्यं तेषां कथमिह महोत्पातरहितं
कृते सत्कारेऽपि प्रसरति खलत्वं च परितः ।।

that is, the third-house-placed Saturn causes struggle and loss in the individual's efforts for earning money. His fate is full of hindrances. By nature he is crooked and insolvent. He cheats even his own people and friends.

According to Mahasagar such a Saturn is fatal for both the elder and younger brothers of the individual. Otherwise, excepting this evil effect, the individual is fortunate. Money, children, prosperity and countrywide fame are the good results. In his words :

सहजमन्दिरगे तपनात्मजे भवति सर्वसहोदरनाशकः ।
तदनुकूलनृपेण समो नरः स्वसुखपुत्रकलत्रसमन्वितः ।।

Dhundhiraj also accepts such a placement of Saturn as beneficial for a lot of reasons. As in the following :

राजमान्यशुभवाहनयुक्तो ग्रामपो बहुपराक्रमशाली ।
पालको भवति भूरिजनानां मानवो हि रविजे सहजस्थे ।।

The individual has the auspicious sympotoms for leadership or headship. He remains in the good books of authority or state power. He is honoured in his town or city and happens to be its chief. The life of lots of people depends on him. He is extremely industrious and valiant.

Means of comfort such as vehicle etc. are easily available to him.

Astrologer Mahesh reiterates these results. Jaidev adds the following to them– cooperation of both friends and enemies and the cause of fame being widespread generosity.

Mantreshwar mentions minus points like lethargy, sorrow and misunderstanding, along with good qualities like intellectual ability and noble conduct :

विपुलमतिमुदारं दारसौख्यं च शौर्ये

जनयति रविपुत्रश्चालसं विक्लवं च ।।

In the opinion of Narayan Bhatt :

तृतीये शनौ शीतलं नैव चित्तं जनादुद्धामाज्जायते युक्तभाषी ।

अविघ्नं भवेत् कर्हिचिन्नैव भाग्यं दृढाशः सुखी दुर्मुखः सत्कृतोऽपि ।।

Constant lack of peace of mind is the result of Saturn's placement in the 3rd house. Occasions of discord with friends and relatives and failure even after hard work trouble the individual. Between good fortune and the reticent individual, there are lots of impediments. Incomplete happiness, lack of peace of mind, bitterness, wickedness and thanklessness are the negative results of Saturn placed in the 3rd house.

But Kashinath considers such Saturn as beneficial in total opposition to this. He maintains that :

छायात्मजे तृतीयस्थे प्रसन्नो गुणवत्सलः ।

शत्रुमर्दी नृणां मान्यो धनी शूरश्च जायते ।।

which means that with Saturn placed in the 3rd house, the individual is likely to be cheerful, appreciater of virtues, subduer of enemies, honourable, prosperous and brave.

Contrary to this Jageshwar has clearly mentioned ill effects of such Saturn. In every sphere of life, problems created by Saturn crop up :

यदा विक्रमे मन्दगामी कदुष्णं भवेन्मानसं भाग्यविघ्नः सदा स्यात् ।
भवेत् पालको वै बहूनां नराणां रणे विक्रमी भाग्यवान् हस्तरोगी ।।
भवेद् भ्रातृकष्टं विदेशे प्रयाणं गृहे नो विरामं लभेद् बन्धुतोऽपि ।
भवेन्नीचसक्तो विरक्तोऽर्थधर्मे यदा विक्रमे सूर्यसूनुर्नराणाम् ।।

that is, he is not clean hearted. Lots of obstructions occur in the rising of fortune. Lots of people are dependent on him. Relations with brothers are fraught with tension and cause pain. Hands are afflicted with diseases. Though the individual is brave, he is always away from home and so, is deprived of comforts of home. One more effect of 3rd house-placed Saturn is carelessness towards money and virtuous life due to undesirable persons' company.

Acharya Varahmihir and Gunakar have mentioned wisdom and valour, while Vashishtha has included popularity among women as results of such Saturn.

According to Gholap Saturn placed in the 3rd house gives sudden and uncertain rise in fortune, prosperity, children, powerfulness, freedom from disease and comforts of home. Such an individual vanquishes his enemies through diplomacy and tach. Driving power and means from authority, he nurtures many persons.

According to Gopal Ratnakar's calculation Saturn in the 3rd house, though fatal for brother, gives courages, followers or servants, luxury and agricultural skill.

Bhrigusutra has a slightly different line of thinking :

उच्चे स्वक्षेत्रे भ्रातृवृद्धिः । तत्र पापयुते भ्रातृद्वेषी ।।

that is, exalted or own house placed Saturn is beneficial

for the brothers. But Saturn combined with malefic planets harms them (the brothers). Another interpretation can be that in the first instance number of brothers will increase and in the latter case the same brothers will show malice towards the individual.

Kalyan Varma holds the opinion that the individual as well as his family are lethargic and filthy bodied. Meanness, generosity, intelligence and skilfulness are also indicated. In his words :

श्यामोऽसंस्कृतदेहो नीचोऽलसपरिजनो भवति सौरे ।
शूरो दानानुरक्तो दुश्चिक्यगे विपुलबुद्धिः ।।

Keeping the tradition of opposite theories alive, Harivansh says :

भूपात् सौख्यं चारुकीर्तिः सुकान्तिः वित्ताधिक्यं वाहनानां समृद्धिः ।
नैरुज्योग्रं पालनं मानवानां भ्रातृस्थाने भानुजातः करोति ।।

that is, Saturn placed in the 3rd house causes favour from authority, world wide fame, healthy-handsome physique and ability to protect people.

Vaidyanath has amended the opinions of other astrologers. According to him the individual is a frugal eater and has superior qualities, money and family. Such Saturn is only fatal for younger brother :

अल्पाशी धनशीलवंशगुणवान् भ्रातृस्थिते भानुजे
सौरिस्तृतीयेऽनुजनाशकर्ता ।

Parashar has underlined profusion of friends. Garg maintains that the individual's life is full of contradictions. Despite being lucky and prosperous like a king, the individual suffers from body pain and has no sibling or child.

तथा तृतीयगे मन्दे स नरो भाग्यवान् भवेत्।
भवेद् दोषस्थिता पीड़ा शरीरे तस्य सर्वदा।।

भ्रातृगो मन्दगः कुर्याद् भ्रातृस्वसृविनाशनम्।
नृपतुल्यं च सुखिनं सततं कुरुते नरम्।।
सौरिर्गर्भविनाशनं च नियतं मंत्रीश्वरो नान्यथा।।

Aryagrantha and Yavan Jataka also do not have very different opinion. But Khankhana considers Saturn placed in the 3rd house absolutely harmless :

जोरावरो यशीलः खुशदाना च मानवः सभ्यः।
अनुचरवृन्दसमेतो भवति यदा वै विरादरे जोहलः।।

He maintains that such an individual can be a wrestler, famous, cheerful, practical and having lots of servants or followers.

In this context the opinions of Western thinkers are worth recalling. Benefic and strong Saturn gives sobriety, discretion, calmness, gentleness, thoughtfulness, concentration, sense of justice, authenticity, cleverness, advisory skill and foresight. Saturn that is debilitated and afflicted causes incomplete education, stay away from home, sorrow, obstructions in writing oblique publication, fickle mind, narrow thinking, friction with friends, relatives and near ones and cold induced problems. The individual is interested in the occult sciences.

When placed in this house and combined with Mars, Saturn helps develop in the individual vices of fraud, treachery and untrustworthiness. Combination of Saturn and Mercury develops the habit of stealing. When coupled with Venus it gives rise to a sense of humour. In the signs of Aries, Leo, Saggitarius, Cancer, Scorpio and Pisces the 3rd house placed Saturn gives comparatively better results.

In male signs Saturn is fatal for brother and can break the home of sisters. In female signs it causes opposition to or from brothers, non-cooperation of brothers, loneliness, untrustworthiness and wickedness. One begets children late. In male signs children come early, but abortions are also possible. Lack of education is also probable.

Saturn is the sign of Virgo-Libra makes for financial difficulties after marriage, loss in business, lack of friends and disturbance in profession. The nature is humorous. Often his qualification and hard work are ignored. One's own near and dear persons put hurdles in progress. Patience is lacking and in times of trouble there is a tendency to run away. Saturn in Cancer also causes death of father or gives a step mother, besides the above mentioned results.

Saturn in Capricorn-Aquarius indicates acute lack of wealth, atheism, active nature, lack of trust, gradual progress, a calm, thoughtful, prudent and forceful disposition.

Saturn in Cancer-Scorpio-Pisces causes constant travelling, selfish nature, greediness, cruelty, carefulness, tremendous hard work and popularity.

3.5 Saturn in the Fourth House

The mysteriousness of Saturn extends its way over the 4th house also. According to the famed astrologer Narain Bhatta :

चतुर्थे शनौ पैतृकं याति दूरं धनं मन्दिरं बन्धुवर्गापवादः ।
पितुश्चापि मातुश्च सन्तापकारी गृहे वाहने हानयो वातरोगी ।।

that is, Saturn in the 4th house deprives the native of

ancestral property and abode. There is constant friction between him and his parents. He has to suffer because of false accusations and opposition of relatives, besides all kinds of losses. He is afflicted with wind-caused diseases.

Acharya Mahesh opines that Saturn placed in the 4th house causes health problems due to bile and wind. The individual is of bad conduct, disorganised, weak bodied, bad tempered and lethargic. In his words :

पित्तानिलक्षीणबलं कुशीलमालस्ययुक्तं कलिदुर्बलांगम् ।
मालिन्यभाजं मनुजं विदध्यात् रसातलस्थो नलिनीशजन्मा ।।

Manasagar holds that ;

बन्धुस्थितो भानुसुतो नराणां करोति बन्धोः निधनं च रोगी ।
स्त्रीपुत्रभृत्येन विनाकृतश्च ग्रामांतरे चासुखदः स वक्री ।।

Direct Saturn placed in the 4th house is detrimental to health and relatives. If retrograde, it is fatal for wife, children and servants. Even after abandoning ancestral house ill-luck keeps dogging the individual.

Jeevanath's view supports the theory of Narayan Bhatta. Kalyan Varma says :

पीड़ितो हृदयहिबुके निर्बाधवववाहनार्थमतिसौख्यः ।
बाल्ये व्याधितदेहो, नखरोमधरो भवेत् सौरे ।।

that is, nails and hair are prominent, there is heart disease and lack of wealth, vehicle, wisdom, happiness, health and near and dear ones.

Bhrigusutra analyses the results of such a Saturn (in the 4th house) in reference to mother :

मातृहानिः । द्विमातृवान् । सौख्यहीनः । निर्धनः उच्चे स्वक्षेत्रे
न दोषः । अश्वांदोलनाघवरोही । लग्नेशे मन्दे मातृदीर्घायुः

सौख्यवान्   रंध्रेशयुक्ते   मात्रारिष्टं   सुखहानिः ।

that is, if Saturn is not the lord of the Ascendant the chances of mother's death and having a step mother are very strong. When Saturn is joined by the lord of the 8th house then also the individual loses his mother to death. Wealth and happiness remain unachieved. But it Saturn is placed in his own house or is exalted, then these evil effects are mitigated. Vashishtha has stressed physical troubles, Varahmihir has underlined happiness and anxiety, while Parashar indicates happiness through contact with low and wicked people.

Garg maintains that the individual is not able to obtain proper, high standard housing. He suffers frequent changes of place, unhappiness and bad health :

भग्नासनोऽगृहो नित्यं विकलो दुखपीडितः ।
स्थानभ्रंशमवाप्नोति सौरे   बन्धुगते नरः ।।

In Kashinath's opinion the individual destroys his wealth, happiness, virtues and contentment through bad company. Close relatives betray him :

सुखं मन्दे सुखैर्हीनो   हतार्थो   बांधवैर्नरः ।
गुणस्वभावो दुःसंगी कुजनैश्च न संशयः ।।

Vrihad Yavan Jatak and Aryagrantha offer nothing new in this context. But Vaidyanath has underlined troubles to mother, deceitful behaviour, immoral conduct and unhappiness :

आचारहीनः कपटी च मातृक्लेशान्वितो
भानुसुते सुखस्थे ।

Gholap has quoted physical debility, inhuman nature,

bad company, suffering from loss of virility, inactiveness and weakness due to wind problems.

Gopal Ratnakar predicts father's death along with that of the mother. According to him illness causing pains and aches, impudence, troubles from the authorities, lack of ancestral money, lack of land & house and daily labour as means of livelihood are also indicated as the evil results of Saturn placed in the 4th house.

In the opinion of Jaideva, it brings wind induced disease, weakness, lethargy and troubles along with wealth and prosperity :

बहुवित्तवातसहितो विबलोऽलसकाश्यदुखसहितः सुखगे ।।

Western astrology experts clearly maintain that in this house if Saturn is posited in Libra, Capricorn and Aquarius then it causes gain of ancestral wealth, greed, untiring hard work for money, comforts of land and house, prosperous agricultural property and an affluent later life. A weak or afflicted Saturn deprives of mother's presence. Every aspect of life proves troublesome. Fourth house placed Saturn make the individual fond of being alone because his life passes facing problems. It has been tested through experience that Saturn in the 4th house causes mother's death prior to that of the father. The individual finds his guardian always opposite to his own mentality. He suffers from physical or mental afflictions.

Saturn posited in Aries, Cancer, Leo, Libra, Saggitarius, Scorpio, Pisces or Gemini gives government or state service. The individual is interested in scientific subjects. There is a possibility of two marriages.

Saturn posited in Taurus, Virgo, Capricorn and Aquarius results in higher success through business rather than service, although in the beginning the business is beset with serious problems. It also indicates a second wife and a step mother. Generally the individual is sober, indifferent, aware, patient, non-violent, large hearted, just, virtuous, giver of charity, suffering from domestic or family feuds, staying away from home and hospitable.

Saturn in Aries, Leo, Saggitarius, Cancer, Scorpio and Pisces indicates lots of children. In Taurus, Virgo and Capricorn Saturn gives some children but in Gemini, Libra and Aquarius it indicates childlessness. A child may die early. When ancestral wealth is destroyed or lost then destiny starts working. The individual may be adopted by someone. From 36th to 56th year is his life's best period. Luck smiles on him only when he is far away from his native place.

Saturn posited in Taurus, Virgo or Capricorn causes accidents related to space or the sky. Regions located in the west are suited for progress. Old age is spent in economic stringgency. All these effects are accentuated if Saturn is malefic or afflicted.

3.6 Saturn in the Fifth House

Practically all astrologers have condemned Saturn placed in the 5th house. Such a Saturn is not considered positive and beneficial :

यदा मन्देऽपत्यं गतवति कथं पुत्रजनितः
सुखं शुद्धा बुद्धिः कथमपि विभूतिश्च परमा।
कलिर्मित्रैः किं नो भवति जठरे किं नहि रुजः
सपर्या देवानां कथमपि च वर्या जनिमताम्।।

The above quoted shloka is a beautiful example of question-answer style. According to it, the individual is without a son, indiscreet or imprudent as well as without riches and friends. He suffers from stomach ailments and does not believe in supernatural powers.

Kashinath maintains that such Saturn deprives the native of fame, prosperity, power of action, beauty and children. He suffers throughout :

पुत्रे मन्दे पुत्रहीनः क्रियाकीर्तिविवर्जितः ।
हीनकोशो विरूपश्च मानवो भवति ध्रुवम् ।।

Astrologer Mahesh has predicted life long illness. The individual always remains weak. His libido is almost dead. Prosperity remains elusive. Children receive undesirable or unfortunate results. Yavan Jatak also has the same view :

सदागदक्षीणतरं शरीरं धनेन हीनत्वमनंगहीनम् ।
प्रसूतिकाले नलिनीशपुत्रः पुत्रस्थितः पुत्रभयं करोति ।।

Dhundhiraj has expressed apprehension that such a native is likely to have problems with his children.

Manasagara deviates somewhat. It says :

शनैश्चरे पंचमशत्रुगेहे पुत्रार्थहीनो भवतीह दुःखी ।
तुंगे निजे मित्रगृहे च पंगौ पुत्रैकभागी भवतीति कश्चित् ।।

that is, Saturn in inimical sign in the 5th house, causes sorrow on account of children and money. But such Saturn, if placed in his own house, exalted or in a friendly house, can give one son.

Gholap and Gopal Ratnakar have called such Saturn the destroyer of all happiness and comforts.

In Kalyan Varma's opinion :

सुख-सुत-मित्रविहीनं मतिरहितमचेतसं त्रिकोणस्थः ।
सोन्मादं रवितनयः करोति पुरुषं सदा दीनम् ।।

Saturn when placed in the 5th house certifies deficiency or absense of intelligence, feelings, friends, health, children and prosperity. The individual suffers from mental disease and remains poor and deprived throughout life.

Varahmihir also holds a similar view.

In astrologer Vaidyanath's view results are a combination of auspicious and inauspicious effects :

मत्तश्चिरायुसुखी चपलश्च धर्मी
जातो जितारिनिचयः सुतगेऽर्कपुत्रे ।

that is, the native is arrogant and lives long but lacks happiness. He is fickle, slayer of enemies and full of religious beliefs.

Sage Parashar has praised Saturn in the 5th house in very determined terms. In his opinion this combination makes the individual prudent, full of intense power of action. He is blessed with lots of sons.

Sage Garg has explicated the effects of such Saturn according to the signs occupied :

सुतभवनगतोऽरिमन्दिरस्थः सकलसुतान् विनिहन्ति मंदगामी ।
समुदितकिरणः स्वतुंगमस्थः कथमपि जनयेत् सुतीक्ष्णमेकपुत्रम् ।।
घटशनिः सुतगः सुतपंचकी मृगशनिश्च सुतात्रयदस्तथा ।

that is, Saturn in the 5th house in inimical sign destroys children. But exalted or own house Saturn grants one son, though belatedly. Power of discretion is lost. Saturn in Capricorn and Aquarius indicates female and male offspring respectively.

Narayan Bhatta opines that :

शनौ पंचमे च प्रजाहेतुदुःखी विभूतिश्चला तस्य बुद्धिर्न शुद्धा।
रतिर्दैवते शब्दशास्त्रे न तद्वत् कलिर्मित्रतो मंत्रतः क्रोडपीडा।।

The main reason of the nature's worries is childlessness.
Wealth and prosperity are uncertain, that is he is never
carefree regarding money matters. He goes astray and his
mind is confused. He believes in hypocrisy. He does not
have faith in religious, cultural & mythological references,
truths, facts or personalities. Because of his deceptive nature
his friends can not cooperate with him. Mantras are
ineffectual. He is totally materialistic and directionless.

According to Mantreshwar, Saturn in the 5th house
weakens the prospects of education, prosperity, progeny
and happiness. The nature is fond of journeys. But he can
not concentrate on his goals.

भ्रान्तो ज्ञानसुतार्थहर्षरहितो धीस्थे शठो दुर्मतिः।

Bhrigusutra has included some new theories :

पुत्रहीनः अतिदरिद्री दुर्वृत्तः दत्तपुत्रः
स्वक्षेत्रे स्त्रीप्रजासिद्धिः।
गुरुदृष्टे स्त्रीद्वयम्, तत्र प्रथमाऽपुत्रा द्वितीया पुत्रवती।
बलयुते मन्दे स्त्रीभिर्युक्तः।

The individual is childless, suffering acute poverty and
of evil conduct. He adopts a son. Saturn placed in his own
house gives daughters. If aspected by Jupiter then the native
marries a second time while his first wife is barren. The
second wife bears him a son. A strong Saturn grants plenty
of pleasure through women.

In the opinion of Khankhana the individual is bereft of
intelligence, full of worries, childless, unhapply, lethargic
and short statured :

बदअक्लो मुत्फकिरः सुतसुखरहितश्च काहिलो मनुजः ।
जोल्हः पंजुमखाने कोतह देहश्च जाहिलो भवति ।।

Western scholars of astrology have done wide and deep deliberations on this point. Saturn in the 5th house when conjoined auspiciously with Sun or Jupiter causes unprecedented success in those fields which are included in his domination such as land, mines, domestic activities and community leadership. The individual receives education of a high standard. A malefic Saturn gives unsuccessful love affairs, emotional and romantic involvement with a person of advanced age and often childlessness also. According to 'Stree-Jataka' women have to suffer acute pain in the stomach. They attain motherhood very late. There may be an interval of 5 to 13 years between two children. Afflicted Saturn causes loss of wealth through lottery, horse-racing or betting. The individual dies either of heart ailment or by drowining. His children are corrupt and unintelligent. In an auspicious trine like the 5th house an evil planet like Saturn usually gives harmful results. Saturn occupying Taurus, Virgo, Libra, Capricorn and Aquarius sign also give unpleasant results. In other signs happy situations are created.

Saturn in Cancer, Scorpio and Pisces causes many children in quick succession. The individual exercies influence on public. His nature is replete with wickedness, quarrelsomeness, selfishness and revenge. Such natives are usually officers in banks, district councils, social institutions, legislative assembly, parliament or railways. They certainly contribute memorably to the society.

Saturn in Taurus, Virgo and Capricorn indicates a gentle temperament, activeness, devoid of intrigues, a cheerful and contented nature, friendliness and poor chances of having the pleasure of children. His wife suffers from gynaecological problems. Stomach ache, irregular periods, unhealthy uterus prove to be the cause of unhappiness. The individual marries several times.

Saturn posited in Gemini, Libra and Aquarius indicates complete education, unreliable nature, extreme selfishness, scant happiness from parents, chances of being adopted and ancestral property. An individual with Saturn in the 5th house achieves success only after long and continuous ancestral property. His wealth is always problem-ridden. Practically all astrology experts have proved an afflicted, malefic Saturn or a Saturn joined with evil planets as harmful. Childlessness, problems on account of children, unworthy children and long intervals-varying from 5, 7, 9 to 11 years-between two children are effects of such a Saturn. The nature suffers from anxiety regarding children throughout life. He is extremely self seeking and a stranger to humanitarian values. But he has authority and powers.

3.7 Saturn in the Sixth House

Several astrologers have expressed their views and opinions on the wide-spread results of Saturn in the 6th house.

According to Jeevnath :

अरौ मंदे चौरादपि नृपकुलाच्छत्रुगणतः
कथं भीतिः पुंसां जननसमये सम्भवति चेत्।
कथं योद्धा युद्धे महति पुरतस्तिष्ठति बलान्-
महिष्यादेर्लाभः सततमभितः कीर्तिरधिका।।

that is, King/state authority, thieves and enemies can not harm the native. He proves to be a formidable warrior and slayer of enemies. Cattle are profitable for him. He gets immense fame.

In the opinion of Kalyan Varma the individual with Saturn in the 6th house is good looking, brave, a voracious eater, wicked-hearted, full of lust and vanquisher of opponents :

प्रबलमदनं सुदेहं शूरं ब्रह्माशिनं विषमशीलम् ।
बहुरिपुपक्षक्षपितं रिपुभवनगतोऽर्कजः कुरुते ।।

Manasagar has asserted mixed effects :

नीचे रिपोर्थे च कुलक्षयं च षष्ठे शनिर्गच्छति मानवानाम् ।
अन्यत्र शत्रून् विनिहन्ति तुंगी पूर्णार्थकामान् जनतां ददाति ।।

which translates into the fact that if such Saturn is in an inimical sign or dibilitated then the individual turns out to be destroyer of his family. Bit if it is exalted or in his own house then the native is granted ability to vanquish enemies, prosperity and satisfaction of lust-fulfilment.

Mahesh maintains that the native is vanqhisher of enemies, appreciater of good qualities, full of noble thoughts, refuge of common people, healthy and strong, fond of lots of food and a thinker :

विनिर्जितारातिगणो गुणज्ञः सुज्ञाभ्यनुज्ञा परिपालकः स्यात् ।
पुष्टांगयष्टिः प्रबलोदराग्निर्नरोर्कपुत्रे सति शत्रुसंस्थे ।।

Jageshwar thinks that the enemies of the individual are subdued by themselves. His mental and physical abilities are of high order. But he suffers from venereal diseases :

शनौ शत्रुगे शत्रवः संज्वलन्ति प्रतापानले राजगेहेऽरिचारान् ।
बलैबुद्धियोगैर्भवेत् कस्तदग्रे परं वा प्रमेही स रोगी नितंबे ।।

Varahmihir, Vaidyanath, Vasishtha, Parashar and Dhundhiraj mention the following special results such as powerful, rich, respected by enemies, victorious and followers of ethical teachings.

Sage Garge analyses Saturn situated in the 6th house
from a different angle :

विद्वेषपक्षक्षपितः शूरो विषमचेष्टितः।
बह्वाशी बहुकाव्यश्चारिदाहो रिपुगे शनौ।
षष्ठे नीचगतः सौरिर्जनयेन्नीचवैरिणम्।
अन्यथा वैरिणं हन्ति निर्वैरं स्वगृहे हतः।।

that is, the individual is a destroyer of enemies totally,
fond of food, brave, expert in writing beautiful poetry and
glorious. But such Saturn when placed in a debilitated sign
encourages petty enemies. Saturn if in his own house,
prohibits enemies. Such a Saturn causes enemies to be
destroyed by themselves.

Kashinath proves Saturn in this 6th house as beneficial.
In his view :

शत्रुस्थाने स्थिते मन्दे शत्रुहीनो महाधनः।
पशु-पुत्रयशोयुक्तो नीरोगी जायते नरः।।

that is, the individual is wealthy, without enemies,
healthy, famous, having sons and owner of cattle wealth.

According to Vrihad Yavan Jataka :

विनिर्जितारातिगणो गुणज्ञः स्वज्ञातिजानां परिपालकश्च।
पुष्टांगयष्टिः प्रबलोदराग्निर्नरोऽर्कपुत्रे सति शत्रुसंस्थे।।
छायासुतो भवेच्चैव शत्रुमातुलनाशकृत।।

that is, destruction of large hordes of enemies,
appreciation of qualities, looking after of relatives are the
traits of the individual. He is healthy, strong, fond of food
and harmful for maternal uncle and enemies.

Aryagrantha has pointed out some other effects :

नीचो रिपौ नीचकुलक्षयं च षष्ठः शनिर्गच्छति मानवानाम् ।
अन्यत्र शत्रून् विनिहन्ति तुंगः पूर्णार्थकामाञ्जनतां ददाति ।।

Debilitated Saturn posited in a low Rashi indicates annihilation of the family. Exalted gives wealth and luxuries. In other signs it destroys enemies.

As different from this, Gopal Ratnakar claims that Saturn placed in the 6th house causes the individual to be with few sons, argumentative, rich, troubled by enemies, deaf and imbecile. While at the same time Gholap considers such Saturn to be good because of many reasons.

Mantreshwar has quoted stubbornness and vanity also along with other effects.

Narayan Bhatta also deals with it in great detail :

अरेर्भूपतेश्चौरतो भीतयः किं यदीनस्य पुत्रो भवेद् यस्य शत्रौ ।
न युद्धे भवेत्संमुखे तस्य योद्धा महिष्यादिकं मातुलानां विनाशः ।।

that is, the individual is carefree regarding enemies, authority in power and thieves. He is an expert in warfare and very brave. He is a good speaker and deft in logic. Keeping, buying and selling of cattle is profitable for him. But unpleasant happenings with the maternal uncle keep cropping up.

Harivansh maintains that :

पुष्टिर्देहे वीर्यमारोग्यतश्च भाग्यं भोगं भूषणं वाहनं तु ।
विद्या वित्तं सौख्यवर्गं तनोति शत्रोर्हानिं शत्रुगोऽशत्रुपुत्रः ।।
प्रसादो भूमिपालतः स्त्रीपुत्रजनितं सौख्यं जन्मे षष्ठगते शनौ ।

the individual is disease free, potent, lucky, owner of riches, comforts, enjoyments, vehicles, servants and favour of the king or authority and suppresser of enemies.

Khankhana especially mentions some unmitigable sorrow along with generosity/ charitable nature and prosperity.

According to Bhrigusutra he has few relatives. All of his efforts do not bear fruit. Saturn conjoined with Mars indicates a stay away from home or native place. Saturn placed in the 8th house gives undesirable results. Pains, wounds and wind induced diseases trouble the individual.

Many non-Indian thinkers have also contemplated in this context, if Saturn is weak and malefic, then the individual suffers from diseases all his life. Problematic situations regarding food, clothing and health always confront him.

He does not keep clean. In a fixed sign Saturn gives cough, inflammation in the bronchial tube, heart problem, urinary trouble etc. In a moving sign Saturn causes diseases of stomach, chest and joints. In common signs Saturn indicates asthama, problem in lungs and pain in the legs. If Saturn is strong and auspicious it causes a position of high authority.

According to astrologer Katve such a Saturn makes the first half of life a store-house of problems. Lack of shelters, lots of fruitless labour, ill-repute and obstructions at every step are the results of Saturn placed in the 6th house. Maternal uncle and aunt may suffer from various troubles or problems.

Such individuals are happy in their marriage. Buffalo among the milch cattle is profitable for him. In old age he has physical and financial difficulties. He keeps staying away from his native place or home. This causes problems. He has business acumen. But he either enjoys fame or prosperity- not both.

3.8 Saturn in the Seventh House

The presence in 'Jaya Bhava' (house of wife) of the mysterious planet Saturn, in certain contexts has been discussed in detail by astrologers.

Jeevnath opines :

यदा दारागारं गतवति दिनाधीशतनये
गदैरार्ता दाराः बलमपि कुतो वित्तमधिकम् ।
अनुत्साहः कृत्ये भवति कृशतातीव भविनां
गदानामाधिक्यं सपदि चपला बुद्धिरभितः ।।

that Saturn in the 7th house destroys or harms the health of the wife of the native. He is powerless, moneyless, lethargic, sick and fickle minded.

Manasagar has discussed it making the marital life as point of focus :

विश्रामभूतां विनिहंति जायां सूर्यात्मजः सप्तमगश्च रोगान् ।
धत्ते पुनर्दम्भधरांगहीनां मित्रस्र् वा वंशभवां मनुष्यः ।।

that is, Saturn in the 7th house creates differences and conflicts, in marital life. The first wife of the individual dies a premature death. He suffers from diseases. Even his second marriage is not as per his wishes. Life becomes devoid of peace. The second wife is arrogant and slightly physically disabled. In short, the native suffers widowhood and second marriage.

Mahesh says that the individual is thin bodied, without means of earning money, restless, deprived of comforts of home, wife and food and impractical :

आमयेन बलहीनतां गतो हीनवृत्तिजनचित्तसंस्थितिः ।
कामिनीभवनधान्यदुःखितः कामिनीभवनगे शनैश्चरे ।।

Dhundhiraj has a similar view point. Mantreshwar mentions relationship with a mean natured woman.

The description of Narayan Bhatta is multifaceted :

सुदारो न मित्रं चिरं चारु वित्तं शनौ धूनगे दम्पती रोगयुक्तौ ।
अनुत्साहसंतप्तकृद्दृहीनचेताः कुतो वीर्यवान् विह्वलो लोलुपः स्यात् ।।

that is, the native is deprived of a comely wife, noble and clean hearted friends and wealth, comfort and enjoyments early in life. Both husband and wife remain afflicted with diseases. Unhappiness and sorrow born of constant problems ultimately render him inactive and incorrigibly lethargic. He becomes apprehensive and timid. Greed takes root. Consequently he cannot maintain the required image at the social level.

According to Parashar :

सप्तमे स्त्रीविरोधनम् । हीना च पुष्पिणी व्याधिदौर्बलिनस्तथा ।

that is, he is humiliated by woman/wife. Usually he cohabits with low, sick or menstruating females. Varahmihir also supports this view. Vaidyanath also mentions broad and full bosom of his wife.

In the words of Vasishtha :

रविजः किल सप्तमस्थः जायां कुकर्मनिरतां तनुसन्ततिं च ।

A characterless/corrupt wife and few children are the ill effects of the 7th house placed Saturn.

Both Gholap and Gopal Ratnakar have accused such Saturn for practically all problems and they maintain the individual remains sick and worried. Death of first wife, a second marriage, evil, fickle, unintelligent, unhappy disposition, wicked friends, sick wife, lack of food and clothing, away from home, dependent on others, immoral conduct, many marriages, pain in naval and ears etc. are the effects of Saturn situated in the 7th house. The native loses money in government disputes.

Kalyan Varma holds the view that :

सततमनारोग्यतनुं मृतदारं धनविवर्जितं जनयेत् ।
धूनेऽर्कजः कुवेषं पापं बहुनीचकर्माणम् ।।

— diseases haunt the individual all his life. From the angle of appearance, nature and social status, he is unattractive and looked down upon. He puts on ugly clothes. His wife dies all of a sudden.

'Vrihad Yavan Jataka' also confirms this theory.

Kashinath opines that :

कलत्रस्थे मित्रपुत्रे सकलत्रो रुजान्वितः ।
बहुशत्रुर्विवर्णश्च कृशश्च मलिनो भवेत् ।।

He as well as his wife are disease ridden, troubled by enemies, deformed, weak and dressed in dirty unsightly clothes. In the opinion of Khankhana the native is of immoral conduct, unhealthy, reticent, unintelligent and dominated by other.

वदरो जनः कृशांगः कमफलमश्च मानवो हिर्जः ।
जानो वा स्याज्जोल्ही हफतुमखाने यदा भवति ।।

Garga underlines the deceitful and fradulent character of the individual.

Bhrigusutra says :

शरीरदोषकरः कृशकलत्रः वेश्यासम्भोगवान् अतिदुःखी
उच्चस्वक्षेत्रगते अनेकस्त्रीसम्भोगी कुजयुते शिशनचुम्बनपरः
शुक्रयुते भगचुम्बनपरः परस्त्रीसम्भोगी ।

— his physique is weak and defective. Wfe keeps ill. He is unhappy and goes to prostitutes. If Saturn is in his own house or exalted,```````` the individual cohabits with many females. If conjoined with Mars, his wife is a nymphomaniac. If Saturn is joined with Venus then he himself is over lusty and always eager for sex.

In the opinion of western astrologers Saturn in the 7th house often results in unpleasant or undesirable influences. Married life remains full of clashes and unhappy. Life partner is lost. Immoral conduct is encouraged. Husband and wife are unhappy, hopeless, dull and lacking communication. Friends are mean natured and can act inimically any time. Working with somebody's active support causes huge loss. No redress is granted by the courts or government authority. Social interference often causes hurt. Unnecessary disputes croup. If Saturn is placed in a common sign, it indicates many marriages. A strong Saturn begets wealth or property from wife's side. Long lasting prosperity is also probable. If such a Saturn is situated in a woman's birth chart then she marries a rich widower, much older than her.

If Saturn is benefic then the individual gets a suitable wife who is predominantly Saturnine. He gets lots of opportunities of progress after marriage. Saturn in Libra indicates happy married life. But a combination of Saturn and Moon adversely affects marital happiness.

Since the 7th house affects several aspects of marriage, presence of Saturn in it creates specific results.

Saturn in Taurus, Virgo, Libra, Capricorn and Aquarius often gives undesirable results. In the opinion of astrologers if a malefic planet is in the centre then the result is not a happy one.

Saturn in Pisces, Aries, Leo, Gemini, Cancer, Scorpio and Saggitarius indicates a good marriage. The couple is happy. Even their disputes are for the sake of fun. The wife is totally devoted to her husband. She displays patience and understanding. She encourages and inspires her spouse. She always makes efforts for his health, prestige, fame and happiness. The wife of such an individual is well versed in house-hold chores and adept and disciplined in social and personal conduct. Her personality plays an important role in domestic matters.

Allen Leo's opinion regarding Saturn in the 7th house is worth considering. This placement indicates no marriage or a late marriage. But if married, the wife is sober, trustworthy, fair-minded, hard working, foresighted, careful and very prudent in spending money. Despite not being the best placement, it makes for a happy conjugal life. The wife expresses her love not through words but her behaviour. She expects the same from her husband.

The 7th house Saturn gives a wife who is patient, sober and matured temperament. Her appearance and temperament can be defined according to the Sign :

1. **Saturn in Aries :** Wife is tall, proportionate and slim bodied, oval faced, with sharp eyes, pretty nose and good hair. Her personality is imbued with pride in a desirable way.

2. **Saturn in Leo-Saggitarius :** Face is round, figure is impressive but not very tall. Complexion is dusky, voice is sweet and nature is cheerful and expressive but behaviour is a little dry.

3. **Saturn in Taurus-Virgo-Capricorn :** The wife has a square face, nature is uncertain, complexion is fair but lack-lustre, hair is thin and she does not talk much.

4. **Saturn in Gemini-Libra-Aquarius :** She is fair, a good conversationalist but a little quarrelsome, has a round glowing, fleshy face, hair is thin but silky.

5.   Saturn in Cancer-Scorpio-Pisces : The wife has a brooding nature. She has a long impressive face, long hair, dry but lustrous.

A speciality of Saturn in the 7th house is that though the wife is beautiful, financial condition remains worrisome. Business is uncertain and unsatisfactory. Professional ups and downs and changes keep happening. Children are few. From 28th year onwards, the individual starts business. Between 36th and 42nd years luck provides many venues for progress. Saturn in Taurus-Virgo-Capricorn creates chances for a second marriage, after which progress takes place. Saturn in the 7th house keeps a strong desire for food and sex always alive.

Saturn in Aries-Gemini-Leo-Saggitarius-Capricorn and Aquarius gives its full effect, attains fame in many fields.

Saturn in Gemini-Virgo-Saggitarius-Pisces helps in the fields of astrology, teaching, editing, mathematics and printing. Either the mother or the father dies in his childhoood. He can be adopted by someone. At the age of 52-55 years, he may lose his wife.

Saturn in Gemini-Libra-Aquarius makes for long interval between the birth of two children. There are many sources of income.

In short, Saturn in the house of wife ('Jaya Bhavastha') often makes the individual uninterested in marriage. He dies before his life partner. Children may come late in life.

3.9 Saturn in the Eighth House

Saturn placed in this house of death has been considered from various angles by the scholars of astrology. According to Jeevanath

यदा रंध्रस्थाने दिनकरसुते जन्मसमये

विनाशो वित्तानां निजजनवियोगः सहजतः।
सदा वक्राकारा मतिरतितरां वा चतुरता
गदव्रातातंकः प्रभवति कलंकश्च भविनाम्।।

Saturn in the eighth house indicates the following results : destruction of wealth, unexpected separation from near and dear ones, crack mentality, suffering due to illness, slander and cleverness.

According to Mahesh :

कृशतनुर्ननु ददुविचर्चिका प्रभवतो भयतोष विवर्जितः।
अलसतासहितो हि नरो भवेत् निधनवेश्मनि भानुसुते स्थिते।।

The individual would be weak, suffering from skin diseases, discontented and conceited.

Manasagar opines that the individual will undergo suffering away from his native place. He has to face charges of stealing other's money and he is murdered by some evil person :

शनैश्चरे चाष्टमगे मनुष्यो देशान्तरे तिष्ठति दुःखभागी।
चौर्यापराधेन च नीचहस्तात् पंचत्वमाप्नोत्यथ नेत्ररोगी।।

In Jyotish-Shyam-Sangraha, causes of death of the individual have been discussed;

बुभुक्षया लंघनेन तथा च बहुभोजनात्।
संग्रहण्याः पाण्डुरोगात् प्रमेहात् सन्निपाततः।।
कंटकैर्व्रणकोपेन हस्तिपादाभिघाततः।
हयतः खरतो मृत्युः मन्दे स्यान्मृत्युभावगे।।

Starvation, fasting, overeating, colitis, jaundice, diabetes, delirium, thornprick, wounds, or an elephant's, horse or donkey's kick may prove to be the causes of the individual's death.

Gholap and Gopal Ratnakar maintain that the individual would be controversial, poor, dependent on or under the power of others, cohabiting with low-class women, crooked, troubled, defamed, hater of good persons, mentally retarded, suffering from eye diseases, with weak semen and blood problems, with few children, suffering from leprosy and with a paunch.

Vashishtha opines that :

सर्वे ग्रहा दिनकरप्रमुखा नितातं
मृत्युस्थिता विदधते किल दुष्टबुद्धिम् ।
शस्त्राभिघातपरिपीड़ितगात्रभागं
सौख्येर्विहीनयति रोगगणैरुपेतम् ।।

The individual would be evil minded, wounded by some sharp weapon, unhappy and afflicted by many diseases.

Acharya Varahmihir and Sage Parashar have mentioned eye diseases, few children, sudden loss and illness.

Kalyan Varma says

कुष्ठभगंदररोगैरभितप्तं ह्रस्वजीवितं निधने ।
सर्वारम्भविहीनं जनयति रविजः सदापुरुषम् ।।

that the individual has a short life, lacks of enthusiasm and suffers from terrible diseases like leprosy and piles.

In the words of Mantreshwar :

शनैचरे मृतिस्थिते मलीमसोऽशंसोऽवसुः ।
करालधीः बुभुक्षितः सुहृज्जनावमानितः ।।

the individual is fond of filthiness, doesn't have property or money, is evil minded, hungry, humiliated by friends and suffering from venereal diseases.

Kashyap has categorised causes of death according to the Signs :

बुभुक्षया लंघनेन तथा प्रायोपवेशनात् ।
बन्धुवर्गादरिकरात् क्षयतः पृभुदद्रुतः ।।
चटकैर्व्रणकोपेन हयपादाभिघाततः ।
हस्ततः खरतो मृत्युर्मन्दे स्यानृमृत्युभावगे ।।

which means that—

Aries–hunger, Taurus–fasting, Gemini–starvation, Cancer–conspiracy by relatives, Leo–enemy, Virgo-tuberculosis, Libra–terrible skin disease, Scorpio–scheming persons, Saggitarius–injury or wounds, Capricorn–kick of a horse, Aquarius–elephant and Pisces–donkey, these are the causes of death as per signs.

Garg also throws light upon the causes of death of the individual :

विदेशतो नीचसमीपतो वा सौरिर्मृति रन्ध्रगतो विधत्ते ।
हृच्छोककासामयवद् विषूची नानाविधं रोगणं विधाय ।।

that is, the individual's death takes place somewhere far away from his house or in some low standard location. Besides he dies of injury, heart disease, cough or cholera like diseases.

Vaidyanath opines :

शूरो रोष्यग्रगण्यो विगतबलधनो भानुजे रन्ध्रयाते ।
मंदे लग्नगतेऽथवाष्टमगते तत्पाकभुक्तौ मृतिः ।।

that is, the individual is brave, hot tempered, loser of power and money. He dies in the period or Dasha of Saturn.

Jageshwar has underlined a few special symptoms :

परं कष्टभाक् क्रूरवक्ता प्रकोपी भवेत् क्षुद्रको धान्यकं नैव सत्वम् ।
परं हासवातादिकं किं तदग्रे यदा मन्दगो मृत्युगो वै नराणाम् ।।

that is, the individual is careless of propriety or impropriety in his speech. He is full of anger and unhappiness, follows some low profession and is bitter natured. He is extremely averse to jokes or light hearted talk.

In the opinion of Kashinath :

क्रोधातुरोऽष्टमे मन्दे दरिद्रो   बहुरोगवान् ।
मिथ्याविवादकर्ता स्याद् वातरोगी भवेन्नरः ।।

that is, the individual is full of anger, lacking wealth, given to irrelevant disputes and discussions and suffers from wind induced diseases.

According to Harivansha, Saturn in the 8th house makes the individual poor, powerless, apprehensive, conceited, engaged in some wicked or bad job, suffering from scabies or a disease connected with semen, and gives a wicked son:

स्याःदायुस्थे दद्रुयुक्तो दरिद्री धातोर्हीनो दुर्बलांगो रुजानाम् ।
सुतौ धूर्तौ भीरुरालस्यधीरो भानोः पुत्रे निन्द्यमार्गप्रगामी ।।

In the words of Bhrigusutrakar :

त्रिपादायुः दरिद्री शूद्रस्त्रीरतः सेवकः ।
उच्चे स्वक्षेत्रे दीर्घायुः ।
अरिनीचगे भावाधिपे अल्पायुः कष्टान्नभोगी ।।

The individual lives upto 75 years, is without property, cohabits with low-born women and faces troubles in earning a livelihood. But if Saturn is placed in his own house or exalted then long life and if debilitated or placed in inimical sign a short life is indicated.

Khankhana has mentioned ill effects like illness, conceit, betrayal, evil nature, fear and miserliness etc. in this context:

वीमाराश्च   हरीशो   दगलवाजश्च   दोजखी   मनुजः।
जोहलो हस्तमखाने भवति बरवीलः कृपालसो भीरुः।।

Yavan Jataka mentions fearlessness, while Narayan Bhatta maintains that :

वियोगो जनानां त्वनौपाधिकानां
विनाशो धनानां स को यस्य न स्यात्।
शनौ रंध्रगे व्याधितः क्षुद्रदर्शी
तदग्रे जनः कैतवं किं करोतु।।

that is, the individual does not stay near wise persons. He is attracted to the company of the wicked. He has to suffer separation from his dear ones. He is troubled by loss of money and health. He is narrow minded and small hearted. He always looks for faults in others. He derives great satisfaction in accusing others. He can be a leader of cheats.

According to western astrologers Saturn gives results in accordance with Rashis or signs. Saturn in Libra, Capricorn and Aquarius causes gain of huge property through marriage. The individual inherits property from some prosperous relative and enjoys life.

A strong Saturn indicates long life and natural death. But Saturn afflicted by evil planets indicates poverty, troubles from poor financial condition after marriage, loss of earned wealth, and death from some terrible and long lasting disease. In Cancer and Aries these bad influences increases even more.

The 8th house belongs to death. Yama or God of death is the synonym of Saturn. The combination of two factors of terrbile characteristics is extremely tragic. Astrologers do not favour this conjunction.

An 8th house placed Saturn increases its evil influence in the signs of Taurus, Virgo, Aquarius, Saggitarius, Pisces and Gemini.

Saturn in Aries, Leo, Libra, Scorpio and Capricorn gives one sided results. From amongst wealth, children and prestige, only one is acquired. Saturn in Cancer indicates multi faceted gain, power, money, children and sudden profits - all come to the individual.

Saturn placed in Saggitarius shelves opportunities of progress after marriage. In Aries, Gemini, Cancer, Leo, Saggitarius and Capricorn Saturn inspires the individual to run his own enterprise. Other signs indicate service. Saturn situated in the 8th house gives happiness either in the first or the later half of life. The wife one gets is patient and pragmatic with lots of good qualities. The 8th house Saturn also indicates death in full consciousness. The individual may even have premonition of his death. His fortune smiles after the 36th year. If Saturn is heavily afflicted then it may cause imprisonment, disease, unhappy marital life, loss of parents at an early age, or father's impoverishment, extreme trouble and a problematic 32nd year. Such Saturn brings about several vulnerable occasions (Yogas) of death.

3.10 Saturn in the Ninth House

Saturn placed in this house of "Dharma" (righteousness) influences the conduct of the native. If affets his fortune and future. The astrologer Garga analyses it in great details :

दंभप्रधानः सुकृतः पितृदैवतवंचकः ।
क्षीणभाग्यः सुधर्मा च स्यान्नरो नवमे शनौ ॥

स्वोच्चे स्वभे शनौ भाग्ये वैकुंठादगतो नरः ।
राज्यं कृत्वा स्वधर्मेण पुनर्वैकुंठमेष्यति ।।

नवमभावगतः स्वगृहे शनिर्भवति चेत् स महेश्वरयज्ञकृत् ।
अतिशयं कुरुते जयसंयुतं नृपतिवाहनचिह्नसमन्वितम् ।।

that is, the individual would be full of good deeds, vain, devoid of faith, lacking good fortune but religious. Exalted or own sign placed Saturn indicates that the native has enjoyed a fine past, has a desirable present and grand future. He may be the performer of great "Yagnas" (such as Maheshwar) and would have royal comforts and vehicles. He would be a victor. Manasagar has the following view :

धर्मस्थपंगुर्बहुदंभकारी धर्मार्थहीनः पितृवंचकश्च ।
मदानुरक्तो विधनी च रोगी पापिष्ठभार्यापरहीनवीर्यः ।।

Saturn in the 9th house deprives one of wealth, patience and righteous conduct. He is overpowered by extreme arrogance. He does not hesitate in deceiving even his own father. He and his wife both are over lustful and sexed, therefore, he suffers from various diseases born of loss of semen.

But Mahesh has somewhat different view point. He says :

धर्मकर्मसहितो विकलांगो दुर्मतिर्हि मनुजोऽतिमनोज्ञः ।
संभवस्य समये यदि कोणः त्रित्रिकोणभवने यदि संस्थः ।।

that is, the individual is religious and performer of good deeds. There may be some physical debility. By nature he is often crooked. But he is good looking. "Kona" and "Tritrikona" are synonyms of Saturn and the 9th house respectively.

The opinion of Jeevanath has special significance :

यदा धर्मस्थानं गतवति शनौ जन्मसमये
सुहृद्वर्गाद्दुःखं प्रभवति गतिस्तीर्थविषये।
गृहद्वारं दीनं द्विजपरिवृतं शीलममलं
वयोऽन्ते वैराग्यं रतिरपि च योगे तनुभृताम्।।

that is, Saturn when placed in the 9th house, causes extreme opposition from the relatives of the individual. Even friends prove to be enemies. But the native can control his desires. In youth he stays in auspicious and sacred places. Easily moved by others sorrows he is generously charitable. His mind is devoid of any blemish. By nature he is detached. In the later half of his life he renounces all enjoyments and comforts and seeks salvation through Yoga.

According to Narayan Bhatta :

मतिस्तस्य तिक्का न तिक्तं सुशीलं
रतिर्योगशास्त्रे गुणो राजसः स्यात्।
सुहृद्वर्गतो दुःखितो दीनबुद्ध्या
शनिर्धर्मगः कर्मकृत् संन्यसेद्वा।।

which means that the individual is full of discernment and wisdom and therefore, abdicating worldly matters and enjoyments he turns towards the path of Divine Bliss. He suffers and begets only sorrows from this world. Yet his conduct is pleasing to others. "Rajoguna" (royal attributes) is predominant in him. He takes interest in Yoga, and its practice. He takes actions to benefit his relatives and friends. But he chooses either activeness or perennial detachment.

In the opinion of Jageshwar :

भवेत् क्रूरबुद्धिस्तथा धर्मनाशो न तीर्थं न सौजन्यमेतस्य गेहे।
तथा पुत्रभृत्यादिचिन्तातुरः स्यात् यदा पुण्यगो मंदगामी नरस्य।।

that is, the individual is of a ruthless mentality, lacks wealth, is worried about children and servants, devoid of gentle behaviour and disinterested in pilgrimages.

In the view of Khankhana the native is wealthy, soft-spoken, full of humanity, fortune and contended :

बख्तबुलन्दः श्रीमान शीरींसखुनश्च मानवो यदि वै।
जोहलो बख्तमकाने बेतालश्च हि कृपालुरपि भवति।।

There is ample contradiction between the views of Varahmihira and Kalyan Varma. According to Varahmihira the individual has wealth, children and happiness. While Kalyan Varma maintains that the individual not only lacks all these but also causes unhappiness and pain to others.

Parashar opines that Saturn in the 9th house causes imprisonment to the friends of the individual. According to Gholap he goes through life without Dharma, noble conduct, health, company of virtuous people, desire for enjoyments and affection of good persons. He may be attacked by wild beasts.

Gopal Ratnakar says that the native is miserly yet builds ponds and temples. He is troubled by his relatives from the father's side. He is gradually separated from his female relatives.

Western thinkers have proved that Saturn in beneficial Libra, Capricorn, Aquarius and Gemini is auspicious. It makes the individual thoughtful, patient, sober, stable minded, reticent, expert in legal matters, studious and a scholar of profound metaphysical subjects. He earns fame through educational and religious institution. He may even start a new school of thought or creed. If Saturn in the 9th house is afflicted by malefic planets then the individual has deceit, stinginess, pettiness, obstinacy, disrespect towards religion and selfishness. He suffers from the side of his wife. He meets failure in book publishing, stays away from home and legal matters.

Combined with benefic influences Saturn indicates successful stay away from home. Otherwise it generates purposeless travelling and confusion.

Saturn placed in the 9th house and in Aries, Leo, Saggitarius, Gemini, Cancer, Scorpio and Pisces gives opportunities of progress after the 36th year. After the 20th year, the individual starts trying to earn money.

In other signs or Rashis problems and troubles keep cropping up. Loss of immovable assets, hurdles in earning money, disturbed/unstable lifestyle, uneasy relation and separation from father and brother are some of the indications of such a Saturn. Marriage takes place late as well as in an unconventional manner. A foreigner wife during stay abroad is also probable. There is a curious mixture of "Yes" and "No" in his nature,

Saturn in "Male sign" indicates complete education. One may have a step mother. Saturn in Cancer, Scorpio and Pisces proves fortunate for younger brother and sister.

3.11 Saturn in the Tenth House

There is a special significance to the placement of Saturn in the 10th house, the house of Karma or action. An all pervading influence of Saturn, negative or positive, becomes manifest on the activities of the individual. In this regard Manasagar says :

शनैश्चरे कर्मगृहे स्थितेऽपि महाधनी भृत्यजनानुरक्तः ।
प्राप्तप्रवासे नृपसद्मवासी न शत्रुवर्गाद् भयमेति मानी ।।

that is, the individual is wealthy, honoured, and admired by his servants owing to his policy, vanquisher of opponents and luxuriates like a king in his stay away from home.

Jeevnath has explicated the special features of the 10th house Saturn in figurative language :

अजा माता बाहुर्जनक उत कल्याणमभितः
शनौ राज्यस्थानं गतवति जयस्तस्य समरे।
प्रभुत्वं कोषस्य क्षितिपतिगृहे दुष्टदमना-
धिकारो यस्य स्वं नहि मिलति पूर्वार्जितमपि।।

that is, the individual survives on goat's milk (because he loses his mother soon after birth). He has to rely on his own efforts and labour (because he loses his father's affection too alongwith his mother). His prosperity is acquired by his own hands. He enjoys all kinds of comforts due to his constant hard work. He is trusted of the king and reaches important position such as that of treasury officer or penal officer. He is not able to enjoy ancestral wealth. But he acquires all luxuries and fame through his own endeavours.

The wise Mahesh has endorsed these very symptoms in a different way :

राज्ञः प्रधानमतिनीतियुतं विनीतं सद्ग्रामवृन्दपुरमेदनकाधिकारम्।
कुर्यान्त्रं सुचतुरं द्रविणेन पूर्णं मेषूरणे हि तरणेस्तनुजः करोति।।

that is, the native is well versed in policy matters. He is gentle and secretary to the authority in power. He enjoys many high privileges. He earns fame and fortune through his own mental calibre.

In the opinion of Maharishi Garga :

भवेद् वृन्दपुरग्रामपतिर्वा दंडनायकः।
प्राज्ञः शूरो धनी मन्त्री नरः कर्मस्थिते शनौ।।
सेवार्जितधनः क्रूरः कृपणः शत्रुघातकः।
जंघारोगी नीचशत्रुराशिस्थे कर्मगे शनौ।।

that is, the individual is endowed with valour, wealth and wisdom. On many occasions or in many ways he heads the city or province. But if Saturn is situated in a debilitated or inimical sign or Rashi then these attributes are changed. The individual then is miserly, cruel and danger to enemies. He earns money by serving others. He suffers from diseases of the thigh region.

Jageshwar has declared such a Saturn as totally condemnable:

शनौ कर्मगे पितृघाती नरः स्यात् परं मातृकष्टं कथं देहसौख्यम् ।
तथा वाहनं मित्रसौख्यं कुतः स्याद् ध्रुवं दुष्टकर्मा भवेत्रीचवृत्तिः ।।

taht is, Saturn located in the 10th house kills the father. It also constantly creates hurdles in the way of getting love or company of mother. The individual is surrounded by vicious friends, evil deeds and vile things. Lack of near and dear ones, dearth of physical comforts and troublesome conveyance are the results of Saturn placed in the 10th house.

Narayan Bhatta maintains that :

अजा तस्य माता पिता बाहुरेव वृथा सर्वतो दुष्टकर्माधिपत्यात् ।
शनैरेधते कर्मगः शर्म मन्दो जये विग्रहे जीविकानां तु यस्य ।।
शनौ व्योमगे विंदते किं च माता सुखं शैशवं दृश्यते किन्नु पित्रा ।
निधिः स्थापितो वा पिता वा कृषिश्च प्रणश्येत् ध्रुवं दृश्यते दैवतो ना ।।

The similarity between the views of Narayan Bhatta and Jeevnath is notable. The individual is not destined to enjoy parents' love and company. He becomes an orphan in infancy. He earns prosperity and happiness through his own efforts and endeavours. He succeeds in his struggles. He is affected by conceit of his authority and status. When in power he behaves in an unbridled manner. He can enjoy not ancestral one, only self earned property.

In the view of Kashinath :

कर्मभावो सूर्यपुत्रे कुकर्मा धनवर्जितः ।
दयासत्यगुणैर्हीनश्चंचलोऽपि भवेत् सदा ।।

that is, the individual is corrupt, without wealth, fickle, impatient, fond of lying and ruthless.

But Vaidyanath has said, admiring such Saturn, that the native is prosperous, well respected, valiant, head of the family, adminitrator and disinterested in worldly pleasures. In his words :

मंदे यदा दशमगे यदि दंडकर्ता
मानी धनी निजकुल प्रभवश्च शूरः ।। विवासः ।।

As opposed to the above, Vashishtha criticises Saturn of the 10th house :

बहुकुकर्मरतं कुपुत्रं दौर्मनस्यं ।

that is, the individual is involved in several vile deeds, is corrupt minded and has bad sons.

In the opinion of Parashar if the 10th house Saturn is in Pisces, then it makes for "Pravraja Yoga" (indicator of renunciation). The individual is prosperous, happy and honoured :

दशमे धनलाभं सुखं जयं
माने च मीने यदि वार्कपुत्रः संन्यासयोगं प्रवदंति तस्य ।

Varahmihir has mentioned the special effects of happiness and valour. Mantreshwar has quoted the individual's interest in agricultural activity : 'कृषिपरः ।'

Harivansh holds the view that if exalted and placed in his own house then such Saturn causes headship of the village, prosperity, honours and recognition from the king or Government and discretion. In other Signs activates constant struggle and danger from enemies :

बुद्धियुक्तं पूर्णवित्तं मनुष्यं ग्रामाधीशं राजमान्यं करोति।
स्वोच्चस्थो वा स्वस्थस्थो वा विशेषात् शेषस्थचेत् वैरिभीत्यं शनिश्च।।

Khankhana has included the auspicious results of Saturn in its own period or Dasha :

शाहमकाने जोहलत्वेषु दशापते च मानवः शाहः।
अथवा भवेन् मुशीरः खुशखुल्कः सुकृती गनी नेही।।

that is, the individual is like a king, minister or secretary of the king, happy, performer of noble deeds, well honoured and full of human qualities. But these results become manifest in Saturn's own period or Dasha.

Gholap has accepted such a Saturn as propitious. In the opinion of Gopal Ratnakar the native spends his entire life staying away from home or native place. There is little happiness from mother's side. He is dominated by bile and is miserly. He may be a farmer or a chief or head. He likes places of pilgrimage.

In the opinion of Bhrigu :

पंचविंशतिवर्षे गंगास्नायी अतिलुब्धः पित्तशरीरी पापयुते कर्मविघ्नकरः
शुभयुते कर्मसिद्धिः केन्द्रे मन्दे षट्त्रिंशद्वर्षादुपरि भाग्यवृद्धिः
जनसेवकः मित्रवृद्धिः समाजकार्ये राजकार्ये च कुशलः सम्मानलाभश्च।

that is, the individual bathes in the Ganges in his 25th year. He is greedy and dominated by bile. If Saturn is joined by malefic planets then there are hurdles in work. If joined with auspicious or benefic planet then jobs are completed. Placed in a kendra (quadrants) Saturn helps in rise of fortune after 36th year. The individual is a helper of people, skilled in official jobs and behaviour, well respected and has many friends.

The western astrologers have ascertained results accepting the supreme importance of conjunction with planets and their effects and the sign falling in the 10th house. Accordingly Saturn when joined with auspicious planets like Capricorn, Libra, Aquarius and Gemini, gives good results. The individual earns fame in the field of law and justice. He attains high status and gets wealth. Constant activeness, high ambition, trustworthiness, foresight, orderliness and grace are the effects in this case. He has allround good fortune. He progresses continually through personal endeavour, coupled with good luck. He displays his abilities in his position as the chief officer in some prestigious and important institution.

When Saturn is afflicted by evil planets then the individual does not discriminate between good or bad in his arrogance born of power and place. He is bad in character, untrustworthy and conspiratorial. He falls as speadily as he rises.

If Saturn is conjoined with Sun, Mars or Jupiter then the ill-effects increase many fold. He loses ancestral property and parents in childhood. Constant failure in earning a livelihood, under employment, disputes with higher autority and bad name in public service are some of the results. There is always a risk present to his prestige and he can not become self dependent.

If Saturn in the 10th house is afflicted by Sun or Moon it gives all kinds of bad results. In this house Ares, Scorpio and Pisces are considered especially unpropitious. H.N. Katve has analysed Saturn in the 10th house in great detail. According to him, father's death, chances of adoptions, exile from the country, constant change in occupation, loans and problems therefore, lack of livelihood, aimlessness and many other losses are indicated. Saturn placed in this house gives trouble to one's parents. The individual may even go to jail for financial crimes. Lots of problems in service, mental confusion, long illness and misfortune become manifest. Bereft of means of earning the individual suffers humiliation from family and society. He has to face terrible struggles even for the bare minimum needs and amenities. He does not have the benefit of ancestral property. His fortune rises when away from his birth place.

Saturn in Aries, Leo, Saggitarius and Gemini causes expertise in serious subjects in learning, teaching, correction and chances of business. In other signs renouncing the world, writing, editing, religious leadership, astrological practice etc. become more pronunced inclination. He may get membership of local administrative institutions.

Saturn in Aries, Leo, Saggitarius, Gemini, Cancer, Scorpio and Pisces indicates full education in the fields of chemistry or law. The individual earns his living through work in courts, police, army or technical jobs.

Saturn in Taurus, Virgo, Libra and Aquarius justifies the proverb "easier said than done". The individual is an expert in his profession. He earns his living through writing, preaching, contractorship or brokerage of imported goods. He does not enjoy the happiness of having a wife or son. e is lustful.

If Saturn is in infelicitous conjunction with Venus or Moon then it causes physical relation with older women. As age increases, his sexual urge increases too. His clothes are untidy. He cares more for social life than his family. He sacrifices his personal good for the sake of social service. He is either extremely lustful or totally godly. He has a special mission in life towards which he devotes entire energy. But if the 10th house Saturn is afflicted by evil planets it creates insurmountable obstacles and problems in the individual's life.

3.12 Saturn in the Eleventh House

The 11th house is the house of profit or gains. Renowned scholar of astrology Narayan Bhatta has expressed his opinion while explicating the qualities of such Saturn in the 11th house in the following words :

स्थिरं वित्तमायुः स्थिरं मानसं च
स्थिरा नैव रोगादयो न स्थिराणि ।
अपत्यानि शूरः शतादेक एव
प्रपंचाधिको लाभगे भानुपुत्रे ।।

that is, the individual turns out to be fortunate in several dimensions. He posses the pleasure and profits of intellect, valour, long life and wealth. He never has to face any serious health problem. He remains carefree, though once in a while his children and fault finding attitude cause mental tension. He is tops in intrigues.

According to Jageshwar, the native is prosperous. He posseses valuable animals such as elephants. Leaving a side some minor problems he generally is very healthy. But he needs to guard against fire :

धनं सुस्थिरं दन्तिनस्तस्य गेहे
भयं चाग्निना जायते देहदुःखम् ।
न रोगा गरिष्ठास्तदंगे कदाचित्
यदा लाभगो मन्दगामी जनानाम् ।।

Vaidyanath has also accepted 11th house Saturn as entirely beneficial :

भोगी भूपतिलब्धवित्तविपुलः प्राप्तिं गते भानुजे ।
दासीदासकृषिक्रियार्जितधनं धान्यं समृद्धिं शनिः ।।

that is, the individual enjoys several benefits from his
own endeavour or through king's or authority's favours. He
is used to prosperity. As regards servants also, he is very
lucky. He reaps huge profits from agriculture. He posses
property and wealth. Vaidyanath does not throw light on
the negative side of this Saturn. Varahmihir has mentioned
immense wealth while Vashishtha mentions fame. Parashar
has especially talked about company of good friends.

Jayadeva has mentioned various sources of income :

कृष्णगोर्णिकाश्वगजनीलबलाढ्यतः स्यात् ।
सद्वस्तुता   भवति   लाभगतेऽर्कसूनौ ।।

The means which generate money for him are
agriculture, wool, fourfooted animals like horses and
elephants, things of blue colour and cottage industry.

Kashinath has also written about livestock. According
to him :

छायात्मजे तु लाभस्थे सर्वविद्याविशारदः ।
खरोष्ट्रमहिषैः पूर्णो राजमान्योऽशुचिर्भवेत् ।।

that is, because of Saturn in the 11th house, the
individual happens to be well versed in several subjects. He
is honoured by the king or government but involved in
undesirable actions. He posseses livestock like buffaloes,
camels and asses and earns huge profits through them.

The author of Manasagara has given some special
attributes :

सूर्यात्मजे चापगते मनुष्यो धनी विमृश्यो बहुभाग्यभोगी ।
मितानुरागी मुदितः सुशीलः सबालभावे भवतीतिरोगी ।।

that is, contentment is the by-word with the individual. He is wealthy, a good thinker, fortunate and fond of luxuries. He suffers from many diseases in childhood. He likes cool places and things.

Astrologer Mahesh expresses the view that if a strong Saturn is placed in the 11th house then dark horses, blue gems, elephants and woollen clothes are among the things he posseses and enjoys.

As in the following :

कृष्णाश्वानामिन्द्रनीलोर्णकानां नानाचंचद्वस्तुदन्ताबलानाम् ।
प्राप्तिं कुर्यान् मानवानां बलीयान् प्राप्तिस्थाने वर्तमानेऽर्कसूनौ ।।

Mantreshwar assures that Saturn in the house of profit or gains is the giver of long life, wealth, valour and health :

बह्वायुः स्थिरसंपरायसहितः शूरो विरोगो धनी ।

Kalyan Varma uses slightly different words :

बह्वायुः स्थिरविभवः शूरः शिल्पाश्रयो विगतरोगः ।
आयस्थे भानुसुते धनजनसम्पद्युतो भवति ।।

In the above description a wealthy family and earning through skill in crafts is worth noting.

Khankhana, describing the effects of the 11th house Saturn, writes :

साहबदर्दो नेकः शोरीसुखन स्तवंगरो वा स्यात् ।
याप्तमकाने जोहलईशाः साविरो रिपुहन्ता ।।

which means that the individual is sensitive, good to others, soft spoken, of noble conduct, propertied, vanquisher of enemies and balanced.

Harivansh mentions state honours, acquiring of knowledge through wise and learned persons and income from various sources :

पृथ्वीपालं मानलाभं धनं च विद्यालाभं पंडितेभ्यः प्रसूतौ ।
नानालाभं सर्वतो मानवस्य लाभस्थाने भानुपुत्रो विदध्यात् ।।

In the opinion of the writer of Bhrigusutra, Saturn of the 11th house does not let any work to be completed without problems. Though longlasting and multidimensional benefits are derived from the state or the ruling authority. Such Saturn when situated in Libra, Capricorn or Aquarius is a promoter of knowledge, fortune, and means of pleasure and comfort :

बहुधनी विघ्नकरः भूमिलाभः राजपूजितः ।
उच्चे स्वक्षेत्रे विद्वान् महाभाग्यभोगः वाहनयोगः ।

Gopal Ratnakar has underlined disturbance in education. He says that both the native and his father do not have an elder brother. He gains profits from land. Gholap concedes virtuous character, glory, defeating of enemies, clean heart and a comfortable, well arranged life in a fine home.

The knowledgeable Garga says :

स्थिरसंपत्तिभूलाभी शूरः शिल्पान्वितः सुखी ।
निर्लोभश्च शनौ कैश्चित् मृतप्रथमजीविकः ।।

that is, the prosperity and landed property of the individual remain stable. He is talanted, happy, contented, humble and valiant. His first child is still-born.

There is considerable similarity in the views of Jeevnath and Narayan Bhatta :

यदा लाभस्थानं गतवति शनौ यस्य जनने
स्थिरं वित्तं चित्तं स्थिरमपि चिरं जीवति च सः।
प्रपंचस्याधिक्यं रणभुवि च शूरत्वमधिकं
कुतो रोगाभोगः कुत उत सुतस्तस्य भवति।।

that is, the individual lives long and is immensely learned and prosperous. He is healthy, valiant and engrossed in worldly matters. He does not beget a son.

Astrologers in other parts of the world maintain that if Saturn in the house of profit i.e. the 11th house, is in Libra, Capricorn or Aquarius (specially when they are auspicious) it gives special benefits from movable and landed property. The later half of life is better. Few relatives and trouble from children are indicated. Sometimes mean progeny, children late in life or death of children also occurs.

When Saturn is afflicted by malefic planets, it may cause troubles and problems from friends or in financial matters. Such Saturn when in conjunction with Sun and Moon causes extreme shortage of money. Such Saturn when situated in moveable signs indicates robbing of every thing by friends and when placed in fixed signs, it gives problems and troubles in early life. When it is placed in common signs it results in allround hopelessness.

Generally Saturn in the 11th house is not beneficial for son—speciality if it is in Gemini, Leo, or Saggitarius. The individual does not enjoy having a son. His middle life is happy. By nature he is stingy, non-greedy, prejudiced, diplomatic, crooked, self centred, non trusting, serious, out-spoken, jealous of friends and suspicious. He has to face many financial ups and downs.

3.13 Saturn in the Twelfth House

Regarding Saturn's placement in the 12th house, as in the case of other houses, the views of different astrologers display an apparent contradiction. According to Dhundhiraj:

दयाविहीनो विधनो व्ययार्त्तः सदालसो नीचजनानुयातः ।
न रोगभंगोज्झितसर्वसौख्यो व्ययस्थिते भानुसुते प्रसूतो ।।

that is, the native is devoid of mercy, money, happiness and contentment. He is plaugued by over expenditure. He is vain, physically handicapped and keeps company of vile and mean persons. Jeevnath opines :

व्ययस्थाने मन्दः प्रभवति तदा कादर उत
त्रपाहीनः शश्वच्छुभकृतिविधौ निष्ठुरमतिः ।
सचेदंगस्वामी परविषयगामी प्रमुदितः
सदा शत्रुध्वंसी यजनकृदसौ वित्तप इव ।।

Saturn in the 12th house makes the individual impervious, ardent and determined for good work. If this Saturn is also the lord of the lagna then chances of progress come one's way only when one is far away from the native place. The individual is a vanquisher of enemies and performs religious rituals involving heavy expenditure. According to Manasagar :

व्यये शनौ पंचगणाधनाढ्यो गदान्वितो हीनवपुः सुदुःखी ।
जंघाव्रणी क्रूरमतिः कृशांगो वधे रतः पक्षिगणस्य नित्यम् ।।

The individual leads several persons. He is physically handicapped, disease-ridden, unhappy, powerless, merciless and killer of birds. He suffers injury in the thigh.

Harivansh expresses the view :

स्वस्य देशे सदालस्ययुक्तो नरो बुद्धिहीनस्तथोद्विग्नचित्तः

बुद्धिभ्रंशं मानभंगं कुसंगं मन्दं शिल्पं देहजाडयं नरस्य ।
बन्धोर्वैरं वित्तहानिः प्रसूतौ कुर्युराजाब्दकुधरे व्यवस्थः ।।

that in his own surrpunding place he is aimless and effortless. His life is spent in foolishness, confusion, restlessness and mental distraction. He works slowly. His relations with his near and dear ones are not cordial. He wastes his wealth.

Khankhana has established that Saturn placed in the house of expenditure i.e. 12th house, is entirely undesirable:

तंगहालो बदफेलः पापासक्तश्च मुफलिसो मनुजः ।
जोहलः खर्चमकाने भवति हरिशः कृपालुरेव स्यात् ।।

that is, the individual is plagued by over expenditure throughout his life. Unexpected and undesirable spending, interest in condemnable activities, indiscrimination between present and past human behaviour are the results of such Saturn. The native is strong.

Varahmihir mentions downfall, Vashishtha says sharpness and Parashar adds on ache in the ribs.

According to Kalyan Varma :

विकलः पतितो रोगी विषमाक्षो निर्घृणो विगतलज्जः ।
व्ययभावगते सौरे बहुव्ययः स्यात् सुपरिभूतः ।।

that is, the individual is without happiness, shame, health, mercy, money, honour, good eye sight and nobility. Vaidyanath claims that the individual is a deceiver by nature. Garga has also deribed such Saturn :

नीचकर्माश्रितः पापो हीनांगो भोगलालसः ।
व्ययस्थानगते मन्दे क्रूरेषु कुरुते रुचिम् ।।

that is, the self indulgent, sinful and merciless individual is involved in vile actions throughout life. He may be physically debilitated.

Kashinath believes that the reason of his poverty is his unnecessary and uncontrolled expenditure. Such a native besides being fickle minded shabbily dressed, is also extremely selfish. He turns off his near and dear one, incurring their opposition to his behaviour :

असद्व्ययी व्यये मन्दे कृतघ्नो वित्तवर्जितः ।
बन्धुवैरी कुवेषः स्याच्चंचलश्च सदा नरः ।।

In the description of Bhrigusutra, alongwith other things, the following are worth noting :

पापयुते नेत्रच्छेदः शुभयुते सुखी सुनेत्रः ।
पुण्यलोकप्राप्तिः पापयुते नरकप्राप्तिः । शुभयुते राजयोगकरः ।।

that is, if Saturn is conjoined with malefic planets the individual is blind and goes to hellish regions after death. But when conjoined with auspicious planets the results are just the opposite.

Gopal Ratnakar adds up being learned alongwith physical debility.

When Saturn is joined with auspicious planets, the native is skilled and knowledgeable in many fields. His eye sight and his mentality is bad.

In Mantreshwara's description special mention is made of being defeated by enemies. According to Jayadeva, the individual is devoid of sensitivity, lacks money, happiness and is averse to conventions. He has an unimpressive physique, as in the follows :

विद्यो विधनः स्वकर्महीनो विसुखो हीनतनुर्व्यर्ययेऽर्कपुत्रे ।

Jageshwar writes about over expenditure, conceit,

sorrows and loss of dear one as results of the 12th house Saturn. The native passes his life working for and serving undesirable persons :

व्यये संप्रयुक्तोऽलसो नीचसेवी
कुतस्तस्य सौख्यं जनो याति नाशं।
यदा सौरिनामा गतश्चान्त्यभावम्।।

The description of Narayan Bhatta supports Jeevanath. Western astrologers hold the view that Saturn in this house gives unpleasant results only. The individual destroys his own happiness, progress and well-being. He suffers exile, fleeing or false accusations. Imprisonment is also possible. He may be poisoned. Hurdles are put in his way constantly by unseen enemies. He is at risk from animals. Gradually he becomes a loner or inclined towards renouncing the world.

All these ill effects are aggravated when Saturn is influenced by malefic planets. When conjoined with auspicious planets or with positive influences, benefit accrues from hospitals, prisons, beggar houses etc. The unfortunate conjunction of Mercury and Saturn may even cause insanity. With Mars it can cause bloodshed, suicide, or death by accident or sudden attacks. When unpleasant conjunction is present with Sun and Moon the demise of some dear one causes deep sorrow. The individual becomes disinterested in life and the world.

In general Saturn in Aries, Gemini, Cancer, Leo, Scorpio, Saggitarius and Pisces gives favourable results. There may be some inherent contradictions. The individual achieves remarkable fame due to his intelligence being expert in some field or founder of some institution, expert in legal matters or a politician. He has to stay away from home several times. He may be penalised in a struggle for power. With few children, being conventional and having secret sex life, these individuals earn fame. The wife is of sober disposition. One eye may be defective. They are slim. Their family does not progress much.

Saturn in Taurus, Virgo, Libra, Capricorn and Aquarius also gives the same contradictions for livelihood. There is education and position. The first born of the native is a duaghter, and family is big. He suffers from a flaw like self centredness, yet receives affection from elders. His sociability is doubtful.

Saturn in Gemini, Scorpio and Aquarius signs creates a revolutionary and fiery personality and gives eternal fame.

The above mentioned view points are the outcome of a thorough observation and examination of Saturn's effect as per its placement in the twelve houses of a horoscope by some of the most prominent astrologers. These results have been practically tested also on the basis of personal experiences.

It is notable that often the descriptions show variations and differences due to signs, influence of aspect and strength. The learned scholars and discerning readers would be able to find after a thorough study the positions and situations where most of these statements and descriptions synchronise with one another.

It needs no mention that a "Shastra" (discipline of knowledge) becomes meaningful only when its principles are interpreted according to a reference to the correct context, the specific person and the occasion. A detailed explication of Saturn's placement in the twelve houses is fully competent in laying bare the outer as well as the innermost mysteries of a personality.

4 Saturn in Twelve Signs and Aspects

Inference as to any planet's influence consists of a multi-dimensional analytical method. Future happens to be a live conglomerate of millions of visible and invisible rays. Deciphering nature or providence's mysterious script, therefore, entails a moment to moment examining of the individual's all round consciousness.

The enigmatic Saturn renders varied results when placed in various signs or Rashis besides its placement in the several houses. Scholars of astrology have minutely analysed this fact. The ace amongst them, Kalyan Varma, has anylytically dealt with Saturn's placement in the twelve signs especially in the 29th chapter of his "Saravali".

Saturn in Aries

When Saturn is in the sign Aries, it makes the individual extremely wrathful, inclined towards evil deeds, devoid of virtues, wicked and cruel. Such a person looks for disputes. He becomes habitual of picking enemy with others. All his tendencies become negative :

मेषेऽर्कजे सुरोषो जघन्यकर्मा च लब्धदोषोऽपि।
प्रियवैरो नैकृतिको नृशंसकोऽसूयकः पापः।।

He is garrulous, stubborn, foe to his own kith and kin, involved in worldly disputes, burdened with worthless labour and fiery by disposition. He is also unintelligent, full of deceit, a wanderer with lean physique. He is always restless. All in all, Saturn in Aries is unpleasant.

Saturn in Taurus

सौरे वृषभं याते भवति च जातः परांगनाप्रेष्यः।
नैकृतिकः स्फुटदृष्टो बहुक्रियासंगतो मूढः।।

The native behaves peculiarly in relation to women. In order to exploit them, he even serves them. Apparently he is frank. Even his wickedness is charming and stylish. He takes initiative in varied jobs but suffers because of his foolishness and wickedness. Servility predominates in him. Financially he is ordinarily placed. Not fated to enjoy family life, he is mysteriously popular amongst women. Even women senior to him in status or age are eager to do everything for him. His friends also are of undesirable types. His conduct is full of falsehood.

Saturn in Gemini

The individual spends his life mainly travelling. Continuous journey and living away from his native place is his destiny. Because of his spendthrift habits, he is always in financial difficulties. Consequently he feels trapped. He is enterprising. With his sweet and glib speech, he earns popularity, He is adept at putting up appearances, is secretive in his life style and an expert in official work. He is full of lust :

छलकृच्च मन्युदुष्टः क्रियातिशायी शठः कुशीलश्च।
बन्धनविहारसक्तो बाह्यक्रीडानुगो मिथुने।।

He is full of deceit, anger and meanness. Extrovert by nature, he likes freedom and restraint both, takes too long to do any work.

Saturn in Cancer

परबाधको विशिष्टो बन्धुविरुद्धो विलोमशीलश्च ।
मध्ये भूपतितुल्यः परभोगविवर्धितः शशिभे ॥

This individual always puts hurdles in other people's way, but earns fame for his own achievements. He is somewhat intolerant in his dealings with near and dear ones. His behaviour is full of contradictions. The middle period of his life brings him prosperity and fame along with competition. Despite being good looking and fortunate, he has a childhood full of struggles. He suffers from diseases during this period. He lacks maternal love. He is devoted to work of his own liking. Ill health is his destiny. He is soft spoken and readily performs noble deeds. If there is relation with the 7th house in any way, he may marry twice. There are signs of timidness also.

Saturn in Leo

As a result of Saturn being placed in Leo, the individual is truly committed to the field of study, research and writing. Despite being widely knowledgeable, he is the centre of controversy. Consequently he becomes rude and cold. He hardly enjoys conjugal happiness. Usually he has to earn his living through servile means. He is full of resentment with his closest people and is also ignored by them. He has few children. Often he receives objects of comforts from his adversities. He may beget wealth and honour from his wife's family.

नीचक्रियासु निरतो निवृद्धरोषो मनोरथैर्दान्तः ।
भाराध्वश्रमदुःखैः प्रकीर्णदिहो यमे सिंहे ॥

The native remains busy with degrading actions, suffers from lack of control over his desires and afflicted by excess of responsibilities and labour. Physically he is not very tall.

Saturn in Virgo

अधमः परोपकारी कन्याजनदूषकः क्रियानुरतः ।
कन्यायां रवितनये ह्रवेक्ष्यकारी पुमान् जातः ।।

The native is a do-gooder of the lowest kind. He considers a woman as thing of pleasure, though active, full of love and broody.

He is also reticent, affluent and goes on pilgrimages. If there is an inauspicious influence, he is a debauch, impersonating as eunuch, skilled in some handicraft and dependent on others. He is remarkably ambitious and crooked. He is also averse to friendship and discontented. He possesses a lean body. Saturn in Virgo leads to an explosion of arrogance.

Saturn in Libra

Saturn in Libra is highly acclaimed from a materialistic viewpoint. According to scholars, the individual is prosperous, leading a life fit for a king, well versed in various fine arts, fond of collecting precious things, full of aesthetic taste and achiever of name and fame through his stay abroad or away from home.

वृन्दसभानां ज्येष्ठो वयःप्रकर्षात्कृतास्पदः साधुः ।
कुलटानटीविटस्त्रीभरणो   रविजे   तुलायाते ।।

The individual is capable of establishing the power of his superior personality in a crowd of similars. He achieves a status befitting his age, but has a strong inclination for worldly and sensual pleasures.

He is the chief in his family, very generous and possesses heroic qualities. He attains a lot of renown.

Saturn in Scorpio

बाह्यो मंगलवाचैर्नृशंसकर्मा ह्वनेकदुःखः स्यात्।
अष्टमराशौ रविजे क्षयव्ययव्याधिभिस्तप्तः ।।

The native displays aversion to performing propitious rituals and acts. He has a crooked mind. Also, he runs the risk of being poisoneed, or injured by some weapon. By temperament, he is cruel and wrathful, avaricious, arrogant and misappropriator of others' wealth. He commits many mean and low acts. He also suffers losses, over expenditure and diseases. His life is full of hurdles. Often he does not beget a son. He is adamant, though troubled by conspiracies of his enemies. He has to suffer direct or indirect punishment.

Saturn in Saggittarius

Saravali considers Saturn in Sagittarius good. As in the following :

व्यवहारबोध्यशिक्षाश्रुतार्थविद्याभिधानुकूलमतिः ।
पुत्रगणैर्विख्यातः स्वधर्मवृत्तेश्च शीलैश्च ।।

अन्त्ये वयसि च लक्ष्मीं भुनक्ति परमां प्रलब्धमानस्तु।
अल्पवचा बहुसंज्ञो मृदुर्यमे कार्मुकस्थे स्यात् ।।

that is, the individual is given to scholarly pursuits and well versed in practical knowledge of various disciplines. He becomes renowned for his noble conduct, behaviour and nature. His son ably carries forward his fame. This soft spoken reticent native attains enormous wealth, prestige and honour in the later half of life. He enjoys a happy family life with children and wife. He is trusted and favoured by persons in authority. He is a leader of the community.

Saturn in Capricorn

स्थानविभूषणनिरतः क्रियाकलाङ्गः प्रवासशीलश्च।
कोणे मृगभे जातः प्रज्ञातशौर्योपचारः स्यात्।।

The individual is fond of good places and ornaments. He has practical knowledge of various arts. He is an expert in the use of medicines. He constantly stays away from home. He is extremely industrious.

The native is able to enjoy other men's wealth, property and women. He is honoured by eminent persons for his scriptual scholarship and knowledge of arts and crafts. He is also accorded honour in several places by followers of different faiths.

Though trusted by authority, king-like and enjoying perfumed goods, he suffers from eye problems. He also begets lots of lasting wealth.

Saturn in Aquarius

Unanimously scholars of astrology hold Saturn in this sign as condemnable. The individual is an inverterate liar, crooked, deceitful, lethargic, addicted to drugs and a womaniser. He is a conman and his companions and colleagues are also given to mischief. His temperament is explosive :

ज्ञानकथास्मृतिबाह्यः परांगनार्थः सुकर्कशाभाषी।
रवितनये   कुम्भस्थे बहुक्रियारम्भकृतयत्नः।।

that is, the individual is a womaniser, yet forthright and initiator of many actions. He has no interest in ethical or moral issues or religious discourse. He gains prosperity (often through windfall of others' wealth) troubled by adversaries and steeped in worldly pleasures.

Saturn in Pisces

धर्मव्यवहाररतो विनीतशीलो गुणैः समायुक्तः।
मीने भास्करतनये पश्चाद्धावास्पदं पुरुषः।।

The individual is disciplined and righteous in conduct. He is gentle, humble, full of good qualities and peace loving. He attains special status in later part of his life.

He likes performing auspicious rituals like the "Yagna". He is a capable craftsman. Knowledgeable in the deep issues of policy and ethics, he is wealthy and most eminent in his family and amongst his relatives. He is a connoisseur of gems, very practical, possessor of royal dignity, every body's well-wisher, happy with his wife and children, trusted by the authorities and an appreciator of positive abilities.

In order to predict the results of a planet, a study of the aspects of other planets also is very necessary. In the following account, the results of the aspects of other planets on a planet in various signs have been analysed.

Saturn in the sign of Mars and Aspects of Planets

Saturn aspected by the Sun results in the individual being prosperous through milch cattle, wealthy, expert in agriculture and involved in welfare work. Saturn aspected by Moon gives a wicked guardian to the subject. He is restless by nature. He destroys his wealth, name and happiness through involvement with mean and low type of women.

Saturn aspected by Mars inspires individual towards cruelty. He is totally involved in prohibited activities. He patronises swindlers. He is addicted to drugs and women. He is motivated by lower instincts but attains fame. Saturn aspected by Mercury causes an individual to be liar, garrulous, glutton, poor, unhappy, a notorious cheat, irreligious and contemptible.

Saturn aspected by Jupiter makes the native fortunate, pious, ethical, prominent among a group of advisers and happy.

Saturn aspected by Venus renders the native perverted, womaniser, very unstable and unhappy.

Saturn in the Sign of Venus and Aspects

Such a Saturn aspected by the Sun makes the native learned, dependent on others, lean in body, frank and poor.

Saturn aspected by Moon makes the subject close to womenfolk, respected by his kin and honoured by the authority. His power increases with the help and patronage of women.

Saturn aspected by Mars makes the native well versed in skill of warfare. He is peace loving, talkative and has a happy and prosperous family.

Saturn aspected by Mercury makes the individual wicked minded. He is infatuated with barren women and entertains others with his clownish acts.

The native with Saturn aspected by Jupiter is full of sympathy, popular, hard working and conceived with social welfare.

Saturn aspected by Venus makes the subject extremely powerful. He enjoys all kinds of luxuries and comforts. He begets precious jewels and ornaments.

Saturn in the Sign of Mercury and Aspects

Such a Saturn aspected by Sun makes the native religious, sober, averse to anger, patient, poor, unhappy and troubled.

Saturn aspected by Moon makes the native protector of women's interests, admired by women, having authority and owner of beautiful complexion.

Saturn aspected by Mars makes the Jataka a weight lifter, expert in warfare, a wrestler, sentimental yet crooked minded.

The native with Saturn aspected by Mercury, is expert in warfare, skilled dancer, musician, famous painter, intelligent and prosperous.

Saturn aspected by Jupiter causes the person to be blessed with noble qualities, favoured by officers, loved by relatives and prosperous.

Saturn aspected by Venus makes the subject naturally interested in womenfolk, having knowledge, both theoretical and practical, of yoga and skilled in marital affairs.

Saturn in the Sign of Moon and Aspects

Such a Saturn aspected by Sun deprives the native of his father in childhood. He is contented with non standard comforts and food etc. Evil minded, he remains deprives of wealth and wife. Saturn aspected by Moon gives the native wealth yet he suffers at the hands of his siblings. He may lose his mother also.

Saturn aspected by Mars makes the individual worrisome though rich. He gets involved with women of low repute, but he achieves power of status. Saturn aspected by Jupiter gives the person all kinds of comforts. He is lucky too.

Saturn aspected by Venus makes the native unhappy and discontented despite being born in a good family.

Saturn in the Sign of Sun and Aspects

Such a Saturn aspected by the Sun makes the native addicted to intoxicants, given to lying, unhappy, poor, stingy, disorganised and slave-like, being dressed in dirty, shabby clothes.

Saturn aspected by Moon makes the native enjoy all comforts and happiness provided by sons, wife, money, power and status.

Saturn aspected by Mars results in the individual being a constant vagabond, criticised/ abused, staying in hiding, mean, prone to stealing and without wife or children.

Saturn aspected by Mercury makes the person a fraud. He is fond of drinks, a slave of women, unhappy, poor and infamous.

Saturn aspected by Jupiter makes the native virtuous, full of leadership qualities, head of his community and prosperous.

Saturn aspected by Venus makes the subject good looking, rich, comfortable in old age, misogynist and prone to worries.

Saturn in the Sign of Jupiter and Aspects

Such a Saturn aspected by the Sun makes the native father of adopted sons. He gets riches, honour and fame through them. Saturn aspected by Moon deprives the individual of his mother, he has two names, good of conduct and possesses wealth, wife and children.

Saturn aspected by Mars results in the native being

extremely malicious. He suffers from wind or gas induced diseases and is involved in hateful deeds.

Saturn aspected by Mercury makes the subject enjoy luxuries fit for a king. He is a leader of community, good looking, fortunate, gentle in action and respectable.

Saturn aspected by Jupiter confers the highest rewards of power and position on the native. He is a diplomat, expert in military matters and capable in adversity. He is a master of policy.

Saturn aspected by Venus makes the person involved in many professions but he is industrious. He spends his life either in a forest or hilly region. There is a possibility of two parents i.e. stepfather, stepmother as well as own parents.

Saturn in Own Sign and Aspects

Saturn aspected by Sun makes the person dependent on others, worrisome and troubled with diseases. He has to carry loads and spend his life with an ugly wife.

Saturn aspected by Moon makes the native of unstable disposition, a fraud and wicked. He suffers during travelling and proves quarrelsome for his maternal relatives.

Saturn aspected by Mars renders the individual chief leader, hard working, bold, famous, virtuous, sharp and valiant.

Saturn aspected by Mercury makes the native good looking, resentful, ordinarily well off, well known and clever.

Saturn aspected by Jupiter gives the subject all the comforts and benefits of high position and a long life span which is free from illness. He acquires good qualities and fame easily.

Saturn aspected by Venus makes the individual fortunate, rich, involved with several women. He gets to enjoy all kinds of comforts and luxuries without much effort.

Different Planets in the Sign of Saturn and Planetary Aspects

It is also important to see what results are there when different planets aspect various planets situated in Capricorn or Aquarius. Astrologers have given much importance to this aspect in predictive astrology.

(1) Sun in Saturnian Sign :

1. If aspected by Moon, it causes fondness for ostentation, instability and hurdles. The native destroys his wealth and happiness due to desire for women.

2. If aspected by Mars, it makes the native jealous by nature. He suffers at the hands of wicked persons and diseases. He receives injury from some fatal weapon.

3. If aspected by Mercury, it makes the person industrious but feminine in temperament. He suffers from seminal diseases and has an attractive body. He covets other persons' possessions.

4. If aspected by Jupiter, the native is highly intelligent, famous, disciplined, industrious and the centre of hope for many people.

5. If aspected by Venus, the individual enjoys the company and property of wicked women. He deals in the sale and purchase of precious stones.

6. If aspected by Saturn, the individual gets support from the ruling power, has influence and capability of vanquishing his enemies.

(2) **Moon in Saturnian Sign :**

1. If aspected by Sun, the individual is of a nomadic nature, unhappy, helpful for others, an artist, vain and poor. He may be involved in farming and is valiant.

2. If aspected by Mars, the individual shows conflicting traits. He is prosperous but argumentative and vainn. He possesses vehicles and attains fame, but has an unstable mind.

3. If aspected by Mercury, the native is ever desirous of women. He is an expert in song and music and other self indulging sexual arts. He travels a lot but is not very prosperous. His mind is always confused.

4. If aspected by Jupiter, the individual has poer, money, sons, wife, land, orchards, servants, vehicles and fame.

5. If aspected by Venus, he has a perverted mind and is always eager for others' women and money. He is scared and unhappy. He is not respected by noble people and is involved in unsocial activities. He also invites trouble because of his bad temper.

6. If aspected by Saturn, the native is vain, ill dressed, over powered by lust, given tc fraudulent activities, undisciplined and wicked. He earns wealth through forest produce. He treats women folk as objects of pleasure.

(3) **Mars in Saturnian sign :**

1. If aspected by Sun, the individual is of a rude temperament, industrious, of dark complexion and possesses family and wealth.

2. If aspected by Moon, the individual is noble, unstable, hater of his mother, non-serious in friendship. He possesses jewels and ornaments.

3. If aspected by Mercury, the individual is soft spoken, insincere, wicked, lacking in wealth and irreligious and suffers from incomplete efforts and works.

4. If aspected by Jupiter, the native enjoys longevity, is influential, skilled, appreciated by colleagues and full of qualities required for acquiring power.

5. If aspected by Venus, the person is controversial, a womaniser and fond of comforts.

6. If aspected by Saturn, the individual is powerful and has authority and wealth. He begets many children and is learned and valiant. But he is unhappy and discourteous towards women.

(4) Mercury in Saturnian Sign :

1. If aspected by Sun, the individual has a strong physique, sweet-tongued, famous, hard-hearted and expert in wresting.

2. If aspected by Moon, the individual has a huge body and is vain. He earns prosperity through trading in liquid products. He may also deal in flowers, drugs and edible tubers.

3. If aspected by Mars, the individual is vain yet shy, gracious yet talkative. He is comfortable and talented.

4. If aspected by Venus, the individual is ugly, stupid, wicked and lustful. His family life is deplorable but he has many sons.

5. If aspected by Saturn, the individual is involved in evil deeds, lacks wealth and is unhappy and exploited.

(5) Jupiter in Saturnian Sign :

1. If aspected by Sun, the individual is good lookin and

manly. He enjoys wealth and happiness. Has many good qualities and possesses power and authority.

2. If aspected by Moon, the individual brings glory to his family. He has learning, good conduct, noble thoughts, and also money. He helps others and serves his father.

3. If aspected by Mars, the individual is an expert in warfare, handsome, well-known, respected, manly and proud.

4. If aspected by Venus, the individual lacks nothing. He has food, drinks, house, assets, ornaments, clothes, a wife and is contented.

5. If aspected by Saturn, the individual enjoys some high post of authority, has unparalleled qualities of character, possesses movable and immovable property and is happy.

(6) Venus in Saturnian Sign :

1. When aspected by Sun, the individual enjoys women freely. He is given to lust with impunity. He is prosperous, brave, patient and truthful.

2. When aspected by Moon, the individual possesses good looks, valour, wealth, influence and is very lucky.

3. When aspected by Mars, the individual suffers from diseases and love affairs. He also is troubled by over-work and is a breaker of rules and discipline.

4. When aspected by Mercury, the individual is full of learning, truthful, happy, prosperous, possessor of permanent property and qualities.

5. When aspected by Jupiter, the individual is soft and expert in the art of music. He gets a beautiful and

accomplished wife, and enjoys good clothes, ornaments, perfumes etc.

6. When aspected by Saturn, the individual is impressive looking despite being dark complexioned. He has many followers and is prosperous.

The above analysis underlines the effects caused by various planets located in the sign – Capricorn and Aquarius– of Saturn. Without proper understanding of positive or negative effects caused by the aspects of malefic or benefic planets, forecasting remains uncertain and vague. Astrology is a very complex discipline. Future cannot be properly ascertained if a one sided view is taken. In this context, the importance of the location of different planets in Saturnian signs and aspects of planets thereon is enormous.

●

5 Different Positions of the Mysterious Saturn

वैदूर्यकान्तिविमलः शुभकृत् प्रजानां,
बाणातसी कुसुमवर्ण निभश्च शस्तः ।
यंचापि वर्णमुपगच्छति तत्सवर्णन्,
सूर्यात्मजः क्षपयीतति मुनि प्रवादः ।।

(Brahatsamhita Ch.10/Shloka-21)

"Planet Saturn resembles the shining bright, glorious and with emitting peaceful light like stone, known as Cat's eye, as well as blue as the 'Alsi' flower, which whenever travels in direct motion, brings plenty of prosperity, pleasure and happiness in the lives of natives. Sages say that Saturn destroys the persons of black complexion similar to that of its own."

In astrological parlance, Saturn is primarily responsible for such experience as misery and grief, struggle and frustration, poverty and filth, pain and punishment, decay, destruction and death. It is not that Saturn gives only bad results all the time. Planets offer results as warranted by a native's past karma. No power can stop the effects of one's karma from fructifying them in any manner. When good things in life are promised by past karma, Saturn does give them in full measure. But the difference, however, is in Saturn's process of giving such results.

Karmic fruits are in the form of enjoyment or sorrow concerning some aspect of senses and biological existence. Actual experience of these results, therefore, is the sum-total of impressions registered on the objective mind, consequent to the happenings brought about by planetary influences. As we know, the objective mind is connected with the brain and the external world through the senses. These impressions are momentary and fade away as fast as new impressions follow. Whereas, karmic results are brought about by the influence of Saturn in particular, such experiences transcend to the subjective mind and do not cease just at the level of senses. The subjective mind is a link between the soul and the objective mind. It possesses latent memory and hence the impressions on the subjective mind are enduring and formative. As coral takes shape under the ocean, the experiences on the subjective mind mould the inner character.

The natives with such horoscopes wherein the influence of Saturn predominates are very much likely to be in the melting pot of life's experiences. Irrespective of the merits of such horoscopes and the environmental conditions prevailing, they are bound to be simmering with mental turmoil in the form of disappointments, disillusions or disenchantment. If it is Cursed Destiny, the mental metamorphosis stems from poverty, failures and obstacles in life dogging every step. With regard to Blessed Destiny the change within is brought about by the very success and prosperity, consequent to realization of futility of achievements in materialistic sense. In either case, the outcome would be the same; an urge for freedom, to run away from everything, to seek solitude ultimately leading to detachment and renunciation. An in-depth study of such horoscopes would reveal that they belong to souls who are highly evolved and have reached the end of their journey towards Moksha. The mental turmoil they are undergoing in this life is in actuality, a process of purification.

We can better appreciate the mode of dispensing karmic results by Saturn once we realize that pain and pleasure, success and failure, sorrow and happiness are relative concepts and are inseparable. One ceases to be meaningful in the absence of the other. In its final analysis, both are illusions as they are mere impressions registered on the objective mind. Powerful impact may either numb the sense of experience or distort the impressions: Nausea develops from plenty and disillusion out of easy success. In delivering results, Saturn incites a sense of misery and frustration even while endowing one with success, power and pelf by shattering the illusion shrouding the objective mind through the experiences of karmic results and in doing so turns it into a melting pot of mental turmoil. In this process, the dirt and muck of kama (lust), krodha (anger), moha (delusion), lobha (avarice), mada (infatuation) and matsarya (jealousy) that are deeply embedded within, get burnt and destroyed and the mind is completely liberated from illusion (Maya).

A purified mind is the first stage in developing spiritual tendency, in re-programming life by accepting right values and in finding a purpose higher than mere sensual pleasures and physical existence. In this context, Saturn is a purifying crucible from which the mind emerges cleansed and purged.

If the influence of Saturn be of malefic kind then the impressions received by the subjective mind would get distorted in the process, leading to mental imbalance. On the other hand, when the influence of Saturn is of benefic nature, and strong, it results in power of concentration. Most of the products of the genius are the outcome of impressions of the subjective mind. In interpreting the role of Saturn in a horoscope, wherein it is in Kendra to the Moon, the inferences reached could be diametrically opposite unless based on a realistic evaluation of the nature and strength of Saturn's influence. But the fact remains that, other things being equal. this horoscopic pattern depicts a mind that is serious, brooding and deep while being devoid of buoyance and sparkle. It gives a tendency to keep the head down involved in tedious and meticulous kind of occupation with a negative attitude towards enjoyment of sensual pleasures. In brief, sufferance is the badge of this tribe even were they to be housed in a palace.

The role of Saturn in moulding the basic pattern of life would be more pronounced under two distinct formats. One is where Saturn and the Moon are in mutual kendras (square) or conjunct. The other is when Saturn is in Lagna Kendra (square to Ascendant). In other words, the 1st, the 4th, the 7th or the 10th sign from Ascendant in one case and from the Moon in the other. Other things being equal, the chart with Saturn in Kendra to the Moon is indicative of delays and obstacles in life's progress and a visible condition of mental depression; a sluggish response to the joys of life.

An altogether different picture emerges in respect of horoscopes with Saturn posited in Kendra to the Ascendant. It spells success and material progress. In horoscopic interpretation, the ascendant is the vital clue as to the scope and opportunity in life within the ambit of which karma results are to materialize. Influence of Saturn being conducive to the application of one's efforts, effectively contributes in a large measure to converting the opportunities into achievements. Commensurate with strength of Saturn and its disposition with reference to the relative strengths of other planets, the achievement could reach dizzy heights with the material prosperity well consolidated. Even under adverse conditions, the success may be slow to come by dogged by delays and obstacles, but the native will rise above the average level and mark his presence. But one should not lose sight of the fact that while such activities involving application of one's efforts find success, other aspects of life concerning experiences emanating from senses would suffer. In consequence, the achievement and success in life instead of strengthening the bond of sensual attachment to worldly affairs will cause detachment. This comes about by the realization of the truth that success exists only as illusion. Their involvement in activities would, however, continue despite success or failure. Under beneficial influences, the natives of such horoscopes would be the workers and their work invariably oriented towards the benefit of society or the well being of mankind and least for their own personal ends. This pattern of horoscope provides a good foundation for the emergence of a life of Nishkama karma.

The reason for such a condition is not far to seek. Kendra is a key position in a horoscope as it provides clear and unobstructed reach to its counterpoints in all the four directions. When Saturn is in Kendra to the Moon, the full impact of Saturn's influence would be on the Moon. The inevitable consequence of it, from the point of astrological delineation, would be that mind would lose some of its buoyancy. A buoyant mind responds to the impressions of karmic results with vigor and sparkle, through the senses. It is an exuberant, vibrant and responsive mind. Because of its buoyancy, the impressions on the objective mind are rebounded and the subjective mind is thus shielded. Once the buoyancy of objective mind is deflated, it is slow in its responses. The impressions of karmic results will then infiltrate into the subjective mind, which results in brooding over every little happening around. Such a condition is, of course, best suited for concentration or meditation but certainly not conducive to enjoyment of sensual pleasures.

An imprint of both the patterns in one, thus placing Saturn in Kendra to the Moon as well as the ascendant makes the horoscope very significant. With Saturn in sufficient strength and supported by benefic influences of other planetary forces, the native of such a horoscope would leave his footprints on the sands of time by way of enduring achievements. Should the environment be not conducive to material success, it may result in a high degree of achievement on the spiritual side. The horoscope of every eminent personality who has risen to great heights by dint of his efforts is likely to have this pattern as its foundation. It would be the 'in' thing to take up for purposes of illustration such horoscopes of eminent people. But the temptation in such cases to tailor the astrological brief to suit the known facts would be too great to resist. Hence, we propose to take up for discussion a horoscope which holds potential but the results are yet to materialize, so that delineation would necessarily follow dictates of astrological reasoning only.

The horoscope which hold great promise often proves deceptive. Invariably this would be due to presence of Yogabhanga forces extant in the chart. Before proceeding with delineation of a chart with apparent strength, it is desirable to ascertain, in the first instance, that it is free from nullifying influences. There are a number of combinations attributed to cause Bhanga or cancellation of Rajayogas. We may recount here a few of them that are simple to identify and proven to be effective by and large. If the lord of the 10th occupies the 3rd Bhava it is said to nullify the effects of Rajayoga that may be present in the chart. More disastrous in effect is the mutual exchange of houses in Navamsa chart by the Sun and the Moon. This is said to drive the native to a condition where even to have a square meal a day would be an uphill task.

Another interesting feature, in this context, is the scrutiny of each sign and attributing a specific degree as Mrityubhagas or fateful portion with reference to each of the planets and also Lagna. Under this scheme, the Mrityubhagas attributed to Saturn in each of the signs commencing from Aries (Mesha) in that order would be 10, 4, 7, 9, 12, 16, 3, 18, 28, 14,13 and 15. If Saturn were to be posited right on these points, the results attributed to Saturn may be a complete wash out. On the same lines, Mrityubhagas for the Moon are said to be 26, 12,13, 25, 24, 11, 26, 14, 13, 25, 5 and 12 in the order from Aries to Pisces. The horoscope would be drained of its potency, if the Lagna point falls on Mrityubhagas which are identified as 1, 9, 22, 22, 25, 24, 23, 18, 20, 24 and 10 in each of the signs from Aries onwards.

As a course for academic study, astrology makes an easy subject. But mere erudition in the subject need not necessarily confer mastery in interpretation of horoscope in a meaningful way. It warrants, in addition to scholarship, an inbuilt sense of judgment to pick the correct meaning of the symbolic clues appropriate to each individual horoscope.

5.1   Retrograde Saturn : Resultant Outcome

Saturn is the most mysterious among all the nine planets. It is by and large wrongly understood and supposed be a significator of miseries, death, poverty, sufferings, ailments, failures, panes, delay, obstacles and frustration etc. This is only the dark side of the Saturn. On the other hand, Saturn is the King Maker. It gives immense power, prosperity, popularity, victory over rivals, long life, etc. A good and well placed Saturn elevates the native to the top position of power like the Prime Minister, the President, The Head of the Department, Chairman, Chief Secretary and the like. A lot has been written about Saturn but, still there remains a lot to be looked into. Our humble observation with regard to retrograde Saturn is as under.

Let us have a short look on the position of Saturn in

all the 12 houses. This will help us to understand retrograde Saturn and its effect.

Saturn in *Lagna* : makes one poor, sick, lustful, dirty and lisping if the ascendant is one among the seven signs, namely, Aries, Taurus, Gemini, Cancer, Leo, Virgo and Scorpio. If the ascendant is one among the remaining five signs, good effects are brought about.

The 2nd house : rich, but the riches confiscated by the Government, and suffering from diseases on the face.

The 3rd house : intelligent and valorous.

The 4th house : devoid of happiness at all times.

The 5th house : poor and unlucky with regard to children.

The 6th house : over-powering enemies.

The 7th house : made unhappy through wife and other women.

The 8th house : wind or suffering from eye diseases.

The 9th house : rich, happy and having good children.

The 10th house : learned and conquering others.

The 11th house : immensely wealthy.

The 12th house : fallen from high position or *dharma*.

It follows then that Saturn will be favourable if posited in the 3rd, 6th, 9th, 10th and the 11th and unfavourable in the remaining houses.

Here are certain other results of Saturn placed in different positions as detailed in various sources. When Saturn is in deep exaltation (22° Libra), it is capable of making the native the head of a country and enjoy worldly comforts. But when it occupies the rest of Libra (i.e. between 23° and 30°), the native is driven out of his country and subjected to mental agony, wrath of government and loss in business, etc. Saturn in association with an exalted planet is inclined to confer good effects, but conjoining a debilitated planet, it produces just the opposite results. Occupying its own debilitation, Saturn is bad indeed. Saturn gives mixed results when it is posited in its own sign and the signs of friendly planets. Good effects are attributed when it occupies the sign of a very friendly (*atibandhu*) planet.

Saturn aspected by benefics is capable of producing good effects even as when it receives the aspect of good planets. Logically, therefore, bad effects accrue when it receives the aspect of an evil planet or is conjoined with an evil planet.

It is a widely accepted dictum that whenever a planet occupies its sign of debility but is in a *navamsa* identical with its sign of exaltation, it should confer good effects. But this is not true in case of Saturn.

When Saturn is placed in its *neecha* (debilitation) sign and is in exalted *navamsa*, it brings about sorrows in the beginning of its *dasa* and leads to distress at the end. On the other hand, when it is placed in its exalted sign having attained *navamsa* of his debilitation, it bestows happiness in the beginning of *dasa* and gives evil effects at the end.

There is yet another condition in which Saturn makes the life of a native miserable. To this we propose to bring the attention of the readers. Retrogression of Saturn; retrograde Saturn has the power to pull down one gradually to a pitiable state of affairs. According to *Saaraavali* the period of a retrograde planet rotates a man even as the pot maker rotates his wheel, and brings about agony and enemies.

In the period of retrograde Saturn, no action bears fruits, obstruction betakes all attempts, misery follows and even destruction of brothers (and all those who try to help the native) takes place.

Prasnamaarga summarises the effects of good and evil planets. If good planets are powerful, they bestow immense good on a native, but in contrast, if evil planets are weak, they bring about untold miseries. So, then a powerful evil planet should necessarily bless one with favourable effects. Retrogression definitely makes a planet powerful.

A planet in its retrogression is identical in power with its placement in the sign of exaltation. That is how *Uttarakaalamrita* extols a retrograde planet.

But, when it comes to the question of what is stored during the period of Saturn in retrogression, all the strength that the Saturn assumes is translated into a sad tale of misfortune. The native is virtually spun around even as a pot-makers's wheel is, as *Saaraavali* puts it. Even though this is a general rule applicable to both the evil planets, Mars and Saturn, there is a difference: Mars gets really powerful when in retrogression (*vakrecha balaadhyah*). As regards Saturn, it is strong while in its direct motion. It follows then that in retrogression, the opposite should hold good. Perhaps that explains the adverse effects the retrograde Saturn confers upon the natives.

There is, however, one exception. While retrograde, if Saturn receives the full aspect of the Sun, then its *dasa* will produce good effects. The full aspect can take place only when Saturn is placed in the 7th sign as counted from the Sun. In such a situation, Saturn will be retrograde too.

Intricate indeed are the rules upon which the edifice of predictive astrology is based. The deeper we delve into its depths, the richer we become by the shining gems that we come by.

Here we would like to explain certain well tested experienced research points on the planet Saturn. How does Saturn behave in various stages, signs and houses?

1. Yoga Karaka Saturn in the 10th House

For Libra ascendant, Saturn is a Yoga Karaka planet and its placement in the 10th house gives enormous professional rise.

Any person having such placement of Saturn in the 10th house will become a king, ruler, administrator, minister, Governor, Chairman, or the like even if he is born in a very poor family. Hitler was born in Libra ascendant having Saturn in 10th house and that made the history.

2. Mutual exchange of the 10th and 5th lords for Libra ascendant

Moon becomes the lord of the 10th house and Saturn is the 5th lord. If there is a mutual exchange between Moon and Saturn or both are conjoined in the 10th or 5th house one becomes equal to a King, P.M. or Chief Minister or head of a very big organisation.

This has also been observed that the afflicted Saturn snatches a lot and brings a heavy downfall when the period is over.

3. Saturn in the 7th House

Saturn's placement in the 7th house especially when retrograde causes delay in marriage. If the Sun is placed in the ascendant and Saturn in the 7th house and both of these planets are almost at same degrees, marriage will be completely denied.

Conjunction of Saturn and Rahu in the 7th house is extremely adverse and causes separation after marriage.

If Saturn is placed in the ascendant and has direct motion, the rivals and opponents are destroyed by the grace of God automatically.

If Saturn is retrograde in the ascendant and is aspected by malefics and unaspected by benefics, one becomes a murderer and is not caught. However, the benefic aspect of Jupiter or Venus will prevent him to become a killer.

If Saturn becomes a 'Markesh' and it is placed in an airy sign *i.e.* Gemini, Libra or Aquarius, one dies due to poison. If Saturn falls in fiery sign *i.e.* Aries, Leo or Sagittarius, one dies due to poison, but placement of Saturn in earthy sign such as Taurus, Virgo or Capricorn will cause death due to war, quarrel or murder. If 'Markesh' Saturn falls in Watery sign such as Cancer, Scorpio or Pisces, one dies due to adverse or negative effects of medicine. However, 22nd Dreshkaan should also be taken into consideration before arriving at any conclusion for the cause of death.

4.   Saturn in the 8th House

Saturn's placement in the 8th house gives a good longevity *i.e.* a long span of life. However, the diagnosis of the disease is always deceptive in such case and old age is tough as far as health is concerned.

Placement of Saturn in the ascendant in Capricorn or Aquarius will eliminate all opponents and rivals automatically. However, if retrograde Saturn occupies the ascendant and ascendant lord Saturn is affected by malefic, the person will be hanged to death. If Saturn is strong and it is aspected by the benefics the native will become a killer but such tendency may be present.

5. Saturn's Transit in 8ᵗʰ house gives enormous wealth

When Saturn transits in the 8ᵗʰ house, one receives appreciable amount of wealth from any old person, male or female. This is not our finding but we found this observation correct not only in our case but many more cases. However, this rule should be used only for timing this event, provided such indication of getting money or property through legacy or so is there. Such a property, wealth or job can be received when Saturn transits at 1 deg. of the sign falling in the 8ᵗʰ house.

6. Paralysis and Saturn

If Saturn and Rahu afflict the 8ᵗʰ house or these have concern with the 8ᵗʰ house in one or other way or both Rahu and Saturn are placed in the constellation of each other and one of these is positioned in the 8ᵗʰ house, one will suffer from paralysis. If Venus is also involved, the combination becomes harmful.

If Saturn becomes a killer and falls in airy sign *i.e.* Gemini, Libra or Aquarius, one may die due to poison.

7. Saturn in the 6ᵗʰ House and Chronic Ailments

One suffers from various ailments such as gout, rheumatism, gastric disorder, spondylitis, arthritis, asthma, troubles connected with veins, polio, disorder of limbs, trouble in legs. respiratory complaints, early decay of hair and teeth etc. If Saturn is placed in the 6ᵗʰ house especially in airy sign such as Gemini, Libra or Aquarius.

8. Saturn Mahadasa in the 4ᵗʰ House

If Saturn Madadasa is the 4ᵗʰ reckoned from the balance Mahadasa of birth, one will suffer a lot. He will become poor and diseased. He may lose all his money and be prosecuted. He will be charge-sheeted and face a lot of defamation, humiliation, frustration, tension and failure in undertakings, deaths of near and dear ones. However, though this is an important rule of astrology but we have not found it applicable in all cases. But in our case Saturn Mahadasa is the 4th one, this is the best Mahadasa of human life so far and certainly superior to previous 3 Mahadasas.

9. Saturn in the 6th House in Cancer

For Aquarius ascendant Satunr's placement in the 6th house in Cancer gives innumerable diseases but if it is posited in the 8th house, in Virgo, it gives a long span of life, but problems in lower extremities and waist etc.

10. Saturn in the 11th House

Saturn's placement in the eleventh house gives wealth through illegal means. This is further multiplied if Saturn is debilitated in the eleventh house. However, there is a mismatch between wealth and income for a while. Placement of Mercury in the 11th house also gives illegitimate income.

In a number of cases, Mercury of the 11th house makes the native a successful businessman. the Mahadasa of Mercury causes a lot of income through unrighteous means and by manipulation. Conjunction or mutual aspect or exchange of signs between Saturn and Mercury identical to the 11th house, multiplies illegal income through manipulations.

11. Saturn and Venus combination

Saturn and Venus combination of Saturn and Venus is extremely adverse for maintaining moral values. This causes tendency towards physical relations of advance age or with the person of same sex, we have explained this in detail in the chapter 'Pointers to Carnality' in our book "Predicting Marriage".

12. Saturn in the 4th House

Saturn obstructs fortune especially if it is posited in the 4th house. Though the fortune has no concern with the 4th house, even then Saturn's placement in the 4th house is one of the worst combinations for a proper rise of fortune at proper age and time. Such a Saturn also gives rise to diseases connected with lungs such as asthma, T.B. bronchitis, and pleurisy etc. One does not tell his secrets to anyone.

Nobody can understand such expressions easily. This also causes imprisonment to the native but other combination should also be judged before reaching to any conclusion. This is the worst position as regards the placement of Saturn (in the 4th house).

13. Saturn in the 12th House

Saturn's placement in the 12th house gives huge wealth to the native. Yet a powerful downfall of post, position, rank, wealth and prosperity definitely comes one day.

If Saturn is afflicted and indicates income, the native will earn money by unrighteous means such as theft, smuggling, deceit, misplaced confidence, dacoity, illicit relation and evil deeds.

Conjunction of the Sun and Saturn or their opposition is very adverse for marriage especially if the longitudes are nearly the same. We have discussed a lot about the combination earlier.

Placement of Saturn in the 12th house is extremely damaging. Even a prosperous and rich person may have to face imprisonment, poverty, funerals and prosecution etc. A rich will lose everything gradually, if Saturn falls in the 12th house and that is weak and afflicted. Adversities will be more prominent if the ascendant is weak. First 6 years and 4 month will be adverse; another 6 years and 4 month will be prosperous full of gains, acquisitions, elevation, name, fame, honour etc. but last 6 years and 4 month will snatch everything given by Saturn during its Mahadasa.

14. Favorable signs for Sadhe Saati Saturn

For persons born in Capricorn or Aquarius, Sadhe Saati of Saturn doesn't cause much adversity. Similarly, persons born in Libra and Taurus also do not suffer during the Sadhe Saati of Saturn.

15. Saturn in Sagittarius or Pisces

Jupiter and Saturn have a peculiar relationship, which we have explained earlier. However, Saturn bestows very good and auspicious results during the major or sub-period of Saturn if that is placed in Sagittarius or Pisces. The native gets power, authority, position, prosperity and happiness on that account. It has been observed that Saturn gives result like that of exhalation if falls in any sign of Juptiter. However well placed Saturn is beneficial for persons born in Taurus, Libra, Sagittarius, Capricorn, Aquarius and Pisces.

16. Saturn in the 9th House

If a well fortified Saturn is placed in the 9th house, one will be blessed with powers and respect in the society. He will not believe in superstitions. It has been found that Saturn in the 9th house makes the native religious. One is deeply involved in spiritualism. However if there is a mutual exchange between 4th and 9th lord, a Raja Yoga is formed and in that case one enjoys wealth, power, prosperity and happiness but that native is fully dedicated to the Almighty.

17. Conjunction of Saturn and Moon

If Saturn conjoins with Moon, one will suffer from headache and if the combination is death inflicting, one will die due to water as Moon is the significator of water. The combination causes T.B. or pleurisy if occures in the 4th house or affects the 4th house.

18. Combination of Saturn and Sun

If Saturn is conjoined with the Sun, the native will suffer heart trouble especially if the 4th house is involved in one or the other way.

19. Saturn Signifies

Saturn governs strike, labour problems, tensions, impotency, humiliation, worries, frustations, pain, falling of hair and teeth, untraditional things, intercaste and illegitimate marriage. It destroys the balance of mind and one treats enemy as friend and well wishers as rivals.

20. Saturn and Mercury

Both these planets are eunuchs. If these are placed in the 8th house impotency and nervous disorder will be there. One may suffer nervous breakdown if Rahu is also involved. Combination of Mercury and Saturn causes all kinds of illegitimacy. In the 5th house, this combination will give illegitimate birth of children. Similarly in the 7th house that may cause illegitimate relationship with women and so on.

21. Saturn at same Degree of Lagna

If Saturn has same degree as that of Lagna, that is

extremely bad. The native will have bad health throughout his life.

22. Saturn in the 5ᵗʰ House

Saturn in the 5ᵗʰ house causes delay in birth of children. Many times the birth may be completely deined if Saturn and Rahu are there and the combination is afflicted. In watery sign Saturn gives birth to male children whereas Jupiter gives daughter in watery signs in the 5ᵗʰ house *i.e.* Cancer, Scorpio or Pisces. Saturn in fiery sign gives birth to female children *i.e.* if Saturn is placed in Aries, Leo or Sagattarius, female children will be born unless other strong combinations of male children are not present. Jupiter in fiery sign in the 5ᵗʰ house gives male children.

23. Saturn in the 6ᵗʰ House in Airy Signs

If Saturn is placed in the 6ᵗʰ house in Gemini, Libra or Aquarius, one will suffer from one or the other trouble throughout life especially from chronic ailments. If Moon is also there with Saturn, it is impossible that the native would be cured.

24. Major period of Saturn will be the best, if one is born in the major period of the Sun. It means that if natal Moon falls in Krittika, Uttara Phalguni or Uttarashadha constellation, then the major period of Saturn will be the 6ᵗʰ dasha and that will be operative over the native only after 53 years of age. That period of Saturn for 19 years will be the best one for the native. Exact results will depend on the location of Saturn in the birth chart.

A few most important points with regard to Saturn and its transit are given below :

25. Sadhe Saati of Saturn

This name of Sadhe Saati of Saturn is very well known to all the readers. Sadhe Saati of Saturn runs for Seven and a half years during the Saturn's transit in the 12th sign from the natal Moon, over the sign occupied by the natal Moon and the 2nd sign from the natal Moon. Sadhe Saati of Saturn curtails the good effect and produces inauspicious events that occur during these Seven and half years.

Following shloka may be referred to the Sadhe Saati of Saturn :

द्वादशे जन्मगे राशौ, द्वितीये च शनैश्चरः।
साधार्धानि सप्तवर्षाणि तदा दुःखैर्युतो भवेत्।।

26. Laghu Kalyani Dhaiya of Saturn

कल्याणी प्रदाक्षति वै, रविसुतो राशेश्चतुर्थाष्टमे।

Laghu Kalyani Dhaiya of Saturn runs, when Saturn transits in the 4th and the 8th house from the natal Moon. Both of the Dhaiya of Saturn effect the native for seven and half years each and curtail auspicious results of the birth-chart. Negative and inauspicious happening and occurring rise during the Dhaiya of Saturn.

5.2 Entry of Transiting Saturn in Various Legs (Paads)

जन्मांगरुद्रेषु सुवर्णपादं द्विपंचनन्दे रजतस्य वदन्ति।
त्रिसप्तदिक् ताम्रपदं वदन्ति, वेदार्क साष्टेऽपिवह लौहपादम्।।

(ज्योतिषतत्त्वप्रकाश/श्लोक-140/पृष्ठ-572)

Transiting Saturn enters through Gold legs, whenever, it transits over the natal Moon, the 6th and the 11th house. Saturn enters through Silver legs for the particular signs, when it transits the 2nd, 5th or 9th house from natal Moon. Transiting Saturn enters through Copper legs for the signs, where it transits in the 3rd, 7th and 10th house from the natal Moon. Saturn's transit in the 4th, 8th and 12th house from the natal Moon is adverse because Saturn enters through Gold legs for the native born in such a sign from where, it is 4th, 8th or 12th.

1. Transiting Saturn stays in a sign for almost two and a half years and enters in the next sign thereafter. Whenever, Saturn enters in another sign, it is good or bad depending on whether the transiting Saturn is entering in a particular sign through Gold legs (स्वर्ण पाद), Silver legs (रजत पाद), Copper legs (ताम्र पाद) and Iron legs (लौह पाद).

Gold Legs : When Saturn transits over the natal Moon or 6th or 11th from there, it comes on Gold legs. In that case, it provides prosperity, happiness, success, gains, elevation, extension and accomplishment of ambitions etc.

Silver Legs : Saturn comes on Silver legs, when it transit in 2nd, 5th or 9th signs from the natal Moon. This is also a good entry, through Silver legs, as it gives the native happiness, increase in income, promotion, fame, honour and success in endeavors.

Copper Legs : Transiting Saturn comes on Copper legs for the signs from where, it transits in the 3rd, 7th or 10th house. This gives ordinary results but this is not adverse,

Iron Legs : Saturn's transits with Iron legs for the native born in such a sign from where Saturn's transit is 4th, 8th or 12th. Saturn's entry through Iron legs is worst as it provides immense adversities, satbacks, tensions, failures of undertakings, frustration, tensions, ill health, humiliation and unwelcome changes.

2. Saturn's entry on Gold legs is the best. It comes next, if the entry of Saturn takes place on Silver legs. Saturn's entry into a sign on Copper legs is not good but not bad as well. However, the transit of Saturn on Iron legs is most undesirable and it gives rise to many tensions and problems.

3. Sadhe Saati of Saturn or Laghu Kalyani Dhaiya there of should also be taken into consideration for finding out the exact outcome of the transit of Saturn in a particular sign and houses.

Our experience with regard to Saturn's transit is the same which should be taken into consideration not only from the natal Moon, but from the natal ascendant as well.

5.3   Means of Saturn's Conveyance

All planets move from one place to another by means of their conveyance. Saturn also moves through different means conveyances and different stages. Entry of the transiting Saturn from one constellation to another compels Saturn to change its conveyance.

The conveyance of Saturn should be determined in the following manner :

a. Find out the constellation occupied by the natal Moon.

b. Also find out the constellation in which, the Saturn is transiting.

c. Count the number of constellation from that of natal Moon to the constellation of the transiting Saturn.

d. If the numbers are more than 9, divide by 9. The remainder will present the kind of conveyance through which transiting Saturn, will move.

e. Conveyance of Saturn represents the kind of effects the native will receive during the transiting of Saturn in a particular constellation. This gives remarkable and

amazing results but the calculation should be carefully
done.

1. Ass or
   Donkey   Argument, unhappiness
2. Horse   Pleasure, prosperity and journey
3. Elephant   Delicious food, Pleasure & profits
4. Goat   Adversities, ailments, Deformation, Fear
5. Jackal   Fear and Problems
6. Lion   Victory, Profit, Honour and Fame
7. Crow   Mental agony and tensions or sat-back
8. Deer   Winning or Victory, Recognition & profit
9. Peacock   Pleasure and profit

5.4   Vedic Mantra on Saturn

Viniyoga :   शन्नो देवरिति मन्त्रस्य दध्यङ्ङाथवर्ण ऋषिः, गायत्री
छन्दः, आपो देवता शनि प्रीत्यर्थे जपे विनियोगः ।

Om shanno devriti Mantrasya
dadhyangvarna rishih; Gayatri chandah
aapo devta shani preetyarthey jape
viniyogah.

ॐ शन्नोदेवीरभिष्टय आपो भवन्तु पीतये । शंय्योरभिस्रवन्तु नः ।

(Om Shannodevirbhishtyey aapo bhavantoo peetyeh)

5.5   Pauranik Mantra of Saturn

ॐ नीलांजनसमाभासं रविपुत्रं यमाग्रजम् ।
छायामार्तण्डसम्भूतं तं नमामि शनैश्चरम् ।।

(Om Neelanjansamabhasnam Raviputram yamagrajama
Chayamartandsambhutnam tam namami shanashcharam)

5.6   Tantrik Mantra of Saturn

प्रां, प्रीं, प्रौं शनये नमः ।

(Om Pram, Preem, Prom shanayeh namah)

Vedic Mantra should be recited only by those, who wear Yagyopavit or Janeyu. All others are not permitted to recite the Vedic Mantra of Saturn. They are advised to recite Pauranik or Tantrik Mantra only.

Vedic Mantra, Pauranik Mantra or Tantrik Mantra of Saturn should be recited for at least 23,000 times alongwith dashansh havan, tarpan, marjan and Bhahmin Bhojan etc. to minimize or curtail the adversties due to Saturn. However, the sages have suggested that the specific number of Mantra, should be enhanced four times in kalyug. It means that the mantra of Saturn will be effective, when done for 92,000 times alongwith dashansh havan, tarpan, marjan and Bhahmin Bhojan etc.

Root of Saturn : Root of the Shami tree.

Gems of Saturn : Blue Sapphire, Lajvart, Firoza, Amethist (Jamania)

Metal : Ring of Iron or that of the Nail taken out from the lower portion of boat, that is the portion of boat, which always remains in the water.

The horse shoe (naal) of the feet of black horse, if found somewhere on the way, should be picked up and a ring of the size of middle finger may be prepared by the blacksmith on Saturday during the constellation of Saturn. This ring should be purified by recitation of 23,000 Vedic Mantra of Saturn. Thereafter, it should be worn in the middle finger on Saturday morning.

Articles to be donated : Articles to be donated to rectify or prevent the adversity caused due to malefic Saturn– Til, Kali Urad, Oil, Blancket, Black cloth, Wool, Iron, Shoes,

Sleeper, Neel, Nail, Iron Bucket, Iron Tawa, Iron Chimta, Umbrella, Buffalo, Shani Patra, Kastoori and money in particular. It may be noted that the donation of Saturn remains incomplete and ineffective, if money has not been included in the same.

Time for the donation of the articles of Saturn : Donation should be made around noon *i.e.* mid day. Proper Sankalp for the donation of Saturn should be pronounce properly and correctly. Seven rounds of the Peepal tree should be taken alongwith Shani dev darshan on Saturdays preferably in the day time at noon.

Special Prevention of Saturn : There are so many preventions, but the recitation of Mantras of donation of Saturn and Vrat for Saturn are most useful, which are explained at various places in this work.

We have mentioned extremely useful, very effective and rarely known rectificational measures for the prevention of adversities caused due to malefic Saturn or to nullify the inauspicious results of the Sadhe Saati of Saturn. Number of preventive measures against the adversities of Saadhe Saati have been detailed and explained in our thought provoking work entitled "Saturn : Maladies & Remedies."

Here we have discussed very briefly about various stages of mysterious Saturn. In fact, each & every point may be dealt with minor specifications & explanations in one complete chapter. The book on Saturn has already covered so many pages and volumes that we have decided to pen other books on our humble findings on Saturn, at some other time. If, our prestigious, learned and talented readers desire so.

नीलाञ्जनसमाभासं रविपुत्रं यमाग्रजम् ।
छायामार्तण्डसम्भूतं तं नमामि शनैश्चरम् ।।

6 The Transiting Saturn: The Determinant of Marriage

Whether marriage will be delayed or completely denied cannot be determined without an examination of the position of Saturn. If Saturn afflicts both the lumanaries, the 7th house, and the 7th lord, it delays marriage appreciably. If the Sun-Saturn or Moon-Saturn have anything to do with the 7th house or posited in Cancer or Leo at the same degree, marriage is completely denied. If Saturn is associated with Mars at the same degree or Saturn and Mars have mutual aspect at the same degree the marriage is denied. Retrograde Saturn in the 2nd or 7th house or the aspect of retrograde Saturn on the houses concerned or on the 7th and 2nd lords, or on the significator Venus, creates havoc. Marriage gets appreciably delayed or takes place only after the age of 30 years, if Saturn is posited in the 7th house under retrograde motion. On the contrary, if strong and well placed Saturn in respect of the 7th house in own or exaltation sign with a friendly *navamsa*, it gives rise to early and happy marriage. This helps a lot in determining the time of marriage which is as given below.

6.1 The Transiting Saturn and Marriage

While timing the marriage of any native in general the determines it cannot but be Saturn as the lord of marriage. It is commonly seen in several charts that a native enters marital relationship under the following conditions.

1. When transit Saturn aspects natal Saturn by its 3rd house aspect.

2. When Saturn transits the natal Saturn with a margin of 10° on either side of natal Saturn or when Saturn transits the sign occupied by natal Saturn 0°-30°.

3. When transit Saturn aspects natal Saturn or is in opposition (180°) which is its 7th house aspect.

4. When transit Saturn aspects natal Saturn with its 10th house aspect.

Of these four conditions, we find the first two as more effective than the other two. This becomes even more effective in the case of women.

Whenever the transiting Saturn aspects natal Saturn it would cause marriage. It can also be said with equal force that when Saturn transits natal Saturn completely without giving marriage, then there are chances of extreme late marriage when the 10th house aspect occurs. But by that time the native would be in his mid thirties. The brightest possibility is when transit Saturn aspects natal Saturn by its 3rd house aspect. Because, at that time the native would be around 24 years as Saturn would be 2 to 3 signs away from its natal position.

The exact time of marriage can be predicted from the transits of Venus, Jupiter, Mars and Moon, corresponding with the *lagna* and the 7th lord.

Saturn's role as the lord of marriage is supreme. But Venus in fixed signs also has a distinct effect.

A word of caution, afflicted Saturn normally destroys the *Bhava* or the house it aspects by its 3rd, 10th and 7th aspects, if the houses are not its own or if they are not otherwise beneficially occupied or aspected by other planets. Saturn when afflicted by the Sun, its arch rival, and badly placed in a house or at 0° or 29°, while transiting its birth position, may not yield the desired results or may even destroy married life. As Saturn causes marriage and finds its time too, so also can it deny a marriage indefinitely or disturb it.

Yet another interesting fact is the sudden, unforeseen transformation of benefics Jupiter and Venus into malefic. *Karako Bhavanashaya* is a famous line every astrologer is aware of, which means when the *Karaka* of a *Bhava* is in the relevant *Bhava* it will invariably destroy the *Bhava*. For instance, if Venus is in the 7th as the *Karaka* for that house it will always deny a happy married life. The same is true in cases when Venus is afflicted either by Mars and Rahu or the Sun, despite the aspect of Jupiter on Venus. <u>But if Saturn is with Venus or even aspects it, it cancels these ill effects and purifies Venus ensuring marital happiness abundantly.</u>

The so called divinely benefic Jupiter can be a disastrous malefic if it is badly posited. Jupiter in a *Kendra*, especially the 7th can be dangerous. It will turn worse if it is exalted or debilitated and placed in the 7th house. *Stana Hani Karoti Jeevaha* and *Stanavriddhi Karoti Mandaha Jeeva* or Jupiter normally harms the place of its occupation while Manda or Saturn improves the house it is placed in.

Even when benefics turn into malefic and mar marriages, Saturn, the so-called malefic, acts virtually as a benefic and ensures marital happiness. Although it is slow and sluggish it averts marital accidents; it gives long lasting marital bliss, and is the real lord of marriage.

The lord of time, Saturn, times events. As the lord of longevity, it determines the death of natives. The *saadhe sati* occurs in all charts at least twice. This period grooms natives into perfect human beings, by exposing them to untold miseries.

Marriage takes place when transiting Saturn aspects or passes over the natal Saturn. Transiting Jupiter also plays a prominent role in the settlement or ceremonisation of marriage. Jupiter must have a positive aspect over the 5th house or its lord during its transit for the settlement of marriage. Thus transiting Saturn indicates a slot of two and a half years in which marriage will take place. Transiting Jupiter will help in minimising their time slot to the year only. Practise and experience can make one perfect in determining the signs in which transit of Saturn and Jupiter will finally settle the marriage of the native.

After determining the exact transit of Jupiter, transit of Mars should be examined. Transiting Mars will have a positive or favourable aspect over the 7th house or its lord. Venus also plays the similar role in the chart of males in particular.

Illustration : 6.1　　　　　　*Horoscope No.: 1*

Date of birth, time and place withheld.

Pln	Degree	Rasi	Nakshatra	Pad
Asc	29:35:08	Vir	Chitra	2
Sun	23:41:43	Can	Aslesa	3
Mon	12:49:15	Ari	Aswini	4
Mar	15:03:08	Leo	P Phalguni	1
Mer (C)	15:53:47	Can	Pushya	4
Jup (R)	22:36:08	Aqu	P Bhadrapad	1
Ven	0:40:33	Can	Punarvasu	4
Sat	19:55:32	Gem	Ardra	4
Rah (R)	23:58:28	Sco	Jyestha	3
Ket (R)	23:58:28	Tau	Mrigshira	1

Lagna Chart

		Mar	
	7	5	Sun
Rah 8			4 Mer
	6		Ven
	9	3 Sat	
	12		
10		2 Ket	
11		1	
Jup		Mon	

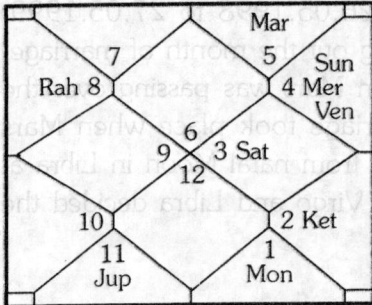

Navamsa Chart

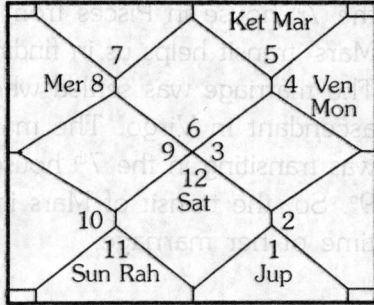

		Ket Mar	
	7	5	
Mer 8			4 Ven
	6		Mon
	9	3	
	12		
	Sat		
10		2	
11		1	
Sun Rah		Jup	

Balance of Vimshottari Dasa of **Ket   0Y 3M 6D**

She was decently married on 28.04.1999. She was born in Virgo ascendant with Saturn in Gemini. At the time of marriage Saturn was transiting in Aries and it aspected the natal Saturn by its 3rd aspect. Jupiter was transiting in Pisces from 26.05.1998 to 27.05.1999 that is in her 7th house. At the time of marriage Mars was transiting in the 7th house from natal Moon. When Mars was transiting in ascendant in Virgo her marriage was finally settled. Her marriage took place during the major period of the Sun and the sub period of Mercury. The Sun is the *Atma Karaka* planet as well as the strongest planet in the birthchart as it obtains 1.77 *Shadabala*. Mercury is the lord of the 10th house or the ascendant and is posited in the 11th house in Cancer as well as in Saturn's constellation *Pushya*. Saturn aspects the 7th house in the natal chart. Marriage took place when the Sun was transiting in its sign of exaltation Aries over the natal Moon which was transiting in the ascendant in own constellation *Hasta*. Thus, the marriage of the woman was destined to take place in Aries from 17.04.1998 to 07.06.2000. This transit of Saturn gives a slot of 2nd and half years in which marriage will take place. For further preciseness the transit of Jupiter in the

7th house should be examined. Here Jupiter transited in the 7th house in Pisces from 26.05.1998 to 27.05.1999. Mars' transit helps us in finding out the month of marriage. The marriage was settled when Mars was passing over the ascendant in Virgo. The marriage took place when Mars was transiting in the 7th house from natal Moon in Libra at 9°. So, the transit of Mars in Virgo and Libra decided the time of her marriage.

Illustration : 6.2   *Horoscope No.: 2*

Date of birth : 07.11.1985   Time of birth : 00:10:00 hrs
Place of birth : Agra   Lat 27:09 N Long 78:00 E
Ayanamsa   : 23:39:21   Sidereal Time : 2:55:41

Pln	Degree	Rasi	Nakshatra	Pad
Asc	25:44:50	Can	Aslesa	3
Sun	20:38:22	Lib	Vishakha	1
Mon	2:03:15	Leo	Magha	1
Mar	12:41:49	Vir	Hasta	1
Mer	13:33:47	Sco	Anuradha	4
Jup	15:21:37	Cap	Sravna	2
Ven	2:46:27	Lib	Chitra	3
Sat (C)	5:07:45	Sco	Anuradha	1
Rah	15:35:38	Ari	Bharani	1
Ket (C)	15:35:38	Lib	Swati	3

Lagna Chart

```
        Mon
    5            3
 Mar 6           2
         4
 Sun Ven 7   1 Rah
 Ket    10
        Jup
 Mer 8           12
 Sat  9      11
```

Navamsa Chart

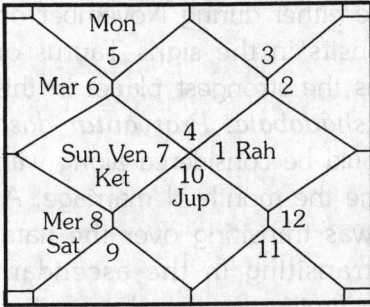

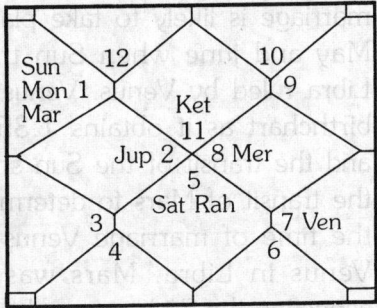

```
 Sun    12       10
 Mon 1           9
 Mar         Ket
             11
      Jup 2  8 Mer
          5
        Sat Rah
     3           7 Ven
     4       6
```

Balance of Vimshottari Dasa of **Ket 5Y 11M 1D**

The marriage of this charming pretty girl took place on 27.11.2009 during the sub period of Mercury in the major period of Saturn which was running from 09.10.2007 to 09.08.2010. 7th lord Saturn occupies the 5th house identical to Scorpio. Transiting Saturn entered in Virgo on 10.09.2009 and aspected the natal Saturn and she was married immediately therafter in 2009. Jupiter was transiting in Aquarius at the time of marriage which is the 7th from the natal Moon. In fact, Jupiter entered in Aquarius on 02.05.2009 and stayed there till 02.05.2010. this was the high time for her marriage, as per the rules of transiting Saturn and Jupiter. Both the prominent planets strongly indicate the year of marriage.

Transiting Mars may be taken into consideration for predicting accurate month of marriage that should influence the 7th house or its lord either by conjunction or aspect. At the time of marriage on 27.11.2009 Mars was transiting in Capricorn at 22°52' and was aspecting the 7th house and 9th lord Jupiter. There are other methods related to *navamsa* chart, transiting Sun and Jupiter for fining up the time of marriage. Exact month of the marriage can be predicted by the examination of *pratyantar dasa* and the Sun's transit in the sign of planets whose *dasa bhukti* is operative. For example, major period of Venus indicates marriage is likely to take place either during November or, May and june when Sun transits in the signs Taurus or Libra ruled by Venus. Venus is the strongest planet in this birthchart as it obtains 1.35 *shadabala*. *Pratyantar dasa* and the transit of the Sun should be considered along with the transit of Mars to determine the month of marriage. At the time of marriage Venus was transiting over the natal Venus in Libra. Mars was transiting in the ascendant aspecting the 7th house and the Jupiter was exactly transiting in Capricorn i.e. the 7th house from ascendant. In fact, Jupiter resumed retrograde motion 30.07.2009 to 12.10.2009 and again resumed direct motion on 12.10.2009 to 20.12.2009 in Capricorn only. Thus, the marriage of the girl took place exactly when Jupiter was transiting in Capricorn in the 7th house over the natal Jupiter. Saturn was aspecting natal Saturn from its 3rd aspect. Mars was transiting in the ascendant and having the aspect over the 7th house and 9th lord Jupiter. Venus was transiting over the natal Venus and Moon was transiting in *Uttara Bhadrapada* ruled by the 7th lord Saturn and in the sign Pisces ruled by Jupiter, the planet that occupies the 7th house. Research minded scholars will certainly be able to find out the exact month and even the date of marriage if they work hard on the subject and practice it everyday by application of role of transiting Saturn, Jupiter, Mars, Venus and Moon in the natal chart. We give the longitudes of the transiting planets as on the date of marriage as on 27.11.2009. We are giving the longitudes of the transiting planets as on the date of marriage as under: Sun 10°50' of Scorpio, Moon 7°03' of Pisces, Jupiter 26°20' of Capricorn, Mars 22°25' of Cancer, Saturn 8°70' of Virgo, Venus 29°47' of Libra.

Illustration : 6.3   *Horoscope No.: 3*

Date of birth, time and place withheld.

Pln	Degree	Rasi	Nakshatra	Pad
Asc	20:15:26	Lib	Vishakha	4
Sun	0:02:03	Sco	Vishakha	1
Mon	21:35:43	Cap	Sravna	2
Mar	14:41:13	Cap	Sravna	1
Mer (D)	29:51:02	Lib	Vishakha	1
Jup	0:51:30	Lib	Chitra	2
Ven	13:13:04	Lib	Swati	4
Sat (R)	10:37:33	Ari	Aswini	2
Rah (R)	25:13:14	Aqu	P Bhadrapad	3
Ket (R)	25:13:14	Leo	P Phalguni	1

Lagna Chart

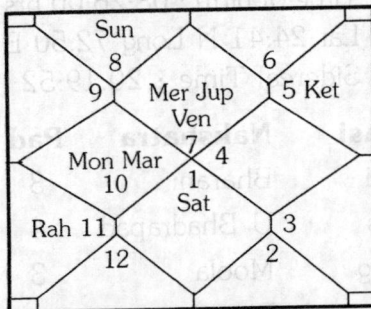

Navamsa Chart

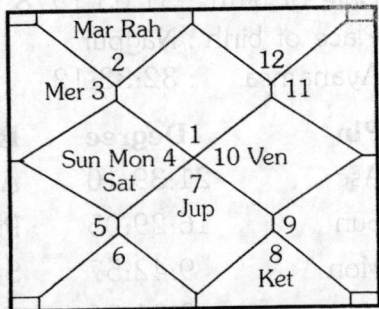

Balance of Vimshottari Dasa of **Mon   1Y 3M 19D**

The native was married on 21.02.2000 with a beautiful, well educated, talented and modest girl of sweet temperament. *Yogakaraka* Saturn occupies the 7th house under retrograde motion so it may be noted that *Yogakaraka* Saturn in the 7th house gives a good wife along with conjugal bliss instead of ugly or quarrelsome wife or spouse as generally believed. At the time of marriage Saturn was transiting in Aries. So, the transiting Saturn was crossing over the natal Saturn. Jupiter was also transiting in Aries in the 7th house from ascendant. Transiting Mars, when aspects the 7th house from the ascendant or Moon, marriage takes place. Mars was transiting in Pisces and was speedily moving towards the 7th house. Thus, transiting Saturn and Jupiter were simultaneously in Aries i.e. in 7th house from ascendant over the natal Saturn at the time of ceremony. However, the ascendant lord and the significator Venus transited in Capricorn over the natal Moon. We are giving the longitudes of the transiting planets as on the date of marriage as under: Saturn 7°55' of Aries, Sun 8°29' of Aquarius, Jupiter 7°17' of Aries, Mars 13°25' of Pisces, Moon 7°30' of Virgo, Venus 10°27' of Capricorn.

Illustration : 6.4   *Horoscope No.: 4*

Date of birth : 31.03.1978	Time of birth : 08:26:00 hrs
Place of birth : Nagpur	Lat 24:41 N Long 72:50 E
Ayanamsa : 32:33:12	Sidereal Time : 20:19:52

Pln	Degree	Rasi	Nakshatra	Pad
Asc	21:39:10	Ari	Bharani	3
Sun	16:29:05	Pis	U Bhadrapad	4
Mon	9:42:57	Sag	Moola	3
Mar	3:06:06	Can	Punarvasu	4
Mer	2:25:40	Ari	Aswini	1
Jup	4:54:17	Gem	Mrigshira	4
Ven	3:02:05	Ari	Aswini	1
Sat (R)	0:39:47	Leo	Magha	1
Rah (R)	12:14:07	Vir	Hasta	1
Ket (R/C)	12:14:07	Pis	U Bhadrapad	3

Lagna Chart

```
              Ket Sun
       2         12
  Jup 3           11
        Mer Ven
           1
     Mar 4    10
           7
  Sat 5          9 Mon
      6        8
      Rah
```

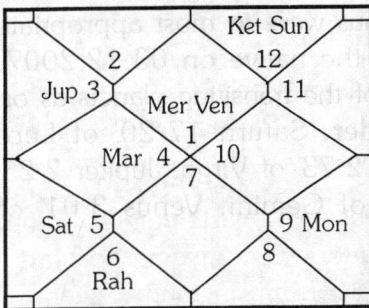

Navamsa Chart

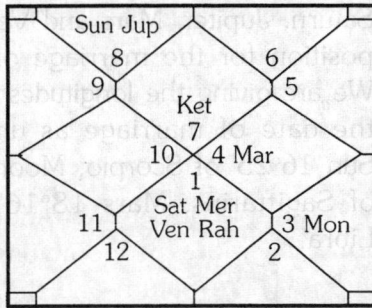

```
     Sun Jup
        8          6
     9               5
           Ket
            7
        10   4 Mar
            1
         Sat Mer
     11  Ven Rah   3 Mon
       12          2
```

Balance of Vimshottari Dasa of **Ket   1Y 10M 24D**

The native was decently married on 03.12.2007 with a decent girl. The native is born in Aries ascendant with 10th and 11th lord Saturn placed in the 5th house in inimical sign Leo. Natal Saturn is almost at 1° of Leo. The marriage of the native took place on 03.12.2007 when transiting Saturn was crossing the natal Saturn. As per our findings when transiting Saturn is at 10° on either side of natal Saturn or when Saturn transits the sign occupied by natal Saturn 0°-30° marriage takes place, which holds good here as well. Transiting Jupiter must influence the 7th house either from ascendant or from Moon. Moon sign is Sagittarius and the marriage took place when transiting Jupiter was passing over natal Moon was aspecting the natal Jupiter as well. Saturn transited over the natal Saturn, the Jupiter transited over the natal Moon and is in opposition to natal Jupiter when the marriage was ceremonised. 7th lord Venus which is the significator of marriage as well may also be examined particularly in case of males to find out accurate time of marriage. Venus was transiting in Libra in the 7th house from the ascendant and had a mutual aspect with natal Venus. Transit of Mars is equally important to decide the time of marriage. It must have an influence over the 7th house from the ascendant or the moon. Mars was transiting in Gemini which is 7th from the Moon. Thus, Saturn, Jupiter, Mars and Venus were in most appropriate position for the marriage of the native on 03.12.2007. We are giving the longitudes of the transiting planets as on the date of marriage as under: Saturn 17°20' of Leo, Sun 16°25' of Scorpio, Moon 2°73' of Virgo, Jupiter 2°25' of Sagittarius, Mars 18°16' of Gemini, Venus 3°01' of Libra.

Illustration : 6.5   Horoscope No.: 5

Date of birth : 09.06.1968   Time of birth : 22:20:00 hrs
Place of birth : Agra   Lat 27:09 N Long 78:00 E
Ayanamsa   : 23:24:52   Sidereal Time : 15:14:28

Pln	Degree	Rasi	Nakshatra	Pad
Asc	12:48:47	Cap	Sravna	1
Sun	25:28:10	Tau	Mrigshira	1
Mon	9:11:05	Sco	Anuradha	2
Mar (C)	28:48:05	Tau	Mrigshira	2
Mer (R)	8:10:07	Gem	Ardra	1
Jup	5:47:13	Leo	Magha	2
Ven (D)	22:32:13	Tau	Rohini	4
Sat	29:22:54	Pis	Revati	4
Rah (R)	23:29:19	Pis	Revati	3
Ket (R)	23:29:19	Vir	Chitra	1

Lagna Chart

```
        11          9
Rah 12         8 Mon
Sat
          10
       1    7
          4
  Ven  2           6 Ket
Mar        3      5
Sun     Mer     Jup
```

Navamsa Chart

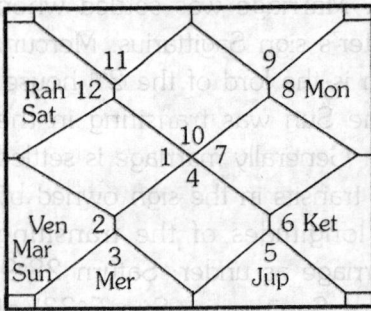

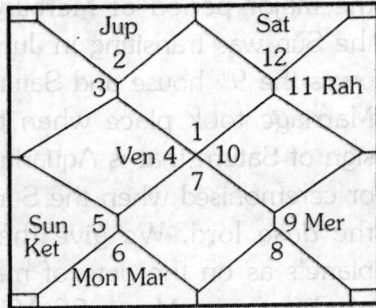

```
     Jup         Sat
      2           12
     3              11 Rah
              1
        Ven 4   10
              7
  Sun  5           9 Mer
  Ket      6       8
        Mon Mar
```

Balance of Vimshottari Dasa of **Sat 10Y 7M 28D**

The native was married on 18.02.1993 when Saturn was transiting in Capricorn at 28°. The native is born in Capricorn ascendant with Saturn in Pisces at 29°. On 18.02.1993 transiting Saturn was at the same degree in Capricorn as in Pisces in the natal chart. Transiting Saturn was aspecting the natal Saturn by its 3rd aspect. Transiting Jupiter's influence on the 5th house is essential for the settlement of marriage either from ascendant or from Moon. Jupiter was transiting in Virgo in the 9th house from ascendant aspecting the 5th house and 5th lord Venus in addition to its aspect on ascendant. However, Jupiter was aspecting the 5th house and natal Saturn if reckoned from moon. Thus, Jupiter's transit in Virgo and Saturn's transit in Capricorn were the determinants of the time of marriage. Mars was transiting in Gemini and was aspecting the ascendant. In fact, when Mars was transiting the 7th house from Moon in Taurus the marriage was settled. However, Moon was transiting in the ascendant on the date of marriage and aspecting its own 7th house. Transit of Venus on natal Saturn in Pisces too was a deciding factor as it is the 5th from natal Moon under the aspect of transiting Saturn.

The marriage took place during the sub period of Saturn in the major period of Mercury. Marriage was settled when the Sun was transiting in Jupiter's sign Sagittarius. Mercury owns the 9ᵗʰ house and Saturn is the lord of the 2ⁿᵈ house. Marriage took place when the Sun was transiting in the sign of Saturn that is Aquarius. Generally marriage is settled or ceremonised when the Sun transits in the sign owned by the *dasa* lord. We give the longitudes of the transiting planets as on the date of marriage as under: Saturn 28°9' of Capricorn, Moon 26°19' of Sagittarius, Sun 5°33' of Aquarius, Jupiter 20°18' of Virgo, Mars 17°5' of Gemini, Venus 18°23' of Pisces.

Illustration : 6.6   *Horoscope No.: 6*

Date of birth : 06.08.1961   Time of birth : 16:00:00 hrs
Place of birth : Fatehpur   Lat 27:10 N Long 87:12 E
Ayanamsa   : 23:19:05   Sidereal Time : 13:17:42

Pln	Degree	Rasi	Nakshatra	Pad
Asc	12:47:23	Sag	Moola	4
Sun	20:23:26	Can	Aslesa	2
Mon	25:12:19	Tau	Mrigshira	1
Mar	0:00:52	Vir	U Phalguni	2
Mer (C)	11:27:35	Can	Pushya	3
Jup (R)	7:23:26	Cap	Uttarasadha	4
Ven	9:50:48	Gem	Ardra	1
Sat (R)	1:55:47	Cap	Uttarashadha	2
Rah (R/C)	3:57:19	Leo	Magha	2
Ket (R)	3:57:19	Aqu	Dhanistha	4

Lagna Chart

```
        Jup Sat
         10           8
  Ket 11              7
            9
         12   6 Mar
          3
         Ven
     1           5 Rah
       2        4
      Mon    Mer Sun
```

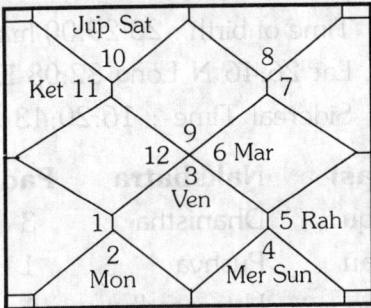

Navamsa Chart

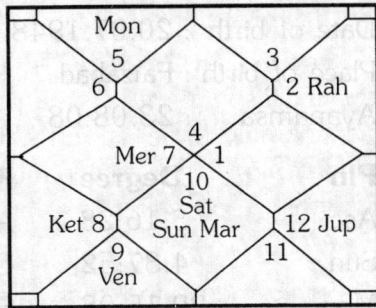

```
        Mon
         5           3
         6           2 Rah
            4
       Mer 7  1
            10
            Sat
   Ket 8  Sun Mar  12 Jup
       9        11
      Ven
```

Balance of Vimshottari Dasa of **Mar 6Y 0M 6D**

The native is born in Sagittarius ascendant with Saturn and Jupiter in the 2nd house. Saturn is retrograde therefore it will give the effect of Sagittarius and not that of Capricorn. Similarly Jupiter will do so, as per the general concept of retrograde planet. The marriage took place on 25.11.1989 when Saturn was transiting in Sagittarius in association with Venus and Jupiter was transiting in Gemini in the 7th house from ascendant. Mars was transiting in Libra at the time of marriage from where it was aspecting the ascendant lord Jupiter. Venus was transiting in the ascendant. It will not be out of place to mention that Mars in case of females and Venus in case of males mostly influence the 7th house at the time of marriage during their transit. In this horoscope transit of Mars is not fullfiling the condition but Venus is very much in appropriate position as discussed earlier since it was transiting over the ascendant on 25.11.1989. We give the longitudes of the transiting planets as on the date of marriage as under: Saturn 17°44' of Sagittarius, Sun 8°57' of Scorpio, Jupiter 15°57' of Gemini, Moon 1°28' of Libra, Mars 20°17' of Libra, Venus 27°53' of Sagittarius.

Illustration : 6.7   Horoscope No.: 7

Date of birth : 20.07.1948   Time of birth : 20:29:00 hrs
Place of birth : Faizabad   Lat 26:46 N Long 82:08 E
Ayanamsa   : 23:08:08   Sidereal Time : 16:20:43

Pln	Degree	Rasi	Nakshatra	Pad
Asc	3:16:28	Aqu	Dhanistha	3
Sun	4:37:52	Can	Pushya	1
Mon	29:15:08	Sag	Uttarasadha	1
Mar	8:50:36	Vir	U Phalguni	4
Mer	14:51:37	Gem	Ardra	3
Jup (R)	27:01:31	Sco	Jyestha	4
Ven	1:51:52	Gem	Mrigshira	3
Sat	29:18:30	Can	Aslesa	4
Rah (R)	17:43:11	Ari	Bharani	2
Ket (R)	17:43:11	Lib	Swati	4

Lagna Chart

```
          _____
         |\           |           /|
         | \    12    |    10    / |
         |  \ Rah 1   |   9 Mon /  |
         |   _____|_____/   |
         |    |\     11|     /|    |
         |  2 | \   ___|___ / |    |
         |    |  \ |  8 Jup| /     |
         |    | 5 \|_____|/      |
         |    |   /|   6   |\      |
         | Mer|  / |       | \ 7 Ket|
         | 3  | /  |       |  \    |
         |Ven |/   |       |   \   |
         |   4/____|_____|____\  |
         |  / Sun Sat |  Mar  \   |
         | /          |         \ |
         |/_____|_____\|
```

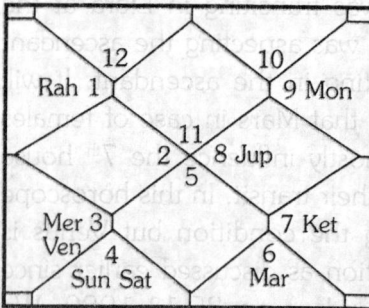

Navamsa Chart

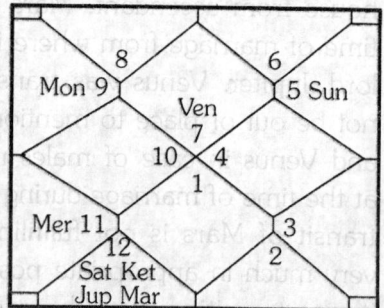

```
          _____
         |\           |           /|
         | \    8     |    6     / |
         |  \ Mon 9   |   5 Sun /  |
         |   _____|___Ven__/   |
         |    |\      |   7 /|     |
         |    | \  10 |   /4 |     |
         | Mer|  \____|__/___| 3   |
         | 11 |  /|   1   |\  |    |
         |    | / |       | \ |    |
         |   /|/  |   12  |  \|\   |
         |  / Sat Ket     |   \ 2  |
         | / Jup Mar      |    \   |
         |/_____|_____\|
```

Balance of Vimshottari Dasa of **Sun 4Y 10M 1D**

She was born in Aquarius ascendant with Mars in the 8th and, the Sun and Saturn in 6th house. She was married at 20 years at age on 24.11.1968 Saturn was transiting in Pisces and Jupiter was transiting in Virgo at the time of marriage. Saturn's transit in the triangular position from the natal Saturn brings marriage. Here natal Saturn is posited in Cancer and transiting Saturn in Pisces i.e. 9th house, which had given rise to marriage. It was almost exact 240° from natal Saturn. Jupiter was transiting in Leo at the time of settlement of marriage but was transiting in Virgo over natal Mars at the time of ceremonisation. Jupiter and Mars were associated with each other in transit in Virgo at the time of marriage. However, both Jupiter and Mars were transiting in the 7th house in Leo at the time of marriage. Thus, in a few cases of early marriage it has been observed that when Saturn transits in triangular position from natal Saturn, the marriage takes place. We are giving the longitudes of the transiting planets as on the date of marriage as under: Saturn 25°56' of Pisces, Sun 8°20' of Scorpio, Moon 29°36' of Sagittarius, Jupiter 7°51' of Virgo, Mars 15°28' of Virgo, Venus 17°30' of Sagittarius.

Illustration : 6.8   *Horoscope No.: 8*

Date of birth : 18.09.1979   Time of birth : 05:35:00 hrs
Place of birth : Kanpur   Lat 26:27 N Long 80:19 E
Ayanamsa   : 23:34:18   Sidereal Time : 5:11:34

Pln	Degree	Rasi	Nakshatra	Pad
Asc	25:34:58	Leo	P Phalguni	4
Sun	0:55:12	Vir	U Phalguni	2
Mon	24:03:13	Can	Aslesa	3
Mar	2:15:56	Can	Punarvasu	4
Mer (C)	5:01:12	Vir	U Phalguni	3
Jup	4:07:22	Leo	Magha	2
Ven (C)	7:17:38	Vir	U Phalguni	4

Sat (C)	24:36:45	Leo	P Phalguni	4
Rah	14:59:10	Leo	P Phalguni	1
Ket	14:59:10	Aqu	Satabhisha	3

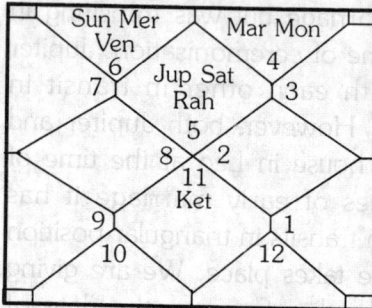

Lagna Chart   **Navamsa Chart**

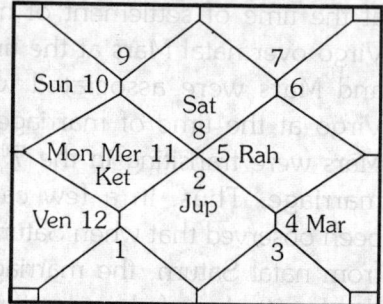

Balance of Vimshottari Dasa of **Mer 7Y 6M 29D**

The native was born in Leo ascendant with Jupiter and Saturn placed therein. The marriage of the native took place on 14.04.2009 when Saturn was transiting in Leo over the radical ascendant, Saturn and Jupiter. This fullfills all the three conditions of accurate timing of marriage. Marriage was settled when Venus was transiting in the 7th house in Aquarius. Mars was also transiting in the 7th house from ascendant at the time of settlement as well as ceremonisation of marriage. This is the way to find out the time of marriage by examination of transiting Saturn, Jupiter, Mars and Venus.

It may be noted that Saturn's sub period in the major period of Venus was operative at the time of marriage. Saturn is the 7th lord and Venus is stationed at 2nd house in Virgo. Venus obtains the *navamsa* of exaltation and Saturn obtains the *navamsa* of *yogakaraka* Mars. Saturn is 7th lord as well and lends its aspect on 7th house. Venus is significator of marriage and is very well placed in the 2nd house. Marriage was settled during the last week of January 2009 when the Sun was transiting in the sign of Saturn Capricorn. Implementation of these observations on number of practical birth chart can make one perfect in predicting accurate month of marriage. We give the longitudes of the transiting planets as on the date of marriage as under: Saturn 21°50' of Leo, Sun 0°10' of Pisces, Moon 21°01' of Scorpio, Jupiter 27°24' of Capricorn, Mars 29°20' of Aquarius, Venus 5°30' of Pisces.

Illustration : 6.9   *Horoscope No.: 9*

Date of birth : 19.11.1973   Time of birth : 22:35:00 hrs
Place of birth : Allahabad   Lat 25:27 N Long 82:50 E
Ayanamsa   : 23:29:47   Sidereal Time : 2:26:39

Pln	Degree	Rasi	Nakshatra	Pad
Asc	19:05:05	Can	Aslesa	1
Sun	3:43:56	Sco	Anuradha	1
Mon	4:11:54	Vir	U Phalguni	3
Mar (R)	2:04:38	Ari	Aswini	1
Mer	17:03:37	Lib	Swati	4
Jup	12:57:41	Cap	Sravna	1
Ven	20:41:41	Sag	Purvasadha	3
Sat (R)	10:15:01	Gem	Ardra	2
Rah (R)	5:34:57	Sag	Moola	2
Ket (R)	5:34:57	Gem	Mrigshira	4

Lagna Chart

Ket Sat
5   3
Mon 6   2
4
Mer 7   1 Mar
10
Jup
Sun 8   12
9   11
Ven Rah

Navamsa Chart

Sat   Ket
10   8
Mon 11   7 Ven
9
Mer 12   6
3
Mar 1   5 Sun
Jup   2   4
Rah

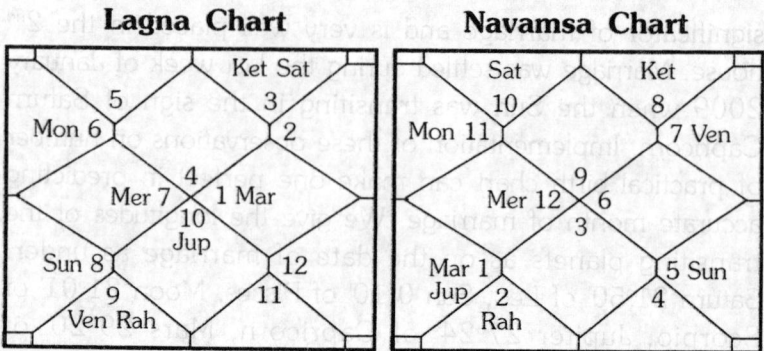

Balance of Vimshottari Dasa of Sun 2Y 7M 10D

The native was born in Cancer ascendant with Saturn in Gemini. The native was married on 12.12.2002 when Saturn was transiting in Gemini over natal Saturn and Jupiter was transiting in Cancer and was aspecting the 5th house, 9th house and the 9th lord Jupiter which occupies the 7th house identical to Capricorn. Mars and Venus were transiting in Libra from where Mars was aspecting the 7th house and the natal Mars. Venus was also transiting in Libra which was the 7th from extremely strong and *yogakaraka* Mars. We given below the longitudes of the transiting planets as on the date of marriage as under: Saturn 2°10' of Gemini, Moon 29°22' of Aquarius, Sun 25°50' of Scorpio, Jupiter 24°7' of Cancer, Mars 12°48' of Libra, Venus 13°33' of Libra.

Illustration : 6.10   *Horoscope No.: 10*

Date of birth : 18.09.1949   Time of birth : 06:01:00 hrs
Place of birth : Faizabad   Lat 26:46 N Long 82:08 E
Ayanamsa   : 23:09:11   Sidereal Time : 5:45:57

Pln	Degree	Rasi	Nakshatra	Pad
Asc	3:42:20	Vir	U Phalguni	3

Sun	1:36:23	Vir	U Phalguni	2
Mon	0:48:51	Can	Punarvasu	4
Mar	13:36:31	Can	Pushya	4
Mer	25:27:40	Vir	Chitra	1
Jup (R)	29:11:03	Sag	Uttarasadha	1
Ven	10:44:36	Lib	Swati	2
Sat (C)	18:22:38	Leo	P Phalguni	2
Rah (R)	23:43:08	Pis	Revati	3
Ket (R)	23:43:08	Vir	Chitra	1

Lagna Chart   Navamsa Chart

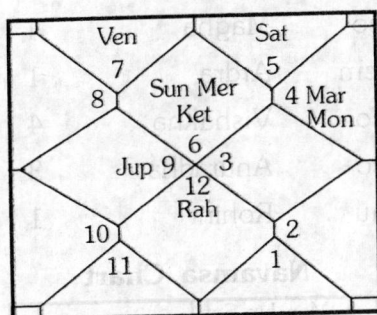

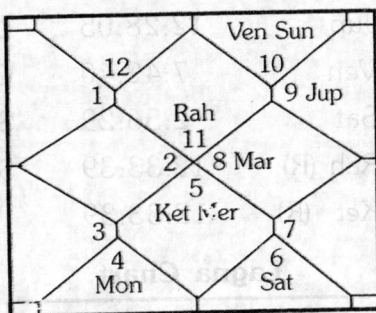

Balance of Vimshottari Dasa of **Jup 3Y 0M 8D**

The native is born in Virgo ascendant with Saturn in Leo. The native was married on 01.07.1975 with Saturn in Gemini from where it was aspecting natal Saturn in the 7th house. Mars was transiting in Aries which is 7th from significator Venus and Venus was transiting in cancer over the natal Moon and Mars. We are giving the longitudes of the transiting planets as on the date of marriage as under: Saturn 1°10' of Virgo, Moon 25°15' of Cancer, Sun 15°57' of Aquarius, Jupiter 11°9' of Leo, Mars 10°43' of Leo, Venus 28°70' of Pisces.

Illustration : 6.11   *Horoscope No.: 11*

Date of birth : 06.08.1956   Time of birth : 03:34:00 hrs
Place of birth : Allahabad   Lat 22:39 N Long 88:23 E
Ayanamsa   : 23:15:19   Sidereal Time : 0:55:13

Pln	Degree	Rasi	Nakshatra	Pad
Asc	28:22:01	Vem	Punarvasu	3
Sun	20:09:43	Can	Aslesa	2
Mon (C)	12:12:24	Can	Pushya	3
Mar	0:14:50	Pis	P Bhadrapad	4
Mer	6:57:22	Leo	Magha	3
Jup	12:28:05	Leo	Magha	4
Ven	7:42:40	Gem	Ardra	1
Sat	2:56:29	Sco	Vishakha	4
Rah (R)	12:33:39	Sco	Anuradha	3
Ket (R)	12:33:39	Tau	Rohini	1

Lagna Chart

Sun Mon 4	Ket 2	1
Jup 5 Mer	Ven 3	
6 9	12 Mar	11
7 8 Sat Rah	10	

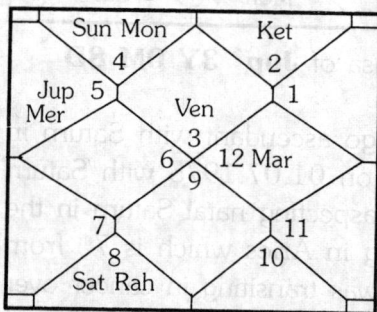

Navamsa Chart

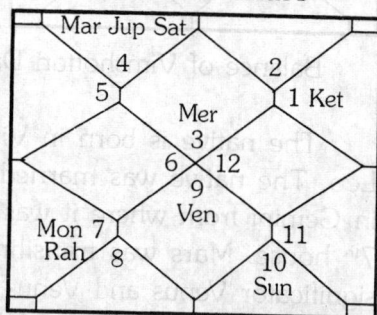

Mar Jup Sat 4	2	1 Ket
5	Mer 3	
6 9	12 Ven	11
Mon 7 Rah 8	10 Sun	

Balance of Vimshottari Dasa of **Sat 6Y 4M 8D**

She was born in Gemini ascendant with Saturn in Scorpio. She was married on 16.11.1978. Saturn was transiting in Leo at that time and was crossing the radical location of the 7th lord Jupiter. Jupiter was transiting in Cancer over the natal Moon from where it was aspecting natal Saturn. Mars was transiting in Scorpio over the natal Saturn which is the 5th from the Moon sign. In fact, Mars was transiting over the 7th lord Saturn as reckoned from Moon. She was passing through Mercury Saturn *dasa bhukti*. Saturn is the 9th lord and Mercury is the lord of the ascendant Saturn obtains *navamsa* of Moon. Mercury obtains own *navamsa*. Saturn is quite strong as it obtains 1.23 *shadabala* and falls in *Vikshkha* constellation ruled by the 7th lord Jupiter. Thus, marriage is very much justified at 23 years of age when she was running under the sub period of Saturn in the major period of Mercury. Longitudes of planets as on the date of marriage: Sun 0°27' of Scorpio, Moon 22°6' of Taurus, Mars 17°2' of Scorpio, Venus 15°33' of Libra, Jupiter 15°21' of Cancer, Saturn 18°4' of Leo.

Illustration : 6.12   *Horoscope No.: 12*

Date of birth : 06.11.1951   Time of birth : 19:59:00 hrs
Place of birth : Farrukhabad   Lat 22:39 N Long 88:23 E
Ayanamsa   : 23:11:09   Sidereal Time : 23:22:31

Pln	Degree	Rasi	Nakshatra	Pad
Asc	7:46:54	Gem	Ardra	1
Sun	20:11:03	Lib	Vishakha	1
Mon	24:13:08	Cap	Dhanistha	1
Mar	26:31:00	Leo	P Phalguni	4
Mer	4:25:51	Sco	Anuradha	1
Jup (R)	12:00:22	Pis	U Bhadrapad	3
Ven	3:46:04	Vir	U Phalguni	3
Sat	16:50:06	Vir	Hasta	3
Rah (R)	14:10:36	Aqu	Satabhisha	3
Ket (R)	14:10:36	Leo	P Phalguni	1

Lagna Chart

```
        4            2
Ket  5                    1
Mar
              3
    Ven Sat 6     12 Jup
              9
   Sun 7           11 Rah
        8         10
        Mer       Mon
```

Navamsa Chart

```
                        Mar
        10          8
Rah 11                   7 Jup
Ven
              9
      12     6
              3
      Sun 1   Sat    5 Ket
        2          4   Ker
                       Mon
```

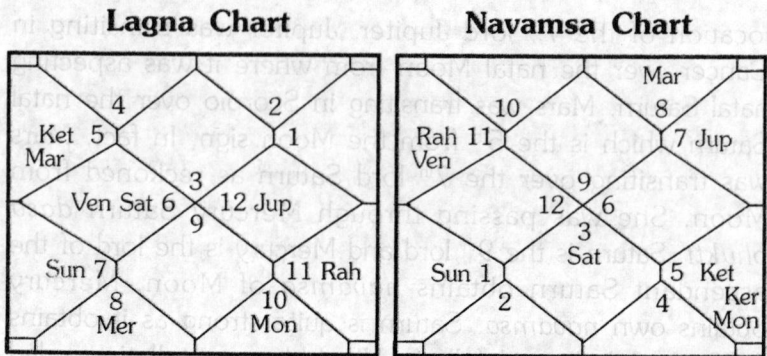

Balance of Vimshottari Dasa of **Mar 6Y 6M 12D**

The native was born in Gemini ascendant with Saturn in Virgo. He was married on 16.11.1978 when Saturn was transiting in Leo over the lord of *lagna*, Mercury. In fact, the natal Saturn is at 16°50' of Virgo and transiting Saturn was at 19°14' i.e. Saturn transited within 30° of the location of natal Saturn at the time of marriage. Jupiter transited in Cancer which is 7th from natal Moon and is aspecting natal Jupiter. It may be noted that when natal Jupiter and transiting Jupiter aspect each other with regard to the 7th house or ascendant marriage takes place provided other conditions for marriage are fulfilled. Mars was transiting in Scorpio where it was receiving the aspect of natal Jupiter and transiting Jupiter. Marriage took place during Jupiter Saturn *dasa bhukti*. Venus is the significator of marriage and is quite strong as it obtains 1.33 *shadabala*. Jupiter is the 7th lord and Saturn is the lord of the 9th house. Saturn is posited in the 4th house under mutual aspect with Jupiter. Thus, Jupiter Saturn *dasa bhukti* is most appropriate for a happy married life. We have not discussed the rules of timing of marriage here in this chapter. This has been discussed in detail in our other book "Vivah Vimarsh". Here we have shown the application and implementation of the rules regarding dasha and transit for accurate timing of marriage. Longitudes of planets as on date of marriage : Sun 0°24' of Scorpio, Moon 22°6' of Taurus, Mars 17°2' of Scorpio, Jupiter 15°21' of Cancer, Venus 16°38' of Libra, Saturn 19°7' of Leo.

6.2 Conclusion

In chapter entitled as **'Saturn : The Timer'**, we have tried to express our humble opinion about the astonishingly accurate timing through the examination of transiting Jupiter. Whenever Saturn transits over the 10th lord either from the ascendant or Moon it gives rise to settlement of the native by getting a suitable job, business or service i.e. a rewarding and progressing period for success.

Similarly, Saturn's transit helps a lot in timing marriage accurately and precisely. Practice and practical experience can make one perfect in the art of the study of transiting Saturn. There are various oppurtunities in one's life when marriage is likely to take place; if the first opportunity is not availed by the parents of the native for the marriage of their child they should not ignore the 2nd or 3rd opportunity.

The first opportunity of marriage comes when the transiting Saturn aspects the natal Saturn or when the distance of the transiting Saturn is less than 90° from the natal Saturn. The 3rd aspect of the transiting Saturn on the natal Saturn gives rise to marriage. Here Saturn stays for about two and a half years which is an important time slot in which marriage takes place. Now see the position of Jupiter which should be transiting in the 5th or 7th house from the ascendant or Moon or otherwise the transiting Jupiter and natal Jupiter must aspect each other.

If the 1st opportunity of marriage does not materialise

for any reason the second opportunity will appear when Saturn will transit exactly over the natal Saturn. There may be a difference of 10° on either side between the natal and transiting Saturn in the same sign. This may be termed in other words that marriage takes place when transiting Saturn crosses the natal Saturn.

Other conditions of the transit of Jupiter, Mars and Venus are the same as explained above.

The third opportunity comes when Saturn transits almost 120° apart from natal Saturn from where it lends aspect over the natal Saturn. This happens in the case of late marriage when transiting Saturn reaches in the 4th sign from the natal Saturn and aspects the natal Saturn. Bleak opportunity of a very late marriage around 45 years may come in evidence when natal Saturn and transiting Saturn are opposite to each other and have mutual aspect. Other transits like that of Jupiter, Mars and Venus will act in the same way as given here.

First of all, appropriate *dasa bhukti* for marriage should be determined, thereafter, transiting rules of Saturn should be implemented intelligently. Thereafter transit of Jupiter, Mars and Venus will help in finding out a period of one and a half month for the marriage of the native. *Navamsa* rule and the rule of transit of the Sun in the signs owned by the major period lords will help us a lot to find out very accurate and precise time of marriage. If *pratyantar dasa* is also considered the correct week or the fortnight of marriage will be the outcome in which marriage is to take place. Practice, excercise and experience can make one perfect in timing the correct year, month and even the fortnight in which the marriage will be ceremonised.

7 Nadi Principles about Saturn's Transit

A very interesting fact in Hindu Predictive Astrology is that many principles or secrets are found in the *Nadi Granthas*, and we commonly call them as *Nadi* principles. The research students of Hindu Astrology can study these principles and apply them to their horoscopic analysis for higher preciseness and amazing results. Following principles of the transit of Saturn are simple and easy to apply. This can be assured that appropriate appreciation of the following principles of the transit of Saturn will give acurate observation, if synchronised with Dasa Bhukti etc. Position of the placement of Saturn in the birth chart and that of transiting Saturn should be systematically analysed.

According to ancient *Nadi Granthas* Saturn's transit result can be delineated from four different phases of Saturn as follows:

1. Degree wise transit results of Saturn over and in trines to the seven planets and the nodes.

2. Transit results of Saturn through or from certain houses as counted from its *Chandra Navamsa*.

3. House wise transit results of Saturn.

4. Degree wise transit results of Saturn over the lords of the 8th house or its trines from each house.

PHASE-I :

Degree wise transit results of Saturn over and in trines to the seven planets and the nodes:-

When Saturn transits over a position which is identical

degree wise to the natal position of any planet or its trine positions, it gives unfavourable results pertaining to:

I.   That natal planet (as significator);

II.   The house/s owned by that planet;

III. The house occupied by that planet.

1. The Sun:

रविविंत्रिकोणगे मन्दे पितृपीड़ा
भवेत् कष्ट पितृवर्गेहरिष्टदम् ।

Meaning, when transit Saturn coincides identically with the natal position of the Sun or its trines, the native's father's health will be afflicted or the native himself will be troubled or death of some elderly male relative will take place.

Additional Results: Grief on account of a close relative, misunderstanding with father or reproaches from him, mental anguish to father, heavy expenditure, one becomes indebted, prestige at stake, demise of father, troubles in vocation or service or business, change of place of residence etc.

2. The Moon:

चन्द्रत्रिकोणगे मन्दे मातृपीड़ा
भवेत् कष्टं मातृवर्गेहरिष्टदम् ।।

Meaning, when transit Saturn coincides identically with the natal position of the Moon or its trines, the native's mother's health will be afflicted or the native himself will be troubled or death of an elderly female relative will take place.

Additional results: Mental agony to mother due to

misdeeds of her brethren, loss of status, loss of wealth, sickness of mother causing worries to father, mental agony, demise of mother, misunderstanding with mother, devaluation of landed property etc.

3. Mars:

कुजत्रिकोणगे मन्दे भ्रातृपीड़ा
भवेत् कष्ट भ्रातृ वर्गेहरिष्टदम् ।।

Meaning when transit Saturn coincides identically with the natal position of Mars or its trines, the native's brother's (or sister's) health is afflicted or the native himself will be troubled or death of brother or sister will occur.

Additional results: Blood impurities, humiliation, fear of criminal proceedings, quarrels for assets, low ebb in business activities, demotion, worries on account of brethren, loss of wealth or property, wound by weapon or physical injury, fear of accident etc.

4. Mercury:

When transit Saturn coincides identically with the natal position of Mercury or its trines, the native's maternal uncle's or aunt's health will suffer.

Additional results: Increase in debts, financial stringency in business or trade, misfortune or death in mother's paternal family, hindrances in education and mental anguish on account of it, sickness of a close friend, mental disorders, etc.

5. Jupiter:

गुरुत्रिकोणगे मन्दे पुत्रपीड़ा
भवेत् कष्टं पत्रवर्गेतरिष्टदम् ।

Meaning, when transit Saturn coincides identically with the natal position of Jupiter or its trines, health of the native's son (or daughter) is afflicted or the native himself is troubled or death of son (or daughter) takes place.

Additional results: Worries or troubles from family members, mental anxiety and anguish on account of one's children, hindrance in religious pursuits or studies, demise of son or daughter, etc.

6. Venus:

शुक्रत्रिकोणगे मन्दे कलत्रपीडा महद्भयम् ।

Meaning, when transit Saturn coincides identically with the natal position of Venus or its trines, the native's wife will have major health problems or great fear is impending.

Additional results: Disgrace on account of wife and consequent mental anguish, obstacles from in laws, separation from wife, demise of wife, absence of reciprocal love, marital relations strained, troubles in wife's paternal family, etc.

7. Saturn:

When transit Saturn coincides identically with its natal position or its trines, the native will experience major physical ailments lasting over long duration.

Additional results: Disputes with and troubles from family members, absence of peace of mind on account of problems concerning landed property and great loss of money, abnormal increase in miseries and sufferings, demise of native himself, etc.

8. Rahu:

राहुत्रिकोणगे मन्दे देहपीडा मनोव्यथा स्वसमानजनावधिः ।

Meaning, when transit Saturn coincides identically with the natal position of Rahu or its trines, the native is grieved by physical pain or mental agony or death of a nearer relative occurs.

Additional results: Relations with Government strained, setback in health, reputation at stake, happening of some untoward incident in his own family, death of a close friend or a cousin, performs obsequies for a dead relative, food poisoning, snake or insect bite, shifting of residence to a distant place, etc.

9. Ketu:

When Saturn coincides identically with the natal position of Ketu or its trines, the health of the native himself is likely to be afflicted seriously.

Additional results: Quarrels in family, demise in maternal uncle's family, mental tension due to family dispute over inheritance, kidney disprders, calamity, hospitalization etc.

PHASE–II :

Transit results of Saturn through or from certain houses are counted from the *Chandra Navamsa Rasi.*

रायुभीतिर्मनस्तापमन्तश्रिव दकलापवान् ।
चंद्रांशराशिगे मन्दे गोचरे जन्मगेहथवा । ।

(*Chandra kala nadi* part I, Pg. 314,Verse 3124)

Meaning, when Saturn transits *Chandra Navamsa Rasi* (rasi represented in the natal chart by the Moon's occupied *navamsa rasi*) or the sign occupied by the Moon (in Rasi chart), the native suffers from fear of enemies, mental anguish and humiliation from secret blemish.

चंद्रांशराशि मारभ्य गोचरे त्वष्टमे शनौ।
राहुदाये महत्कष्टं योगभडगौ विनिर्दिशेत्।।

(*Chandra kala nadi* part I, Pg.201, Verse 2044/45)

Meaning, when Saturn transits the 8th sign from the *Chandra Navamsa Rasi*, the native will suffer great calamity during Rahu's period and will have termination of a running favourable *yogaphala* or *yogabhanga* results.

चंद्रांशराशि मारभ्यं गोचरे सप्तमे शनो।
राहुदाये वक्रभतौ देहजाडये विनिर्दिशेत्।।

(*Chandra kala nadi* part I, Pg.235, Verse 2385)

When Saturn transits the 7th sign from the *Chandra Navamsa Rasi*, the native gains obesity during Mars' sub period in Rahu's period (if it coincides).

The above rules give us a clue to study transit results of other slow moving planets through *Chandra Navamsa Rasi*. Similarly, their transits through *Navamsa* signs occupied by the remaining six planets should be looked into.

PHASE-III :

House wise transit results of Saturn :

Chandrakala Nadi (Madras Government Oriental series 1952 and 1956) gives the following verse at many places:

यद् भावस्याष्टमे मन्दे यद भावस्याष्टमेक्षिते।
तद् भावः क्लेशमाप्नोति मूर्त्यादिफलभीरयेत्।।

(Vol. I pg.100 verse 1058; Vol. II part I pg. 106, verse 913; and Vol. II part II pg 240 verse 4827)

Meaning, the house from which the 8th house when transited by Saturn and the other three houses from which the respective 8th houses when aspected by Saturn, suffer afflictions. One has to obtain Saturn's transit results from the ascendant onwards, in the same way.

In order to understand the above verse we have to take first the house through which Saturn in transiting and the three houses which Saturn aspects. The suffering and afflictions are felt on account of those houses from which the above four places become the 8th houses.

The whole *Nadi* principle contained in the verse could be explained clearly as follows:

1. When Saturn transits the ascendant, it is the 8th from the 6th house; Saturn's 3rd house aspect falls on the 3rd house, it is the 8th from the 8th house; Saturn's 7th house aspect falls on the 7th house; it is the 8th from the 12th house; and Saturn's 10th house aspect falls on the 10th house; it is the 8th from the 3rd house. Therefore, the native who has the transit of Saturn in the ascendant, will suffer unfavourable results in matters connected with the 6th, 8th, 12th and 3rd houses.

2. When Saturn transits the 2nd house, it is the 8th house from the 7th house; 3rd house aspect falls on the 4th house; it is the 8th from the 9th houses; Saturn's 7th house aspect falls in the 8th house, it is the 8th from the ascendant; Saturn's 10th house aspect falls on the 11th house, it is the 8th from the 4th house. Therefore the native will suffer afflictions in matters connected with the 7th, the 9th, the ascendant and the 4th house.

In the same way, Saturn's transit and its influences from the 3rd house onwards to the 12th house can be judged. It may be emphasized here that the above transit results are to be borne by the native throughout the transit of Saturn in a particular sign.

PHASE-IV :

Degree wise transit results of Saturn over the lord of the 8ᵗʰ house or its trines from each house.

तत्तद् भावाष्टमेशांशे गोचरे शनि संस्थिते ।
तत्तद् भावविनाशोने क्लेशं प्राप्नोति भूरिशः ।।

Meaning, (of two verses): when transit Saturn coincides identically with the natal position of the lord of 8ᵗʰ house from a particular house or its trine positions, the native will experience mental upsets due to denial of results signified by that particular house (these two verses are complimentary to each other).

A

Bhrugu Nadi describes the following transit results of Saturn over the lords of the 12 houses.

लग्नेशांशे   शयुपीडा   मातुजनावधिः ।
धनेशांशे दारपीडा सौख्यांशे देहजाडयता ।।

सुखेशांशे पितारिष्ट स्वप्रभोश्च तथा भवेत् ।
सुतेशांशे मित्रपीडा राजराष्ट्र विनाशकृत् ।।

षष्ठेशांशे पितृव्यस्थ देहबाधा भविष्यति ।
दारेशांशे प्रवास स्यात् मातामहजनावधिः ।।

रन्ध्रेशांशे देहपीडा भाग्येशांशे धनक्षयम् ।
कर्मेशांशे व्याधिकयं श्वशुरारिष्टमादिशेत् ।।

लाभेशांशे मात   हानिः व्ययेशांशे पुत्रपीडा ।
मूर्त्यादिव्य भावान्तं शनिचारवशात्फलम् ।।

When transit Saturn coincides identically with the natal position of the lord of:

1. The first house the native will be subjected to trouble from his enemies or the maternal relatives will be afflicted. (1st house being the 8th from its 6th house).

2. The 2nd house- native's spouse will be subjected to trouble (2nd house being the 8th from the 7th house).

3. The 3rd house- native will become obese (3rd house being the 8th from the 8th house).

4. The 4th house- native's father or employer will be subjected to trouble and affliction (4th house being the 8th from the 9th house).

5. The 5th house- native will be subjected to trouble from friends or trouble from government or state agencies (5th house being the 8th from the 10th house).

6. The 6th house- native's paternal uncle or aunt will be physically injured (6th house being the 8th from the 11th house).

7. The 7th house- native will undergo unnecessary journeys or will get news about the demise of maternal grandfather (7th house being the 8th from the 12th house).

8. The 8th house- native's health will be afflicted (8th house being the 8th from the 1st house).

9. The 9th house- native will experience reduction in his assets or properties (9th house being the 8th from the 2nd house).

10. The 10th house- native will experience increase in expenditure or health problem concerning his father-in-law (the 10th house being the 8th from the 3rd house).

11. The 11th house- the native may lose his mother or affliction to her (11th house being the 8th from the 4th house).

12. The 12th house- native will experience problems concerning his children (the 12th house being its 8th from the 5th house).

Transit results of Saturn are to be judged beginning from the 1st house upto the 12th house. In *Bhrigu Nadi* only transits over its natal planets are considered.

PHASE-IV :

B

Chandrakala Nadi gives exhaustive details of the effects of Saturn's transit, in about 350 verses out of a total of 9152 verses. There are two improvements in this masterpiece as compared with *Bhrigu Nadi-*

a) The author gives importance to the trine positions of a natal planet also.

b) Saturn's transit effects through sign/s aspected by natal planet are also taken into account as stated below:-

लग्नेशांशे तत्तिरकोणे स्फुटयोगं गते शनौ
मातृलारिष्टमाप्नोति मातुर्माता मनोव्यथाम् ।।

Meaning, when transit Saturn coincides degreewise with the lord of the ascendant or its trine positions, there will be affliction to one's maternal uncle and consequently maternal grandmother will have mental agony.

Additional results: Physical injury from a weapon, native's father grieved due to loss of his brother or sister, grief to native's mother or maternal grandmother, worries to maternal uncle or aunt, death of maternal uncle or aunt, one becomes indebted, loss or fear from thieves, etc.

धनेशांशे तत्तिरकोणे स्फुटयोग गते शनौ ।
धनेशदृष्टिराशौ तु दारहानि विनिर्दिशेत् ।।

Meaning, when transit Saturn coincides degree wise with the lord of the 2nd house or its trine positions or passes through sign/s aspected by that lord (on the same degree) there will occur death of the native's wife.

Additional results: Loss in vocational activities, death of someone in wife's paternal family, wife gaining obesity so far as to destruct free movement of her body, worries to wife, death of wife, want of marital happiness, etc.

Regarding the 3rd house or *Sahodarasthana*, no specific verse is found in the text. The 3rd house being the 8th from the 8th house, matters connected with that house will be involved such as ill health, gaining obesity, grief, inheritance, accident, debts, poverty, medical operation etc.

सुखेशांशे तत्तिरकोणे स्फुटयोगं गते शनौ ।
स्वपित देहजाडयादि दृष्टिराशौ महाविपत् ।।

Meaning, when transit Saturn coincides degreewise with the lord of the 4th house or its trine positions; native's father will gain obesity and when Saturn passes through sign/s aspected by that lord, he will suffer major calamity.

Additional results: Death of the native's father and consequent mental agony to mother and to paternal uncle or aunt, mother much worried, grief to father due to loss of his spouse, calamity to father's brethren, father's sickness, etc.

सुतेशांशे तत्तिरकोणे स्फुटयोगं गते शनौ ।
प्रतयकदाये सोदरस्य सन्तानारिष्टमादिशेत् ।।

Meaning, when transit Saturn coincides degree wise with lord of the 5th house or its trine positions, there will be death of brother's or sister's child provided at that time native's running *Dasa* is the 5th one (Pratyaridasa) from birth *Dasa*.

Additional results: Loss of paternal wealth, serious sickness of a friend, ill health or death of wife's mother death in wife's paternal family, death of a child in one's own family etc.

षष्ठेशांशे तत्तिरकोणे स्फुटयोगं गते शनौ ।
षष्ठेशदृष्टिराशौ   तु सोदरस्य मनोव्यथा ।।

Meaning, when transit Saturn coincides degree wise with the lord of the 6th house or its trine positions or passes through sign/s aspected that lord, the native's brother or sister will suffer mental agony.

Additional results: Death of an elder brother or sister, loss of status or position, change of place of residence, great mental agony and much fear to native, death of paternal relative (i.e. father's brother or sister), miseries to elder brethren, etc.

मदेशांशे तत्तिरकोणे स्फुटयोगंह गते शनौ ।
मदेशदृष्टि राशौ तु मातामहविनाशनम् ।।

meaning, when transit Saturn coincides degreewise with the lord of the 7th house or its trine positions or passes through sign/s aspected by that lord, death of native's maternal grandfather is indicated.

Additional results: Unexpected and heavy expenditure, death of maternal uncle or afflictions to or death of native's father's mother.

रन्ध्रेशांशे तत्तिकोणे स्फुटयोगं गते शनौ ।
रन्ध्रेशदृष्टिराशौ तु स्वजनारिष्टमादिशेत् ।।

meaning, when transit Saturn coincides degreewise with the lord of the 8th house or its trine positions or passes through sign/s aspected by that lord, death of a nearer relative (family member) takes place.

Additional results: One's own death, fear from opponents, native suffers from severe diseases and is confined to hospital, wife's health suffers, death of a bosom friend, worries on account of children, blemish to family, loss of property or wealth, native feels exhausted and becomes emaciated, fear of death due to accident etc.

भाग्येशांशे तत्तिकोणे स्फुटयोगं गते शनौ ।
स्वमातृभगिनी पुत्रनाशं च मनुरब्रवीत् ।।

Meaning, when in transit Saturn coincides degreewise with the lord of the 9th house or its trine positions, demise of son of native's mother's sister, will occur, so says the great seer Manu.

Additional results: Quarrels with bad people (Goondas), eye disease, disease in throat, loss of wealth, quarrels in a family, mental disability, etc.

कर्मेशांशे तत्तिकोणे स्फुटयोगं गते शनौ ।
कमोशदृष्टिराशौ तु भगिन्याश्च मनोव्यथा ।।

Meaning, when transit Saturn coincide degreewise with the lord of the 10th house or its trine positions or passes through sign/s aspected by that lord, the native's sister suffers mental anguish.

Additional results: Calamity in wife's paternal family, native himself hospitalised, severe sickness or death of brother or sister and consequent grief to native, affliction to or death of wife's father etc.

लाभेशांशे तत्तिकोणे स्फुटयोगं गते शनौ।
लाभेशदृष्टिराशौ तु मातृपीडा विनिर्दिशेत्।।

Meaning, when in transit Saturn coincides degree wise with the lord of the 11th house or its trine positions or passes through sign/s aspected by that lord, trouble to native's mother is indicated.

Additional results: Desertion of one's birth place, sickness of friend's wife, quarrels on account of or loss of landed property, grief to mother due to death of maternal uncle or aunt, death of a maternal relative, over worried, mental agony to mother, afflictions to or death of mother, etc.

व्ययेशांशे तत्तिकोणे स्फुटयोगं गते शनौ।
व्ययेशदृष्टिराशौ तु सन्तानारिष्टमादिशेत्।।

Meaning, transit Saturn coincides degreewise with the lord of the 12th house or its trine positions or passes through sign/s aspected by that lord, demise of the native's child is indicated.

Additional results: Setback in studies or failure in examination, sickness of elder brother's wife or elder sister's husband, sickness of children, demise of grandfather, loss of wealth, afflictions to son or daughter or misunderstanding with them, etc.

8 SATURN
The Great Timer

Timing Prominent Events Through Saturn's Transit

To predict the exact spell of time, for any event to happen, is one of the most arduous tasks in astrology. There are innumerable systems, that help in timing the events in various ways. *Vimshottari dasa* system and transits are the most customary procedures, which are considered one of the vital tools of an astrologer. Apart from various kinds of *dasa* systems such as *Vimshottari, Ashtottari, Yogini, Kalchakra* and *Jaimini*, solar return charts and transits of planets also help us in precise predictions as far as the timing of an event is concerned.

Transit of Saturn is a supporting tool in pinpointing the period of occurrence of important events, and more so the turning points in one's life. The study of the role of Saturn in any horoscope is quite complicated and tough exercise, which may be correctly and successfully worked out only after a thorough study and wide experience of the subject. In fact, generally, we know very little about predictions on the basis of transiting planets and more so about the transit of Saturn. There are a few veteran scholars, who are able to predict all important, good or bad, events and their periods, only on the basis of transiting planets, without taking any help of *dasa-bhukti* etc.

Whenever Saturn transits over the natal Sun, many adversities take place, especially with regard to the matters of the house owned by the Sun. Suppose, Scorpio is the ascendant and the 10th lord Saturn is posited in Cancer in the 9th house. Whenever Saturn will transit over the 10th lord Sun, in Cancer, serious problems are bound to arise in professional matters.

Saturn is a planet of paramount importance. It covers one's career and moulds it according to its placement in the birth chart. Saturn indicates the accumulated power of *Karmas* of past life and the outcome of the *Karmas* of the past life comes as evidence in the present life. From Saturn's transit, in relation to the natal position in the chart, one can find out the changes, promotions and demotions in the career, or which may cause recognition, or otherwise affect the native.

Saturn's transit is quite important with regard to the 10th house, or professional matters, that may cause promotion, appreciation, recognition, expansion, extension and all-round professional success. Contrary effects may also be experienced. What will be the exact result depends on the 10th lord and the position of the 10th lord, both from ascendant and Moon. In case of mutual exchange of the 10th lord with any other planet, transit of Saturn over the other planet will bring prosperity and popularity in all professional matters. If the 10th lord, or the planet of mutual exchange, is inimical to Saturn, negative results appear, as soon as Saturn transits over that particular planet.

Saturn stays two and a half years in one sign. An expert and experienced astrologer may foresee whether this two and a half year period is favourable or unfavourable. The life of a person may be covered in three or four circles of Saturn's transit. Each cycle of thirty years may be divided into twelve segments of two and a half years each. Saturn will transit for two and a half years in each sign. One zodiacal sign contains two and a quarter constellations, nine *navamsa* signs and thirty degrees. There will be different dates or time periods when Saturn transits in different asterisms and *navamsas*. Saturn transits in one constellation for 13 months and 10 days and in one *navamsa* for 3 months and 10 days approximately, and these segments of time span are of great significance and use, with regard to determination of correct events. But it requires expert experience and practice with regard to transiting planets. A few important points should be kept in view quite distinctly.

1. Transiting planets do not create events. If any event is not indicated in the birth chart i.e. the event, which is not promised by natal chart, it will not take place. Transiting planets help in precise timing of any event.

2. Saturn indicates losses, sickness, obstacles, restriction, worries and pains. If Saturn is in a negative transit, its occupation, aspect or conjunction with any house or lord thereof, will certainly cause problems. However, if Saturn's transit is positive, quite encouraging results will be experienced with regard to the house concerned.

3. The exact result of the transit of Saturn depends on the nature of sign through which it is passing. If Saturn is a *Yogakaraka* and transits over the sign of exaltation, or own sign, the benefic results will be the outcome. If it transits in its sign of debilitation or inimical sign, the negative results will come up.

RULE-1

Whenever Saturn transits over the natal Mars, the life takes a prominent turn. When Saturn transits 4th, 7th, and 11th as reckoned from natal Mars, vital changes with prominence are experienced. These are the turning points of life. One should be quite cautious at the time of change of sign during the transit of Saturn. This turning point may either be favourable or unfavourable, which depends on the position and ownership of natal Mars.

Illustration : 8.1   *Horoscope No.: 13*

Date of birth : 20.07.1952   Time of birth : 12:45:36 hrs
Place of birth : Jabalpur   Lat 23:10 N Long 79:57 E
Ayanamsa   : 23:11:50   Sidereal Time : 8:27:27

Pln	Degree	Rasi	Nakshatra	Pad
Asc	10:21:44	Lib	Swati	2
Sun	4:18:02	Can	Pushya	1
Mon	15:55:18	Gem	Ardra	3
Mar	17:03:49	Lib	Swati	4
Mer	0:24:49	Leo	Magha	1
Jup	23:44:51	Ari	Bharani	4
Ven (C)	11:18:34	Can	Pushya	3
Sat	16:16:51	Vir	Hasta	2
Rah (R)	28:26:31	Cap	Dhanistha	2
Ket (R)	28:26:31	Can	Aslesa	4

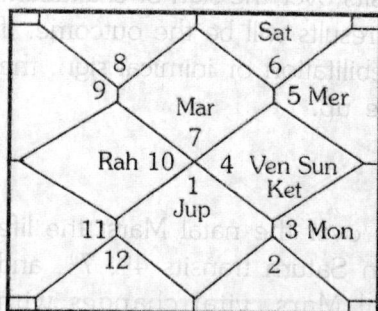

Lagna Chart   **Navamsa Chart**

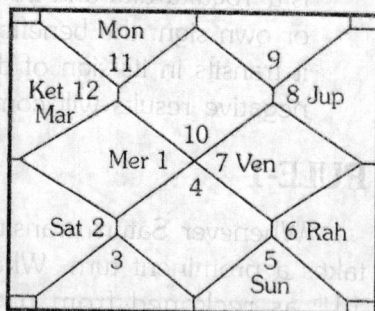

Balance of Vimshottari Dasa of **Rah 5Y 6M 2D**

In the case of above illustration, the native was a famous, very well established and well-known business magnet. He was running many large units of Plastic industry.

Everything was quite fine and bright. There were at least two cars for each member of the family. The native had a turn over of approximately one billion rupees per annum. Suddenly, an abrupt & steep descent came in his business w.e.f. May 1998, when Saturn was transiting in Aries. Saturn transited in Aries from 17.4.1998 to 7.6.2000. The native was born in Libra ascendant with Mars. Saturn's transit in Aries should be properly studied.

Transit of Saturn was the 11th from radical Moon. With that reason, auspicious and benefic results should have come but it was just the opposite. Saturn's transit in Aries was 7th from natal Mars and that changed the course of life of the native by bringing a heavy downfall. The transit of Saturn in Aries wrecked the empire of the native. All factories were locked out, cars and land were sold. The native was compelled to dispose off his valuable gems, ornaments, machines and the like. Here, the transit of Saturn through Aries changed the life of the native in the most unprecedented manner. This downward trend has not yet stopped, even after nearly 10 years. We humbly opine that the transit of Saturn, just opposite natal Mars in a birth chart, brings negative U-turn in one's life, if Mars is a negative planet for that particular ascendant.

The native had to undergo imprisonment from 5.3.2003 to 14.3.2003, when Saturn was transiting over the lord of the 10th house i. e. the natal Moon. He was again locked up on 29.7.2007, when Saturn entered in Leo and aspected natal Mars. The native has reached bankruptcy. His relations with almost all his friends and relatives have become strained. Thus, the transit of Saturn over the natal Mars is extremely adverse. Let us derive the positive side of the transit of Saturn in the same case. Saturn transited in Libra from 7.10.1982 to 30.12.1984. The native was working as the Chief Engineer in a private firm. He resigned there and came to Lucknow with bag and baggage. He started independent Plastic business during the transit of Saturn through Libra and got astonishing success in a short span of time. From Rs. 5000/- he started earning billions of rupees. The growth, expansion and regular flow of income continued all through the transit of Saturn from Libra to Pisces and downfall started w.e.f. transit of Saturn through Aries as discussed above.

Mars is a negative planet for Libra ascendant, but it gives positive results in the 11th, 3rd and 10th house, in spite of the lordship of the 2nd and 7th house. The transit of Saturn, in the 4th, 7th and 11th house, as reckoned from natal Mars, brings prominent changes and turnings in life. These are not the events but the change of course of events. These are the prominent turning points, which are over and above the *dasa-bhukti*. All those who know astrology will find our observation very useful when sudden positive or negative changes are not explained by *dasa-bhukti*.

Illustration: 8.2   *Horoscope No.: 14*

Date of birth : 05.09.1963   Time of birth : 11:24:00 hrs
Place of birth : Kanpur   Lat 26:27 N Long 80:19 E
Ayanamsa   : 23:20:42   Sidereal Time : 10:09:46

Pln	Degree	Rasi	Nakshatra	Pad
Asc	1:35:09	Sco	Vishakha	4
Sun	18:36:41	Leo	P Phalguni	2
Mon	7:52:44	Pis	U Bhadrapad	2
Mar	1:56:00	Lib	Chitra	3
Mer	11:38:50	Vir	Hasta	1
Jup (R)	24:59:14	Pis	Revati	3
Ven (D)	20:17:55	Leo	P Phalguni	3

Sat	(R)	24:45:59	Cap	Dhanistha	1
Rah	(R)	25:40:45	Gem	Punarvasu	2
Ket	(R)	25:40:45	Sag	Purvasadha	4

Lagna Chart   **Navamsa Chart**

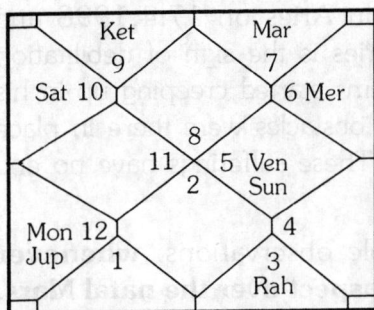

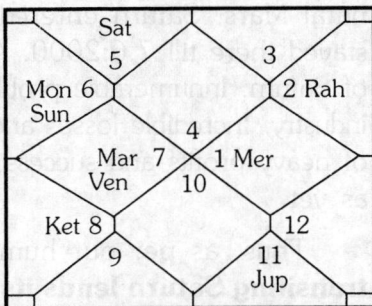

Balance of Vimshottari Dasa of **Sat 12Y 6M 8D**

The native entered in business only at the age of 16 years and became one of the leading businessmen within 15 years. The native was running a very large security printing press and was earning millions of rupees per month. He decided to enter into dairy business at a large scale during the year 1991. He implemented his idea and soon a large dairy was commissioned in the beginning of 1993, when Saturn was transiting in Capricorn from 5.1.1991 to 30.3.1993.

The native was born in Scorpio ascendant. Mars occupies the 12th house in Libra. Saturn's transit in Capricorn was a turning point of his career because natal Mars was aspected by transiting Saturn from Capricorn. The transiting Saturn completely changed the course of life of the native. It was a positive change. It was so, because Saturn was transiting in own sign, Capricorn, where Mars gets exalted. Dairy started functioning very nicely, which was beyond the expectation of the native. Dairy was running round the clock. The native made many expansions and extensions in the dairy. He started producing dry milk, ghee and other products as well. Each and every thing of the business was running perfectly well in all aspects as long as transiting Saturn did not lend its aspect over the natal Mars. Saturn entered in Aries on 17.4.1998 and stayed there till 7.6.2000. Aries is the sign of debilitation of Saturn. Innumerable problems started creeping up in his industry. Incredible losses and obstacles were there in place of heavy profits and success. These sufferings have no end as yet.

Thus, as per our humble observations, **whenever transiting Saturn lends its aspect over the natal Mars, it becomes a landmark or the turning phase of one's life. Also, transit of Saturn over radical location of Mars, brings prominent change in one's life and gives a sharp turn, in one or the other way. This change may be positive or negative, depending upon the ascendant, sign occupied by the natal Mars, and the sign in which Saturn transits.** This is our view based on the study of these two and many other horoscopes. Our research on this point can be said to be in a nascent stage. Learned readers may verify these findings in their own studies as well. We are sure that similar results will be obtained.

For the judgement of the time of important events of one's life, Saturn's transit is very useful. Certain findings have prompted us to share our humble views with our learned readers. A few rules of Saturn's specific transits have been explained, whose reliability may carefully be examined by the readers and scholars alike.

We know very little, how the transit of Saturn helps in timing events about it. Certain researches and repeated observations, if made keenly, will be of immense benefit. We have been keen scholars of astrology for almost four decades. Saadhe Sati of Saturn is supposed to curtail auspicious results of Dasha Bhukti and enhances the adversities, problems, tensions, distress, disappointment along with theft, deceit, demotions, unwelcome transfers, losses, changes etc.

Now we intend to illustrate, how prominent events can be predicted with the help of the transit of Saturn through various positions. This is a thorough research area, which we are exploring since 1984 and have got enormous success in our observations and timing events by the judgement of birth charts. In fact, Saturn is the slowest moving planet, so the transit of Saturn, if studied properly, will help in pointing out the time of the occurrence of the prominent events of life. We will try to specify and explain a few of the prominent transits of Saturn, which we have examined and found highly accurate precise and useful. This needs thorough study, experiment and experience. These transits should be judged along with the result of dasha bhukti to pin point the time of the concerning events like promotions, progress, rewards, achievements, appreciations, recognition or other wise problems, downfalls, tensions, losses, thefts and deceits etc.

Following observations and findings are the outcome of our experience and study made during the last so many years.

RULE-2

Whenever, Saturn transits over the Ascendant, it brings prominent change in life. This is partially so, when Saturn aspects the Ascendant, during its transit. This change may be beneficial or problematic

and it depends on various factors, which require deep experience and art of judgement.

In the example Horoscope No. 3 (RT)

Saturn's transits over the Ascendant : Saturn transited in Scorpio i.e. over the Ascendant of the native from 30.12.1984 to 02.01.1988. The native went to U.S.A. on 20.08.1986 for higher education in Electrical Engineering. Saturn transited in the 7th house from the Ascendant from 07.06.2000 to 23.07.2002. The native was promoted as M.D. of a famous bank.

Transiting Saturn aspects the ascendant and the natal Moon

RULE-3

Transiting Saturn aspects the ascendant and the Moon simultaneously that brings promotion, elevation, appreciation, expansion of responsibilities and extensions of power. This will be so even when Saturn will transit over the Moon and will aspect the ascendant.

Ex.-1: Here Saturn's movement in Taurus is important because Saturn lends its aspects over the natal Moon and the ascendant. In fact, Saturn's transit in Taurus was there from 07.06.2000 to 23.07.2002, when the native was promoted Managing Director of CREDIT SUISSE BANK during December, 2001. He enjoyed all kinds of prosperity and pleasure. This can be seen in the example horoscope No. 3 of Rajiv Tewari.

Ex.-2: When Saturn transited in Aquarius over the natal Moon from 30.03.1993 to 07.03.1996. Saturn's transit in Aquarius was auspicious for the native. He was appointed in a very prestigious organization and worked there from June 1994 to September, 1995. During the same transit of Saturn in Aquarius, the native was appointed in further better organization in September, 1995, named CREDIT SUISSE.

It will not be out of place to mention that Saturn's transit, whenever affects the ascendant and the Moon both that becomes most prominent event and auspicious period of two and half years for the native.

Illustration : 8.3   *Horoscope No.: 15*

Date of birth : 02.05.1967   Time of birth : 20:59:00 hrs
Place of birth : Lucknow   Lat 26:50 N Long 80:54 E
Ayanamsa   : 23:23:51   Sidereal Time : 11:32:02

Pln	Degree	Rasi	Nakshatra	Pad
Asc	19:06:16	Sco	Jyestha	1
Sun	18:08:08	Ari	Bharani	2
Mon	1:52:42	Aqu	Dhanistha	3
Mar (R)	25:17:41	Vir	Chitra	1
Mer (C)	7:55:32	Ari	Aswini	3
Jup	3:41:34	Can	Pushya	1
Ven	27:54:11	Tau	Mrigshira	2
Sat	13:50:12	Pis	U Bhadrapad	4
Rah (C)	13:26:18	Ari	Bharani	1
Ket	13:26:18	Lib	Swati	3

Lagna Chart   **Navamsa Chart**

Lagna Chart	Navamsa Chart
Ket 7, 9, 10, 6 Mar, 8, Mon 11, 5, 2, Ven, Sat 12, 1, 4 Jup, 3, Rah, Sun Mer	Sat 8, 10, Ket 11, 7 Mon, 9, 12, 6 Ven, Sun, 3 Mer, 1, Rah, 5 Jup Mar, 2, 4

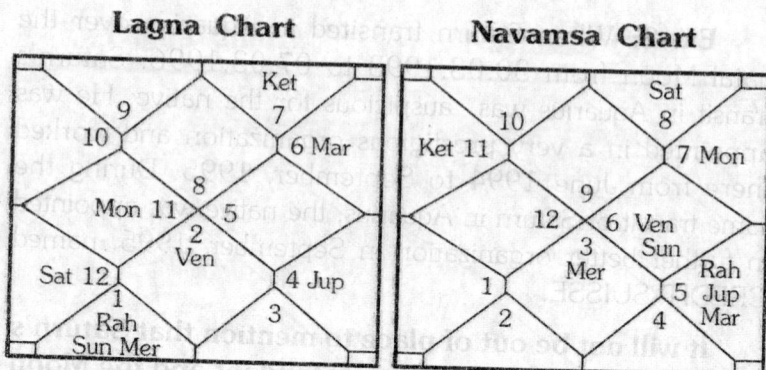

Balance of Vimshottari Dasa of **Mars 2Y 6M 5D**

It also makes clear that if Sadhe Sati of Saturn, corresponds with the ascendant and the Moon both, the positive events and progress will be there instead of disappointments, humiliations, distress, sorrows, losses, demotions etc. It may be noted that two and half years of Saturn's transit in a particular sign, may effect the ascendant and Moon both and that period of Saturn's transit will be quite promising and rewarding.

In the horoscope of Mr. Rajiv Tewari, transit of Saturn's in Aquarius, was extremely important and promising for his professional promotions and positive changes.

RULE-4

When transiting Saturn has an influence over the 10th lord from the ascendant or the Moon, either by association or aspect this two and a half years of Saturn's transit is quite promising and rewarding for the native in connection with occupation, securing job, starting business or settlement.

Ex.-1: The 10th lord Sun is exalted in the 6th house.

Saturn's transited in Aries from 17.04.1998 to 07.06.2000. The native's marriage with Anuragini took place on 23.06.1994. The native was settled in the career during the same period before his marriage.

Saturn's transit in Taurus from 07.06.2000 to 23.07.2002 was extremely eventful for the native. This transit of Saturn is not only the 10th from the 10th house but that is important because transited over the 7th house and its lord Venus. The native decided to marry a beautiful girl Maneesha and to divorce his wife Anuragini. Maneesha and Rajiv were together almost throughout this period.

During the same transit of Saturn in Taurus, the native was promoted as Managing Director because the Saturn's transit in Taurus had an influence by its benefic aspects over the ascendant and Moon simultaneously.

Ex.-2: (Amitabh Bachchan)

Most popular and famous Film actor Amitabh Bachchan was born in Aquarius ascendant and Libra Moon sign. The lord of the 10th house Mars is posited in Virgo. Saturn was transiting in Pisces from 26.04.1966 to 02.07.1968. Amitabh Bachchan got first break in the film industry during the same period. He got a break in *Saat Hindustani*, which was the first film of Amitabh Bachchan and was released in 1969.

In the horoscope of Amitabh Bachchan, the lord of the 8th house is Moon itself and the Moon is posited in Libra. Saturn was transiting in Aries from 02.07.1968 to 29.04.1971. This was one of the most prominent periods of the life of Amitabh Bachchan, when he got a chance to work in the Box Office hit film *Janzeer* and *Abhimaan* etc.

Illustration : 8.4

Date of birth : 11.10.1942
Place of birth : Allahabad
Ayanamsa : 23:03:18

Horoscope No.: 16

Time of birth : 17:00:00 hrs
Lat 25:27 N Long 81:50 E
Sidereal Time : 17:14:52

Pln	Degree	Rasi	Nakshatra	Pad
Asc	21:32:44	Aqu	P Bhadrapad	1
Sun	24:25:19	Vir	Chitra	1
Mon	10:54:00	Lib	Swati	2
Mar (D)	22:37:51	Vir	Hasta	4
Mer (R/D)	23:36:31	Vir	Chitra	1
Jup	0:32:30	Can	Punarvasu	4
Ven (C)	15:14:27	Vir	Hasta	2
Sat (R)	19:13:48	Tau	Rohini	3
Rah (R)	10:21:42	Leo	Magha	4
Ket (R)	10:21:42	Aqu	Satabhisha	2

Lagna Chart

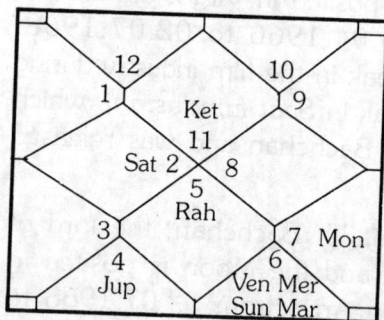

Navamsa Chart

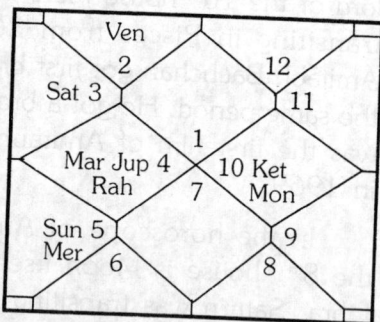

Balance of Vimshottari Dasa of **Rah 12Y 3M 12D**

Saturn's transit in Virgo over the 10th lord Mars made Amitabh Bachchan the Super Star. Taking over the title by Rajesh Khanna. The prominence of his career was continued by super-duper hit films, when Saturn transited in Libra over the natal Moon.

Amitabh Bachchan suffered his very serious injury at the set of film *Coolie* on 26th July, 1982, when Saturn was transiting in Virgo over the 10th lord Mars, 7th lord Sun, 8th lord Mercury and yogakaraka Venus, through 8th house from the ascendant. This may be pointed out that Saturn's transit over natal Mars corresponding with any of the Trik house may cause serious injury, accident or health problem as well.

It has been invariably observed that the transiting Saturn over the lord of 10th house either from the ascendant or from the Moon is a period of progress, promotion, prominence or settlement in job or business. Same results will be experienced, if transiting Saturn lends its aspects over the lord of the 10th house either from the ascendant or from the Moon.

RULE-5

If the 10th lord is involved in an exchange of house with a particular planet Saturn usually gives more remarkable results in respect of success or rise in career or undertaking, when it during its transit, aspects or is united with that particular planet, with whom the 10th lord has exchanged his position. Such a nativity offers scope for application of the previous rule also.

The rule operates fairly well even when the 10th lord owning two houses simultaneously is involved in the exchange and not the 10th house directly.

Ex.-1: A famous capitalist and business tycoon was born in Libra ascendant. The 10th lord Moon is posited in

Aquarius and 5th lord Saturn occupies the 10th house. Thus there is an exchange of 5th and 10th lord the Saturn and the Moon identical to Cancer and Aquarius. The birth chart may be seen at the end, where implementation of the rules has been explained.

Saturn was transiting in Libra from 06.08.1982 to 30.12.1984 over the natal ascendant of the native. Transiting Saturn was aspecting natal Saturn. This was the most prominent period so far as professional progress is concerned. The native started a small organization, which progressed very speedily. The organization was started from Rs. 2000/- only in the year 1982, which has now reached millions of crores. This has become an organization of international prominence, popularity and prosperity.

Saturn's transits in Capricorn from 05.01.1991 to 30.03.1993 was also important as transiting Saturn was aspecting natal Saturn. The native entered into aviation line. However, Jupiter's transits in Aquarius over the natal Moon from 30.03.1993 to 07.03.1996 was extremely promising and rewarding for the native, when so many schemes of Housing, Aeronautics, Products and a dream city came in existence.

RULE-6

The transit of Saturn, over the 10th house from the 10th lord is remarkable for professional advancement, progress and prosperity. However, if the 10th sign is reckoned from the 10th house owned by Saturn or i.e. the exaltation sign of Saturn, the professional prosperity will be further higher and rewarding. It means, if the 10th house from the 10th lord is Libra, Capricorn or Aquarius, professional prosperity and progress will certainly be highlighted during the transit of Saturn in either of these signs.

Ex.-1:

This beautiful and captivating woman was born in Aquarius ascendant. The lord of the 10th house Mars is posited in Aries. The 10th sign from Mars is Capricorn, where Sun is posited. Saturn transited from 05.01.1991 to 30.03.1993 in Capricorn, which was highly rewarding period for her in almost all the aspects of life.

Illustration : 8.5 　　　　*Horoscope No.: 17*

Date of birth : 26.01.1957　Time of birth : 09:09:00 hrs
Place of birth : Unnao　　　Lat 26:32 N Long 80:30 E
Ayanamsa : 23:15:42　　　Sidereal Time : 17:21:40

Pln	Degree	Rasi	Nakshatra	Pad
Asc	23:28:13	Aqu	P Bhadrapad	2
Sun	12:40:15	Cap	Sravna	1
Mon	20:33:51	Sco	Jyestha	2
Mar	5:15:19	Ari	Aswini	2
Mer	19:08:07	Sag	Purvasadha	2
Jup (R)	8:23:08	Vir	U Phalguni	4
Ven	23:21:58	Sag	Purvasadha	4
Sat	18:28:53	Sco	Jyestha	1
Rah (R)	3:12:51	Sco	Vishakha	4
Ket (R)	3:12:51	Tau	Krittika	2

Lagna Chart

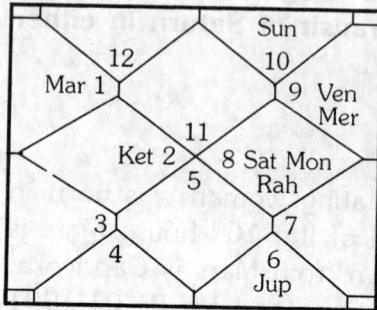

Navamsa Chart

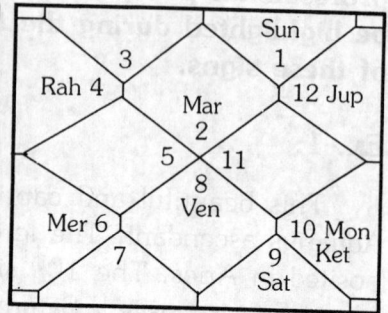

Balance of Vimshottari Dasa of **Mer   12Y 0M 11D**

Ex.-2:

This is the horoscope of one of the most competent, prosperous and famous business tycoons of the country. His name is the symbol of success in business world. He started his career from a very low position and reached enormous heights.

Illustration : 8.6   *Horoscope No.: 18*

Date of birth : 15.10.1954   Time of birth : 07:16:00 hrs
Place of birth : Kanpur   Lat 26:27 N Long 80:19 E
Ayanamsa   : 23:13:47   Sidereal Time : 8:39:30

Pln	Degree	Rasi	Nakshatra	Pad
Asc	12:10:30	Lib	Swati	2
Sun	27:56:35	Vir	Chitra	2
Mon	8:22:26	Tau	Krittika	4
Mar	2:41:02	Cap	Uttarasadha	2
Mer	20:53:45	Lib	Vishakha	1
Jup	4:59:24	Can	Pushya	1

Ven	4:46:48	Sco	Anuradha	1
Sat	16:21:41	Lib	Swati	3
Rah (R)	15:28:33	Sag	Purvasadha	1
Ket (R)	15:28:33	Gem	Ardra	3

Lagna Chart

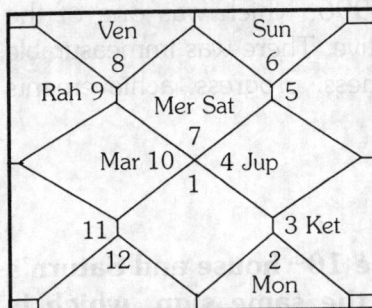

Navamsa Chart

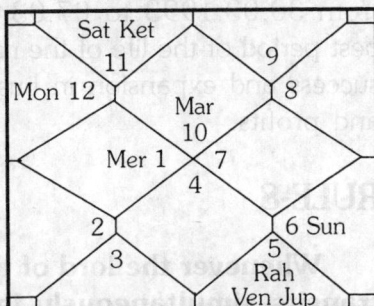

Balance of Vimshottari Dasa of **Sun   0Y 8M 23D**

He was born in Libra ascendant. The 10th lord Moon occupies Taurus. The 10th from Taurus is Aquarius. Saturn transited in Aquarius from 30.03.1993 to 07.03.1996. The expansion of the business of native was quite miracles and astonishing during the transit of Saturn in Aquarius. This transit took place around his 40 years of age. He established dozens of very large size factories of plastic packaging within the same period. However, Saturn transit over the 10th lord Moon in Taurus from 07.06.2000 to 23.07.2002 was also quite rewarding and progressing so far as the expansion of packaging industry is concerned. He entered in various other ventures with immeasurable success.

RULE-7

If the 10th lord joins Capricorn or Aquarius, Saturn can exchange his position with the 10th lord,

during his transit, when he enters and moves through the house owned by the 10th lord. During this transit of Saturn, career will take upward turn. New activities and endeavours will bring sweet results.

Ex.-1 : In the following horoscope the 10th lord Saturn occupies Aquarius. Transits of Saturn in Aquarius was there from 30.03.1993 to 07.03.1996, which was one of the best period of the life of the native. There was immeasurable success and expansion in business, progress, achievements and profits.

RULE-8

Whenever the lord of the 10th house and Saturn's transits simultaneously in the same sign, which is identical to the own or exaltation sign of Saturn (i.e. Libra, Capricorn or Aquarius) or that of the 10th lord the outcome is a sudden change or promotion by superseding others, upward progressing career and rewarding. The period will be extremely auspicious prosperous rewarding. The results will almost be the same, whenever Saturn transits in Libra, Capricorn or Aquarius and aspects the 10th lord.

Ex.-1:

In this horoscope, the transit of Saturn in Libra will be quite auspicious in various ways, when the 10th lord Sun will transit either in Libra or in Aries sudden rise and progress will come in evidence. The transit of Saturn in Libra from 15.11.2011 to 02.11.2014. Saturn's transit in Aries will be there from 15 April to 15 May and 15 October to 15 November of 2012, 2013 and 2014. These will be most rewarding and progressing months for the native, when sudden elevation and promotions are bound to come.

RULE-9

Rahu and Ketu, when placed in quadrant, give a rise to a Rajyoga, if associated with triangle lords. Rajyoga will again be formed, if Rahu or Ketu occupies the triangle, and associated with an triangle lord. The results of Rajyoga will appear when transiting Saturn will cross the natal position of Rahu and its association or Ketu with the association or otherwise, when Saturn will lend its aspect over this combination. If the quadrant lord is the Sun, Moon or Mars and that is associated with Rahu or Ketu in a triangle, the transit of Saturn over that, this combination will bring miseries, problems, tensions, frustration, disgrace, humiliation, disappointments and failures, but soon thereafter will promote the effect of the Rajyoga.

Suppose, the 10th lord Sun occupies the 9th house in Cancer, adverse results in the beginning of transiting Saturn in Cancer will be there, but that will not last long, because Rahu's association with the 10th lord has also formed the Rajyoga. Good effects will appear during the later half of the transiting of Saturn in Cancer.

In the case of Scorpio ascendant with Rahu and Sun in the 9th house, the native had gone under serious problems and miseries during the Saturn's transit in Cancer from 16.07.1975 to 28.08.1977. The miseries, humiliation, conflicts, oppositions, revelry and false charges were there from 16.07.1975 to May, 1976. Thereafter, the transfer of the native took place to the desired place, where he enjoyed the best outcome of this Rajyoga.

It should, however, be clearly kept in mind before attempting a hasty implication of this rule that transiting Saturn's effect with Rahu or Ketu, is generally seen to generate certain malefic results as well, such as death of relations or of self, set-back in undertaking or even imprisonment. A blemished Rahu, though he creates a Rajyoga, can produce all these and even more. Therefore, this rule must be applied very clearly and carefully. Death or imprisonment etc. should not be predicted before the examination of complete horoscope thoroughly. Good and bad results of this combination have been observed from time to time.

RULE-10

शनिवत् राहुवे, कुजावत् केतवे *i.e.* Rahu acts like Saturn and Ketu acts like Mars. If Saturn owns quadrant of triangle and it is united with Rahu or Ketu, prominent results of Saturn will appear, when transiting Saturn will aspect the natal Saturn and Rahu. Similarly, Mars and Ketu are conjoined, the adverse results will appear, when Ketu will transit over with its position. Such a position giving arise to adversities will appear when Ketu will transit over the natal Rahu or Rahu will transit over the natal Ketu.

When Saturn transits in Libra, Capricorn or Aquarius and passes over the natal position of Rahu, the adverse results as mentioned above will appear. Similarly, when Mars transits in Aries, Scorpio or Capricorn over the natal position of Ketu, the fructification of aforesaid results will be there. This is remarkable and noteworthy rule of the transit of Saturn and Mars as well over the natal position of Rahu and Ketu or that of the aspect of transiting Saturn and Mars over Rahu and Ketu.

RULE-11

If the 10th lord is associated with Rahu or Ketu and that is not posited in a quadrant or triangle, the downfall, reversion or suspension may take place during the adverse transits of Rahu and Ketu provided the 10th lord is unexpected or uninfluenced by the Saturn's transits. It will not be out of place to mention that such adverse results will be highly pronounced, when the 10th lord occupies any of the Trik houses and that too with natal Rahu and without Saturn's benefic effects during its transit over the 10th lord. Without examination of complete horoscope, negative results should not be predicted.

RULE-12

If there occurs a Rajayoga, generated by Rahu or Ketu, lodged in a Kendra and united with or aspected by lord of a Kone or vice versa, and if such a yoga is further indicative of a set-back in career or disposition on account of Rahu's or/and Ketu's simultaneous connection with lord of an evil house, then the negative results fructify, when Saturn becomes delinked with Rahu or/and Ketu or when the natal positions of Rahu and Ketu fall in the 6th, 8th or 12th from moving Rahu and Ketu.

Similar results also accrue during Rahu's transit over his own or Ketu's natal position, provided such a yoga as stated above is aspected by or associated with Saturn in the horoscope, as explained earlier, particularly when Mars and Saturn, owing to evil houses, do not act as producers of Rajayoga.

Whenever, Saturn's transits over his natal location that period generally exhibits auspicious or inauspicious results depending upon the exact location of Saturn in a particular house or sign. Whenever, Saturn passes over the ascendant that period of seven and half years is a turning point in ones career. If Saturn is posited in the ascendant as a benefic and that is aspected by transiting Saturn or Saturn's transits over the same period is most benefic with regard to the houses it owns.

Ex.-1

The native is working in Health and Family Welfare Department and is looking after Medico Legal cases. The native is extremely intelligent. His childhood was full of frustration and problems. His father behaved inimically with him due to the opposition of Saturn and the Sun in this horoscope identical with the ascendant and 7th house.

Implementation of the aforesaid rules in this horoscope will help the readers to understand how the transit of Saturn decides the time of events.

Illustration : 8.7   *Horoscope No.: 19*

Date of birth : 02.02.1976   Time of birth : 17:32:00 hrs
Place of birth : Batala   Lat 31:48 N Long 75:17 E
Ayanamsa   : 23:31:37   Sidereal Time : 1:50:24

Pln	Degree	Rasi	Nakshatra	Pad
Asc	13:38:07	Can	Pushya	4
Sun	19:14:50	Cap	Sravna	3
Mon	14:46:02	Aqu	Satabhisha	3
Mar	22:09:36	Tau	Rohini	4
Mer (R)	29:56:38	Sag	Uttarasadha	1
Jup	25:50:59	Pis	Revati	3
Ven	15:20:30	Sag	Purvasadha	1
Sat (R)	4:55:56	Can	Pushya	1
Rah (R)	24:00:02	Lib	Vishakha	2
Ket (R)	24:00:02	Ari	Bharani	4

Lagna Chart

```
          5          3
   6             2 Mar
        Sat
         4
      Rah 7  X  1 Ket
        10
        Sun
     8              12 Jup
      9         11
   Mer Ven     Mon
```

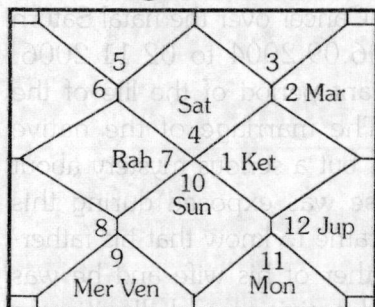

Navamsa Chart

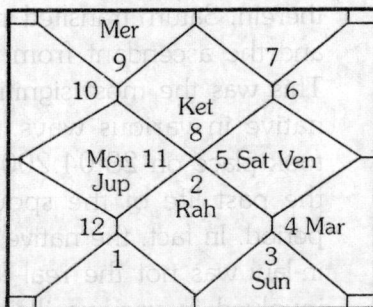

```
            Mer
            9         7
       10          6
             Ket
              8
       Mon 11 X 5 Sat Ven
       Jup     2
               Rah
        12          4 Mar
         1          3
                    Sun
```

Balance of Vimshottari Dasa of **Rah   7Y 0M 23D**

1. The ascendant lord Moon occupies the 8th house corresponding with sign Aquarius, which is the 10th from the 10th lord Mars. Saturn transited in Aquarius over the natal Moon from 30.03.1993 to 07.03.1996. This period brought remarkable event in the life of the native. He was appointed in Health and Family Welfare Department on 13.07.1995 and his father who was inimical to him, expired on September, 1993 and that was a great relief to him.

2. Yogakaraka Mars is posited in Taurus in the 11th house. Saturn's transited in Taurus from 07.06.2000 to 23.07.2002. This was most remarkable period for the native and brought a positive U-Turn in the life of the native. In fact, Mars is the 10th lord from the ascendant and Moon as well. Saturn's transit over Mars was quite rewarding preferably. He lived like a King and enjoyed the comfort of a number of cars, money, luxury, power, position, popularity etc. He was honoured everywhere, due to his outstanding intelligence and capability of solving the intricate and complicated problems of others. In fact, he was properly settled in the office. This period was quite rewarding for the native.

3.   The native was born in Cancer ascendant with Saturn therein. Saturn transited in Cancer over the natal Saturn and the ascendant from 06.09.2004 to 02.11.2006. This was the most significant period of the life of the native in various ways. The marriage of the native took place on 23.04.2004 but a serious mystery about the past life of the spouse was exposed during this period. In fact, the native came to know that his father-in-law was not the real father of his wife and he was involved in various illegal activities and illegitimate relationships. There were a lot of problems in the life of the native with regard to his marriage. The marriage was at the verge of divorce. The native managed to send his father-in-law to the jail due to his wrong activities and unlawful involvements. However, he was blessed with a very fortunate daughter on 15.07.2006. The transit of Saturn in Cancer was a landmark in his life.

4.   There is mutual exchange between Moon and Saturn in this horoscope. The Lagna lord Moon falls in Aquarius and 8th lord Saturn joins Cancer in the ascendant. The transit of Saturn in Leo from 02.11.2006 to 10.09.2009 was extra-ordinary and auspicious for the native. Here Saturn aspected the 10th lord Mars and ascendant lord Moon simultaneously. The native came in our contact during this period and became highly religious. All problems and tensions of his life gradually disappeared. He got prominence and professional prosperity in addition to money. He built his own house and left the house of his aunt, who was always asking him to divorce his wife. The native was leading extremely unhappy and miserable married life due to the intervention of his aunt and father-in-law. He was able to realize his mistake and started living happily

with his wife and also started loving her from the core of his heart. In fact, Jupiter's transit in Leo was a boon for the native, which resulted into this radical change. It may be seen that ascendant lord Moon, the 10th lord Mars and transiting Saturn are in mutual Kendras. Transiting Saturn was aspecting Mars and Moon, where as natal Mars and Moon were aspecting transiting Saturn simultaneously.

5. Transit of Saturn in Scorpio from 02.11.2014 to 26.01.2017 will aspect the 10th lord Mars. This will bring huge professional success to the native. His progress and prosperity will be rewarding.

Ex.-2 :

1. This woman was born in Taurus ascendant. The 10th lord Saturn joins the 11th house in Pisces. Saturn transited in Pisces from 07.03.1996 to 17.04.1998. She was employed in a prestigious organization during this transit of Saturn recently. The important point to note that Saturn was transiting in the 8th house from natal Moon, which gives plenty of miseries, problems, tensions and failures of undertaking. Here, it is just reverse due to transit of Saturn in Pisces, over the 10th lord natal Saturn, which resulted into a prestigious occupation. The Moon is posited in Leo and Venus is the lord of 10th house from Moon, which occupies the ascendant Taurus itself. Saturn transited in Taurus from 07.06.2000 to 23.07.2002. She got a remarkable promotion during this period but it was an extremely adverse period for her married life. She was almost separated. It was so because Mars was conjoined with Venus and Rahu in Taurus ascendant. The Saturn's transit over the Taurus ascendant and natal Mars (Markesh) and 7th lord brought a U-turn in her life as

mentioned by us in this Chapter. It may be noted that transit of Saturn over the natal Mars may bring prominent change in the life of the native depending upon the natal position, lordship etc. of Mars.

2. The transit of Saturn over the natal Sun is also quite important as the Sun and Saturn are extremely inimical.

3. In this case, transit of Saturn in Gemini over the natal Sun from 23.07.2002 to 06.09.2004 resulted into disappointment, failure of undertakings and unwelcome changes of place.

Illustration : 8.8   *Horoscope No.: 20*

Date of birth : 24.06.1966   Time of birth : 03:25:00 hrs
Place of birth : Roorkee   Lat 29:52 N Long 77:53 E
Ayanamsa   : 23:23:06   Sidereal Time : 21:13:00

Pln	Degree	Rasi	Nakshatra	Pad
Asc	9:28:24	Tau	Krittika	4
Sun	8:34:37	Gem	Ardra	1
Mon	16:41:51	Leo	P Phalguni	2
Mar (C)	24:50:49	Tau	Mrigshira	1
Mer	3:04:20	Can	Punarvasu	4
Jup (C)	17:04:21	Gem	Ardra	4
Ven	3:35:08	Tau	Krittika	3
Sat	6:02:33	Pis	U Bhadrapad	1
Rah (R)	1:17:37	Tau	Krittika	2
Ket (R)	1:17:37	Sco	Vishakha	4

Lagna Chart

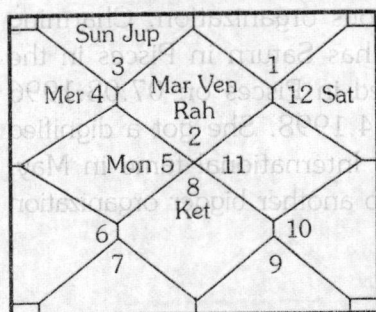

Navamsa Chart

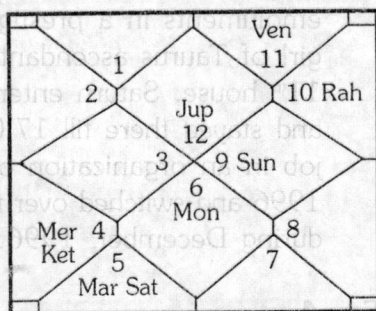

Balance of Vimshottari Dasa of **Ven 14Y 11M 13D**

Ex.-3

1. In a strong nativity of Libra ascendant, Saturn is posited in the ascendant itself with 9th lord Mercury. He was an struggling businessman and was a Sale Agent.

2. Saturn's transit over the ascendant Libra from 06.08.1982 to 30.12.1984, when the native started an independent business of Plastic manufacturing and packaging. Within two and half years of the transit of Saturn in Libra, the native was able to span his business to whole of India and in so many other country as well. This shows that the transit of Saturn over the ascendant with Yogakaraka Saturn brings prominent success and enormous income. Saturn's transit over the ascendant only is a turning point in one's life.

3. A native of Scorpio ascendant enjoyed promotion, prosperity and prays and power, when Saturn transited over the ascendant i.e. in Scorpio from 30.12.1984 to 02.01.1988.

4. If Saturn is well placed in a birth-chart and the transiting Saturn passes over the natal Saturn, one may get a

decent service or he/she may be appointed at good emoluments in a prestigious organization. Charming girl of Taurus ascendant has Saturn in Pisces in the 11th house. Saturn entered in Pisces on 07.03.1996 and stayed there till 17.04.1998. She got a dignified job in an organization of International fame in May, 1996 and switched over to another bigger organization during December, 1996.

Ex.-4 :

The native was born in Libra ascendant. The lord of the 10th house Moon occupies the 5th house corresponding sign Aquarius and 5th lord Saturn falls in the 10th house. Thus, there is mutual exchange between 5th and 10th lords Saturn and Moon.

Illustration : 8.9   *Horoscope No.: 21*

Date of birth, Time and Place withhold.

Pln	Degree	Rasi	Nakshatra	Pad
Asc	14:02:12	Lib	Swati	3
Sun	25:33:20	Tau	Mrigshira	1
Mon	7:52:15	Aqu	Satabhisha	1
Mar	21:54:21	Ari	Bharani	3
Mer	18:49:52	Gem	Ardra	4
Jup (R)	26:24:18	Lib	Vishakha	2
Ven	2:38:47	Tau	Krittika	2
Sat	12:35:31	Can	Pushya	3
Rah (R)	9:17:41	Tau	Krittika	4
Ket (R)	9:17:41	Sco	Anuradha	2

Lagna Chart

Ket 8		6
9	Jup 7	5
	10 1 Mar	4 Sat
Mon 11	12	3 Mer
	2 Rah Ven Sun	

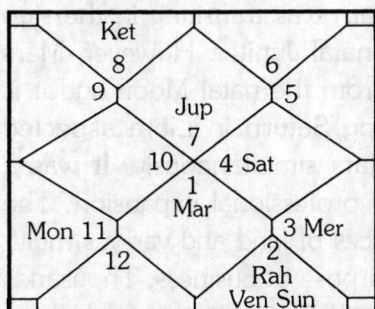

Navamsa Chart

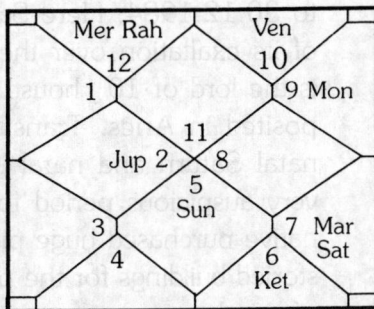

Mer Rah 12		Ven 10
1	11	9 Mon
	Jup 2	8 5 Sun
3		7 Mar Sat
4	6 Ket	

Balance of Vimshottari Dasa of **Rahu 16Y 4M 14D**

1. As per the above Rules, transiting Saturn passed over the natal Saturn in Cancer from 16.07.1975 to 28.08.1977. The native was settled properly in his career. The native was blessed with children. He started working and earned unexpected success and prosperity within this period of about twenty five months.

2. Saturn entered in Leo on 28.08.1977 and stayed there till 19.07.1980. The transit of Saturn in Leo was exceptionally good for the native, when it aspected the 10th lord Moon and ascendant lord Venus. Transiting Saturn also had an aspect over the ascendant and natal Jupiter, during all these three years. Most important is the fact that Saturn's transit in Leo had an aspect over the natal Moon, which is posited in the sign of Saturn Aquarius. This period was extremely remarkable and rewarding for the huge progress, prosperity, popularity and power for the native. He purchased the whole organization, in which he was working earlier. His untiring hard work raised the native to the dizzy height within a short span. The organization of the native spread all over the world.

3.   Saturn's transit in Libra was there from 06.08.1982 to 30.12.1984. Here Saturn was transiting in the sign of its exaltation over the natal Jupiter. However, Mars is the lord of 10th house from the natal Moon and it is posited in Aries. Transiting Saturn in Libra aspected natal Saturn and natal Mars simultaneously. It was a very auspicious period for professional expansion. The native purchased huge pieces of land and various multi-storied buildings for the purpose of business. Thousands of employees were engaged. The native started many new ventures. However, Mars and Saturn are inimical. Similarly, Moon and Saturn are also inimical. There is mutual exchange between Moon and Saturn as well. Mars is strong Markesh for Libra ascendant. Therefore, the transiting Saturn in Libra resulted into adversity in health of the native. He suffered from some kind of ailment for the first time in life, due to the aspect of transiting Saturn on the Mars and Moon as well.

4.   Rahu, Venus and Sun occupy the 8th house. Here Venus is the ascendant lord. Saturn's transit in Scorpio from 30.12.1984 to 02.01.1988 and aspected Rahu, Sun and Venus. This was an adverse period for the health of the native. He suffered a serious sat-back in profession as well. which is beyond description.

5.   Saturn's transit in Cancer was there from 06.09.2004 to 02.11.2006. Here Saturn transited over the natal Saturn and aspected natal Mars, which was auspicious professionally but it was extremely inauspicious for the health of the native. It was so because there is a mutual aspect between the natal Mars and Saturn in this horoscope and the transiting Saturn in Cancer had an influence over the natal Saturn and Mars simultaneously. Saturn is Yogakaraka and Mars is a

killer for Libra ascendant. Therefore, transit of Saturn through Cancer had a negative impact over the health of the native. Unfortunately, the native was passing through the sub-period of the Sun in the major period of Mercury from 17.01.2005 to 24.11.2005. The Sun was heavily afflicted in the 8th house by the association of inimical Rahu and Venus. Moreover, the Sun falls in Mrigshira constellation, ruled by Mars and that is also 12th from the Mahadasha lord Mercury. Mercury is posited in Rahu's constellation Aridra. The Sun is strongest planet in this birth chart and its affliction in the 8th house is certainly adverse. However, Saturn's transit in Cancer was quite unhappy and unhealthy situation for the native.

6. It will not be out of place to mention that Saturn will again be transiting in Libra from 15.11.2011 to 02.11.2014. This transit of Saturn will be extremely auspicious for the expansion and the professional success. Many new ventures and schemes will bring fruits. Most of the plans will be executed with success. Present organization, which was started by the native in the year 1978, when Saturn was transiting in Leo will take the shape of a public sector/private sector bank.

7. We are doubtful that the transit of Saturn through Libra may not be good for the health of the native as the transiting Saturn will aspect the natal Mars and natal Saturn. Saturn's transit in Libra will be there from 15.11.2011 to 02.11.2014. It will resume retrograde motion from 06.02.2012 to 16.05.2012 and again from 18.02.2013 to 18.07.2013; from 03.03.2014 to 21.07.2014. Retrograde transit of Saturn in Libra will exhibit the results of debilitation of

Saturn. This will be adverse so far, as the aspect of the health of native is concerned.

Here, we have discussed the result of the transit of Saturn in Libra. However, these results should be blended properly with Dasha-bhukti results.

(i) The native will be passing through the sub-period of Jupiter in the major period of Mercury from 09.11.2010 to 14.02.2013 and sub-period of Saturn in the major period of Mercury from 14.02.2013 to 26.10.2015. Both the sub-periods of Jupiter and Saturn in the major period of Mercury will be largely covered by the transit of Saturn in Libra. Proper study of the Dasha-bhukti results along with the results of the transit of Saturn in Libra will give very precise and accurate results.

(ii) For more accuracy and preciseness, the transit of Saturn in all the three constellation – Chitra, Swati and Vishakha should be examined.

8. This is the way in which the Saturn's transits in various signs may be examined for timing of events.

The transit of Saturn –

(i) over the 10th lord from the ascendant or natal Moon.

(ii) over the 10th house from the 10th lord from the ascendant and the Moon.

(iii) over the natal Saturn over the ascendant is quite remarkable and rewarding for the professional progress and prosperity.

9. The transit of Saturn over the inimical sign Leo and Cancer is generally adverse. That may bring professional prosperity but will bring tension, frustration, failure of undertakings, unhappiness etc. because these are the most inimical signs with regard to the transit of Saturn.

10. Whenever, Saturn will transit over the natal Moon for Libra or Taurus ascendant for which Mars is a killer planet, certain adversities of health will take place.

11. Saturn's transits over the natal Mars bring a prominent change in one's life. Such changes also appear, when Saturn aspects the natal Mars.

Ex.-5 :

This horoscope belongs to the General Manager of a prestigious organization, who has done M.B.A. after doing Mechanical Engineering in the year 1994.

Illustration : 8.10   *Horoscope No.: 22*

Date of birth : 17.11.1972   Time of birth : 00:35:00 hrs
Place of birth : Bijnor   Lat 29:22 N Long 78:09 E
Ayanamsa   : 23:28:55   Sidereal Time : 4:01:22

Pln	Degree	Rasi	Nakshatra	Pad
Asc	10:39:53	Leo	Magha	4
Sun	1:03:09	Sco	Vishakha	4
Mon	3:10:44	Pis	P Bhadrapad	4
Mar	7:05:26	Lib	Swati	1
Mer (R)	18:54:10	Sco	Jyestha	1
Jup	14:25:13	Sag	Purvasadha	1

Ven	26:59:43	Vir	Chitra	2
Sat (R)	25:22:12	Tau	Mrigshira	1
Rah (R)	24:56:26	Sag	Purvasadha	4
Ket (R)	24:56:26	Gem	Punarvasu	2

Lagna Chart

```
            Ven
             6              4
  Mar 7                         3 Ket
                    5
     Sun Mer 8         2 Sat
                 11
  Jup    9                   1
  Rah    10             12
                        Mon
```

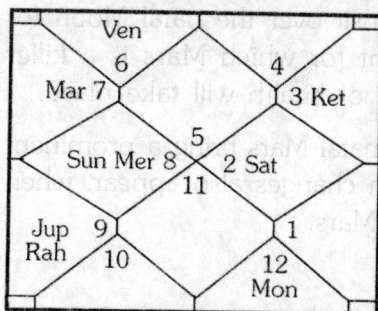

Navamsa Chart

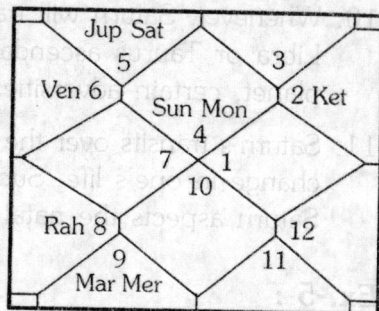

```
         Jup Sat
            5              3
  Ven 6                       2 Ket
              Sun Mon
                  4
           7     1
                10
  Rah 8                      12
       9                11
    Mar Mer
```

Balance of Vimshottari Dasa of **Jup 6Y 7M 12D**

1. The native was born in Leo ascendant. The 10th lord Venus is posited in Virgo in the 2nd house. Saturn was transiting in Pisces from 07.03.1996 to 17.04.1998 and then Saturn was directly aspecting the 10th lord Venus, the 10th house and natal Saturn, placed in the 10th house. Thus, the transit of Saturn in Pisces was quite eventful for the native. He got the first job in August, 1997 in a Telecommunication Organization of international fame. We want to draw attention of the readers that Saturn was transiting over the natal Moon in Pisces, which is identical to the 8th house from the ascendant. Thus, the Sadhe Sati of Saturn from Moon and Ashtam Shani from the ascendant was there to harm the native, but it did not happen so at all. On the contrary, the native got a regular and permanent occupation. Thus his first earning started,

when Saturn was transiting over the natal Moon in the 8th house from the ascendant identical to sign Pisces.

2. Mars happens to be a Yogakaraka for Leo ascendant and that is posited in the 3rd house in Libra in this horoscope. Transit of Saturn in Aries was there from 17.04.1998 to 07.06.2000. Here, the Saturn was transiting in the sign of its debilitation. The third phase of Sadhe Sati of Saturn was also under progress. Transiting Saturn aspected Yogakaraka Mars during its stay in Aries from 17.04.1998 to 07.06.2000. The native got married on 28.04.1999. His marriage was decently ceremonised during the Saturn's transit in Aries. Prosperity also took place when Yogakaraka Mars was aspected by transiting Saturn.

3. Saturn occupies the 7th house in this horoscope identical to Taurus. Saturn transited in Taurus from 07.06.2000 to 23.07.2002. This transit of Saturn in Taurus over the natal Saturn was quite promising for the native, when he was blessed with a son on 4th May, 2001 and soon thereafter, he got a promotion by superseding others on 10.05.2001.

4. The 10th lord Venus occupies Virgo and 10th from the 10th lord Venus in Gemini. Saturn transited in Gemini from 23.07.2002 to 06.09.2004. The transiting Saturn aspected natal Rahu and Jupiter. The native had a welcome change of organization sometime in May, 2003 and once again he had a tremendous change with betterment of designation, salary and place in February, 2004, when he was posted at Lucknow in TATA Indicom. We have mentioned in this chapter that Saturn's transit in the 10th house from the 10th lord is quite fortunate one, so far as the job profit is concerned. The native had two welcome and

progressing changes when Saturn was transiting in Gemini for the 10th lord Venus

5.   Saturn was transiting in Cancer from 06.09.2004 to 02.11.2006. Transiting Saturn aspected the 10th hord Venus during this period. The native again had a welcome change of job with a high emoluments and post during August, 2005, when he was posted at Chandigarh. This transit of Saturn in Cancer also blessed the native with the birth of his 2nd Son on 15.08.2006.

6.   Saturn's transit in Leo from 02.11.2006 to 10.09.2009. This transit of Saturn over the ascendant is most remarkable, because it was aspecting the 10th house, natal Saturn and yogakaraka Mars as well. This brought altogether a great revolutionary change in the profession of the native, when he joined the new telecommunication organization named ETI-SALAT as General Manager and Head on 29th September, 2009. This transit of the Saturn in Leo over the ascendant of the native resulted in a welcome transfer of the native as A.G.M. in Airtel and he stayed there from November, 2006 to September, 2009. He also purchased a beautiful flat during the same period at the tail end of this transit Leo. He decided to switch-over for a better job at Bangalore.

7.   The change as General Manager and Head of the Department of ETI-SALAT took place on 29.09.2009 immediately after the beginning of transit of Saturn in Virgo from 10.09.2009 to 15.11.2011. Here Saturn again transited over the 10th lord Venus in Virgo. This transit of Saturn is likely to bring a few more welcome changes. Soon after the Saturn resuming direct motion in Virgo from 31.05.2010 to

24.01.2011 and once again from 13.06.2011 to 15.11.2011. Saturn in Virgo will transit in Hasta constellation of 01.09.2010 to 21.09.2011. This is quite an important period for welcome changes of place and organization as well. Saturn will enter in Chitra first pada on 21.09.2011 and will stay there till 15.11.2011 before entering into Libra. Mars is a yogakaraka planet and is well placed in this horoscope. Saturn's transit in Chitra first pada and 2nd pada will bring prominent and welcome changes in the professional life of the native.

8. However, Saturn's transit in Libra from 15.11.2011 to 02.11.2014 will be a land-mark for the native, when transiting Jupiter will be passing over the natal Mars and will aspect Jupiter, which is the 10th lord from the natal Moon. Thus, during the transit of Saturn in Libra will elevate the native to the very high position in his occupation. He will also get possession of the flat, purchased by him during Saturn's transit in Leo. Overall, the transit of Saturn in the sign of its exaltation, which will be the 8th from natal Moon, will be quite rewarding and promising for him except that of the health of father due to obvious reasons.

Saturn is the timer of events and the transit of Saturn should be studied properly and thoroughly, keeping various aspects in view.

Here we have discussed the transit of Saturn in various signs with regard to professional changes, elevations, promotions and transfers etc. This discussion of the transit of Saturn in various signs is a quite important tool for timing events and professional prosperity etc. These Rules should not be applied verbative. Dasha-bhukti should also be analyzed alongwith the transits of the planets as well.

We have intentionally not taken Dasha-bhukti and other planets in consideration. The discussion otherwise would have gone very much longer. Readers can easily blend the results of Dasha-bhukti etc. alongwith the transit of Saturn in various signs with regard to rules as explained above.

We humbly request our readers to test the observation of the transit of Saturn as a prominent tool of timing events. They should make further and deeper research on this subject for the sake of betterment of mankind and the Science of Astrology.

9 SATURN
The King Maker

Saturn, if well fortified in any birth chart, makes the native an Emperor, the King or the Head of the country or State. Strong well placed and *Yoga* forming Saturn makes one Prime Minister, Chief Minister or Cabinet Minister. Number of industrialists also have powerful Saturn in the 10th house. Saturn's prominent position in the horoscope with regard to the 10th house can bestow unaccountable success and prosperity to the native with regard to the aspect of his occupation. On the contrary, adversely disposed Saturn brings miseries, loss of power and fall from a high position. Results of Saturn, should be examined very carefully, systematically before any conclusion.

We have experienced that Saturn has a great prominence in the birth charts of celebrities, kings, industrialists and most of all in the horoscopes of powerful and strong persons. This factual finding has been proved again and again, during our study as well as while writing our book **"The Biography of Celebreties : An Astrological Explanation"**. At that moment, we made up our mind for further research on the above mentioned finding of ours and we decided to pen down our research for our beloved readers that Saturn makes one King or equal to King with regard to power, prosperity and fame.

It is not only Saturn, that can make one a King or equivalent, so long as it is well fortified, unafflicted, unblemished, well aspected as well as associated with benefics and strong in *Shadabalas, Navamsa,* etc. Before proceeding further, we would like to recall and revise preliminary essentials about and its significance. Let us study a few prominent and essential points with regard to Saturn– its effect, aspect, association, conjunction and the like, which are explained here under.

9.1   Preliminary Essentials and Significance of Saturn:

Saturn is the owner of the malevolent and feminine sign Aquarius and of the benevolent and masculine sign Capricorn. Being an earthy planet, Saturn yields good results in earthy signs Taurus, Virgo and Capricorn. But Aquarius is an airy sign, thereby it is seen that Saturn has ambivalent nature. The Sun is inimical to Saturn but Saturn shares neutral relationship with the Moon, Mars, Mercury and Jupiter, and Saturn is friendly to Venus. His friends are Venus and Mercury; enemies are the Sun, the Moon and Mars; and neutral is Jupiter. Aquarius is strong by day while Capricorn is strong by night.

In human body, Saturn governs the spleen, upper stomach, endocardium, ribs, bones, hair, nails, cold, and diseases of exposure, rheumatism, consumption, bronchitis, asthama, gout, constipation and Bright 's disease.

Saturn is the planet of limitation, and yet it is the most philosophical planet. It gives endurance, economy, thrift, industry, patience, perseverance, power of retaining secrets, stability, self control, sense of duty towards man and God, accuracy, precaution, etc. A developed individual finds Saturn contributing to truth, concentration, sincerity, prudence, and asceticism. Saturn represents creative power. All through, one should judge this planet as any other by its ownership, location, association, aspects received and strength.

Saturn signifies right ear, body fluids, urine, pneumogastric nerve, peristalsis, bones, spinal cord, pancreatic gland, ivy, barley, hellebore, aconite, thistle, plantain, and leguminous seeds.

मन्दस्तुलामकर   कुम्भगृहे   कलत्रे
याम्यायने निजदृगाणदिने दशायाम् ।
अन्ते   गृहस्या   समरे यदि कृष्णपक्षे
वक्रः समस्तभवनेषु बलाधिकः स्यात् ।।

(Jataka Paarijata 2/67)

Saturn is strong in Libra, Capricorn and Aquarius, in the 7th house, in its passage to the South of the equator, in his own deoanate, on Saturday, towards the end of a sign, in the dark half of the month, and in any sign when it is retrograde. When Saturn becomes a benefic it gives aspiring nature, carefulness in speech, cautiousness, control, justness, patience, practicality, responsibility, seriousness and thrift. As a malefic it gives depression, dogmatic nature, dullness, fear, grasping habits, limitation, meanness, severity, uninspired behaviour, and an inartistic nature.

सुरगुरुरिनसूनुः कारकाः स्युर्विलग्नात् ।

(Jataka Paarijata 2/51)

Saturn is the *karaka* if the 12th house.

आरार्कार्ज्यदिनेशशुक्रशशभृत्तारासुताः कीर्तिताः ।

(Jataka Paarijata 2/28)

Saturn governs muscles.

Saturn's *guna* is said to be *tamas*, and of four *upayas*, Saturn also *bheda*, division.

शक्रारचन्द्रझसुरेज्यमन्दा बसन्तमुख्यत्वीधिपा दृगाणैः ।

(Jataka Paarijata 2/23)

The last two seasons of the *Hindus* (mid-January to mid-March) come under him.

मुख्या दिवाकरमुखादाधिदेवताः स्युः।

(*Jataka Paarijata* 2/20)

Saturn is the planet signifying iron and it is presided over by Lord Brahma.

शनिः स्यातुहिनाचलान्तः।

(*Jataka Paarijata* 2/25)

The geographical landscape in India, governed by Saturn lies between the Ganga and the Himalayas.

आयुर्जीवन मृत्युकारण विपत्सम्पत्प्रदाता शनिः।
सर्पेणैव पितामहं तु शिखिना मातामहं चिन्तयेत्।।

(*Jataka Paarijata* 2/50)

Saturn determines longevity, cause of death, livelihood, adversity, and prosperity.

जाड्ग्यादिप्रति बन्धकाश्वगजचर्माय प्रमाणानि संक्लेशो
व्याधिविरोधदुः खगरणस्त्री सौख्यदासीखराः।।
चण्डाला विकृताङ्गिनो वनचरा बीभत्सदानेश्वरा-
आयुर्दायनपुंसकान्त्यजखागास्त्रेधाग्नि दासक्रियाः।
आचारेतर रिक्तपौरुषमृषावादित्वदीर्घानिला
वृद्धस्नायु दिनान्तवीर्य शिशिरत्वत्यन्तकोपश्रमाः।।
कुक्षेत्रोदित कुण्ड गोलकजनिर्मालिन्यवस्त्रं गृहं
ताद्ग्वस्तुमनोविचार खलमैत्री कृपण पापानि च।
क्रौर्य भस्म च नीलधान्यमणि लोहैदार्यसंवत्सराः।
शूद्रो विट्पितृकारकोऽन्यकुल विद्यासङ्ग्रहः पंगुता।।
तीक्ष्णं कम्बलवस्त्रपश्चिममुखं सञ्जीवनोपायका

ऽधोदृष्टी कृषिजीवनायुधगृह ज्ञातिर्बहिः स्थानकाः ।
ईशान्यप्रियनागलोकपतनं सङ् ग्रामसञ्चारिता
शल्यं सीसकदुष्ट विक्रमतुरुष्का जीर्णतैलेऽपिच ।
दारुब्राह्मणतामसे च विषभूसञ्चारकाठिन्यके ।
भीतिर्दीर्घनिषादवैकृतशिरोजाः सर्वराज्यं भयम् ।
छागाद्या महिषादयो रतिरतो वस्त्रादिशृंगारता
मृत्यूपास कसारमेयहरणाः काठिन्यचित्तं शनेः ।

(Uttara Kaalamirita 5/46-50)

Saturn signifies laziness, obstruction, skin, gain, sickness, distress, misery, misunderstanding, death, outcaste, disfigured limbs, sacred fires, servile duty, unrighteous conduct, falsehood, manliness, wind, old age, muscles, anger, exertion, wicked, cruelty, evil, black grains, nobility, father, defective legs, severity, harshness, agriculture, cousins, serpents, downfall, battles, wanderings, iron, lead, *tamas*, hard-heartedness, fear, dander, fondness for the other sex, worship of *Yama* or *Rudra*.

आयुष्यं मरणं भयं पतितां दुःखावमानामयान्
दारिद्र्यं भृतकापवादकलुषाष्याशौचनिन्दापदः ।
सधैर्यं नीचजनाश्रयं च महिषं तन्द्रीमृणं चायसं
दासत्वं कृषिसाधनं रविसुतत्कारागृहं बन्धनम् ।।

(Phal Deepika 2/7)

Longevity, death, fear, degradation, misery, humiliation, sickness, poverty, labour, reproach, sin, impurity, censure, misfortune, debt, servitude, captivity and the like come under Saturn.

Saturn also refers to the stubborn nature of the native, impetuosity, servitude, idiosyncrasys, despondency, imprisonment, bondage, evil purposes, demoralisation, sorrows, risks, thieves, miners, bricklayers, drunkenness, gambling, oils, seeds, pots, woollen fabrics, architectural skills, cereals, conservatism, hair, teeth, houses, spoils, sinners.

The key words that describe Saturn are limitation and coldness. The urge towards limitation makes one self-controlled and cautious, and the native may be chilled physically or emotionally, even if there is a strong effort to overcome difficulties.

We are here under describing the various results of Saturn in various signs starting from Aries:

1. Stupid sorrowful, miserable, slovenly, indolent, wanderer, insincere, peevish, resentful, cruel, fraudulent, immoral, boastful, quarrelsome, gloomy, perverse, mischievous.

2. Poor, ugly face, evil courses, lives abroad, deceitful, successful, powerful, unorthodox, clever, likes solitude, persuasive, cool, contagious diseases, self restraint, worried nature.

3. Devoid of money, liberal, intelligent, happy, inactive, wanderer, miserable, untidy, thin, subtle, ingenious, few children, interested in chemical and mechanical sciences, narrow minded, speculative.

4. No maternal affection, unhappy, sickly during early life. Poor, weak teeth, pleasure seeking, few sons, slow dull, cunning, rich, selfish, deceitful, malicious, stubborn, devoid of domestic happiness.

5. Disrepute, wandering, unhappy, evil minded. Middle stature, severe, obstinate, few sons, stubborn, unfortunate, conflicting, hard worker, good worker, evil minded, severe.

6. Less wealth, few children, voracious, stubborn, self conceited, dark complexion, malicious, poor,

quarrelsome, erratic, narrow minded, rude, conservative, taste for public life, weak health. Long term results will be good.

7. Leader of community or town, distress, wandering, bad wife, famous founder of institutions, rich, tall, fair, self conceited, tactful, powerful, sound judgement, antagonistic, charitable, proud.

8. Cruel heart, unclean, poor, suffers from piles, rash, indifferent, adventurous, petty, self conceited, reserved, unscrupulous, violent, danger from poisons and weapons and fire, wasteful and happy.

9. Dignified life, bereft of fortune and family, wicked. Pushing nature, artful and cunning, famous. Peaceful, faithful, pretentious, apparently generous, courteous, dutiful children, troubles with wife.

10. Liked by the ruler, minister, ruler, and brave, rich, famous. Harmony and felicity in domestic life, intelligent, selfish, covetous, peevish, learned, reflective, suspicious, revengeful, prudent, melancholic.

11. Wealth, long life and riches. Practical, able, diplomatic, ingenious, slightly conceited, prudent, reflective, intellectual, philosophical, vanquished by enemies.

12. Energetic and virtuous, imprudent, stupid, clever, pushful, gifted profile, happy, good wife, trustworthy, scheming, helpful.

We are further discussing the various results of Saturn in various houses starting from the 1st *Bhava*:

1. Foreign customs, perverted mind, bad thoughts, evil nature, tyrannical, unscrupulous, strong mind, cunning, thrifty, passionate, aspiring, curious, deformed, sickly, exploring, licentious. Gives nervousness, timidity and diffidence in youth, boldness in middle age,

despondency, love of solitude or silent work. Success comes slowly after much hard work and patience. There will be many obstacles in life.

2.   Marital trouble, deformed face, unpopular, broken education, weak sight, unsocial, harsh speech, addicted to drink. There is a struggle for money. This position does not help material welfare. When strong, Saturn brings success from public position, buildings, farming, and business in minerals. One becomes sensible and orderly about financial matters.

3.   Intelligent, wealthy, wicked, loss of brothers, police, adventurous, bold, eccentric, cruel, courageous, obliging, farming. Disagreement with relatives delays, bad for brothers. If Saturn is afflicted here, there will be deceitful tendencies, dishonesty, and hypocrisy. Otherwise things will turn better even if there is scanty education.

4.   Danger to mother, unhappy, sudden losses, colic pains, crafty, narrow-minded, good thinker, good patrimony, success abroad, political disfavour, broken education, licentious. This position suggests bad domestic environment, unfavourable circumstances towards the end of life, and separation from parents. If aspected well, there is gain through cultivation and building; otherwise there will be losses.

5.   Narrow minded, no children, perverted views, tale bearer, royal displeasure, troubled life. The location is bad for speculation, love affairs and contracts. There is loss of children. There may be sorrow from bereavement. All pleasures are likely to end in some trouble or other. One is attracted towards older people.

6.   Obstinate, sickly, deaf, few children, quarrelsome. Clever active, indebted, loose morals. There will be

trouble with servants, susceptibility to chronic diseases, and lessened vitality. These results are negative when Saturn is unafflicted, but when Saturn is all by itself, there is a responsibility to take, and this is through work or health.

7.   More than one wife, enterprising, sickly, colic pains, deafness, ambitious, travelling, dependent, dissimulation, foreign honours, political or diplomatic success. There will be delays and obstacles in marriage, unhappy married life, opposition from public, and loss in partnership. There can be frustration and disappointment.

8.   Struggling, poor, obscure, loose life, few children, corpulent, drunkard, licentious, impious, clever, well informed, asthma, danger from poison, consumption, dishonest, cruel, long life, ungrateful children. This position can suggest a slow and lingering death. There may be danger of drowning. If well aspected, Saturn prolongs life and confers prosperity. One acquires responsibility through the affairs of others, and has a careful interest in psychic matters.

9.   Legal success, founder of charitable institutions, miserly, thrifty, scientific, irreligious, logical, fond of ceremonial activities. One develops bigoted religious beliefs, taste for astrology and philosophy, and losses by travel and litigation. This is not a happy position for Saturn in many cases. There is much seriousness in religious problems.

10.   Visits to sacred shrines and rivers, great worker, good farmer, sudden elevations and depressions, bilious, residence in foreign lands, ascetic in later life. Saturn gives peculiar ambitions life. There is an ability to rise in life, it is usually followed by a severe downfall. If well aspected, Saturn gives responsibility, authority,

love of power and independence; otherwise there will be slanders, disrepute, and the early death of a parent.

11. Deformed, squint eyes, losses in trade, learned in the occult, poor, spendthrift, dexterous, many enemies. One leads a retired life, and may have an enforced seclusion. One is liable to be imprisoned. This position bad for material and social success. It indicates general absence of good spirits, often arising from sorrows borne in secret; and these may be of the native's own making.

Coming to Saturn's own aspects one can only broadly generalise in a paper like this. Usually in India the aspect is from sign position to sign position. This reads to be modified. Saturn at 1° *Thula* (Libra) cannot aspect a planet on 20° *Dhanus* (Sagittarius) only. Keeping this in mind, let us consider aspects. According to all ancient authors, *every planet aspects the 3rd and the 10th, the 4th and the 8th, the 5th and the 9th, and the 7th* from the sign it occupies. In the case of Saturn, the aspect on the 3rd and the 10th is most powerful. Then Saturn's aspects begin at 60°, 90°, 120°, 180°, 210°, 240° and 279° from the degree Saturn occupies in a given chart. The most powerful aspects are at 60°, 180° and 270° only.

पापलोकितसंयुतो निजदशायां भावनाशावहः ।

(*Phal Deepika* 15/8)

Saturn during its major period destroys the *Bhava* (house) Saturn occupies.

तत्तद्भावादष्टमेशस्थितांशं तत्त्रिकोणगे ।
व्ययेशस्थितभांशे वा मन्दे तद्भावनाशनम् ।।

(*Phal Deepika* 17/1)

The only exception is the 8th house where Saturn

promotes longevity. If by transit Saturn arrives at *Rasi* and *Navamsa* occupied by the lord of the 8ᵗʰ or the 12ᵗʰ as reckoned from the *Bhava* concerned, one should expect the total destruction of that *Bhava*. The same result appears when Saturn transits the houses that are triangular to these houses.

रन्ध्रेशो गुलिको मन्दः खरद्रेक्काणपोऽपि वा ।
यत्र तिष्ठति तद्भांशत्रिकोणे रविजे मृतिः ।।

(*Phal Deepika* 17/2)

As certain *Rasi* and *Navamsa* occupied by the lord of the 8ᵗʰ, *Gulika*, Saturn, or lord of the 22ⁿᵈ decanate counted from *Lagna*; when Saturn transits that *Rasi* or *Navamsa* or its triangular position, death can happen.

लग्नेशहीनयम कण्टकभांशकोणं
प्राप्तेऽथवा शनिविहीनहिमांशुभांशम् ।
याते गुरौ स्वमरणन्त्वय राहु हीन-
भूसूसुभांशकगुरौ सहजप्रणाशः ।।

(*Phal Deepika* 17/6)

Subtract the figures of *Yamakantaka* from those of the lord of *Lagna*; subtract the figures of the moon from those of Saturn; then find the *Rasi* or *Navamsa* indicated or their *trikonas* : that gives the time of the native's death.

अर्केण मन्दः, शनिना महीसुतः
कुजेन जीवो गुरुणा निशाकरः ।
सोगेन शुक्रोऽसुरमन्त्रिणा बुधो
बुधेन चन्द्रः खलु वध्यते सदा ।।

(*Jaataka Paarijata* 2/60)

Saturn, Jupiter, Mars, Mercury and Venus, when

retrograde or in conjunction with the Moon, are said to be victorious in planetary war. Yet in planetary war Saturn is overpowered by the Sun.

भानोः कण्टकवर्जितस्य भवनांशे वा त्रिकोणे गुरौ ।
तातो नश्यति कण्टककोनगुलिकक्षर्शात्रिकोणे शनौ ।
अर्कोनेन्दुगृहांश   कोषगगुरौ   चन्द्रोनमन्दात्मज-
क्षेत्रे ऽ॒श॒ेऽप्यथवा त्रिकोणगृहगे मन्दे जनन्या मृति ।।

(Phal Deepika 17/7)

Leaving this aside, subtract the degree of *Mandi* from those of *Yamakantaka*; when Saturn transits this degree, death is likely. The same can happen when Saturn transits the degree indicated by subtracting the degree of *Mandi* from those of the Moon or its triangular position.

मान्दिस्फुटे   भानुसुतं   विशोध्य
राश्यंशकोणे रविजे प्रतिः स्यात् ।
धूमादिपञ्चग्रहयोग   राशि-
द्रेक्काणयातेऽर्कमुते च मृत्युः ।।

(Phal Deepika 17/10)

Subtract the degrees of Saturn from those of *Mandi* and find the *Rasi* and its *Navamsa*; when Saturn arrives at this *Rasi* or *Navamsa* or their triangular position, death is likely. The same can happen when Saturn comes to the *drekkana* of the sign indicated by the aggregate of the five degrees of the five paragraphs reckoned from *Dhuma*. There are many other positions indicating the time of death, as given by *Mantreshwara*.

If Saturn, the Moon and Mars are in the 4th, the 7th and the 10th, there is death by drowning. Afflicted Mars and Saturn indicate death by suffocation. Saturn with a malefic in Taurus suggests hanging. Saturn aspecting the

Sun or the Moon rising may suggest death in a prison. Many other combinations can be gleaned from experience.

मूढस्थोऽपि भृगुः शनिश्च बलवान् भौमोऽरिगो वा बली ।।

(*Uttara Kalamrita 4/15*)

Even when Saturn is eclipsed (combust), Saturn does not lose its strength.

क्रूराश्चोपचयास्थिता रविशनी धर्मस्थितौ ञेऽष्टमे ।

(*Uttara Kalamrita 4/16*)

The Sun and Saturn will be favourable in the 9th house. When Saturn is in exaltation, own house, or a house owned by Jupiter, it will do good even if it were to be *Lagna*.

नृणां द्वादशवत्सरा दशहता ह्यायुः प्रमाणं परै-
राख्यातं परमं शनेस्त्रिभगणं यावत्परैरीतिम् ।
कैश्चिच्चन्द्रसहस्र दर्शनमिह प्रोक्तं कलौ किंतु यत्
वेदोक्तं शरदः शत हि परमायुदयिमाचक्ष्महे ।।

(*Phal Deepika 22/26*)

During saturn's own major period, it might bring ill-health. The sub-periods of Mercury, Venus and Jupiter are said to be good by *Mantreshwar*. The full life span of a person is said to be the time taken by Saturn to make three complete revolutions.

शनिवद्गुलिके प्रोक्तं गुरुवद्यभकण्टके ।
अर्धप्रहारे बुधवत्फलं काले तु राहुवत् ।।

(*Phal Deepika 25/20*)

Saturn is a *Chhadaka* for the 2nd and the 12th houses from its location. It is a malefic for those born in Aries, Leo and Pisces. It is a *Yogakaraka* for Taurus and Libra ascendant. For other ascendants Saturn is more or less a neutral. *Gulika* is said to be similar to Saturn in producing effects.

परिपेषे   जले   भीरुर्जलरोगश्च   बन्धनम् ।
इन्द्रचापे शिलाघातः क्षत शस्त्रैशंषच्युतिः ।।

(*Phal Deepika* 20/24)

If Saturn's major period happens to be the 4th, it proves dangerous.

Some authors take Saturn to be benefic for Pisces ascendant. We have seen birth charts showing that Saturn in the 6th for Pisces has done extremely ill or well, only Saturn fails in killing the native. This may be because Jupiter is not the enemy of Saturn. Jupiter and Saturn can together contribute to be a *Yoga* for some ascendants.

If Venus and Saturn are posited in their exaltation, own house, or are *vargottama*, and if they are strong and powerful to cause a *Yoga*, their mutual major and sub periods will bring suffering, misery, troubles, and worries. If one of these alone is strong, the stronger one will give the *Yoga*.

In *Uttara Kalamrita* mentions that if both Saturn and Venus are weak and placed in the 6th, the 8th and the 12th each from the other or if they happen to own such houses or be conjoined with the lords of these houses, they become auspicious. They become favourable if both of them are malefic.

If Saturn and the Sun are placed in their own or exaltation signs or in the corresponding *Navamsas*, if they are in a *Kona* (trine) or a *Kendra* (angle), or if they own these houses, they bring royal favour and wealth in the sub-period of the Sun, and happiness and wealth in the sub-period of Saturn.

भुक्तौ सूर्यजपार्थिवो प्रदशिती व्यत्यासतः स्वं फलं
राश्यङ्गाधिपती मिश्रः श्रयगतौ तद्राजयोगप्रदौ ।

(Uttara Kalamrita 89)

During the major period of Saturn, we find that Saturn
gives the results of Mars, and in Mars' minor period Saturn
gives its own results.

उदयर्क्षाशस्फुटतुल्यांशे निवसन् पूर्ण फलमाधत्ते ।
शनिवद्राहुः कुजवत्केतुः फलदाता स्यादिह संप्रोक्तः ।।

(Phal Deepika 8/34)

In the matter of the effects emerging during their
periods, it is said Rahu functions like Saturn, Ketu like
Mars.

Mantreshwar does not appear to be acceptable to the
author of *Uttara Kalamrita*. Yet the prescriptions given in
Uttara Kalamrita are found to agree in many charts. Still
one has to be cautious because a blanket application of
any principle is harmful. One has to consider many other
factors before pronouncing a judgement.

शशी दृगाणे रविजस्य संस्थितः कुजार्किदृष्टः प्रकरोति तापसम् ।
कुजांशके वा रविजने दृष्टो नवांशतुल्यां कथयन्ति तां पुनः ।।

(Phal Deepika 27/3)

The Moon in a decanate owned by Saturn and aspected
by Saturn and Mars, makes one an ascetic. If the Moon
occupies a *Navamsa* owned by Mars and is aspected by
Saturn, one is likely to become an ascetic.

जन्माधिपः सूर्यसुतेन दृष्टः शेषैरदृष्टः पुरुषस्य सूतौ ।
आत्मीयदीक्षां कुरुतेऽवश्यं पूर्वोक्तमत्रापि विचारणीयम् ।।

वेदान्तज्ञानिनं वा यतिवरममरेड्यो मृगुलिङ्गवृत्तिं ।
व्रात्यं शैलूषवृत्तिं शनिहित पतितं वाऽथ पाषण्डिनं वा ।।

(*Phal Deepika 27/4, 27/5*)

Usually in the charts of many genuine ascetics we notice Saturn and Jupiter in retrogression.

It is said by ancient authorities that Saturn is beneficial when retrograde in any sign. Retrogression only means that the planet is away from the Sun. However, Saturn as retrograde becomes very powerful in certain signs and for some specific ends.

कण्डूमसूरिरिपुकृत्रिककर्मरोगैः
स्वाचारहीनलघुजातिगणैश्च केतुः ।।

(*Jaataka Parijata 2/80*)

Saturn in an unfavourable position is said to bring out distress because of friends, thieves, poverty, and diseases affecting the joints.

रविकुजसितसौम्या मन्दजीवेन्दवश्च ।

(*Jaataka Parijata 2/29*)

In the case of an ailment brought about by Saturn, one can predict that it is a longstanding one and that it may take years to recover.

वृक्षाश्मक्षतिमाह कश्मलगणैः पीडां पिशाचादिभिः ।।

(*Phal Deepika 14/8*)

Saturn brings on diseases caused by wind and phlegm, paralysis, weariness, mental aberration, pains in the stomach, heart troubles, injury to the ribs and limbs, and possession.

मन्दारान्वितवीक्षिते व्ययघने चन्द्रारुणौ चाक्षिरुक्
शौर्याया्ञ्गिरसो यमारसहिता दृष्टा यदि श्रोत्ररुक् ।
सोग्रे   पञ्चमभे   भवेदुदररुग्रन्ध्यारिनाथान्विते ।
तद्द्वत्सप्तमनैधने सगुदरुक्छुक्रे च गुह्यामचः ।।

(Phal Deepika 14/10)

If the 12th and 2nd houses are occupied by the Moon and the Sun, and if these are conjoined with or aspected by Saturn and Mars, the result is eye disease.

Saturn in the 6th or the 8th brings nervous complaints. Saturn with the Moon in the 6th or the 8th explains enlargement of spleen. Saturn in the 8th house causes wind disease or typhpoid. This planet may be responsible for many ailments, but it appears to be a key factor in cases of insanity and thrombosis. This only heightens its importance as a philosophical planet. Even the classical texts refer to Saturn when they speak of various kinds of *pravrajya* or renunciation. That is, Saturn is not merely a malefic planet.

Saturn rules over the element air and yet Saturn is said to be harsh by nature. *Uttara Kalamrita*, however, states that the origin of Saturn is from *Akash* or ether or space. That is, Saturn is intimately bound up with the self, and this fortifies our contention that Saturn is a philosopher.

9.2 Saturn in Sagittarius or Pisces : Best results

A good Saturn transforms iron into gold, this has been experienced by all the keen scholars of astrology. Saturn's placement in the 12th house in Jupitarian sign, Sagittarius or Pisces, under the benefic aspect by exalted Saturn, makes one a true saint or *Mahatma*. This point of the placement of Saturn in the 12th house requires further examination as under.

Generally, Saturn is regarded extremely adverse in the 12th house and it chiefly brings the downfall from power and prosperity. In Sagittarius and Pisces, Saturn in the 12th house is not adverse. Generally Saturn in the 12th is bad, opined that Saturn in the 12th, a Jovian house Pisces, and well aspected by exalted Jupiter, lord of 9th, gives high yoga and may indicate *sanyasa* or asceticism.

Saturn is an inherent malefic, who is well placed in the 3rd or the 6th or the 11th, especially in the 3rd or the 11th, and more especially in the 11th (*dhana upchaya*). So normally Saturn in the 8th or the 12th is a grave defect, causing frequent and much expenditure. Saturn in the 12th may generally cause expenses on another woman, on litigation, worries due to secret enemies. But, when Saturn is in Pisces in the 12th and aspected by Jupiter from Cancer, Saturn gets transformed and even "sublimated". According to classical works even if a planet is ill-placed in the 6th or the 8th or the 12th (especially the 8the or 12th), if the planet is in own or exaltation or friendly sign and *Asma* and aspected by a benefic, it becomes auspicious.

If the Sun's son, viz., Saturn is in a house of Jupiter and aspected by Jupiter, the native becomes chief, a kingly person or a military commander of police superintendent, etc.

For Aries ascendant, Saturn is the excellent lord of the 10th and also becomes *badhaka,* as the lord of the 11th. Aquarius being the *Moolatrikona* house of Saturn, its lordship of the 11th or *Badhaka* dominates, according to an ancient dictum as "the Sun's son Saturn is a *naisargika* or inherent malefic, its evil tendencies prevail over its good, even where the good lordship is of its *Moolatrikona* house, as in the case of Gemini ascendant". Even if *karmabadhaka* may be in the 12th, it becomes auspicious and fortunate, only if the said Saturn in the 12th house in Pisces is blessed, controlled and transformed by exalted Jupiter, the lord of the 12th house and of the 9th (fortune). Saturn in the 12th may make one an ascetic at heart, who does not care for money. But, Jupiter and the Moon will give a native a princely position and life. For actual renunciation or *sanyasa yoga*, there must be a strong *pravraja yoga* due to four planets, including the lord of the 10th being together in a good place or Jupiter and Saturn being in *thapo*-mood, and not mundane position and prosperity. If Venus is saturn's boson friend, (so that Venus-saturn yoga is good for wordly prosperity), Jupiter is saturn's venerable preceptor, so that sage *Garga* praises Saturn in a jovian house, Sagittarius or Pisces (more especially the former). If a good and powerful Jupiter blesses such a Saturn by his aspect, Saturn transforms iron into gold.

However, let us come to our own observation regarding Saturn as a King Maker. Democracy is a government, by the people, for the people and of the people. Democracy comes under the control of Saturn. Saturn rules over the population and public in general. In earlier times states were ruled by the kings but now the power has been changed altogether. Kings began to be gradually replaced by elected or self styled leaders. We find Jupiter, even if reluctantly making way for Saturn for making the subject a king, minister or secretary etc. Saturn has a potency to disrupt the mightiest, just when everything is going very good.

Jupiter enhances auspicious results of Saturn and reduces the malefic influences. The positions of Saturn and Jupiter are of great importance in the determination of the basic strength or weakness of a horoscope. Harmony between these two planets is a powerful asset even to an ordinary horoscope. Saturn unaided and unchecked by the influence of Jupiter is a lurking evil which can manifest in misfortune and cause havoc when the occasion demands. Is Saturn is powerful in *vakrabala* strength and/or is afflicted this will only enhance its propensity to cause evil. The alleviating influence of Jupiter curbs this tendency to a great extent.

Saturn can be viewed from two different angles, the first as the hour hand in the clock of destiny. Momentous incidents affecting a person's personal life are heralded by its passage through various signs of the zodiac. The movement of transit Saturn in relation to the position of natal Saturn in one's horoscope is a particular point to be noted. Transit Saturn passes in the 10th from natal Saturn when the native is about 22 years. Saturn passes over natal Saturn in the 30th year of the native's life; passes in the 4th from his position when the native is about 36 years, and in the 7th from this position when the native is about 44 years old. Transit Saturn passing over natal Saturn is a particular point to be noted. Prosperity during such a period denotes a good position of Saturn in relation to one's destiny. Saturn's sojourn over the 12 houses tends to highlight certain characteristic features of the individual's life. It will also be found that the second cycle of transit Saturn in relation to one's horoscope brings to relief certain basic similarities experienced in the first cycle of transit Saturn over the 12 signs.

The second angle from which Saturn can be viewed is as a natural malefic. Saturn by itself signifies worries, frustration, delay, misfortune, etc. Of course there are horoscope in which Saturn plays a constructive role, but it is only when Saturn is without any blemish. Generally Saturn pinpoints, by its placement, some negative aspect of our life. The afflictions to Saturn come in many forms, e.g., by its situation in a malefic constellation, conjunction or association with malefic like Mars, Rahu or Ketu, by its inimical disposition to the Sun (especially the dreaded opposition) and by virtue of its possessing high *vakrabala* or strength of retrogression.

Jupiter on the other hand has a constructive role to play. Saturn signifies expansion, higher ideals and thoughts, good fortune and other positive attributes. The most remarkable horoscopes are those which contain a harmonious disposition between Jupiter, Saturn and the Sun.

9.3 Practical Illustrations

Sheikh Mujibur Rehman

Illustration : 9.1   *Horoscope No.: 23*

Date of birth : 17.03.1920   Time of birth : 22:38:00 hrs
Place of birth : Faridpur   Lat 28:12 N Long 79:32 E
Ayanamsa   : 22:44:47   Sidereal Time : 10:06:00

Pln	Degree	Rasi	Nakshatra	Pad
Asc	0:43:02	Sco	Vishakha	4
Sun	4:04:13	Pis	U Bhadrapad	1
Mon	0:01:31	Aqu	Dhanishtha	3
Mar (R)	16:18:38	Lib	Swati	3
Mer (R/C)	8:55:10	Pis	U Bhadrapad	2
Jup (R)	15:49:59	Can	Pushya	4
Ven	6:06:30	Aqu	Dhanishtha	4
Sat (R)	14:05:53	Leo	P Phalguni	1
Rah (R)	24:07:14	Lib	Vishakha	2
Ket (R)	24:07:14	Ari	Bharani	4

Lagna Chart

	Rah Mar	
9	7	
10		6
	8	
Mon 11 Ven	5 Sat	
	2	
Sun 12 Mer		4 Jup
1		3
Ket		

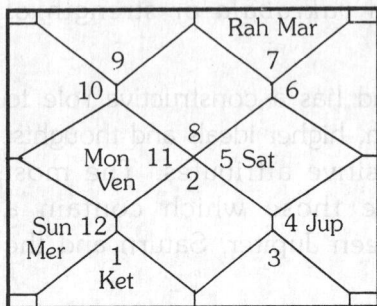

Navamsa Chart

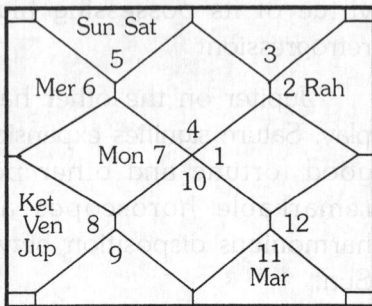

	Sun Sat	
	5	3
Mer 6		2 Rah
	4	
Mon 7		1
	10	
Ket Ven 8 Jup		12
	9	11 Mar

Balance of Vimshottari Dasa of **Mar   3Y 5M 25D**

Sheikh Mujibur Rehman was born in Scorpio ascendant with his Saturn in 10th house. Saturn is retrograde in Leo corresponding with Poorva Phalguni constellation ruled by Venus. In fact, 4th lord Saturn, the 9th lord Moon and 7th lord Venus has mutual aspect on each other. Saturn is extremely powerful in 10th house and obtains 1.51 *shadbala*. The 10th lord the Sun is posited in the 5th house giving rise to *Kendra trikona raja yoga*, in Pisces and receives the aspect of exalted Jupiter. Thus, the 10th house is under the influence of Saturn, Jupiter, Venus and 9th lord Moon which made Sheikh Mujibur Rehman, the Prime Minister of Bangladesh. Mars is *Atmakaraka* planet in this horoscope and obtains *navamsa* of Saturn; Whereas, Saturn obtains *vargottama navamsa* in Leo, whereas the Sun obtains own *navamsa* in Leo. Jupiter and Venus obtain the *navamsa* of Mars which provided him a strong impressive and influential personality with an intense feeling of patriotism. Opposition of Saturn and Mars in *navamsa* chart identical to Leo and Aquarius signs resulted into his assassination when he was in power.

We see that Sheikh Mujibur Rehman who fought for the freedom of Bangladesh, got ultimate success and became

Prime Minister finally. Prominent role of the Saturn and Jupiter with regard to the 10th house is quite in his horoscope.

Amitabh Bahchan

Illustration : 9.2   *Horoscope No.: 24*

Date of birth : 11.10.1942   Time of birth : 17:00:00 hrs
Place of birth : Allahabad   Lat 25:27 N Long 81:50 E
Ayanamsa   : 23:03:18   Sidereal Time : 17:14:52

Pln	Degree	Rasi	Nakshatra	Pad
Asc	21:32:44	Aqu	P Bhadrapad	1
Sun	24:25:19	Vir	Chitra	1
Mon	10:54:00	Lib	Swati	2
Mar (D)	22:37:51	Vir	Hasta	4
Mer (R/D)	23:36:31	Vir	Chitra	1
Jup	0:32:30	Can	Punarvasu	4
Ven (C)	15:14:27	Vir	Hasta	2
Sat (R)	19:13:48	Tau	Rohini	3
Rah (R)	10:21:42	Leo	Magha	4
Ket (R)	10:21:42	Aqu	Satabhisha	2

Lagna Chart

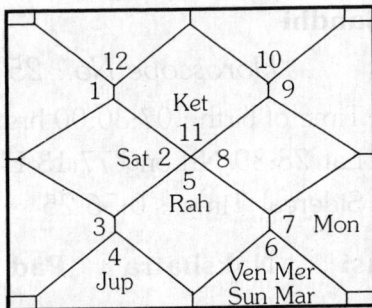

Navamsa Chart

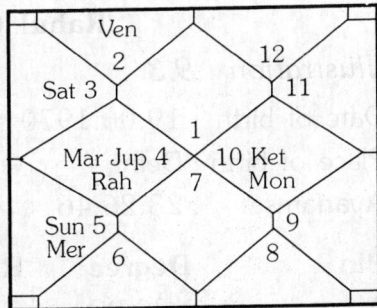

Balance of Vimshottari Dasa of **Rah 12Y 3M 12D**

Amitabh Bachchan was born in Aquarius ascendant. The lord of the ascendant Saturn occupies the 4th house and aspect the 10th house. Lord of the 11th and 2nd is posited in the 6th house and aspect the 10th house. Thus, the 10th house receives the aspect of *lagna* lord Saturn and exalted Jupiter which has made Amitabh Bachchan the most popular, famous and worldwide cinema star. It may be noted that *Lagna Adhi Yoga* which is a very rare one, is also present in this birth chart.

Amitabh Bachchan was running through the major period of Saturn from 10.11.1971 to 10.11.1990 which was most auspicious one for him. Almost all his films were hit. He worked, during Saturn's major period in films like Zanjeer, Deewar, Sholey, Kabhie-Kabhie, Anand, Namak Haram, Abhiman, etc. Saturn obtains 1.29 *shadabala* and joins Taurus identical to Gemini *navamsa*. *Navamsa* and *Rashi* lords Venus and mercury are friendly to Saturn and Saturn is retrograde in the horoscope of Amitabh Bachchan. Thus, Saturn becomes extremely strong. Let us conclude that the joint aspect of *lagna* lord Jupiter and 2nd lord, exalted Jupiter, on the 10th house has provided amazing and historical success to Amitabh Bachchan, and made him a King of Bollywood, i.e. a *Shehenshah*.

Rahul Gandhi

Illustration : 9.3   *Horoscope No.: 25*

Date of birth : 19.06.1970   Time of birth : 07:30:00 hrs
Place of birth : Delhi   Lat 28:39 N Long 77:13 E
Ayanamsa   : 23:26:46   Sidereal Time : 0:56:25

Pln	Degree	Rasi	Nakshatra	Pad
Asc	1:00:03	Can	Punarvasu	4
Sun	3:56:28	Gem	Mrigshira	4

Mon	28:01:38	Sco	Jyestha	4
Mar (C)	17:36:27	Gem	Ardra	4
Mer	15:05:36	Tau	Rohini	2
Jup (R)	2:39:09	Lib	Chitra	3
Ven	9:18:49	Can	Pushya	2
Sat	24:25:38	Ari	Bharani	4
Rah (R)	11:45:01	Aqu	Satabhisha	2
Ket (R)	11:45:01	Leo	Magha	4

Lagna Chart

```
        Ket          Mar Sun
         5              3
      6        Ven          2 Mer
               4
         Jup 7      1 Sat
            10
      Mon 8              12
         9              11
                        Rah
```

Navamsa Chart

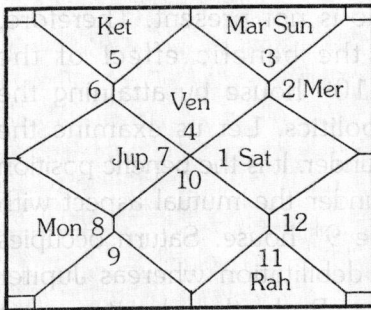

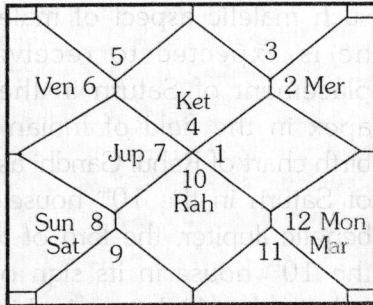

```
                  5              3
      Ven 6        Ket          2 Mer
                   4
         Jup 7      1
              10
              Rah
      Sun  8              12 Mon
      Sat    9         11   Mar
```

Balance of Vimshottari Dasa of **Mer 2Y 6M 5D**

Rahul Gandhi can be compared with Mohandas Karamchand Gandhi. He is extremely popular among all the politicians as well as celebrities just like Mahatma Gandhi, without holding any political power. He is the grandson of Mrs. Indira Gandhi and worthy son of Mr. Rajeev Gandhi. Rahul Gandhi was born in Cancer ascendant with Saturn in the 10th house. Let us examine his horoscope to establish that unafflicted Saturn in the 10th house does not causes downfall after attaining the dizzy heights. We have analysed the a few horoscopes like that of Sheikh Mujibur Rehman, Napoleon Bonaparte and Benazir Bhutto who reached to the topmost position due to placement of strong and well fortified Saturn in the 10th house. However, they suffered steep downfall, unnatural and untimely death, destruction, dethronement, loss of power in the most astonishing way. Here we humbly opine that it is not the Saturn of the 10th house which resulted in their destruction but that is in fact, the affliction of Saturn by malefic planets in one or the other way. The 9th, the 10th and the *lagna* was also afflicted either by placement of their lords with malefics or in *trika* houses or due to adverse aspect of malefic over the ruler of concerning houses.

In the birth chart of Rahul Gandhi such affliction and such malefic aspect of malefic is not present. Therefore, he is expected to receive the benefic effect of the placement of Saturn in the 10th house by attaining the apex in the field of Indian politics. Let us examine the birth chart of Rahul Gandhi as under. It is the benefic position of Saturn in the 10th house under the mutual aspect with benefic Jupiter, the lord of the 9th house. Saturn occupies the 10th house in its sign of debilitation whereas Jupiter falls in the 4th house in Libra. Both, the planets aspect each other as well as the 10th lord Mars which is a *Yogakaraka* for cancer ascendant and also receives the aspect of Saturn and Jupiter. Thus, the Saturn and Jupiter are well fortified and have helped Rahul Gandhi a lot in attaining world wide popularity, name, fame and honour.

Saturn obtains *navamsa* of Mars i.e. Scorpio and occupies Martian sign, Aries. Saturn and Venus have exchanged there constellations. This is called *Vinimay Nakshatra Parivartan Raja Yoga*. Venus falls in the ascendant corresponding with *Pushya* constellation which is ruled by Saturn and Saturn occupies the 10th house in Aries corresponding with *Bharini* constellation ruled by Venus. Jupiter and the ascendant obtain *Vargottam Navamsa*. The Sun obtains the *navamsa* of its exaltation.

There is mutual exchange of *navamsa* between Jupiter and Venus. These are extremely auspicious combination in this horoscope. Both, the luminaries the Sun, the Moon, and Venus are very strong in *shadabala*. Rahul Gandhi is passing through the major period of Moon from 24.12.2005 to 24.12.2015. Moon is the lord of the ascendant and *Atmakaraka* as well. The Moon obtains *navamsa* of Jupiter and falls in *Jyeshtha* constellation which has blessed him with immense hospitality, humanity and patriotism. He is likely to become Prime Minister of India during Moon – Venus period.

Role of Saturn in this horoscope is the most important combination to make Rahul Gandhi a King or equal to a King i.e. the most eligible and deserving Prime Minister. Transit of Saturn in Sagittarius will be most promising as per our research observation with regard to the transit of Saturn and professional promotions.

Adolf Hitler

Illustration : 9.4   Horoscope No.: 26

Date of birth : 20.04.1889   Time of birth : 18:30:00 hrs
Place of birth :   Lat 48:00 N Long 13:00 E
Ayanamsa   : 22:18:22   Sidereal Time : 8:26:00

Pln	Degree	Rasi	Nakshatra	Pad
Asc	4:27:18	Lib	Chitra	4
Sun	8:30:00	Ari	Aswini	3
Mon	14:19:39	Sag	Purvasadha	1
Mar (C)	24:04:25	Ari	Bharani	4
Mer (C)	3:21:37	Ari	Aswini	2
Jup	15:56:18	Sag	Purvasadha	1
Ven (R)	24:23:15	Ari	Bharani	4

Sat	21:09:11	Can	Aslesa	2
Rah (R)	22:44:50	Gem	Punarvasu	1
Ket (R)	22:44:50	Sag	Purvasadha	3

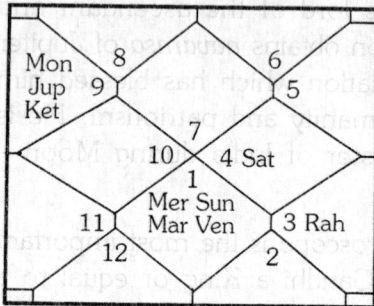

Lagna Chart   **Navamsa Chart**

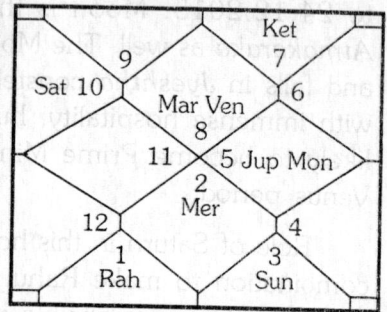

Balance of Vimshottari Dasa of **Ven   18Y 6M 3D**

It is the horoscope Adolf Hitler who has been recognised, appreciated and known for the Saturn. He was born in Libra ascendant with strong Saturn in the 10th house. In fact, Saturn is posited in Cancer corresponding to *Ashlesha* constellation. Saturn obtains own *navamsa* Capricorn. Saturn happens to be a *yogakaraka* for Libra ascendant and if so well placed in 10th house can make one equal to a king provided Jupiter has a concern with the professional aspect of the native. It was not only Saturn in the 10th in Cancer with 1.52 *shadabala* which made Hitler equal to a king. Lord of the 10th house Moon is conjoined with 3rd and 6th lord Jupiter and aspects the 9th house and 9th lord mercury. Mars and the *lagna* lord Venus occupy the 7th house in association with 11th lord the Sun in the sign of exaltation and *swakshetriya* Mars. Thus, Mars and Saturn both have mutual aspect over each other. This is a very rare combination of the conjunction of exalted Sun and *swakshetriya* Mars in 7th house, under malefic aspect of Saturn and Jupiter. This birth chart signifies that Hitler was extremely fortunate person because Karmic Control planets Jupiter and Mercury are placed in triangular position from each other. The Sun is exalted, Mars occupies its own sign in *Kendra* giving rise to *Ruchhaka Yoga*. Jupiter falls in own sign Sagittarius in association with 10th lord Moon with Ketu. Venus is *Atmakaraka* planet in this birth chart and obtains *navamsa* of Mars in association with Mars. Venus and Mars are also associated in rasi chart under the aspect of Jupiter. This is a strong indication of being the Chief of Army. 10th lord Moon obtains own *navamsa* i.e. Moon is *Karmansha Yukta*. Mercury obtains *vargottama navamsa*, Saturn and Mars obtain own *navamsa*. The Sun, the Mars, Venus and Saturn are exceptionally strong planets in this birth chart. However, we intend to say that Saturn's placement in 10th house as a *Yogakaraka* is King Maker combination provided it is strong, unafflicted and the 10th house, its lord is supported by Jupiter. Thus, Saturn can make one a King or equal to a King if Jupiter plays a prominent role with regard to professional aspect of the native.

Albert Einstein

Illustration : 9.5   *Horoscope No.: 27*

Date of birth : 14.03.1879   Time of birth : 11:30:00 hrs
Place of birth : Ulm   Lat 48:23 N Long 10:00 E
Ayanamsa   : 22:10:27   Sidereal Time : 22:36:40

Pln	Degree	Rasi	Nakshatra	Pad
Asc	15:15:00	Gem	Ardra	3
Sun	1:19:11	Pis	P Bhadrapad	4
Mon	22:09:34	Sco	Jyestha	2
Mar	4:43:47	Cap	Uttarasadha	3

Mer (C)	10:56:35	Pis	U Bhadrapad	3
Jup	5:18:23	Aqu	Dhanishtha	4
Ven	24:47:37	Pis	Revati	3
Sat (C)	12:00:49	Pis	U Bhadrapad	3
Rah (R)	10:28:38	Cap	Sravna	1
Ket (R)	10:28:38	Can	Pushya	3

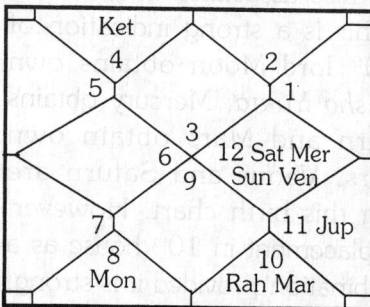

Lagna Chart   **Navamsa Chart**

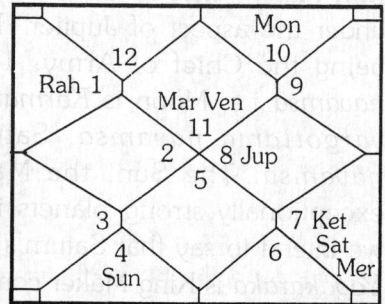

Balance of Vimshottari Dasa of **Mer 9Y 11M 29D**

Albert Einstein was a Nobel Prize winner scientist, who was awarded the Nobel Prize for his Photoelectric Effect. He was born in Gemini ascendant. There is a exchange of the 9th lord Saturn with 10th lord Jupiter corresponding with Pisces and Aries. In fact, the 10th house is occupied by Saturn, Venus and Mercury, whereas, the 9th house is tenanted by the 10th lord Jupiter. Venus is *Atmakaraka* and it is exalted in the 10th house in association with Saturn and Mercury which is a rare combination of conjunction of all the three planets Saturn, Mercury, Venus. *Malavya Maha purusha Raja Yoga* has also been formed along with *Neecha Bhanga Raja Yoga* by Mercury. Mutual exchange of 9th and the 10th lord has also given rise to *Mahabhagya Yoga*. It may be noted that 9th lord Saturn falls in own constellation *Uttarabhadrapada* and obtains the *navamsa* of its exaltation. *Gajakesari Yoga, Parijaat Yoga, Vipreeth raja yoga,*etc., are also present and extremely strong the Sun, Jupiter and Venus, these combinations made him world renowned scientist and Nobel prize winner. In fact, the exchange of the 10th lord Jupiter with 9th lord Saturn must be examined in addition to the conjunction of three closed friends Saturn, Mercury and Venus in the 10th house. Thus, Saturn and Jupiter made Elbert Einstein equal to King among all the scientists of the world. His name will remain immortal undoubtedly.

R.N.Goenka

Illustration : 9.6   *Horoscope No.: 28*

Date of birth : 18.04.1904   Time of birth : 06:05:00 hrs
Place of birth : Kashipur   Lat 29:13 N Long 78:58 E
Ayanamsa   : 22:31:11   Sidereal Time : 19:47:51

Pln	Degree	Rasi	Nakshatra	Pad
Asc	14:47:04	Ari	Bharani	1
Sun	5:02:37	Ari	Aswini	2
Mon	0:01:24	Tau	Krittika	2
Mar (C)	15:47:56	Ari	Bharani	1
Mer	24:26:44	Ari	Bharani	4
Jup	18:59:13	Pis	Revati	1
Ven	13:28:36	Pis	U Bhadrapad	4
Sat	26:57:25	Cap	Dhanishtha	2
Rah (R)	4:39:56	Vir	U Phalguni	3
Ket (R)	4:39:56	Pis	U Bhadrapad	1

Lagna Chart

```
          Mon        Ven Jup Ket
           2              12
      3     Sun Mar          11
            Mer
             1
         41       10  Sat+
              7
         5              9
         6              8
        Rah
```

Navamsa Chart

```
          Sat
           6              4
      7         Mar Ket      3
                   5
         Mer  8      2  Sun
         Ven      11
         Jup 9    Rah      1
           10            12
          Mon
```

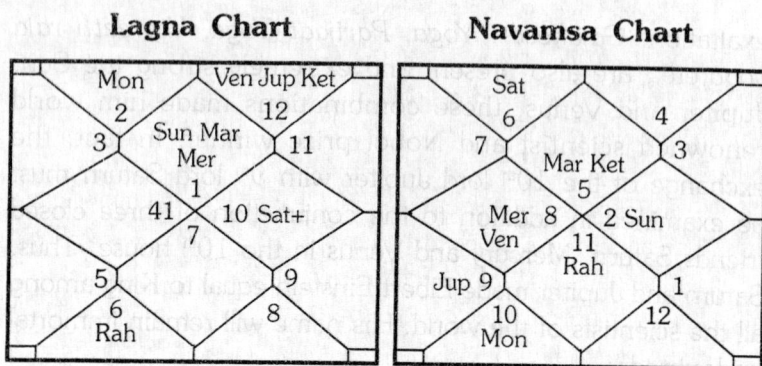

Balance of Vimshottari Dasa of **Sun   4Y 5M 26D**

He was born in Aries ascendant with Saturn in the 10th house in own sign Capricorn. This is *Shasha Mahapurusha Raja Yoga*. Mars and the Sun are conjoined in Aries with 3rd and 6th lord Mercury. Ram Nath Goenka came to India during partition and he was the founder of Goenka Group of Industries, The Indian Express group, etc. Moreover, he was absolutely a self made man. A wonderful and rare placement of planets is present. In fact, Mars, Saturn and Jupiter are posited in their own signs whereas the Sun, Moon and Venus are exalted. The 10th lord Saturn aspects Jupiter. Here Saturn is *Atmakaraka* planet and lends its aspect over 9th lord Jupiter. Thus, the Saturn's influence over Jupiter and various other combinations of planets made Ram Nath Goenka one of the most successful, dynamic, dashing and successful industrialist. He was not less than a King of his time as far as prosperity, progress, popularity and power is concerned.

Saturn occupies its own sign in Capricorn in the 10th house and is not aspected by any malefic planet. Saturn is *atmakaraka* and obtains 1.35 *shadabala*. Saturn obtains the *navamsa* of Mercury and is absolutely unafflicted, the ascendant is also strong enough as the Sun and Mars join the ascendant corresponding with Aries. *Ruchhaka Mahapurusha Raja Yog* and *Shasha Mahapurusha Raja Yoga* have also been formed. 9th lord Jupiter falls in own sign and obtains own *navamsa* and is associated with exalted Venus. Moon and the Sun are also exalted. Therefore, R.N.Goenka was a refugee became a world renowned journalist and shook the whole nation through his world recognised journal The Indian Express etc. Mrs. Indira Gandhi had to try her level best to cease the publication of The Indian Express group but she was not successful in her endeavours. Thus Saturn of the 10th house was unafflicted in this birth chart and hence there was no destruction as there is such a belief.

Jamna Lal Bajaj

Illustration : 9.7   *Horoscope No.: 29*

Date of birth : 04.11.1889   Time of birth : 08:00:00 hrs
Place of birth : Sikar River   Lat 17:21 N Long 78:32 E
Ayanamsa : 22:18:49   Sidereal Time : 10:54:11

Pln	Degree	Rasi	Nakshatra	Pad
Asc	15:51:21	Sco	Anuradha	4
Sun	19:35:21	Lib	Swati	4
Mon	7:10:42	Pis	U Bhadrapad	2
Mar	3:32:34	Vir	U Phalguni	3
Mer	1:30:16	Lib	Chitra	3
Jup	13:10:43	Sag	Moola	4
Ven	24:08:38	Vir	Chitra	1
Sat	10:08:29	Leo	Magha	4
Rah (R)	12:09:11	Gem	Ardra	2
Ket (R)	12:09:11	Sag	Moola	4

Lagna Chart

```
      Jup Ket        Mer Sun
         9              7
      10                   6 Ven
                8            Mar
      11      5 Sat
          2
   Mon 12            4
       1          3
                 Rah
```

Navamsa Chart

```
                       Mer
         9              7
   Rah 10                  6 Mon
                8
      Mar 11     5 Ven
          2
   Sun 12            4  Ket
       1          3    Sat
                       Jup
```

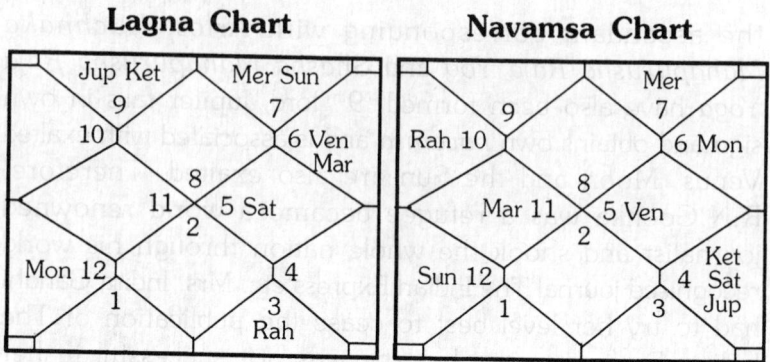

Balance of Vimshottari Dasa of Sat 13Y 6M 7D

Jamna Lal Bajaj was a famous industrialist who was the founder of Bajaj Group of Industries. He was born in Scorpio ascendant with Saturn posited in 10ᵗʰ house in Leo and obtains the *navamsa* of Gemini. Here Saturn is the lord of 3ʳᵈ and 4ᵗʰ house and obtains 1.3 *shadabala* i.e. Saturn is the strongest planet in this birth chart. Saturn is aspected by 2ⁿᵈ and 5ᵗʰ lord Jupiter which made Mr. Jamna Lal Bajaj equal to King of his time. Saturn and Jupiter are associated with each other in *navamsa* chart corresponding with Cancer. Thus, if Saturn has anything to do with the profession of native in one or the other way, and Jupiter also has an influence on Saturn or on the profession of the native he or she is likely to reach at the top. In this birth chart of Jamna Lal Bajaj Jupiter is tenanted in its own sign Sagittarius and it aspects the 10ᵗʰ house and Saturn. Therefore, Jamna Lal Bajaj was one of the leading industrialists of his time.

Saturn is the lord of 3ʳᵈ and 4ᵗʰ house and joins the 10ᵗʰ house corresponding with Moon's *navamsa*. Jupiter is extremely benefic planet for Scorpio ascendant and it lends its favourable aspect over Saturn. Jupiter is posited in own sign Sagittarius in association with Ketu and in the constellation of Ketu as well. Generally the placement of Ketu in the 2nd house, if afflicted makes one extremely rich. Here Saturn is unaspected by any malefic planet. The ascendant is well fortified as its lord Mars is associated with benefic Venus in the 2nd house. 9th lord Moon and ascendant lord mars aspect each other. Here Saturn's occupation in the 10th house is unafflicted and strong. Therefore, there was no downfall of Jamna Lal Bajaj.

Prophet Mohammad

Illustration : 9.8   Horoscope No.: 30

Date of birth : 20.04.0571   Time of birth : 04:00:00 hrs
Place of birth :   Lat 21:20 N Long 40:14 E
Ayanamsa   : 03:57:47   Sidereal Time : 15:08:35

Pln	Degree	Rasi	Nakshatra	Pad
Asc	3:10:47	Aqu	Dhanistha	3
Sun	26:58:52	Ari	Krittika	1
Mon	14:03:29	Leo	P Phalguni	1
Mar	28:53:08	Gem	Punarvasu	3
Mer	1:07:23	Ari	Aswini	1
Jup (R)	28:27:45	Lib	Visakha	3
Ven	7:41:00	Tau	Krittika	4
Sat (R)	0:40:13	Sco	Visakha	4
Rah (R/C)	3:27:59	Tau	Krittika	3
Ket (R)	3:27:59	Sco	Anuradha	1

Lagna Chart

```
        12        10
  Mer  1        9
  Sun
          11
       Ven 2   8  Ket
       Rah   5    Sat
            Mon
    Mar 3         7 Jup
         4      6
```

Navamsa Chart

```
         8        6
  Sun 9        5  Ket
                  Mon
            7
         10   4 Sat
            1
            Mer
  Rah 11        3  Mar
         12    2   Jup
         Ven
```

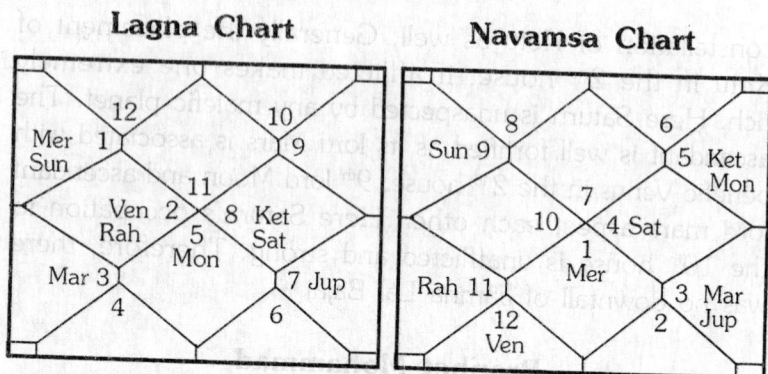

Balance of Vimshottari Dasa of **Ven 18Y 10M 29D**

Prophet Mohammad was the leader of Muslim religion. He was born in Aquarius ascendant with the Saturn in the 10th house. *Yogakaraka* Venus occupies its own sign in the 4th house and aspect the *lagna* lord Saturn. Here Saturn falls in the Jupiter's constellation *Vishakha*. Jupiter also falls in own constellation *Vishakha*. Mutual aspect between Saturn and Venus is extremely auspicious because both these planets are very strong, well fortified and well placed. The 10th lord Mars is *atmakaraka* and falls in the 5th house giving rise to *Kendra trikona raja yoga* corresponding with Jupiter's constellation *Punarvasu*. Here we see that Saturn and Venus are associated with Ketu and Rahu respectively due to which Prophet Mohammad had to struggle a lot. However, Jupiter's aspect on the 10th lord Mars, the 5th lord Mercury, 7th lord the Sun and the ascendant is splendid. The Saturn of the 10th house in Martian sign Scorpio with mutual aspect of Venus made Prophet Mohammad the Head of the country.

Guru Nanak

Illustration : 9.9   *Horoscope No.: 31*

Date of birth : 08.11.1470   Time of birth : 23:30:00 hrs
Place of birth :   Lat 31:39 N Long 74:47 E
Ayanamsa   : 16:28:47   Sidereal Time : 3:15:59

Pln	Degree	Rasi	Nakshatra	Pad
Asc	8:32:42	Leo	Magha	3
Sun	8:50:06	Sco	Anuradha	2
Mon	6:42:48	Tau	Krittika	4
Mar (C)	1:59:04	Sco	Vishakha	4
Mer (C)	21:21:45	Sco	Jyeshtha	2
Jup	12:26:54	Vir	Hasta	1
Ven	4:45:07	Lib	Chitra	4
Sat (R)	6:54:27	Tau	Krittika	4
Rah (R)	20:54:29	Sag	Purvasadha	3
Ket (R)	20:54:29	Gem	Punarvasu	1

Lagna Chart	Navamsa Chart

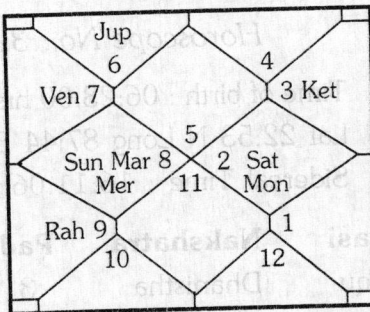

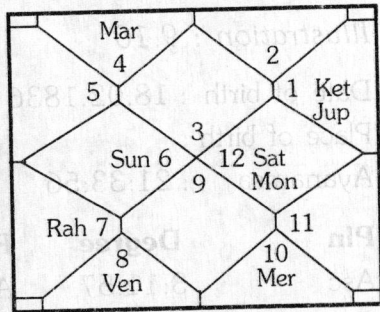

Balance of Vimshottari Dasa of **Sun 1Y 5M 22D**

Guru Nanak was born on 8.11.1470 in Leo ascendant
with Saturn and Moon in the 10th house. The 5th lord Jupiter

is posited in the 2nd house and lends its favourable aspect over the 10th house, Saturn and Moon. It may be noted that Saturn and Moon both are very closely associated with each other at 6^0 54' and at 6^042' Saturn and Moon both obtain the *navamsa* of Jupiter. The 10th lord Venus occupies the 3rd house in own sign and is extremely strong as it obtains 1.48 *shadabala*.

One of the most important aspects to be examined is the placement of *Yogakaraka* Mars, the ascendant lord the Sun and Mercury in the 4th house. There is mutual aspect between Saturn and Moon, and the Sun, Mars and Mercury. Here both the enemies of Saturn i.e. the Sun and Mars are quite strong and strong benefics for the Leo ascendant. Therefore, Guru Nanak did not suffer humiliation, defeat, downfall or destruction. The Saturn in the 10th house under the benefic aspect of Jupiter, the Sun, mars and Mercury made him immortal founder of Sikh religion. Guru Nanak departed to heaven at an old age from where he had come. He left the world on 22.9.1539 at around 69 years of age.

Swami Ram Krishna Paramhansa

Illustration : 9.10	Horoscope No.: 32
Date of birth : 18.02.1836	Time of birth : 06:23:00 hrs
Place of birth :	Lat 22:53 N Long 87:44 E
Ayanamsa : 21:33:56	Sidereal Time : 16:11:06

Pln	Degree	Rasi	Nakshatra	Pad
Asc	3:11:57	Aqu	Dhanistha	3
Sun	6:52:33	Aqu	Satabhisha	1
Mon	22:02:54	Aqu	P Bhadrapad	1
Mar (C)	22:15:08	Cap	Sravna	4
Mer (R/C)	15:07:28	Aqu	Satabhisha	3

Jup (R)	14:33:11	Gem	Ardra	3
Ven	9:04:06	Pis	U Bhadrapad	2
Sat (R)	13:41:27	Lib	Swati	3
Rah (R)	2:36:31	Tau	Krittika	2
Ket (R)	2:36:31	Sco	Vishakha	4

Lagna Chart

```
            Ven          Mar
            12    Sun Mon  10
         1                    9
            Rah 2  Mer 11  8 Ket
                     5
         Jup 3              7 Sat
              4        6
```

Navamsa Chart

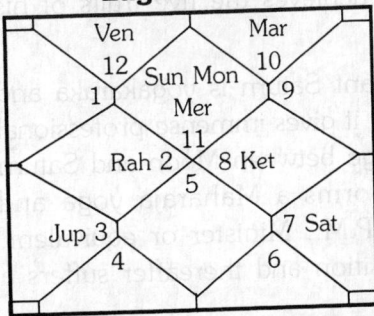

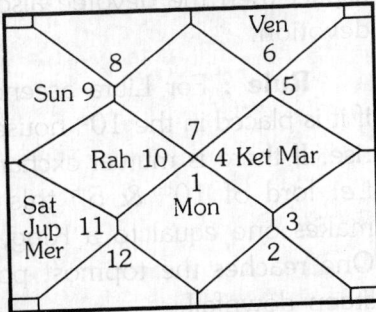

```
                         Ven
            8              6
                            5
      Sun 9        7
         Rah 10      4 Ket Mar
      Sat            1
      Jup 11   Mon        3
      Mer       12       2
```

Balance of Vimshottari Dasa of **Jup 13Y 6M 15D**

In Swami Ram Krishna Paramhansa's birth chart Saturn, lord of lagna and the 12th house is situated in the 9th house in exalted sign of Libra and is aspected by Jupiter, whose benefic aspect is on both the ascendant and its lord Saturn, which gave the native unfathomable devotion to God and spiritual power.

Lord of the 9th and 4th Venus, is yogakaraka is situated in its exalted sign Pisces. Lord of the 10th and 3rd Mars is also in the 12th house in the exalted sign of Capricorn. Saturn, therefore, alongwith Mars and Venus in their respective exalted signs made the native the world's greatest yogi and conferred Siddhi on him.

If Saturn, being the lord of the 4th, is placed in the 9th, then also it produces devotion to God and faults and belief in him. This is possible for the native of Scorpio and Libra ascendant.

When ascendant is Libra, lord of the 9th Mercury is in 4th, and lord of the 4th Saturn is in the 9th then also the native is devoted to good. If such a Saturn is being aspected by Jupiter then feeling of renunciation is very strong. Saturn in the 9th house lessens materialistic desires and worldly concerns. It inspires religious and pious feelings in the native's heart. If Saturn also receives the benefit of Jupiter's aspect then the devotee also achieves the five fruits of his devotion.

Rule : For Libra ascendant Saturn is yogakaraka and if it is placed in the 10th house, it gives immense professional rise. If there is mutual exchange between Moon and Saturn *i.e.* lord of 10th & 5th this forms a Maharaja yoga and makes one equal to a King, P.M., Minister or equivalent. One reaches the topmost position and thereafter suffers a steep downfall.

Swami Vivekanand

Illustration : 9.11   Horoscope No.: 33

Date of birth : 12.01.1863   Time of birth : 06:33:00 hrs
Place of birth :   Lat 22:40 N Long 88:30 E
Ayanamsa   : 21:56:57   Sidereal Time : 13:57:03

Pln	Degree	Rasi	Nakshatra	Pad
Asc	25:58:38	Sag	Purvasadha	4
Sun	29:25:21	Sag	Uttarasadha	1
Mon	17:26:24	Vir	Hasta	3
Mar	6:19:23	Ari	Aswini	2
Mer (C)	11:46:19	Cap	Sravna	1
Jup	4:00:49	Lib	Chitra	4
Ven (C)	7:06:07	Cap	Uttarasadha	4
Sat	13:34:24	Vir	Hasta	2

Rah (R)   23:34:13   Sco   Jyestha   3
Ket (R)   23:34:13   Tau   Mrigshira   1

Lagna Chart   **Navamsa Chart**

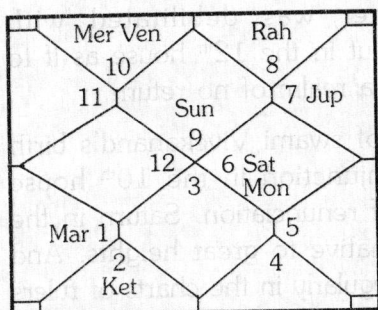

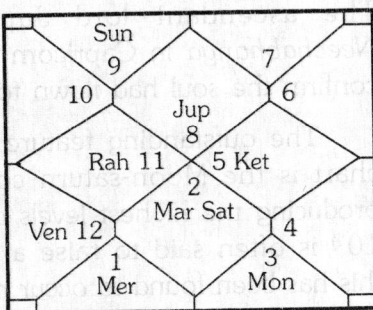

	Mer Ven 10	Rah 8	
11	Sun 9	7 Jup	
12	3	6 Sat Mon	5
Mar 1 2 Ket			4

	Sun 9		7
10	Jup 8	6	
Rah 11	2	5 Ket	
Ven 12 1 Mer		Mar Sat	3 Mon 4

Balance of Vimshottari Dasa of **Moon 4Y 5M 1D**

Nearly a hundred years ago, the Sun set in the spiritual horizon of the world when that lion among renunciates, Swami Vivekanand, the kingly *sanyasi* of India who took the immortal spiritual wisdom of the country to the west, gave up his body on July 4, 1902. He was in excellent health. Jupiter, the *lagna* lord, aspecting the 3rd made death come, but only at his bidding when he knew his life's task had been completed and he could harken back to those heavenly realms from where he had come.

A week before the end Swami Vivekanand had asked Swami Sudhanand, a brother monk, to bring him the Bengali almanac. He went through it carefully. He was found to be studying the almanac keenly on several occasions later as if looking for something auspicious. Only after his passing away did it occur to his brother disciples that he was selecting an auspicious day for his departure as Sri Ramkrishna had done before him. The last day of the lunar month of *vishakha*, an *amavasya*, was current when the body was shed. The *Manahkaraka* Moon ruling the embodied ego or mind was fast merging and dissolving into the Sun, the *Atmakaraka* ruling the Universal Consciousness. And the rising sign at 9-10 p.m. when his spiritual event occurred was Pisces in Cancer *Navamsa*. The ascendant lord Jupiter was debilitated with *Neechabhanga* in Capricorn but in the 12th house as if to confirm the soul had flown to a realm of no return.

The outstanding feature of swami Vivekanand's birth chart is the Moon-saturn conjunction in the 10th house producing the highest levels of renunciation. Saturn in the 10th is often said to raise a native to great heights. And this has been found to occur regularly in the charts of rulers and leaders. But the same Saturn in the 10th house rarely rests quietly before hurtling down the native mercilessly to abysmal depths of humiliation and defeat. There is mutual exchange between the 10th lord mercury and 2nd lord Saturn which elevated him due to his powerful sermons and preaching. However, Jupiter aspects the 5th house and 5th lord Mars blessed Vivekanand with a powerful, creative and deep understanding about the spiritualism and the all mighty. The 9th lord the Sun joins the ascendant and ascendant lord joins the 11th house whereas the 11th lord and the 10th lord are associated with each other in the 2nd house which provided him a handsome appearance and strong and influential speech. However, Swami Vivekanand never suffered any kind of downfall, defeat or destruction, in spite of Saturn in the 10th house because the 9th, the 10th and *lagna* lords are strongly placed in the birth chart. Saturn obtains the *navamsa* of Jupiter identical with the Moon's constellation *Hasta* whereas moon occupies its own constellation *Hasta*. We have always specified in our writings that if the 8th and the 6th house is associated with 10th house and their lords are well fortified and unafflicted, the aspects of the 10th house is promoted. This is true that the conjunction of *Maraka* planets the Saturn and Moon in the 10th house resulted into his untimely death of Swami Vivekanand at a young age. Thus, it should be properly borne in mind that Saturn in the 10th house does not bring destruction, defeat or steep downfall as is generally believed by astrologers.

The downfall occurs with Saturn's power to hurtle one down, confined to political and materialistic careers alone. But in the charts of those who work for the weal of humanity, Saturn in the 10th house becomes an unparalleled benefic conferring its blessings endlessly. Such natives mesmerise crowds with their spiritual strength and draw the highest respect and reverence for their blemishes renunciation. Swami Vivekanand is a good illustration of such a Saturn.

Wherever Swami Vivekanand went, he never failed to attract the masses. He left them electrified and inspired as never before with his speeches that dazzled both the illiterate as well as the intellectual. Thousands of people fell on top of each other to get close and pay their respects to him. Perhaps no one in that period had such a magnetic influence on the masses as swami Vivekanand. And Saturn in the 10th house must be credited for it.

According to *Jaataka Parijata* (15-20), if Saturn or lord of the ascendant aspect the lord of the sign occupied by Moon, one becomes a mendicant. Here, the lord of the sign occupied by Moon, Mercury, is not aspected by Saturn or *Lagna* lord Jupiter. But Saturn influences Mercury deeply by the *Parivartan* between the two planets, fulfilling the conditions for monkhood. According to 15-40, when the Moon occupies a *Drekanna* of Saturn and is aspected by that planet, it leads to renunciation of the world. Here, the Moon occupies the 2nd *Drekanna* of Virgo which is ruled by Saturn. Instead of being aspected by Saturn, the Moon is with Saturn.

Born to an aristocratic but pious and noble couple,
Vivekanand who was earlier known as Narendra Nath Datta
and endearingly called Noren, had Sagittarius rising in the
ascendant producing in him a stately soul, noble and
magnanimous. Consistent with the fiery nature of
Sagittarius, Naren was a brilliant, outspoken youth
who impressed everyone he met with his silvery speech
and piercing intellect. The 2nd house, *Vakstana*, has
Mercury, Venus and *vargottama* Sun while 2nd lord Saturn
is with the Moon- an ideal combination for extraordinary
eloquence.

Gautam Buddha

Illustration : 9.12   *Horoscope No.: 34*

Date of birth : 14.04.0623   Time of birth : 11:00:00 hrs
Place of birth : Kapilvastu   Lat 27:08 N Long 83:05 E
Ayanamsa   : 12:33:06   Sidereal Time : 23:59:27

Pln	Degree	Rasi	Nakshatra	Pad
Asc	24:06:20	Can	Aslesa	3
Sun	28:58:56	Ari	Krittika	1
Mon	14:25:29	Lib	Swati	3
Mar (D)	26:03:34	Ari	Bharani	4
Mer	20:54:27	Tau	Rohini	4
Jup	9:43:24	Ari	Aswini	3
Ven	3:29:08	Ari	Aswini	2
Sat (C)	24:58:10	Ari	Bharani	4
Rah (R)	24:29:07	Gem	Punarvasu	2
Ket (R)	24:29:07	Sag	Purvasadha	4

Lagna Chart

```
        Rah
   5     3
 6         2 Mer
     4
       Ven Jup
 Mon 7  1 Mar Sun
    10     Sat
   8        12
  9        11
  Ket
```

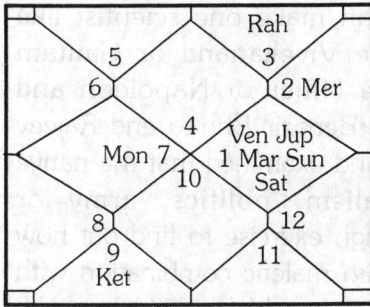

Navamsa Chart

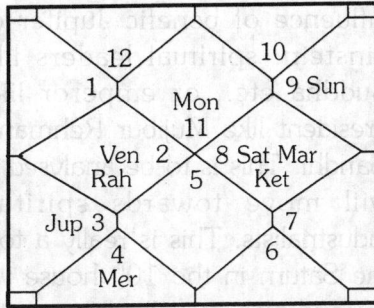

```
    12      10
  1            9 Sun
       Mon
        11
   Ven 2   8 Sat Mar
   Rah  5     Ket
  Jup 3        7
       4       6
      Mer
```

Balance of Vimshottari Dasa of **Rah 7Y 6M 9D**

Gautam Buddha was the founder of Buddhism. He was born in Cancer ascendant with Saturn in the 10th. Mars, Saturn, Jupiter, Venus and the Sun in the 10th house as well. Moon occupies the 4th house in Libra and has given rise to *Adhi yoga, Ruchhaka Mahapurusha Raja Yoga, Dharmakarmadhipati Yoga. Kuhu Yoga, Gajkesari Yoga, Chattus Sagar Yoga, Amsavatara yoga, chamar Yoga, Kendra Trikona Raja Yoga, Guru Mangal Yoga,* etc, are present in this birth chart. Here Saturn obtains *Neecha Bhanga raja Yoga* and obtains the *navamsa* of Mars. The Sun is exalted in its own constellation *Kritika* whereas Mars and Saturn are closely associated in *Bharini* constellation corresponding with Scorpio *navamsa*. Venus obtains own *navamsa*. This is extremely powerful birth chart with the placement of Saturn in the 10th house. Gautam Buddha is honoured as a reincarnation. Thus, we see that Saturn's placement in the 10th house has made the native a spiritual head of a very high order and founder of a religion and he has been the most recognised spiritual leader. Placement of Saturn in the 10th in the birth chart of Gautam Buddha, Guru Nanak, Swami Vivekanand, Prophet Mohammad, Guru Govind Singh, etc., made them spiritual leaders, heads or founders of one or another religion.

Therefore, Saturn's placement in the 10th house under the influence of benefic Jupiter can make one scientist like Einstein, spiritual leaders like Vivekanand or Gautam Buddha etc., or emperor like Hitler or Napoleon and president like Mujibur Rehman, Benazir Bhutto and Rajeev Gandhi. This is to be analysed and examined that the native will move towards spiritualism, politics, army or industrialists. This is really a tough exercise to find out how the Saturn in the 10th house with malefic combination with various planets will take a native to which particular field. Anyway, natives will reach dizzy heights in their respective fields.

Sant Namdeo

Illustration : 9.13   Horoscope No.: 35

Date of birth : 26.10.1210   Time of birth : 06:00:00 hrs
Place of birth : Pandharpur   Lat 17:42 N Long 75:24 E
Ayanamsa   : 12:51:31   Sidereal Time : 8:43:51

Pln	Degree	Rasi	Nakshatra	Pad
Asc	25:47:28	Lib	Vishakha	2
Sun	26:38:58	Lib	Vishakha	2
Mon	10:42:29	Cap	Sravna	1
Mar	4:33:58	Vir	U Phalguni	3
Mer (R/C)	2:23:39	Sco	Vishakha	4
Jup	3:22:43	Lib	Chitra	4
Ven	13:17:30	Sco	Anuradha	3
Sat	23:21:13	Can	Aslesa	3
Rah	14:10:29	Sag	Purvasadha	1
Ket	14:10:29	Gem	Ardra	3

Lagna Chart

```
        Mer Ven          Mar
          8               6
   Rah 9       Sun Jup        5
                   7
        Mon 10       4  Sat
                1
       11                  3 Ket
         12          2
```

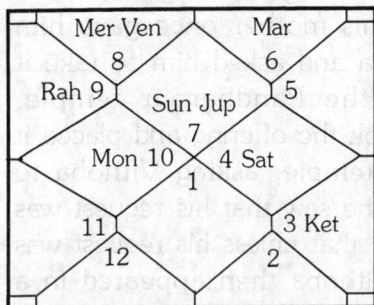

Navamsa Chart

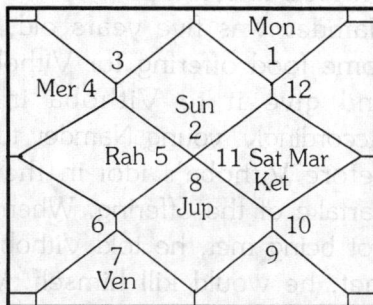

```
                          Mon
            3              1
    Mer 4        Sun          12
                  2
        Rah 5        11 Sat Mar
                8       Ket
            6    Jup
            7              10
          Ven          9
```

Balance of Vimshottari Dasa of **Moon 9Y 5M 19D**

Sant Namdev or Namdev was a prominent religious poet from the Marathwada region of Maharashtra state, India in the Hindu tradition, and was one the earliest writers in the Marathi language. He also wrote some hymns in the Hindi and the Punjabi languages during his about 25 years stay in Punjab. The village which was named after him is now in Pakistan's Punjab. Sixty-one of his compositions are included within Sikhism's holy scripture, the Guru Granth Sahib.

Namdev was born in the village of Naras Vamani, now located in the Satara District in Maharashtra. He was born to a tailor named Damasheti Relekar and his wife Gonai (Gunabai). Soon after his birth, his family moved to Pandharpur in the Solapur district of Maharashtra, where the prominent temple of the Hindu God Vitthal or Vithoba (form of Vishnu) is located. His parents were devotees of Vithoba.

At eleven, Namdev was married to Rajai (Rajabai), a daughter of Govindasheti Sadavarte. Namdev and Rajai had four sons and a daughter. (Some people claiming to be Namdev's descendants reside in Pandharpur.)

Since childhood, Namdev was an ardent devotee of

Vithoba like his parents. According to a legend, when Namdev was five years old, his mother once gave him some food offering for Vithoba and asked him to take it and give it to Vithoba in the Pandharpur temple. Accordingly, young Namdev took the offering and placed it before Vithoba's idol in the temple, asking Vithoba to partake of the offering. When he saw that his request was not being met, he told Vithoba that unless his request was met, he would kill himself. Vithoba then appeared in a personal form and partook of the offering in response to the utter devotion of young Namdev. (The place where, according to the legend, Namdev had waited for Vithoba to partake of the food offering is currently identified in that temple as "Namdev Payari", meaning Namdev's step.)

Namdev traveled through many parts of India, reciting his religious poems. He is said to have lived for more than twenty years in the village of Ghuman in the Gurdaspur district of Punjab, where a memorial commemorates him.

Namdev is regarded to have had a significant influence on the 17th century religious poet Tukaram of Maharashtra.

Namdev's devotional compositions (*"abhangas"*) have been collected in the document known as *Namdev's Gatha*. His work titled *"Teerthavalee"* contains his compositions concerning his travels in the company of Sant Dnyaneshwar.

Sant Namdeo was born in Libra ascendant with Saturn in the 10th house. Jupiter is in the ascendant and the 10th lord Moon falls in the 4th house. There is mutual exchange between Saturn and Moon which has given rise to *Chapa Yoga*. Many other auspicious yoga are present in the birth chart such as *Gaja Kesari yoga, Ubhayachari Yoga, Vasumati yoga,* etc. The Sun is *Atma Karaka* planet and that has obtained *Neecha Bhanga Raja yoga*. Saturn obtains own *navamsa* and Jupiter aspects the 9th house and obtains the *navamsa* of Mars. Mars obtains Saturn's *navamsa* and Venus obtains own *navamsa* which made Sant Namdeo that is a leading name among the true saints.

Sant Tukaram

Illustration : 9.14   *Horoscope No.: 36*
Date of birth : 21.01.1607   Time of birth : 10:00:00 hrs
Place of birth : Dehu   Lat 18:35 N Long 73:51 E
Ayanamsa   : 18:22:21   Sidereal Time : 18:04:13

Pln	Degree	Rasi	Nakshatra	Pad
Asc	12:58:35	Pis	U Bhadrapad	3
Sun	13:30:41	Cap	Sravna	2
Mon	25:15:17	Lib	Vishakha	2
Mar	8:05:43	Pis	U Bhadrapad	2
Mer (R)	28:39:19	Cap	Dhanistha	2
Jup	16:52:44	Aqu	Satabhisha	4
Ven (C)	4:18:02	Cap	Uttarasadha	3
Sat	23:57:16	Sag	Purvasadha	4
Rah (R)	25:07:19	Leo	P Phalguni	4
Ket (R)	25:07:19	Aqu	P Bhadrapad	2

Lagna Chart   Navamsa Chart

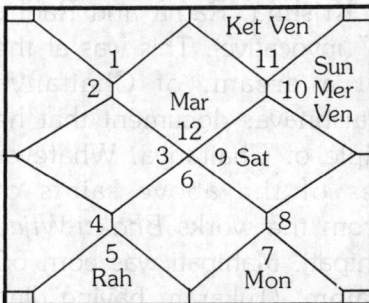

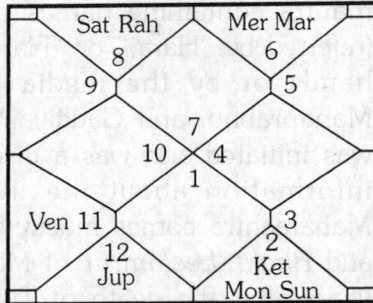

Balance of Vimshottari Dasa of **Jup 9Y 8M 10D**

Tukaram was born and lived most of his life in Dehu, a town close to Pune city in Maharashtra, India. He was born to a couple with the family name "Moray" - the descendent of the Mourya Clan (Ambile) and first names Bolhoba and Kanakai. Through a tradition in India in bygone days, Tukaram's family name is rarely used in identifying him. Rather, in accord with another tradition in India of assigning the epithet "sant" to persons regarded as thoroughly saintly, Tukaram is commonly known in Maharashtra as Sant Tukaram.

Scholars assign various birth years to Tukaram: 1577, 1598, 1608and 1609 CE. The year of Tukaram's death —1650 CE— is much more certain.

Tukaram's first wife, Rakhumabai, died in her early youth. Tukaram and his second wife, Jijabai (also known as Avali), had three sons: Santu or Mahadev, Vithoba, and Narayan.

Tukaram was a devotee of Lord Vittala or Vithoba — an incarnation of Lord Krishna.

Tukaram is considered as the climactic point of the *Bhagawat* Hindu tradition, which is thought to have begun in Maharashtra with Namdev. Dnyaneshwar, Namdev, Janabai, Eknath, and Tukaram are revered especially in the warakari sect in Maharashtra. He has received guru-mantra containing names of Krishna, Rama and Radha (referred by "Hara," or "Hare" invocative). This was at the hands or by the media of a dream, of Chaitanya Mahaprabhu, and Gaudiya Vaishnavas document that he was initiated and was a disciple of Chaitanya. Whatever information about the lives of the above saints of Maharashtra comes mostly from the works *Bhakti-Wijay* and *Bhakti-Leelamrut* of Mahipati. Mahipati was born 65 years after the death of Tukaram, (Tukaram having died 50 years, 300 years, and 353 years after the deaths of

Ekanath, Namdev, and Dnyaneshwar, respectively.) Thus, Mahipati undoubtedly based his life sketches of all the above saints primarily on hearsay.

Tukaram's public religious discourses used to be mixed, by tradition, with poetry, which included some of his own compositions. His discourses focussed on day-to-day behavior of human beings, and he emphasized that the true expression of religion was in a person's love for his fellow human beings rather than in ritualistic observance of religious orthodoxy, including mechanical study of the Vedas. His teachings encompassed a wide array of issues, including the importance of the ecosystem. Tukaram worked for his society's enlightenment in the "warakari" tradition, which emphasizes community service and musical group worship.

Like Namdev, Janabai, and Eknath, Tukaram wrote in archaic Marathi a large number of devotional poems identified in Marathi as *abhang*. A collection of 4,500 *abhang* known as the *Gatha* is attributed to Tukaram. *Mantra Geeta*, a Marathi translation in *abhang* form of the Sanskrit Bhagavad Geeta, is also attributed to him. It is an interpretation of Geeta from a *Bhakti—*devotional—perspective.

Sant Tukaram was born in Pisces ascendant with Saturn in the 10th house. 10th lord Jupiter is posited in the 12th house whereas the Sun, Mercury and Venus occupy the 11th house. 9th lord Mars is posited in the ascendant in Pisces. Thus, both the malefics Mars and Saturn fall in the sign of Jupiter. There is the mutual exchange that is *Vinimay Parivartan Raja yoga* between Jupiter and Saturn which places the name of Sant Tukaram in the galaxy of the few most honoured saints of India.

When Saturn is not placed in the 10th house but rules the native in some other way.

K.D.Singh 'Babu'

Illustration : 9.15   Horoscope No.: 37
Date of birth : 02.02.1923   Time of birth : 04:00:00 hrs
Place of birth : Barabanki   Lat 26:56 N Long 81:11 E
Ayanamsa   : 22:46:57   Sidereal Time : 11:39:08

Pln	Degree	Rasi	Nakshatra	Pad
Asc	4:31:45	Sag	Moola	2
Sun	19:16:50	Cap	Sravna	3
Mon	22:56:41	Can	Aslesa	2
Mar	15:36:22	Pis	U Bhadrapad	4
Mer (R/C)	10:55:26	Cap	Sravna	1
Jup	24:37:00	Lib	Vishakha	2
Ven	2:30:09	Sag	Moola	1
Sat (R)	27:19:07	Vir	Chitra	2
Rah (R)	28:13:13	Leo	U Phalguni	1
Ket (R)	28:13:13	Aqu	P Bhadrapad	3

Lagna Chart

```
          Sun Mer
            10            8
Ket 11              7 Jup
           Ven
            9
Mar 12    6 Sat
            3
    1              5 Rah
      2        4
            Mon
```

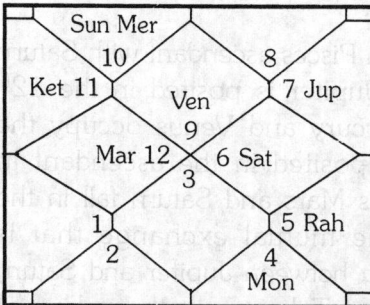

Navamsa Chart

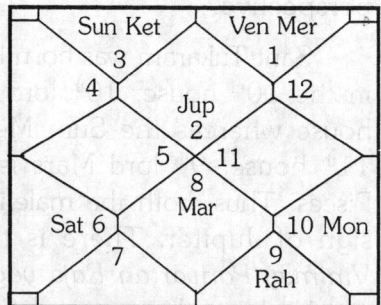

```
          Sun Ket      Ven Mer
            3             1
     4              12
           Jup
            2
        5      11
           8
           Mar
  Sat 6             10 Mon
      7        9
            Rah
```

Balance of Vimshottari Dasa of **Mer 8Y 11M 28D**

The name of K.D.Singh 'Babu' is immortal so far as Indian Hockey is concerned. There are stadiums on his name. He was born in Sagittarius ascendant with Saturn in the 10th house. There is mutual aspect between the 5th lord Mars and 3rd lord Saturn. Jupiter's aspect on the 5th house must be appreciated. However, Saturn is *atmakaraka* planet and obtains *vargottama navamsa*. 10th lord Mercury is placed in the 2nd house and 2nd lord Saturn occupies the 10th house thus, there is mutual exchange between Mercury and Saturn. This provided immense talent and skill of playing hockey to Mr. K.D.Singh. However, the 7th house is aspected by Jupiter, Venus, Mars and Saturn. In one or the other way all these planets are interrelated and influence each other. Placement of Saturn in the 10th house with exchange of the 10th lord raised K.D.Singh 'Babu' to the topmost height.

Jag Jivan Ram

Illustration : 9.16   *Horoscope No.: 38*

Date of birth : 05.04.1908   Time of birth : 11:00:00 hrs
Place of birth : Ara, Bihar   Lat 25:34 N Long 84:40 E
Ayanamsa   : 22:34:15   Sidereal Time : 0:01:09

Pln	Degree	Rasi	Nakshatra	Pad
Asc	18:27:53	Gem	Ardra	4
Sun	22:27:47	Pis	Revati	2
Mon	13:23:01	Tau	Rohini	2
Mar	6:07:30	Tau	Krittika	3
Mer	26:18:27	Aqu	P Bhadrapad	2
Jup	11:02:39	Can	Pushya	3
Ven	6:43:43	Tau	Krittika	4
Sat (C)	9:29:21	Pis	U Bhadrapad	2
Rah (R)	16:21:21	Gem	Ardra	3
Ket (R)	16:21:21	Sag	Purvasadha	1

Lagna Chart

```
       Jup        Mar Mon
        4           Ven
     5          \    2    /
        \   Rah     1
         \   3
          6    12 Sat
          9      Sun
         Ket
      7          11 Mer
      8             10
```

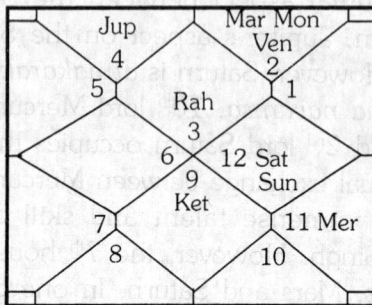

Navamsa Chart

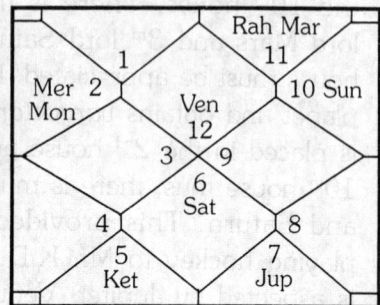

```
                  Rah Mar
           1        11
    Mer  2              10 Sun
    Mon        Ven
               12
             3    9
             6
          4    Sat    8
          5           7
         Ket         Jup
```

Balance of Vimshottari Dasa of Moon 7Y 5M 16D

Babu Jagjivan Ram, known popularly as Babuji was a freedom fighter and a social reformer hailing from the backward classes of Bihar in India. He was instrumental in foundation of the 'All-India Depressed Classes League', an organization dedicated to attaining equality for untouchables, in 1935 and was elected to Bihar Legislative Assembly in 1937, that is when he organized, rural labour movement.

In 1946, he became the youngest minister in Jawaharlal Nehru's provisional government, the First Union Cabinet of India as a Labour minister, and also a member of Constituent Assembly of India, where he ensured that social justice was enshrined in the Constitution. He went on serve as a minister in the Indian parliament with various portfolios for more than forty years as a member of Indian National Congress (INC), most importantly he was the Defence Minister of India during the Indo-Pak war of 1971, which resulted in formation of Bangladesh. His contribution to the Green Revolution in India and modernising Indian agriculture, during his two tenures as Union Agriculture Minister are still remembered, especial during 1974 drought when he was asked to hold the additional portfolio to tide over the food crisis. Though he supported Indira Gandhi during the

Emergency in India (1975-1977), he left Congress in 1977 and joined Janata Party alliance in 1977, along with his Congress for Democracy, he later served as the Deputy Prime Minister of India (1977-1979), then in 1980, he formed Congress (J). He is also famous for "forgetting to pay his taxes" during his years in power.

Name of Jagjivan Ram will remain immortal in the history of Indian politics. He was born in Gemini ascendant with Saturn in the 10th house identical to Pisces. Saturn is associated with inimical the Sun but it is aspected by natal, exalted Jupiter. We have already spoken that Saturn in the 10th house if aspected by Jupiter or Venus, or if it is associated with any of these the results of the 10th house will be largely pronounced. The 9th lord Saturn occupies the 10th house under the benefic aspect of 10th lord Jupiter. This is remarkable *Raja yoga* called *Dharmakarmadhipati yoga* or *Navam Dhasham Sambandh Raja yoga*. This position of Saturn must be highly appreciated in any birth chart. Jagjivam Ram rose to the position of Deputy Prime Minister of India and remained unbeaten throughout as Railway Minister. Here Saturn obtains the *navamsa* of Mercury and falls in own constellation *Uttara Bhadrapada*. Saturn is unaspected by any malefic planet. Thus, Saturn raised the native Jagjivam Ram to the dizzy heights and there was no merciless fall as it has been observed by a number of most recognised, reputed and world famous astrologers of India.

We want to revise the research with regard to the Saturn of the 10th house that it brings miserable and steep fall from the dizzy heights. In fact, in a few birth charts like that of Adolf Hitler, Napoleon Bonaparte, Benazir Bhutto, Richard Nixon, Woodrow Wilson, Sheikh Mujibur Rehman, Martin Luther King Jr., etc. Saturn was posited in the 10th house and they rose to the unexpected heights and became the Head of the State. There had been one or the other tragedies with these world famous personalities which brought the end of their era. After examination of number of such birth charts it was established that Saturn in the 10th house helps the native in his rise to the top most position and thereafter this Saturn throws the native to the bottom. This belief is very firm among all the scholars of astrology. Let us further verify this research work by the examination and verification of a few horoscopes of top level persons having Saturn in the 10th house.

We humbly opine that Saturn of the 10th house may bring downfall, destruction and death only if it is afflicted in one or the other way. If Saturn of the 10th house is aspected or associated by Jupiter or Venus or the 10th lord, Mercury and is unaspected by malefic or *Trika* lords, there will not be any destruction, death or downfall though the native will attain the highest place in his field of work. Jagjivam Ram and Albert Einstein both were born in Gemini ascendant with Saturn in the 10th house under the influence of benefic Jupiter, both are very famous personalities without any suffering and dethronement.

Kalraj Misra

Illustration : 9.17   *Horoscope No.: 39*

Date of birth : 22.11.1938   Time of birth : 19:33:54 hrs
Place of birth : Ghazipur   Lat 25:36 N Long 83:36 E
Ayanamsa   : 23:00:24   Sidereal Time : 23:41:53

Pln	Degree	Rasi	Nakshatra	Pad
Asc	13:45:21	Gem	Ardra	3
Sun	6:36:44	Sco	Anuradha	1
Mon (C)	13:16:27	Sco	Anuradha	3
Mar	24:49:49	Vir	Chitra	1
Mer	28:05:24	Sco	Jyestha	4

Jup	1:18:33	Aqu	Dhanistha	3
Ven (R/C)	2:52:37	Sco	Vishakha	4
Sat (R)	18:39:53	Pis	Revati	1
Rah (R/C)	24:52:01	Lib	Vishakha	2
Ket (R)	24:52:01	Ari	Bharani	4

Lagna Chart

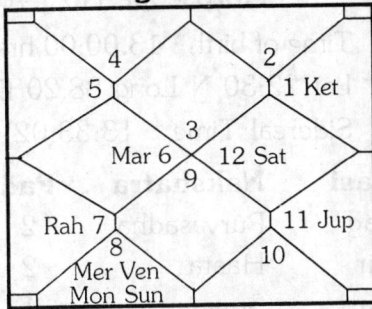

Navamsa Chart

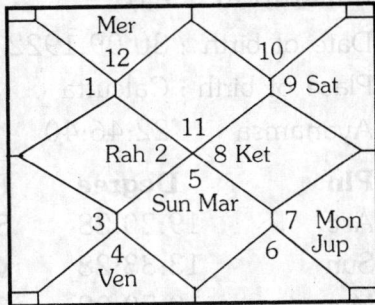

Balance of Vimshottari Dasa of **Sat   4Y 10M 0D**

Kalraj Mishra is an Indian politician and a senior leader of Bharatiya Janata Party (BJP). He was President of Uttar Pradesh state unit of BJP.

Born in 1938 in Ghazipur District of Uttar Pradesh and he passed M.A. from Kashi Vidyapeeth, Varanasi. He joined politics and held many party positions at state and national level. He was Cabinet Minister in Government of Uttar Pradesh holding the portfolios of Public Works, Medical Education and Tourism during March 1997-August 2000 period. He was widely regarded as an incompetent minister. He is currently a member of Rajya Sabha.

Kalraj Misra was Gemini ascendant with Saturn in the 10th house in Pisces. 10th lord Jupiter occupies the 9th house and the 9th lord Saturn falls in the 10th house. This *Dharamakarmadhi yoga* had helped him in reaching to an honourable position and becoming a minister in BJP government. Saturn is undoubtedly strong and obtains 1.26

Shadabala. However, Mars who is the lord of 7th and 12th house occupies the 4th house and aspects Saturn and that has done lot of harm to him. This restricted him to become the Chief Minister.

Hrishikesh Mukherjee

Illustration : 9.18   *Horoscope No.: 40*

Date of birth : 30.09.1922   Time of birth : 13:00:00 hrs
Place of birth : Calcutta   Lat 22:30 N Long 88:20 E
Ayanamsa   : 22:46:40   Sidereal Time : 13:33:02

Pln	Degree	Rasi	Nakshatra	Pad
Asc	19:20:28	Sag	Purvasadha	2
Sun	13:33:28	Vir	Hasta	2
Mon	10:50:02	Cap	Sravna	1
Mar	17:03:06	Sag	Purvasadha	2
Mer	6:56:13	Lib	Swati	1
Jup	1:29:38	Lib	Chitra	3
Ven	28:57:24	Lib	Vishakha	3
Sat (C)	17:21:18	Vir	Hasta	3
Rah (C)	7:04:04	Vir	U Phalguni	4
Ket	7:04:04	Pis	U Bhadrapad	2

Lagna Chart

```
        Mon
        10        8
    11            7  Mer
          Mar        Jup
           9         Ven
    Ket 12    6 Sat Sun
           3     Rah
      1         5
        2     4
```

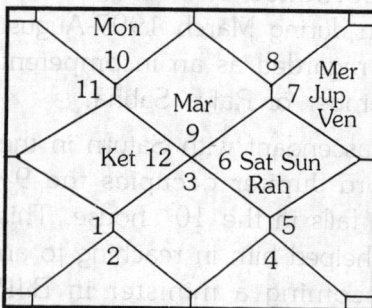

Navamsa Chart

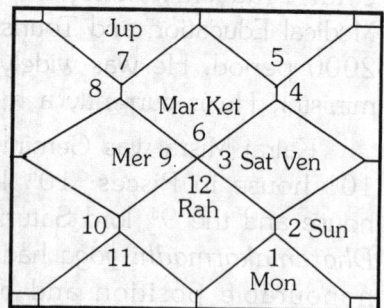

```
        Jup
        7         5
    8             4
        Mar Ket
           6
      Mer 9    3 Sat Ven
           12
           Rah
    10          2 Sun
        11     1
             Mon
```

Balance of Vimshottari Dasa of **Moon** **9Y 4M 15D**

Hrishikesh Mukherjee was a famous Hindi film director known for a number of films, including *Satyakam, Chupke Chupke, Anupama, Anand, Abhimaan, Guddi, Gol Maal, Aashirwad, Bawarchi* and *Namak Haraam*.

Popularly known as *Hrishi-da*, he directed 42 films during his career spanning over four decades, and is named the pioneer of the 'middle cinema' of India. Renowned for his social films that reflected the changing middle-class ethos, Mukherjee "carved a middle path between the extravagance of mainstream cinema and the stark relism of art cinema".

He also remained the chairman of the Central Board of Film Certification (CBFC) and of the National Film Development Corporation (NFDC), and was awarded the 1999, Dada Saheb Phalke Award, India's highest award in Cinema for Lifetime achievement.

He was born in Sagittarius ascendant with Saturn in the 10th house in Virgo. Saturn is associated with the 9th lord the Sun and falls over the axis of Rahu and Ketu. Saturn obtains Gemini *navamsa* in association with Venus and it is extremely powerful as it obtains 1.52 *shadabala*. All the three benefics Jupiter, Venus and Mercury fall in the 11th house in Libra and lend their favourable aspect over the 5th house. Venus is *Atma Karaka* planet and is the significator or film career. Mercury indicates talent, intelligence and skill in the field of film making, direction, acting, etc., which made him an outstanding director and an intellectual. Saturn's position in the 10th house rose him to the position he achieved by his own endeavours.

Munshi Premchand

Illustration : 9.19   *Horoscope No.: 41*

Date of birth : 31.07.1880   Time of birth : 06:00:00 hrs
Place of birth : Varanasi   Lat 25:20 N Long 83:00 E
Ayanamsa   : 22:11:40   Sidereal Time : 2:36:02

Pln	Degree	Rasi	Nakshatra	Pad
Asc	22:23:18	Can	Aslesa	2
Sun	15:55:39	Can	Pushya	4
Mon	8:26:52	Tau	Krittika	4
Mar	14:02:53	Leo	P Phalguni	1
Mer (R/C)	24:58:51	Can	Aslesa	3
Jup	27:14:04	Pis	Revati	4
Ven (C)	20:37:54	Can	Aslesa	2
Sat	6:40:15	Ari	Aswini	3
Rah	13:57:28	Sag	Purvasadha	1
Ket	13:57:28	Gem	Ardra	3

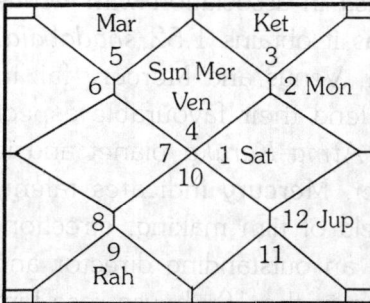

Lagna Chart   Navamsa Chart

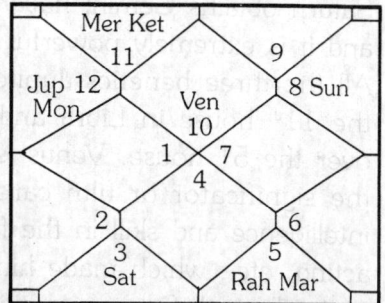

Balance of Vimshottari Dasa of **Sun   0Y 8M 11D**

Munshi Premchand was a famous writer of modern Hindi-Urdu literature. In India, he is generally recognized as the foremost Hindi-Urdu writer during the early twentieth century.

Premchand was born on July 31, 1880 in the village Lamhi near Varanasi to Munshi Ajaib Lal, a clerk in the post office, and his wife Anandi. His parents named him Dhanpat Rai ("master of wealth") while his uncle, Mahabir, a rich landowner, called him Nawab (Prince), the name Premchand first chose to write under. His early education was at a local madarsa under a maulvi, where he studied Urdu. Premchand's parents died young - his mother when he was seven and his father while he was sixteen or seventeen and still a student. Premchand was left responsible for his stepmother and step-siblings.

Premchand wrote about 300 short stories and several novels as well as many essays and letters. He also wrote plays and did some translations. Many of Premchand's stories have been translated into English and Russian.

Godaan (The Gift of a Cow), his last novel, is considered one of the finest Hindi novels. The protagonist, Hori, a poor peasant, desperately longs for a cow, a symbol of wealth and prestige in rural India. The story depicts the human beings' deep-rooted beliefs, and their ability to survive and uphold these beliefs despite great misery.

In *Kafan* (Shroud), a poor man collects money for the funeral rites of his dead wife, but spends it on food and drink.

Some criticize Premchand's writings as full of too many deaths and too much misery. They believe Premchand does not stand anywhere near the contemporary literary giants of India like Sharat Chandra Chattopadhyay and Rabindranath Tagore. But it should be noted that many of Premchand's stories were influenced by his own experiences with poverty and misery. His stories represented the ordinary Indian people as they were, without any embellishments. Unlike many other contemporary writers, his works didn't have any "hero" or "Mr. Nice" - they described people as they were.

Premchand was a contemporary of some other literary giants of that era like Acharya Ram Chandra Shukla and Jaishankar Prasad.

Premchand was born in Cancer ascendant with Saturn in the 10th house in the sign of its debilitation. However, Saturn obtains *Neechabhanga Raja Yoga*. 9th lord Jupiter occupies the 9th house itself and Jupiter aspects the ascendant, the Sun, Mercury and Venus. Saturn is unaspected by any malefic planet. However, Saturn is strongest planet as it obtains 1.5 *shadabala* and falls in the *navamsa* of Mercury. 10th lord Mars that is posited in Leo under *vargottam navamsa* and this combination made him the world famous novelist and story writer. *Graha Malika Raja yoga, Ubhayachari yoga, Vasumati yoga, Durdhara yoga, Vinimay Parivartan Raja yoga* (exchange of 11th lord and lagna lord), *Ekawali Yoga,Chaamar yoga, Lakshmi yoga, Anshaavtaar yoga*, etc., are present in the birth chart. Thus it can be seen that strong Saturn in the 10th house resulted into unusual success of Premchand as a writer and novelist. He became very famous and successful in his lifetime and thereafter as well. All his books, stories, novels etc., have been translated in various languages. There is no hesitation in saying that Premchand was like a King among story writers.

Medha Patkar

Illustration : 9.20　　　　　　　Horoscope No.: 42

Date of birth : 01.12.1954　　Time of birth : 11:00:00 hrs
Place of birth : Bombay　　　　Lat 18:58 N Long 72:50 E
Ayanamsa　　 : 23:13:54　　　Sidereal Time : 14:59:29

Pln	Degree	Rasi	Nakshatra	Pad
Asc	12:32:15	Cap	Sravna	1
Sun	15:15:31	Sco	Anuradha	4
Mon	18:54:33	Cap	Sravna	3
Mar	4:34:31	Aqu	Dhanistha	4
Mer (C)	2:02:58	Sco	Vishakha	4
Jup (R)	6:22:51	Can	Pushya	1
Ven (R)	21:53:29	Lib	Vishakha	1
Sat	21:56:30	Lib	Vishakha	1
Rah	12:37:36	Sag	Moola	4
Ket	12:37:36	Gem	Ardra	2

Lagna Chart

```
        Mar        Rah
        11          9
   12            8   Mer
        Mon            Sun
         10
      1    7 Sat Ven
       4
      Jup
    2              6
      3         5
     Ket
```

Navamsa Chart

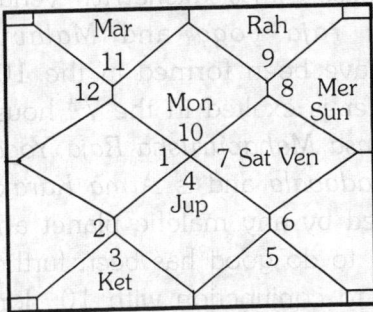

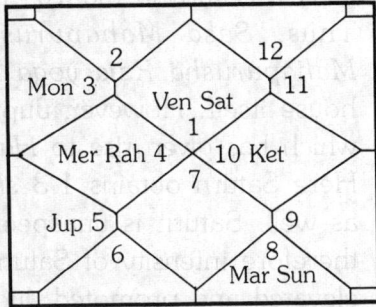

```
           2          12
   Mon 3              11
         Ven Sat
              1
   Mer Rah 4    10 Ket
              7
   Jup 5            9
        6        8
             Mar Sun
```

Balance of Vimshottari Dasa of **Moon 3Y 3M 24D**

Medha Patkar was born in Mumbai, India to Indu and Vasant Khanolkar, a trade union leader and freedom fighter. She was raised by politically and socially active parents. Her father actively fought in the Indian Independence Movement. Medha's mother was a member of Swadar, an organization setup to help and assist women suffering difficult circumstances arising out of financial, educational, and health related problems. Her parents' activism played a role in shaping her philosophical views.

She got her M.A. in Social Work from Tata Institute of Social Sciences (TISS).

Medha Patkar is one of the recipients of Right Livelihood Award for the year 1991. She received the 1999 M.A.Thomas National Human Rights Award from Vigil India Movement. She has also received numerous other awards, including the Deena Nath Mangeshkar Award, Mahatma Phule Award, Goldman Environment Prize, Green Ribbon Award for Best International Political Campaigner by BBC, and the Human Rights Defender's Award from Amnesty International. She was also a Commissioner to the World Commission on Dams.

Medha Patkar was born in Capricorn ascendant with exalted Saturn in the 10th house with *swakshetriya* Venus. Thus, *Sasa Mahapurush raja yoga* and *Malavya Mahapurusha Raja yoga* have been formed in the 10th house itself. However, Jupiter is exalted in the 7th house which has given rise to *Hamsa Mahapurusha Raja Yoga*. Here Saturn obtains 1.3 *shadabala* and is *Atma Karaka* as well. Saturn is unaspected by any malefic planet and therefore intensity of Saturn to do good has been further elevated and promoted due to conjunction with 10th lord and *yogakaraka* Venus. The combination of Saturn and Venus in Libra in the 10th house is exceptionally auspicious which has given a lot of fame, honour and success in her endeavours. The inference may be derived that Saturn if associated with Venus or Jupiter in the 10th house or these planets are in mutual *Kendra* with Saturn in the 10th house or Venus and Jupiter are posited in the triangles with Saturn in the 10th house the progress and success of the native will be there speedily without any blemish or destruction.

Sir Charlie Chaplin

Illustration : 9.21   *Horoscope No.: 43*

Date of birth : 16.04.1889   Time of birth : 20:00:00 hrs
Place of birth : London   Lat 51:30 N Long 00:05 E
Ayanamsa   : 22:18:22   Sidereal Time : 9:40:17

Pln	Degree	Rasi	Nakshatra	Pad
Asc	16:19:53	Lib	Swati	3
Sun	4:41:39	Ari	Aswini	2
Mon	17:05:27	Lib	Swati	4
Mar (C)	21:15:53	Ari	Bharani	3
Mer (C)	25:30:02	Pis	Revati	3
Jup	15:51:47	Sag	Purvasadha	1
Ven (R)	25:48:23	Ari	Bharani	4
Sat	21:07:23	Can	Aslesa	2
Rah (R)	23:08:00	Gem	Punarvasu	1
Ket (R)	23:08:00	Sag	Purvasadha	3

Lagna Chart	Navamsa Chart

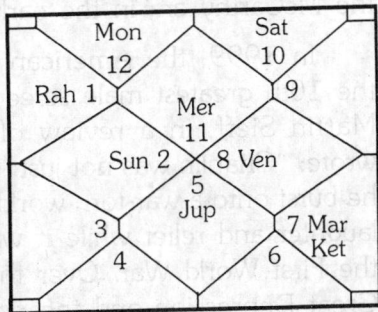

Lagna Chart:
```
          8           6
   Ket  9              5
   Jup       Mon
              7
         10      4  Sat
              1
             Ven
   11     Sun Mar    3  Rah
      12              2
      Mer
```

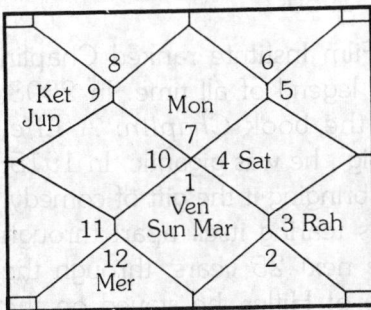

Navamsa Chart:
```
         Mon         Sat
          12          10
   Rah 1              9
            Mer
             11
         Sun 2   8 Ven
              5
             Jup
        3              7 Mar
           4      6    Ket
```

Balance of Vimshottari Dasa of **Rah 3Y 11M 3D**

Sir Charles Spencer "Charlie" Chaplin, KBE was an English comic actor and film director of the silent film era, and became one of the best-known film stars in the world before the end of the First World War. Chaplin used mime, slapstick and other visual comedy routines, and continued well into the era of the talkies, though his films decreased in frequency from the end of the 1920s. His most famous role was that of The Tramp, which he first played in the Keystone comedy *Kid Auto Races at Venice* in 1914. From the April 1914 one-reeler *Twenty Minutes of Love* onwards he was writing and directing most of his films, by 1916 he was also producing, and from 1918 composing the music. With Mary Pickford, Douglas Fairbanks and D. W. Griffith, he co-founded United Artists in 1919.

Chaplin was one of the most creative and influential personalities of the silent-film era. He was influenced by his predecessor, the French silent movie comedian Max Linder, to whom he dedicated one of his films. His working life in entertainment spanned over 75 years, from the Victorian stage and the Music Hall in the United Kingdom as a child performer, until close to his death at the age of 88. His high-profile public and private life encompassed both adulation and controversy. Chaplin's identification with the left ultimately forced him to resettle in Europe during the McCarthy era in the early 1950s.

In 1999, the American Film Institute ranked Chaplin the 10th greatest male screen legend of all time. In 2008, Martin Sieff, in a review of the book *Chaplin: A Life*, wrote: "Chaplin was not just 'big', he was gigantic. In 1915, he burst onto a war-torn world bringing it the gift of comedy, laughter and relief while it was tearing itself apart through the First World War. Over the next 25 years, through the Great Depression and the rise of Hitler, he stayed on the job. It is doubtful any individual has ever given more entertainment, pleasure and relief to so many human beings when they needed it the most". George Bernard Shaw called Chaplin "the only genius to come out of the movie industry".

Sir Charlie Chaplin was born in Libra ascendant with Saturn in the 10ᵗʰ house in Cancer. 10ᵗʰ lord Moon occupies the ascendant and the ascendant lord Venus aspects the ascendant and the Moon. Saturn obtains own *navamsa* and falls in the constellation of Mercury. Saturn is aspected by 2ⁿᵈ and 7ᵗʰ lord Mars. However, the aspect of Jupiter on the ascendant lord Venus, 7ᵗʰ lord Mars and 11ᵗʰ lord the Sun is extremely auspicious and has minimised the adversity of malefic Mars. Placement of the *yogakaraka* Saturn in the 10ᵗʰ house made Chrlie Chaplin most powerful and successful actor of his time. He acting was appreciated by one and all throughout the globe. He won Oscar awards for his performance from time to time. In other words, Sir Charlie Chaplin was crowned king of the Film Industry. Mutual aspect between Saturn and Mars resulted in various problems around the end of his life at 60 years of age. His health started detoriating rapidly and later was not able to communicate and walk as well. He was confined to wheel chair for his last 7 years of life. He died in sleep.

H.G.Wells

Illustration : 9.22   *Horoscope No.: 44*

Date of birth : 21.09.1866   Time of birth : 15:33:00 hrs
Place of birth : Bromley   Lat 51:20 N Long 00:05 E
Ayanamsa   : 21:59:46   Sidereal Time : 15:34:27

Pln	Degree	Rasi	Nakshatra	Pad
Asc	0:07:03	Cap	Uttarasadha	2
Sun	6:24:02	Vir	U Phalguni	3
Mon	28:33:44	Cap	Dhanistha	2
Mar	14:31:36	Gem	Ardra	3
Mer (C)	26:57:42	Leo	U Phalguni	1
Jup	0:26:24	Cap	Uttarasadha	2

Ven	22:41:29	Lib	Vishakha	1
Sat	17:43:14	Lib	Swati	4
Rah (R/C)	10:52:25	Vir	Hasta	1
Ket (R)	10:52:25	Pis	U Bhadrapad	3

Lagna Chart

```
          11              9
   Ket 12      Mon Jup       8
              10
              1
              4
              7 Sat Ven
      2                  6 Sun
      3              5      Rah
      Mar           Mer
```

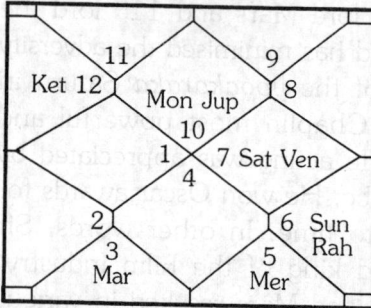

Navamsa Chart

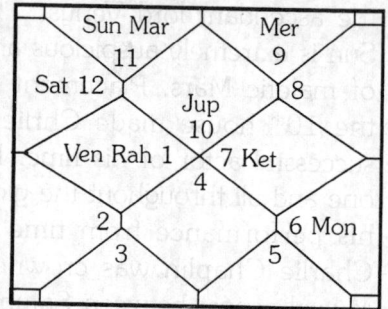

```
          Sun Mar         Mer
             11            9
   Sat 12      Jup           8
              10
   Ven Rah 1
              4
              7 Ket
      2                  6 Mon
      3              5
```

Balance of Vimshottari Dasa of **Mars   4Y 3M 1D**

Herbert George Wells was an English author, now best known for his work in the science fiction genre. He was also a prolific writer in many other genres, including contemporary novels, history, politics and social commentary. Together with Jules Verne, Wells has been referred to as "The Father of Science Fiction".

Wells was an outspoken socialist and sympathetic to pacifist views, although he supported the First World War once it was under way, and his later works became increasingly political and didactic. His middle period novels (1900–1920) were less science-fictional; they covered lower-middle class life (*The History of Mr Polly*) and the 'New Woman' and the Suffragettes (*Ann Veronica*).

H.G.Wells was born in Capricorn ascendant with Saturn and Venus in the 10th house in Libra same as that in the horoscope of Medha Patekar. *Sasa Mahapurusha raja yoga* and *Malavya Mahapurusha Raja yoga* have been formed in the 10th house. Jupiter and the Moon fall in the ascendant giving rise to *Gajakesari yoga*. In this birth chart *neecha bhanga* of Jupiter is there with *Ubhayachari yoga, Vasumati yoga, Paarijat yoga, Shatruhanta Yoga* along with *Anshaawtaar yoga*. The name of H.G.Wells is world famous in the history of writers.

It has been explained that Saturn is a king maker it means that the person becomes a king of his field who has Saturn in his 10th house or who is ruled by Saturn or who is born in the sign of Saturn or if the 10th house is owned by strong and well placed Saturn. This is the prime principle that Saturn is a King Maker. Amitabh Bachchan, Smt. Indira Gandhi, etc., are born with various planetary combinations in different ascendants but their rise was registered during the major period of Saturn only. Thus, Saturn was a King Maker for all such persons. It establishes that Saturn is not foe and there is nothing that is scared of Saturn. Strong Saturn if well placed in the birth chart makes one a king or equal to a king. Afflicted Saturn brings problems, miseries, mishappenings, destruction, delay, denial, death, distress, dejection, despair and disappointments.

Saturn if placed in the 10th house can make one a famous and kingly sanyasi like Vivekanand. It can make one a real Rishi or Maharishi like sant Tukaram, Sant Namdeo, etc. It can make one a founder of a religion or organisation such as Guru Nanak, Guru Govind Singh, Prophet Mohammad, Gautama Buddha etc. It makes one a top ranking writer Premchand, H.G.Wells. it also makes one an industrialist of country wide fame like R.N.Goenka, Jamna Lal Bajaj. This position of Saturn can make one a great politician like Jagjivam Ram, Kalraj Misra. Saturn's placement in the 10th house can make the head of the country Adolf Hitler, Napoleon Bonaparte, Richard Nixon,

Benazir Bhutto, Sheikh Mujibur Rehman, Woodrow Wilson, etc. To establish and confirm the nature of occupation the interested readers may refer our books **'Pointers to Profession'** and **'Astro Equations for Specific Profession'** for the accurate judgement of the nature of the profession. However, Saturn if placed in the 10th house will give enormous success, prosperity and dizzy heights to the native in the concerning field of his work.

Sushma Swaraj

Illustration : 9.23   *Horoscope No.: 45*

Date of birth : 14.02.1953   Time of birth : 12:00:00 hrs
Place of birth : Ambala   Lat 30:19 N Long 76:49 E
Ayanamsa   : 23:12:22   Sidereal Time : 21:13:11

Pln	Degree	Rasi	Nakshatra	Pad
Asc	9:57:38	Tau	Krittika	4
Sun	2:04:26	Aqu	Dhanistha	3
Mon (C)	5:13:06	Aqu	Dhanistha	4
Mar	11:30:13	Pis	U Bhadrapad	3
Mer (C)	10:57:21	Aqu	Satabhisha	2
Jup	20:22:45	Ari	Bharani	3
Ven	18:13:20	Pis	Revati	1
Sat (R)	4:01:07	Lib	Chitra	4
Rah (R/C)	19:09:06	Cap	Sravna	3
Ket (R)	19:09:06	Can	Aslesa	1

Lagna Chart

```
          Jup
    3      1
Ket 4         12 Ven
                 Mar
       2
    5  11 Mon Sun
    8     Mer
  6         10 Rah
 7       9
Sat
```

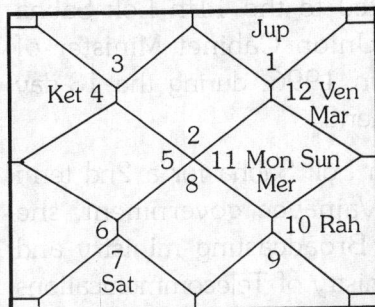

Navamsa Chart

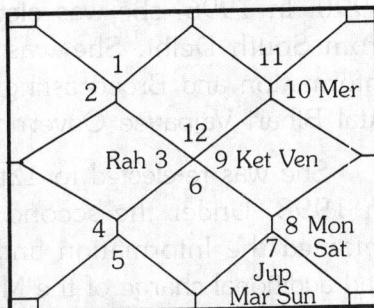

```
      1       11
   2              10 Mer
          12
   Rah 3   9 Ket Ven
           6
   4          8 Mon
      5      7  Sat
          Jup
        Mar Sun
```

Balance of Vimshottari Dasa of **Mars   0Y 9M 3D**

Sushma Swaraj is an Indian politician of the Bharatiya Janata Party (BJP). She is currently the Leader of the Opposition in the 15th Lok Sabha. She is a former union cabinet minister of India and a former chief minister of Delhi. Also she served as the chairperson of the BJP's 19 member campaign committee for the 2009 General Elections.

Sushma Swaraj began her political career as a student leader in the 1970s, organizing protests against Indira Gandhi's government. She was a member of the Haryana Legislative Assembly from 1977–82 and then from 1987-90. As a Janata Party MLA in Devi Lal's government, she was the Cabinet Minister of Labour and Employment (1977–1979). She joined the BJP in 1980. Under a combined Lok Dal-BJP government led by Devi Lal, she was the Cabinet Minister of Education, Food and Civil Supplies (1987–1990). She was judged Best Speaker of Haryana State Assembly for three consecutive years.

In 1980, 1984, and 1989, she unsuccessfully contested the Lok Sabha elections from Karnal in Haryana. All three times, she was defeated by the Congress Party's Chiranji Lal Sharma.

She was elected as a member of the Rajya Sabha in 1990. In 1996, she was elected to the 11th Lok Sabha from South Delhi. She was Union Cabinet Minister of Information and Broadcasting in 1996, during the 13-day Atal Bihari Vajpayee Government.

She was re-elected to 12th Lok Sabha for a 2nd term in 1998. Under the second Vajpayee government, she retained the Information and Broadcasting ministry and had additional charge of the Ministry of Telecommunications from 19 March to 12 October 1998.

She left the Union Cabinet from October - December 1998 to serve as the first woman Chief Minister of Delhi. The BJP lost the assembly elections, and she returned to national politics.

In 1999, she took on a high profile as she contested against the Congress party's President, Sonia Gandhi, from the Bellary constituency in Karnataka, which had returned Congress winners since India's independence. The fervent, high-pitched campaign came to an end with the expected loss of Sushma, Gandhi polled 51.7 percent of the vote, Swaraj coming not too far behind with 44.7 percent.

She returned to Parliament in April 2000 as a Rajya Sabha member from Uttarakhand. She was re-inducted into the cabinet as the Minister of Information and Broadcasting, which she held from September 2000 until January 2003. At that time, she was made the Minister of Health and Family Welfare, and also held the post of Minister of Parliamentary Affairs. She held these posts from January 2003 until May 2004, when the National Democratic Alliance government lost elections.

In a heavily publicized and emotionally charged episode following the elections, Sushma Swaraj threatened to shave her head, don a white saree and eat groundnuts (symbollically mourning) if Sonia Gandhi, the Italian-born Congress leader, became Prime Minister of India.

She was re-elected to the Rajya Sabha in April 2006 from Madhya Pradesh. She served as the deputy leader of BJP in Rajya Sabha. Speculation ran high that Sushma Swaraj was one of the top contenders to be President of the BJP, following Advani's resignation from that role in late 2005. Rajnath Singh ultimately was elected to that post.

She won the 2009 election to the 15th Lok Sabha from the Vidisha constituency in Madhya Pradesh, on a BJP candidacy, by a record margin of 3.89 lakh votes. This is her 10th election.

Sushma Swaraj was born in Taurus ascendant. The 9th and the 10th lord *Yogakaraka* Saturn is exalted in the 6th house under retrograde motion. There is mutual aspect between Saturn and Jupiter identical to the 6th and the 12th house. Major period of Saturn was running over her from 19.11.1987 to 19.11.2006 which was the best period of her life so far as her power, fame, honour and prosperity is concerned in Bharatiya Janta Party as an important leader and successful minister. Saturn obtains 1.3 *shadabala* and Jupiter is *Atma Karaka.* Ascendant lord Venus is exalted in the 11th house and Saturn obtains the *navamsa* of Mars. The Moon sign is Aquarius and Saturn occupies the 9th house from the natal Moon. Thus, Sushma Swaraj is ruled chiefly by Saturn and the major period of Saturn was exceptionally brilliant in almost all aspects of life.

Subhash Chandra Bose

Illustration : 9.24   Horoscope No.: 46

Date of birth : 23.01.1897   Time of birth : 12:29:00 hrs
Place of birth : Cuttack   Lat 20:26 N Long 85:56 E
Ayanamsa   : 22:25:23   Sidereal Time : 20:40:27

Pln	Degree	Rasi	Nakshatra	Pad
Asc	26:55:12	Ari	Krittika	1
Sun	11:09:48	Cap	Sravna	1
Mon	7:33:55	Vir	U Phalguni	4
Mar	19:26:28	Tau	Rohini	3
Mer (R/D)	9:35:33	Cap	Uttarasadha	4
Jup (R)	16:29:26	Leo	P Phalguni	1
Ven	26:19:41	Aqu	P Bhadrapad	2
Sat	6:38:22	Sco	Anuradha	1
Rah (C)	22:51:45	Cap	Sravna	4
Ket	22:51:45	Can	Aslesa	2

Lagna Chart

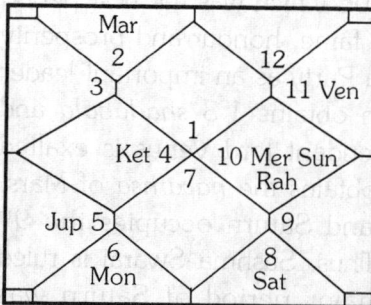

Navamsa Chart

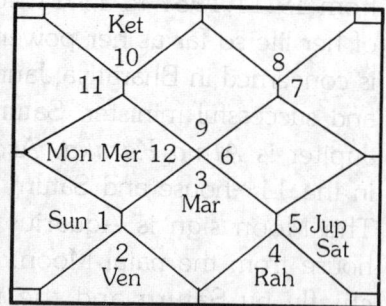

Balance of Vimshottari Dasa of **Sun 1Y 1M 4D**

Subhas Chandra Bose born January 23, 1897;
presumed to have died August 18, 1945, although this is
disputed), popularly known as Netaji (literally "Respected

Leader"), was one of the most influential & one of the greatest leaders in the Indian independence movement.

Bose advocated complete freedom for India at the earliest, whereas the Congress Committee wanted it in phases, through a Dominion status. Other younger leaders including Jawaharlal Nehru supported Bose and finally at the historic Lahore Congress convention, the Congress had to adopt Purna Swaraj (complete freedom) as its motto. Bhagat Singh's martyrdom and the inability of the Congress leaders to save his life infuriated Bose and he started a movement opposing the Gandhi-Irwin Pact. He was imprisoned and expelled from India. But defying the ban, he came back to India and was imprisoned again.

Bose was elected president of the Indian National Congress for two consecutive terms, but had to resign from the post following ideological conflicts with Mahatma Gandhi and after openly attacking the Congress' foreign and internal policies. Bose believed that Mahatma Gandhi's tactics of non-violence would never be sufficient to secure India's independence, and advocated violent resistance. He established a separate political party, the All India Forward Bloc and continued to call for the full and immediate independence of India from British rule. He was imprisoned by the British authorities eleven times. His famous motto was "Give me blood and I will give you freedom".

His stance did not change with the outbreak of the Second World War, which he saw as an opportunity to take advantage of British weakness. At the outset of the war, he left India, travelling to the Soviet Union, Germany and Japan, seeking an alliance with the aim of attacking the British in India. With Japanese assistance, he re-organised and later led the Azad Hind Fauj or Indian National Army, formed from Indian prisoners-of-war and plantation workers from British Malaya, Singapore, and other parts of Southeast

Asia, against British forces. With Japanese monetary, political, diplomatic and military assistance, he formed the Azad Hind Government in exile, regrouped and led the Indian National Army in battle against the allies at Imphal and in Burma.

His political views and the alliances he made with Nazi and other militarist regimes at war with Britain have been the cause of arguments among historians and politicians, with some accusing him of fascist sympathies, while others in India have been more sympathetic towards the inculcation of realpolitik as a manifesto that guided his social and political choices.

He is presumed to have died on 18 August 1945 in a plane crash over Taiwan. However, contradictory evidence exists regarding his death in the accident.

Subhash Chandra Bose is immortal due to his brave, fearless and dynamic activities as a freedom fighter. He was born in Aries ascendant with 10th lord Saturn placed in the 8th house. Saturn aspects the 10th house and the planet placed in the 10th house as well. The 9th lord Jupiter aspects the ascendant. Opposition of Mars and Saturn identical to 2nd and 8th house with mutual aspect between these planets indicate fatal, unnatural and untimely death. His 10th house is ruled by Saturn and Saturn obtains the *navamsa* of the Sun whereas the Sun falls in the 10th house identical to the sign of Saturn. The Sun is aspected by Saturn in the natal chart whereas Saturn obtains the *navamsa* of the Sun as well. Mars, Jupiter and Saturn are in quadrant from each other that is if reckoned from 10th lord Saturn, Mars and Jupiter are 7th and 10th from there, which denotes political career. Venus is *Atma Karaka* planet and that also occupies the sign of Saturn Aquarius. Thus, the 10th and 11th lord Saturn, 2nd lord Venus and the 5th lord the Sun all are under the influence of Saturn in one or the other way. Saturn falls

in own constellation *Anuradha*. Saturn is the key planet
that decidedly made Subhash Chandra Bose an immortal
king.

Guljari Lal Nanda

Illustration : 9.25   Horoscope No.: 47

Date of birth : 04.07.1898   Time of birth : 00:30:00 hrs
Place of birth : Sialkot   Lat 32:29 N Long 74:33 E
Ayanamsa   : 22:26:39   Sidereal Time : 19:17:21

Pln	Degree	Rasi	Nakshatra	Pad
Asc	5:57:43	Ari	Aswini	2
Sun	19:22:16	Gem	Ardra	4
Mon	18:22:51	Sag	Purvasadha	2
Mar	26:48:23	Ari	Krittika	1
Mer (C)	23:34:10	Gem	Punarvasu	2
Jup	9:52:59	Vir	U Phalguni	4
Ven	23:46:33	Can	Aslesa	3
Sat (R)	14:14:25	Sco	Anuradha	4
Rah	25:14:57	Sag	Purvasadha	4
Ket (C)	25:14:57	Gem	Punarvasu	2

Lagna Chart   **Navamsa Chart**

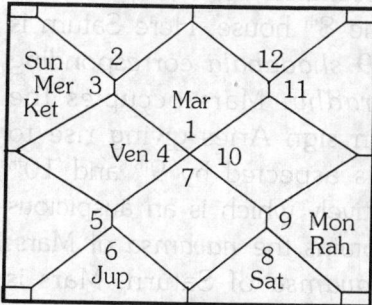

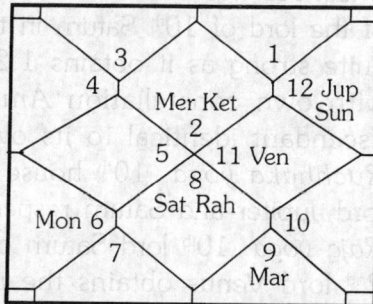

Balance of Vimshottari Dasa of **Ven 12Y 5M 4D**

Gulzarilal Nanda was an Indian politician and an economist with specialization in labor problems. He was the interim Prime Minister of India twice for thirteen days each: the first time after the death of Prime Minister Jawaharlal Nehru in 1964, and the second time after the death of Prime Minister Lal Bahadur Shastri in 1966. (Both his terms ended after the ruling Indian National Congress party procedurally elected a new prime minister.) The Government of India honoured Nanda with the Bharat Ratna Award in 1997.

A principled politician, he found himself out of tune with the changed circumstances. He did not own any property and lived in a rented house in New Delhi's Defence Colony from which he was evicted since he could not pay its rent and moved to Ahmedabad where he lived with his daughter. What sets him apart from almost all the other freedom fighters who held high offices in independent India is his complete insulation from worldly desire. He had no source of income and would not accept funds from his children or from any well wisher. A friend, Sheel Bhadra Yajee, forced him to sign an application for the freedom fighter's pension of Rs 500 per month

Guljari Lal Nanda remained the Prime Minister of India twice. He was born in Aries ascendant with the placement of the lord of 10th Saturn in the 8th house. Here Saturn is quite strong as it obtains 1.29 *shadabala* corresponding with own constellation *Anuradha*. Mars occupies the ascendant identical to its own sign Aries giving rise to *Ruchhaka yoga*. 10th house is aspected by 9th and 10th lord Jupiter and Saturn respectively which is an auspicious *Raja yoga*. 10th lord Saturn obtains the *navamsa* of Mars, 2nd lord Venus obtains the *navamsa* of Saturn. Mars is *Atma Karaka* planet which is posited in the ascendant in Aries. Mars obtains the *navamsa* of Jupiter and that is

Bhagyansha yukta. Saturn and Jupiter's aspect on the 10th house and Saturn being the 10th lord made Gulzari Lal Nanda the Prime Minister twice.

Chandra Shekhar

Illustration : 9.26 Horoscope No.: 48

Date of birth : 17.04.1927 Time of birth : 06:06:00 hrs
Place of birth : Ballia Lat 25:45 N Long 84:09 E
Ayanamsa : 22:50:11 Sidereal Time : 19:49:13

Pln	Degree	Rasi	Nakshatra	Pad
Asc	13:31:06	Ari	Bharani	1
Sun	3:10:42	Ari	Aswini	1
Mon	1:48:23	Lib	Chitra	3
Mar	7:08:30	Gem	Ardra	1
Mer	6:32:21	Pis	U Bhadrapad	1
Jup	27:54:57	Aqu	P Bhadrapad	3
Ven	7:25:12	Tau	Krittika	4
Sat (R)	14:06:23	Sco	Anuradha	4
Rah (R)	7:12:04	Gem	Ardra	1
Ket (R)	7:12:04	Sag	Moola	3

Lagna Chart

```
          Ven        Mer
           2          12
   Rah  3       Sun        11 Jup
   Mar         1
            4    10
               7
              Mon
        5              9 Ket
         6          8
                  Sat
```

Navamsa Chart

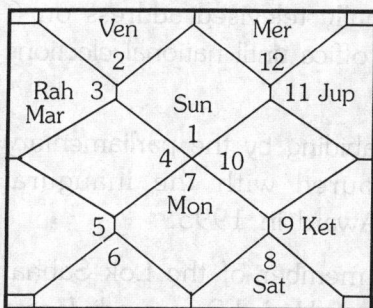

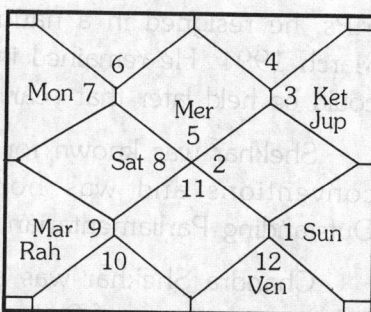

```
              6          4
   Mon 7            Mer       3 Ket
                     5        Jup
         Sat 8     2
                  11
        Mar  9          1 Sun
        Rah   10      12
                    Ven
```

Balance of Vimshottari Dasa of **Mars 2Y 6M 18D**

He was born on 1 July 1927 to a Rajput farming family in Ibrahimpatti - Ballia in eastern Uttar Pradesh. Chandra Shekhar Singh known as Chandra Shekhar did his Master of Arts (MA) at Allahabad University. He was known as a firebrand in student politics. After graduation, he became active in socialist politics.

He came under the spell of Acharya Narendra Dev, a fiery Socialist leader in the beginning of his political career. From 1962 to 1967, Shekhar belonged to the Rajya Sabha, the Upper house of the Parliament of India. He had a nationwide *padayatra* in 1984 to know the country better, which he claimed gave the jitters to Indira Gandhi, the then Prime Minister. He was called a "Young Turk".

After his predecessor, V.P. Singh, resigned, he led a breakaway faction of the Janata Dal, known as the Samajwadi Janata Party (Rashtriya) . The Indian National Congress decided to extend outside support to his government to avoid snap elections, and Shekhar held a bare majority in a coalition with both the Communist parties and the BJP. The relationship crumbled quickly, as the Congress party accused him of spying on Rajiv Gandhi, their leader at that time. The Congress Party then boycotted Parliament and as Shekhar's faction only had about 60 MPs, he resigned in a nationally televised address on 6 March 1991. He remained in office until national elections could be held later that year.

Shekhar was known for abiding by the parliamentary conventions and was honoured with the inaugural Outstanding Parliamentarian Award in 1995.

Chandra Shekhar was a member of the Lok Sabha, India's upper house of Parliament. He led Samajwadi Janata Party (Rashtriya), (Socialist People's Party (National)).

Starting in 1977, he won elections to the Lok Sabha eight times from Ballia constituency in eastern Uttar Pradesh. The only election that he lost was in 1984 against Mr. Jagganath Chaudhary of Congress(I).

Shekhar suffered from multiple myeloma, a form of cancer of the plasma cell. On 3 May 2007, he was hospitalised after his condition had deteriorated. Shekhar died at the age of 80 in New Delhi on 8 July 2007. He was survived by two sons. One of them, Neeraj Shekhar contested and won the Ballia Lok Sabha which was vacated through his father's death.

Chandra Shekhar was born in Aries ascendant with the 10th lord Saturn in the 8th house corresponding with own constellation *Anuradha*. Saturn obtains *Vargottama navamsa* as 10th lord and the major period of Saturn were the best 19 years of his life. Chandra Shekhar was the founder of Janta Dal and he was quite successful in his struggle in his fight against Mrs.Indira Gandhi. He was successful in toppling down the government. The 10th lord Saturn aspects the 10th house and Venus as well. 9th lord Jupiter joins the 11th house and aspects the natal Moon. Saturn is the dispositor of Jupiter as well, where as Jupiter is *Atma Karaka*. Jupiter falls in own constellation *Poorva Bhadrapada* in 11th house identical to saturnine sign Aquarius. Moreover, Jupiter, Saturn and Mars are in mutual *Kendra* that is the 9th, 10th and lagna lord are in quadrant from each other. It is not out of place to mention that Saturn was the King Maker in the horoscope of Shri Chandra Shekhar.

Gyani Zail Singh

Illustration : 9.27　　　　　Horoscope No.: 49

Date of birth : 05.05.1916　　Time of birth : 05:30:00 hrs
Place of birth : Faridkot　　　Lat 10:46 N Long 76:42 E
Ayanamsa　　: 22:41:32　　　Sidereal Time : 19:56:54

Pln	Degree	Rasi	Nakshatra	Pad
Asc	11:16:12	Ari	Aswini	4
Sun	21:28:00	Ari	Bharani	3
Mon	22:54:58	Tau	Rohini	4
Mar	27:09:14	Can	Aslesa	4
Mer	10:57:50	Tau	Rohini	1
Jup	26:46:31	Pis	Revati	4
Ven	6:33:24	Gem	Mrigshira	4
Sat	19:25:24	Gem	Ardra	4
Rah (R)	9:32:21	Cap	Uttarasadha	4
Ket (R)	9:32:21	Can	Pushya	2

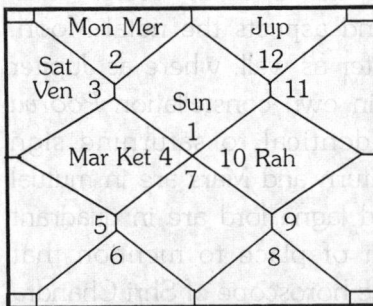

Lagna Chart	Navamsa Chart

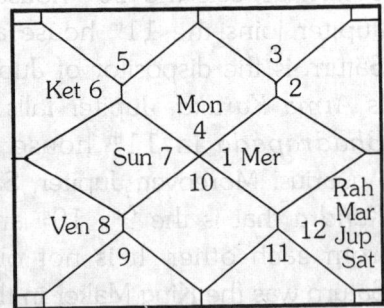

Lagna Chart		Navamsa Chart	
Mon Mer	Jup		3
Sat Ven 3	2 12 11	5 Ket 6 2	
Sun 1		Mon 4	
Mar Ket 4	10 Rah	Sun 7 1 Mer	
7		10	
5	9	Ven 8	12 Rah Mar Jup Sat
6	8	9 11	

Balance of Vimshottari Dasa of **Moon　0Y 3M 22D**

Giani Zail Singh was an Indian politician and member of the Congress Party. He served as the seventh President of India. He was the President of India during Operation

Blue Star, the assassination of Indira Gandhi, and the 1984 anti-Sikh riots.

Sardar Zail Singh, a Sikh by religion, was given the title of *Giani*, as he was educated and learned about Guru Granth Sahib. However, he did not have formal secular education. He had a humble start in life and his father was a Sikh Tarkhan Ramgarhia who was killed in an automobile accident.

Zail Singh's public life was long and varied - freedom fighter, state Congress leader, Chief Minister, Union Home Minister, and the president of India. A fighter against princedom, feudalism and foreign domination in the pre-independence days, he is also remembered for his crusade against communalism, economic disparities and social injustice in the republic. He also served as Chief Minister of Punjab.

Giani Zail Singh was elected to the highest office of the President of India on 15 July 1982 and took the oath of office on 25 July 1982. The media felt that the president had been chosen for being an Indira loyalist rather than an eminent person. "If my leader had said I should pick up a broom and be a sweeper, I would have done that. She chose me to be President,"[3] Singh was quoted to have said after his election.

Giani Zail Singh died in a road accident on 25 December 1994, near Kiratpur Sahib in Ropar district. Following his accidental death, Zail Singh was cremated at Ekta Sthal in the Raj Ghat area.

Gyani Zail Singh was born in Aries ascendant. The lord of 10th house joins the 3rd house in association with 2nd lord Venus and aspects the 9th house. Karmic Control Planets are Saturn and the Moon in this horoscope and Saturn obtains the *navamsa* of Jupiter. The Sun is the strongest

planet that obtains 2.01 *shadabala* and *Atma Karaka* planet
Mars obtains 1.46 *shadabala* and aspects the 10th house.
Saturn, Jupiter and Venus are placed in quadrant from
each other. From Moon sign 9th and 10th Saturn is associated
with Lagna lord Venus in the 2nd house. It will not be out of
place to mention that major period of the 10th lord Saturn
was exceedingly auspicious for Gyani Zail Singh when he
was the Chief Minister of Punjab from 1972 to 1977.
However, in the major period of Mercury and the sub period
of Venus he became the President of India in the year
1982. Saturn as 10th lord aspecting the 9th house and 9th
lord Jupiter made him the President of India that is
equivalent to a King.

Shyama Prasad Mookerjee

Illustration : 9.28   *Horoscope No.: 50*

Date of birth : 06.07.1901   Time of birth : 01:45:00 hrs
Place of birth : Calcutta   Lat 22:30 N Long 88:20 E
Ayanamsa   : 22:29:07   Sidereal Time : 20:37:25

Pln	Degree	Rasi	Nakshatra	Pad
Asc	26:51:49	Ari	Krittika	1
Sun	20:33:29	Gem	Punarvasu	1
Mon	7:47:34	Aqu	Satabhisha	1
Mar	3:02:58	Vir	U Phalguni	2
Mer (R/C)	2:17:46	Can	Punarvasu	4
Jup (R)	15:01:54	Sag	Purvasadha	1
Ven	8:15:11	Can	Pushya	2
Sat (R)	20:36:37	Sag	Purvasadha	3
Rah (R)	28:43:46	Lib	Vishakha	3
Ket (R)	28:43:46	Ari	Krittika	1

Lagna Chart

Navamsa Chart

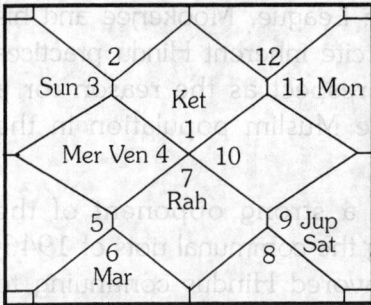

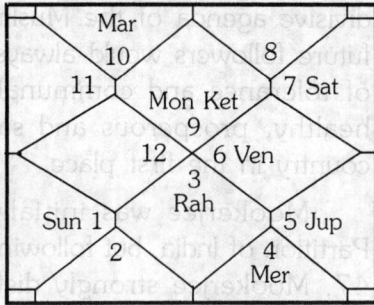

Balance of Vimshottari Dasa of **Rah 16Y 5M 23D**

Shyama Prasad Mookerjee was a nationalist political leader of India, and is considered the godfather of modern Hindutva and Hindu Nationalism.

Mookerjee founded the Bharatiya Jana Sangh, the first nationalist political party of its kind, and closely associated with the Rashtriya Swayamsevak Sangh (RSS).

He was elected as member of the Legislative Council of Bengal, as an Indian National Congress candidate representing Calcutta University but resigned next year when Congress decided to boycott the legislature. Subsequently, he contested the election as an independent candidate and got elected. He was the Finance Minister of Bengal Province during 1941-42.

He emerged as a spokesman for Hindus and shortly joined Hindu Mahasabha and in 1944, he became the President. Mookerjee was political leader who felt the need to counteract the communalist and separatist Muslim League of Muhammad Ali Jinnah, who were demanding either exaggerated Muslim rights or a Muslim state of Pakistan.

Mookerjee adopted causes to protect Hindus against

what he believed to be the communal propaganda and the divisive agenda of the Muslim League. Mookerjee and his future followers would always cite inherent Hindu practices of tolerance and communal respect as the reason for a healthy, prosperous and safe Muslim population in the country in the first place.

Mookerjee was initially a strong opponent of the Partition of India, but following the communal riots of 1946-47, Mookerjee strongly disfavored Hindus continuing to live in a Muslim-dominated state and under a government controlled by the Muslim League.

On 11 February 1941 S P Mookerjee told a Hindu rally that if Muslims wanted to live in Pakistan they should "pack their bag and baggage and leave India... (to) wherever they like".

Shyama Prasad Mookerjee was one of the most important leaders of India and a great freedom fighter. He was the first president of RSS. He was born in Aries ascendant and Aquarius Moon sign. Lord of the 10th house Saturn joins the 9th house in association with 9th lord Jupiter under the mutual aspect with natal Mars and the Sun. Here 10th lord Saturn is afflicted by the aspect of Mars and the Sun both and that resulted into his imprisonment and that resulted into his unnatural and untimely death. Thus, the association of Saturn with Jupiter in the 9th house made him extremely popular but he rose to dizzy heights by his own endeavours. However, the affliction of Saturn by inimical Mars and the Sun resulted into steep downfall and unnatural and untimely demise. He died on 23.6.1953.

Siddhartha

This is the horoscope of a very famous person of India who rose from a very small position to enormous height. No planet is exalted in the birth chart but 3 planets *i.e.*

Mars, Venus and Mercury are placed in their own sign in
7ᵗʰ, 8ᵗʰ & 9ᵗʰ house respectively.

Illustration : 9.29   *Horoscope No.: 51*

Date of birth, Time and Place withhold.

Pln	Degree	Rasi	Nakshatra	Pad
Asc	14:02:12	Lib	Swati	3
Sun	25:33:20	Tau	Mrigshira	1
Mon	7:52:15	Aqu	Satabhisha	1
Mar	21:54:21	Ari	Bharani	3
Mer	18:49:52	Gem	Ardra	4
Jup (R)	26:24:18	Lib	Vishakha	2
Ven	2:38:47	Tau	Krittika	2
Sat	12:35:31	Can	Pushya	3
Rah (R)	9:17:41	Tau	Krittika	4
Ket (R)	9:17:41	Sco	Anuradha	2

Lagna Chart

```
        Ket
         8          6
      9              5
          Jup
           7
       10   4 Sat
            1
            Mar
   Mon 11        3 Mer
        12      2
               Rah
             Ven Sun
```

Navamsa Chart

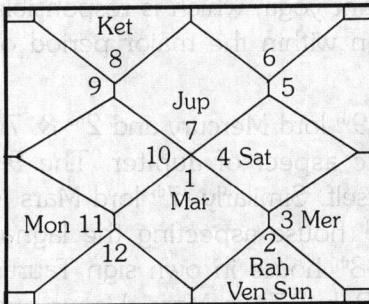

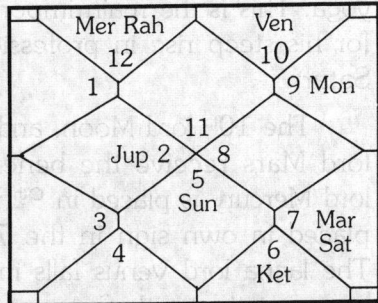

```
      Mer Rah      Ven
         12         10
      1           9 Mon
            11
      Jup 2    8
            5
            Sun
      3           7 Mar
      4          6 Sat
               Ket
```

Balance of Vimshottari Dasa of **Rahu 16Y 4M 14D**

The native is an extremely handsome, fair and
attractive person with magnificent physique. He is a person
of charming and pleasing manners coupled with an

extremely perspicacious mind. A man of humble beginning the native has risen to create his own empire in the world of finance and aviation. He also owns a television channel. Such heights bave been achieved by dint of hardwork and good fortune.

The native has his own demense comprising several well appointed bungalows of latest architecture, a lake, garden, fountains, picnic spot and big halls for holding private and public functions. The mansion in which he resides is comparable to the best anywhere in the world. Thus the native is blessed with exceptionally bright fortune along with innumerable qualities like sharp intelligence, courage, patriotism and organisational ability of highest order. He is meritorious, rich, industrious and energetic.

Let us judge the planetary position of his birth chart :

The Saturn is yogakaraka as it is the lord of 4th & 5th house and is placed in the house of profession *i.e.* the 10th house, whereas the 10th lord Moon falls in 5th house. Thus mutual exchange of Saturn and Moon *i.e.* lord of 10th and 5th has given rise to a Maharaja yoga, Punya Karmadhipati yoga. This is the main important yoga, which is responsible for his steep rise in profession within the major period of Saturn.

The 10th lord Moon, and 9th lord Mercury and 2nd & 7th lord Mars receive the benefic aspect of Jupiter. The 9th lord Mercury is placed in 9th itself. Similarly, 7th lord Mars is placed in own sign in the 7th house aspecting the lagna. The lagna lord Venus falls in 8th house in own sign Taurus in association with Sun and Rahu. Thus Mars, Venus and Mercury are placed in their own sign in 7th, 8th & 9th house respectively. But it is Saturn which is mainly responsible for the rise of the native during Saturn's Mahadasa. Saturn obtains navamsa of it's exaltation. The lord of 11th house Sun also obtains own navamsa which has given him worldwide fame. Saturn falls in own constellation.

Here we see that Saturn is a king maker if it is well placed in the birth chart. Generally, people always have some apprehension regarding this vital planet Saturn, but how wrong this belief is can be very well seen in present birth chart. As far as Sadhe Saati of Saturn is concerned it was auspicious for the native, at least for his professional prosperity. So Saturn can give more to a person if it is Yogakaraka and is placed in the 10th house.

The native is endowed with outstanding nobility manifested through his innumerable philanthropic activities. Almighty has blessed him with an extremely courteous and beautiful wife, loving and decent children, cooperating brothers and sisters.

He is a great patriot as well. He spends crores of rupees towards national cause. He is a true son of the nation. The latest example of his devotion towards the country is the stupendous help of billions of rupees to the families of Kargil martyrs. He is not only a multi billionaire but also a thinker, philosopher, singer, artist, planner and visionary. He started an organisation with a meagre capital, which has developed into a multi thousand crore rupees entity.

Ashok Srivastava

This is the birth chart of a native who spent his childhood in extreme poverty. After facing many problems he managed to earn a living through an ordinary job in the Secretariat. After some time he was promoted to the post of a clerk there. Time's wheel kept moving. Gradually he became an important trade union leader. Name and success made him arrogant. It is then that Saturn started to show the effect of its power and he had to leave his job and leadership both.

Illustration : 9.30   *Horoscope No.: 52*

Date of birth : 05.05.1956   Time of birth : 02:10:00 hrs
Place of birth :   Lat 26:08 N Long 83:33 E
Ayanamsa   : 23:15:05   Sidereal Time : 17:00:47

Pln	Degree	Rasi	Nakshatra	Pad
Asc	16:28:34	Aqu	Satabhisha	3
Sun	21:04:45	Ari	Bharani	3
Mon	10:30:49	Aqu	Satabhisha	2
Mar	19:16:47	Cap	Sravna	3
Mer	11:42:34	Tau	Rohini	1
Jup	28:41:27	Can	Aslesa	4
Ven	4:28:12	Gem	Mrigshira	4
Sat (R)	7:25:11	Sco	Anuradha	2
Rah (R)	15:04:16	Sco	Anuradha	4
Ket (R)	15:04:16	Tau	Rohini	2

Lagna Chart   **Navamsa Chart**

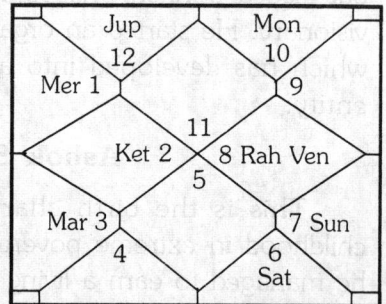

Lagna Chart	Navamsa Chart

Lagna Chart:
```
            Mar
    12       10
 Sun 1          9
        Mon
         11
  Mer Ket 2   8 Rah Sat
         5
 Ven 3           7
    4        6
     Jup
```

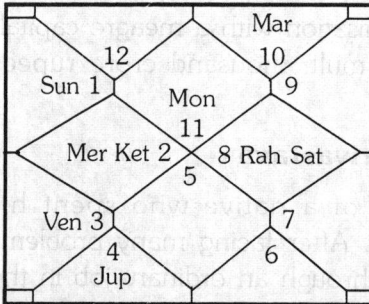

Navamsa Chart:
```
     Jup       Mon
    12          10
 Mer 1           9
         11
   Ket 2    8 Rah Ven
         5
 Mar 3           7 Sun
    4        6
           Sat
```

Balance of Vimshottari Dasa of **Rah   12Y 9M 20D**

As per the birth chart of this native Saturn's major period (Mahadasa) started from 24.1.1985. A pleasant period of progress began in his life. He started a small scale industry. At present this person is a multimillionaire and running big industries successfully. In the birth chart Saturn is the lord of the ascendant and situated in the 10th house in the sign of Scorpio which belongs to Mars. It is also beneficially aspected by an exalted Jupiter, and lord of the 5th Mercury. Jupiter's aspect mitigates Saturn's ferocity but here Saturn is conjoined with Rahu. Rahu, therefore, is enhancing its evil effects. At the same time Jupiter and Mercury are diminishing these evil effects. To analyse the Saturn and the 10th house, it is necessary to consider Mars, the lord of the 10th, as well. Lord of the 10th Mars is in the 12th house in its own exaltation sign Capricorn, and also establishing Vinimaya Parivartana Yoga with Saturn. The aspect of Jupiter 10th house, lord of the 10th Mars and Saturn and Rahu in the 10th house is enhancing the auspicious results of 10th house. The native earned country wide fame after making Cancer hospital "Lavanya" which he started during Saturn Jupiter period. He spends crores of rupees per month in advertisement only. Before reaching a conclusion, the navamsa of Saturn and Mars should also be considered. Saturn is situated in the navamsa of Mercury and aspected by Mars and Jupiter which is in its own navamsa. Therefore, in the navamsa chart also, lord of the ascendant Saturn is influenced by both Mars and Jupiter. A proper study reveals that Saturn will take this native to the top. Because of Mercury being in the navamsa of Mercury the native would prosper only in business, not in a service. Because of Saturn's conjunction with Rahu in the 10th there would always be ups and downs in the business. Lots of success may be followed by continuous losses. A favourable position is created by the aspect of own navamsa placed Jupiter over Saturn. The native will keep moving towards progress. Even in an adverse situation, he will not lose his courage, strength, patience, discretion or intelligence. Soon he will regain his original glory.

We have mentioned earlier that the beneficial effect of Saturn begins in the 36th year of life. The major period of Saturn for this native began in the 29th year - when he started a small scale industry of making telephone parts. At the commencement of the 36th year the sub-period of Mercury began within the major period of Saturn. He came into contact with some important persons. He moved to Delhi (North-West, direction of Mercury) and set up huge industry of making "Pagers" with an investment of billions. The Saturn in the 10th established him amongst the front ranking industrialists of India, from the humble position of an assistant clerk, where he has success, fame, wealth, in short everything. It is therefore, imperative that the position of Saturn should be analysed very carefully.

The late PM and popular leader of Bagladesh Sheikh Mujeeburrahman was born in the Scorpio ascendant. In his birth chart Saturn was in the 10th house while being retrograde, which caused his murder while in office. It was this Saturn in the 10th house which gave him immense popularity despite such a humble start, Pakistan got divided and he became the PM of Bangladesh. Later it was the same Saturn, that caused his terrible end due to its affliction.

Everybody is conversant with the name of Albert Einstein. A scientist like him takes birth once in centuries. He was born with Gemini in the ascendant. The lord of the 8th and 9th Saturn is in the 10th conjoined with Mercury and Venus, and the lord or the 10th house Jupiter is in the 9th house. Here Venus is in its exalted sign which is a highly favourable planet for Gemini ascendant. Lord of the 9th Saturn and lord of the 10th Jupiter are forming Vinimaya Parivartan Yoga, while Mercury also in the 10th house is creating Neech Bhanga Raj Yoga. Lord of the ascendant Mercury, lord of the 5th Venus and lord of the 9th Saturn joined together in the 10th house creating Ishtabala Yoga.

Apart from this because of the mutual exchange of lords of the 9th and 10th another yoga called "Dharma Karmadhipati" has been established. Apart from these extra ordinary yogas it is Saturn in the 10th which gave him worldwide fame.

Hence, if Saturn is in the 10th and in a favourable situation, *i.e.* because of its situation it is gaining beneficence, then the native achieves a very high position in life, in terms of place and designation or becomes highly successful in business or reaches a high, popular level in politics. When such a Saturn is lord of the ascendant, in its own house or in an exalted sign, or being lord of the ascendant is located in the 7th hose – then only such a result would obtain and a prediction may be made to this effect. If Jupiter, Venus or Mercury influence the Saturn placed in the 10th house by aspect or conjunction, downfall would not be there. But if a cruel planet like Mars or Rahu influenced such Saturn, downfall after rise is certain. These features of 10th placed Saturn are worth remembering. While assessing results given by Saturn, its auspiciousness or inauspiciousness should be taken note of carefully.

Acharya Kalyan Varma has stated in Saravali that if Saturn and Jupiter are together in the 10th house then the native becomes very rich, famous and is highly talented. He may become the head of the city. If Saturn is in the sign of Jupiter and Jupiter is aspecting Saturn then the native becomes the chief or chief commander or commander of the army. In this case Saturn does not cause a downfall but if the lord of the sixth or eighth house is in the 10th house and it is not even aspected by Jupiter then downfall takes place.

Plastic King

Illustration : 9.31   Horoscope No.: 53

Date of birth, Time and Place withhold.

Pln	Degree	Rasi	Nakshatra	Pad
Asc	12:10:30	Lib	Swati	2
Sun	27:56:35	Vir	Chitra	2
Mon	8:22:26	Tau	Krittika	4
Mar	2:41:02	Cap	Uttarasadha	2
Mer	20:53:45	Lib	Vishakha	1
Jup	4:59:24	Can	Pushya	1
Ven	4:46:48	Sco	Anuradha	1
Sat	16:21:41	Lib	Swati	3
Rah (R)	15:28:33	Sag	Purvasadha	1
Ket (R)	15:28:33	Gem	Ardra	3

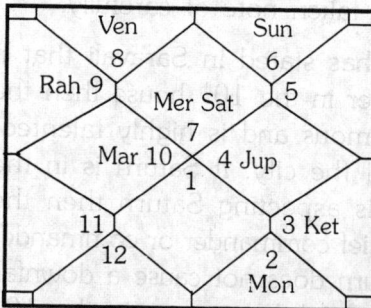

Lagna Chart	Navamsa Chart

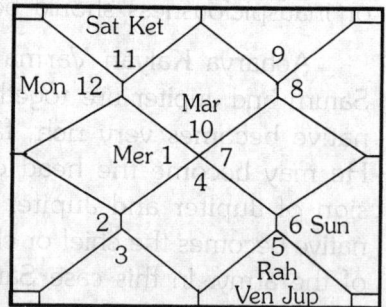

Balance of Vimshottari Dasa of **Sun   0Y 8M 23D**

The native is a great industrialist of Asia dealing in plastic, lamination and packaging material. He started his career from a very low position and bad to do a lot of cycling in the early young age, to make both ends meet. Now he is the owner of unlimited wealth, a number of industries, farms, lands and houses etc.

The native was born in Libra ascendant with exalted Saturn therein. Saturn happens to be a yogakaraka for Libra borns and that has given rise to Sasa Maha Purusha Rajyoga. It is not only Saturn which has done the miracle in such a short period. The following planetary setup is strong enough to elevate the native to the present height.

1. Saturn exalted in Lagna, Mars exalted in the 4th, Jupiter exalted in the 10th and Moon exalted in the 8th house *i.e.* vital planets are exalted and three out of them are exalted in the angles only.

2. The combination of "Bhagyadhipati" (lord of luck) Mercury with yogakaraka Saturn in the ascendant is the best. Lords of both the triangles are associated in the Lagna itself. This combination can elevate any one to a very strong and high position.

3. Saturn obtains own navamsa, Mars obtains Vargottam navamsa in exaltation in navamsa lagna, which has given lot of youth, charm, energy, activeness, dynamism and dashing qualities to the native.

4. The Sun who is the 11th lord obtains Vargottam navamsa. This provided fame, honour, reputation, recognition, prosperity power and popularity to the native.

Mercury is the strongest planet as far as shadabala of planets is concerned. Mercury obtains 11.03 Rupa Shadabala which is an extraordinary high strength. Thereafter Jupiter and Saturn are strong. All the three planets are placed in Kendras. Rahu is also best placed in the 3ed house. These splendid and powerful combinations have given a steep and exceptional professional rise to the native. Till middle of 2010 the business of this tycoon has spread over more than 100 countries including USA, Dubai, UK, Russia, Germany and the like.

Indira Gandhi

Illustration : 9.32   Horoscope No.: 54

Date of birth : 19.11.1917   Time of birth : 23:33:00 hrs
Place of birth : Allahabad   Lat 25:27 N Long 81:50 E
Ayanamsa   : 22:22:52   Sidereal Time : 3:23:05

Pln	Degree	Rasi	Nakshatra	Pad
Asc	2:11:30	Leo	Magha	1
Sun	4:08:25	Sco	Anuradha	1
Mon	5:47:35	Cap	Uttarasadha	3
Mar	16:22:57	Leo	P Phalguni	1
Mer (C)	13:15:08	Sco	Anuradha	3
Jup (R)	15:00:00	Tau	Rohini	2
Ven	21:01:17	Sag	Purvasadha	3
Sat	21:47:15	Can	Aslesa	2
Rah	9:18:39	Sag	Moola	3
Ket	9:18:39	Gem	Ardra	1

Lagna Chart

```
                Sat
         6        4
      7        |  3 Ket
           Mar
            5
   Sun Mer 8  | 2 Jup
          11
   Ven  9      |     1
   Rah   10         12
          Mon
```

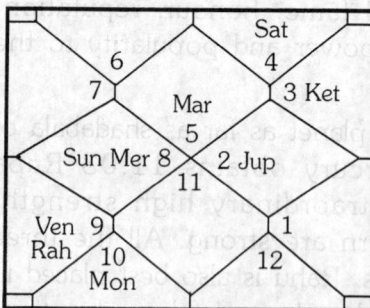

Navamsa Chart

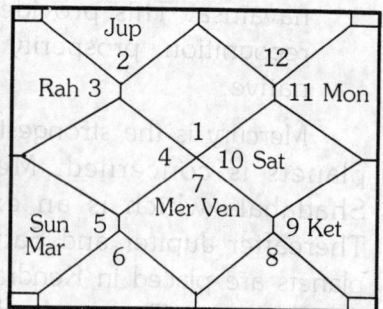

```
            Jup
         2        12
  Rah 3       |  11 Mon
           1
        4  | 10 Sat
           7
        Mer Ven
  Sun  5      |   9 Ket
  Mar    6         8
```

Balance of Vimshottari Dasa of **Sun   1Y 10M 21D**

It is believed that our late PM Mrs. Indira Gandhi, who was born with the Cancer in ascendant, was one of the ablest leaders of the world. Whatever predictions were made during her lifetime proved entirely untrue. That is not to say that all those astrologers were ignorant or incompetent, but that owing to faulty birth time in the birth chart, it was full of errors.

A number of scholars in India had expressed their doubts regarding it. In the English journal of astrology "Planets & Forecasts" published from Orissa, we wrote in December 1983 an article entitled "Indira Gandhi – An Astrological Profile", in which we mentioned the correct time of her birth as 11.33 hours. According to this time Leo was in ascendant at $2^0 28'$. In this article all the major events of her life were astrologically analysed and her end in 1984 was also predicted. Due to Vinimaya Parivartana (Mutual Exchange) Yoga between lords of the 5th and 10th houses, her son Rajiv Gandhi becoming the Prime Minister, was also predicted in the very same article. Satunr's Mahadasha started for Mrs. Gandhi in 1970.

In its early part, she got the victory in Indo-Pak war. From 1970 to 1984 she carried India to remarkable new heights. Of course being lord of the 7th Saturn is also the Markesh–lord of death or the planet causing death. But at the same time there is "Shadashtak" yoga between Rahu and Saturn which renders Rahu also as fatal. On 17.5.1984 Rahu's sub-period within Saturn commenced. During this period only, she was cruelly murdered on 31.10.1984. Saturn only brought her among the front rankers of world politics.

In her birth chart Saturn is making "Vipreet Raj Yoga" and is situated in its own navamsa. Saturn is in the nakshatra of Mercury and vice-versa, Lord of lagna Sun is also in

Anuradha, the nakshatra of Saturn. In a way Indira Gandhi's personality was controlled by Saturn. Her Moon sign was Capricorn, whose lord is also Saturn. Moon and Saturn share Vinimaya Parivartan Raj Yoga. To conclude, for persons with Leo ascendant, Saturn despite being the fatal planet, by virtue of its situational auspiciousness gives prestige, fame, popularity and power.

Gopal Das Neeraj

This is the birth chart of a famous and popular poet of India. Here as a yogakaraka Saturn is retrograde and is situated in an exalted sign Libra in the ascendant, which resulted in the native attaining extensive fame and a top position among contemporary poets. He has received scores of national and international awards. Here Saturn is the

Illustration : 9.33   *Horoscope No.: 55*

Date of birth : 05.01.1925   Time of birth : 02:15:00 hrs
Place of birth : Etawah   Lat 26:46 N Long 79:02 E
Ayanamsa   : 22:48:23   Sidereal Time : 8:56:53

Pln	Degree	Rasi	Nakshatra	Pad
Asc	16:17:41	Lib	Swati	3
Sun	21:12:38	Sag	Purvasadha	3
Mon	24:06:39	Ari	Bharani	4
Mar	17:12:24	Pis	Revati	1
Mer (R)	4:18:00	Sag	Moola	2
Jup (C)	11:13:34	Sag	Moola	4
Ven	24:38:27	Sco	Jyestha	3
Sat	19:33:45	Lib	Swati	4
Rah (R)	21:19:10	Can	Aslesa	2
Ket (R)	21:19:10	Cap	Sravna	4

Lagna Chart

```
        Ven
         8              6
Sun
Mer  9          Sat        5
Jup             7
       Ket 10    4 Rah
              1
            Mon
   11                   3
      12            2
      Mar
```

Navamsa Chart

```
      Sat          Rah
       12           10
    1                   9 Mar
              Ven
               11
       Mer 2      8 Mon
              5
      3                 7 Sun
       4            6
      Jup Ket
```

Balance of Vimshottari Dasa of **Ven 6Y 7M 12D**

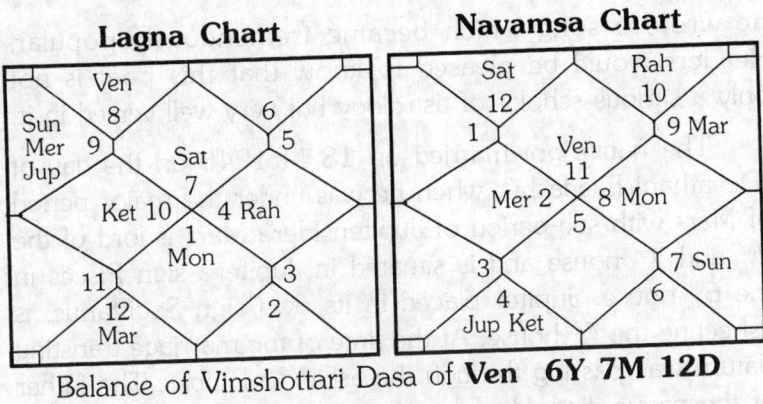

lord of the 4th and 5th and situated in the ascendant. The native is handsome and possesses an impressive personality. Lord of the lagna Venus is in the 2nd house in the sign of Scorpio, hence he also has a melodious voice. He charms his audience with his poetry racital. Saturn's major period is from 20.11.1985 to 20.11.2004. During this period only he has attained maximum honours and awards. Because of the influence of Saturn he received Padmashree as well. This positioning of Saturn in exalted Libra is creating Shasha Mahapurush Rajyoga. Here the position of Moon as the lord of 10th, in the 7th house is also worth considering. Moon is in the sign of Mars' as well as in its navamsa. Lord of the lagna Venus is in Mars sign Scorpio and is also aspected by Mars. Moon is also aspected by Jupiter besides Saturn and is situated in the fourth division of Venus-controlled "Bharani" nakshatra (constellation).

The early life of the native was spent in extreme poverty. Collecting money by diving in the rivers was his means of earning. Then starting from a typist's job, today he is a world renowned poet. For this Saturn in Libra, situated in the ascendant is the main reason. Normally, Saturn starts giving its beneficial results after the 36th year. The rise of this native also occurred from 1962-63 when he wrote a song which became tremendously popular. Readers would be pleased to know that this poet is not only a serious scholar of astrology but very well versed in it.

The native got married on 18.11.1946 on the day of "Devathani Ekadashi", when he was under the major period of Mars with sub-period of Jupiter. Here Mars is lord of the 2nd and 7th house and is situated in Jupiter's sign Pisces in the 6th house. Jupiter placed in its own sign Sagittarius, is aspecting the 7th house. At the time of the marriage transiting Saturn was passing through the ascendant Libra. The father of the native died when he was six and sub-period of Rahu was running in the major period of Sun. Birth of his son took place on 1.6.51, when the sub-period of Moon was continuing under the major period of Mars. Here Moon is lord of the 5th from Mars, being situated in Mars' sign only and is being aspected by the significator of children Jupiter. From 9.2.1960 to 1965 the native wrote songs for films. His mother died on 7.12.1977 when Venus' sub-period was continuing within the major period of Jupiter. The native went to USA for the first time during the sub-period of Rahu within the major period of Jupiter on 13.9.1984 and was conferred with the Padmashree on 26.11.1991 during the sub-period of Mercury within the major period of Saturn. Gopal Das Neeraj has won various honours and rewards due to his unparalleled talent in Indian poetry. Till 2010, he is working at the age of 85 almost round the clock.

A great deal has been written about the mysterious influence of Saturn. But fully understanding it, studying its effect on birth charts and then predicting accurately – this is the very aim of astrology. Several factors concerned with Saturn, if explained thoroughly, would go a long way in assessing the effect of Saturn in the birth charts by the readers.

Saturn is a symbol of poverty and penury and represents the common man. It is considered an evil planet because it is significator of death, murder and imprisonment, long term chronic diseases, unlimited suffering, humiliation and insults, failure and hurdles, as well as separation, bitterness in relationship, and hopelessness – these are all like puppets in the hands of Saturn. Saturn governs labour. People who believe in action are not terrorised by its anger. In other words, those who have a favourable Saturn are industrious, active and laborious. Their hard work frees them from the terror of Saturn and even rewards them. For persons born under Taurus lagna, Saturn is a beneficial and yogakaraka planet, because there it is lord of the destiny as well as lord of profession. In the birth chart of such a native, wherever Saturn may be situated, it enhances the effects of that house.

In its own period, it gives wonderful results. For those born under Libra lagna also Saturn is beneficial and yogakaraka, it is worth noting that for native born in these two lagnas. Saturn's position enhances the effects of the house occupied. Yet the inherent nature and characteristics of Saturn should not be overlooked. For instance, positioned in the 10th house, Saturn would make the native rise to the highest status but he would have to work extremely hard for it and the progress would be gradual and slow. Hard work, efforts and slow speed – these are the qualities of Saturn. While assessing the effects of Saturn, therefore, its nature as well as its characteristic qualities must be considered.

9.4 Saturn in the 10th : Special Information

Saturn situated in the "Upchaya" in the birth chart is beneficial. In any case all malefic planets give beneficial results when placed in the third, sixth or eleventh house.

Within these houses, with which native Saturn would affect better will depent on his lagna (ascendant) and the position of other planets. In the 10th house, Saturn affects occupation more. If the situation is good the native can reach the pinnacle of progress. But an inauspicious situation brings downfall, ill fame, insults and deprivations. One may not get timely promotions and may even have to face humuliation of demotion or suspension, if Saturn is afflicted in the 10th house.

For the Capricorn ascendant, Saturn in the 10th is exalted and very beneficial. In the sign of Libra, if Saturn of the 1th is conjoined with Venus then asctions get enhanced beneficial results. In Aquarius ascendant such Saturn is even better, although here it is placed in a sign governed by its adversary Mars. For Aries ascendant Saturn in the 10th house falls in the sign of Capricorn and a cause of good results. Saturn in the 10th house makes the native reach the top but it is followed by a steep fall from position and status of affliction. This is a fundamental characteristic of Saturn.

It is like a Prime Minister losing an election even for an MP's seat. Ex-PM of India the late Indira Gandhi became world famous due to Saturn but later she could not even win an MP's election. If Saturn in the 10th is placed beneficially, aspects an exalted Venus or joined with it, or is under the influence of an auspicious Jupiter – then such demotion will not occur. For Gemini ascendant Saturn as lord of the 8th or 9th will give similar results for the 10th house. But if Saturn in the 10th is conjoined with Venus or Jupiter then it will not give an inauspicious result. In the same way for Capricorn ascendant Saturn and Venus in the 10th house would give very good results. The ferocity of Saturn is surely mitigated by the influence of Jupiter.

For Taurus ascendant Saturn in the 10th is good almost as much as for Aries ascendant. In both these lagnas Saturn in the 10th is Swagrahi (in his own house), hence it creates "Shasha Mahapurush Rajyoga". But for Aries ascendant sometimes Saturn is considered a "Badhak" obstacle or deterrent since it is lord of the 11th house. Consequently some scholars have started the results of Saturn in the 10th for Taurus ascendant to be better than that for the Aries ascendant. Reference may be made of 48th couplet in the 2nd chapter of "Jataka Parijata", where "Badhak" planets have been explained *i.e.* :

क्रमाच्चराग   द्विशरीर   भानामुपान्त्यधर्मस्मरगास्तरीशाः ।
खरेशमान्दिस्थित राशिनाथा हयतीव बाधकरस्वेचराः स्युः ॥

that is, for movable, fixed and common ascendants 11th, 9th and 7th houses respectively are Badhak places. Planets situated in these houses or those possessing their lordship, are Badhakas and give unplesant results, provided in the signs controlled by them "Mandi" or "Khara" are also present.

This means that firstly it should be found out as to "Mandi" or "Khara" are situated in which sign. If the lord of that sign is situated in Badhak place, or is the lord of a Badhak house, then only it causes problems.

Mandi : It is sub-planet, which is the son of Saturn. It is the most harmful among the evil planets. Cause of greater suffering than that caused by Saturn, enhancer of distress and losses this sub-planet becomes even more malefic if conjoined with or aspected by Saturn. If Mandi is placed in the 8th house the native dies at a young age. Even when several planetary positions giving longevity are there in thr birth chart but Mandi falls in the 8th house, the person has a short life span. It is, therefore, necessary to be informed about Mandi's position when predicting from the birth chart.

Khara : The 56th couplet from the 5th chapter of "Jataka Parijata" is quoted below which talks about Khara :

विलग्न जन्म द्रेक्काणघस्तु द्वविंशति खरः ।
सुधाकरोपगांशक्षाच्चतुः षष्ट्यंशको भवेत् ।।

that is, the planet which owns the 22nd "Dreshkana" from the ascendant is called Khara.

The misconceptions prevalent about Badhak planets are responsible for the belief that for Aries ascendant, Saturn owning the 11th house is considered Badhak. But for both Taurus and Aries ascendant even when Saturn is the lord of the Badhak houses it should not be considered as Badhak unless Mandi or Khara also are not situated in the sign of Capricorn or Aquarius. Whenever well fortified Saturn influences the native, business would prosper but health would cause concern. On prediction disease connected with Saturn will definitely prove its effect.

Causing high rise and then pulling down, a prestigious high status and then sudden downfall – this is the characteristic of Saturn in the 10th, unless here Saturn is the lord of the ascendant, in his own house, is exalted, or yogakaraka. If Saturn in the 10th is under the influence of Jupiter or Venus its ferocity is sufficiently diminished. On the contrary if such a Saturn is conjoined with other evil planets or aspected by them, then is spells absolute decline.

9.5 Auspiciousness of Saturn & Saturn in the Ascendant

In the first, fourth, fifth and ninth house Saturn gives bad results and harms the interests of the house where it is located. But if this fact is accepted on its face value then one would predict wrongly. If Saturn is also lord of the lagna when in these positions while also being their lord, then it gives beneficial results. It is a common principle, enunciated by Laghu Parashari that even evil planets do not harm their own houses, rather they enhance their good effects. Saturn in ascendant is bad. It gives the native long term diseases, body ache, gas problems, spondylitis, hair loss, physical deformity, boils and soars, pimples or other factors diminishing the glow of the face, pessimistic outlook and a disease like arthritis. Saturn in the lagna causes diseases of old age even in youth, and the person concerned looks older than his or her age. In the same way if Mars is placed in the ascendant then the native looks younger than his actual age. The very nature of Saturn is inclined towards diseases of old age, pains and aches etc. Before explaining these facts a proper and thorough analysis of Saturn should be done. If Saturn is in an exalted sign like Libra or in its own sign Capricorn or is placed in the ascendant in Aquarius then the above mentioned ill effects are considerably reduced. Similarly if Saturn is conjoined with Jupiter or aspected with it then also its ferocity is diminished and good effects are enhanced.

Several sages have considered positioning of Saturn in Jupiter's sign Pisces or Sagittarius as beneficial. Rishi Garga has written that if Saturn is in its exalted sign of Libra, Pisces or Sagittarius, in the ascendant then the individual has an immensely attractive personality and physique both. He is like a king. It is stated in Skanda Hora that Saturn in Libra, Sagittarius or Pisces, in the ascendant gives wealth and prosperity. Saturn in Sagittarius appeals better than Saturn in Pisces.

9.6 Combination of Saturn and Venus

Saturn and Venus have a complementary relationship. Both these planets are friends and show their results during earh other's periods and sub-periods. Kalidasa has mentioned in his book "Uttarakalamrita", when Venus's sub-period is running during Saturn's major period then Saturn's influence is seen and vice-versa. These relationship is beneficial. The effects of the house, where they are together, is enhanced. Their conjunction in the 7th house is inauspicious for the marital happiness and the person concerned suffers from low moral values in his character. Saturn's aspect on or conjunction with Venus, lords of the 7th and 2th, or planets in the 7th and 2nd houses causes delays in marriage. Saturn and Venus situated in each other's navamsa give good results in matters relevant to the concerned houses because in Pisces Venus is exalted and Saturn also is favourable.

Saturn and Mercury are also friends, and their mutual relationship also gives good results. If Jupiter is in an inauspicious position with Saturn then the native's life is full of struggles. Financial condition sees ups and downs. If Saturn and Venus are conjoined they make the native a skilled painter, artist or calligraphist. They are often expert cartoonists too. The money position of the native improves with the help of some female. According to Jataka Parijata, the combination of Saturn and Venus makes a person skilled in sports, swimming etc. and animal lover. He loves travelling. He may be a good surgeon, or a successful businessman in timber. When Saturn and Venus are placed in the ascendant the native possesses an attractive personality and has interest in several women. This usually leads to an immoral life style. Despite having several servants he is unhappy.

If Saturn and Venus are conjoined in the 4th house then the individual receives money from women and friends. He is respected by his relatives. In the 7th house conjunction of these two planets gives birth to character depravity. In the 10th house they together make one glorified and prosperous like a king. In the birth chart of people with Capricorn or Aquarius as ascendant this yoga gives the best results. For them Venus is Yogakaraka and Saturn bring lord of the lagna, together with Venus, enhances the effects of the concerned houses and gives good results. For Libra and Taurus ascendants also the conjunction of Saturn and Venus is auspicious. For these ascendant Saturn is yogakaraka and Venus is benefic being the lord of ascendant. Combination of such a Saturn and Venus enhances the effects of the concerned houses and lends them auspiciousness.

According to Hora Sara, if the conjunction of Saturn Venus is in the 1st, 4th, 5th, 9th or 10th house then the native is under the influence of a woman and works in a high position. In other houses the same combination spells poverty and depletes physical strength and energy. If the lagna is Taurus, Libra, Capricorn or Aquarius and Saturn-Venus conjunction is also in one of these signs then the results are very satisfying.

If Saturn is conjoined with Jupiter, then its ferocity and evil are diminished. Saturn attains some auspiciousness, but the auspiciousness of Jupiter is destroyed owing to Saturn's malevolence. That means Saturn-Jupiter combination makes the Saturn's inauspiciousness and Jupiter's auspiciousness a little less. Experience proves that if these two are situated at "Samasaptaka" from each other *i.e.* facing each other, they exchange their effects. Saturn gives Jupiter's results and vice-versa.

9.7 Saturn-Sun Relationship

Saturn and Sun are ideal enemies. In qualities and shortcomings both are opposite to each other. Such animosity is not seen in any other two planets. Saturn rules the West while Sun rules the East. Sun is an indicator of fame, prosperity, and state positions, while Saturn indicates poverty, notoriety and servile work. The planets friendly to Saturn are inimical to Sun excepting Mercury. Likewise planets friendly with Sun are inimical to Saturn. The combination of Saturn and Sun spells troble. The house where they are together, loses its effects. Father and son are against each other. Even if they are not against each other, one or the other suffers misfortune. The renowned scholar of astrology Acharya H.N. Katve has disclosed a well researched fact regarding Sun and Saturn in his book which has proved true in my experience also. It is that when Saturn and Sun are conjoined in the birth chart of a native then he and his father, or he and his son had been enemies in their previous birth. They are born as father and son in this birth so as to take revenge from each other's fortune. Nature, regulated by planets, itself arranges this rigamarale. Often the son's luck is gained by the father. The son is poor, he can not progress, faces numerous hurdles, problems, and difficulties. While after his birth the father constantly prospers, progresses and becomes luckier. This usually happens when the vanquished enemy of the previous birth is father in this birth and by depleting the luck of his former victorious enemy, now his son, avenges himself. If the defeated enemy is the son in this birth then fathers downfall starts after the birth of son. Often the father dies. Imprisonment or suspension may happen. Theft, robbery or accident can also happen. We have dedicated two complete chapter on Sun-Saturns relationship and misogamous role of Sun and Saturn.

In short, the father faces calamities after the birth of his son. If the combination of Saturn and Sun is in the birth chart of the child then it would be injurious to the father or the son, this can be known from experience, test and analysis.

9.8 Saturn-Moon Relationship

Just as Saturn and Sun create adverse relationship between father and son, likewise Moon and Saturn also create clashing relationship between mother-son or mother-daughter. Ill fame, mental illness, suffering, loss of intelligence, mental defects or problems, loss of memory, troubles to the mother, antagonistic mentally etc. are caused by it. But the Saturn Sun combination is worse than the Saturn Moon one.

Saturn is the signs of Leo and Cancer is harmful. In Taurus, Libra, Gemini and Virgo, Saturn gives beneficial results. Scorpio and Aries situated Saturn is also inauspicious. If Saturn in the Aries possesses Neech Bhang Rajyoga, then it gives pleasant results. In its own signs Capricorn and Aquarius Saturn is beneficial. Once again it can be mentioned that Saturn for Libra is the best since it creates great yogas. Period and sub-period of Jupiter and Saturn are good for those with Libra ascendant. For such a native even in the 6th, 8th and 12th houses, Saturn gives favourable results.

For Aries ascendant combination of Saturn and Jupiter in the 9th house is auspicious and creates Raj Yoga. Some books of astrology contradict it but our experience supports it. For Gemini ascendant Jupiter and Saturn are lords of the 10th and 9th respectively. Both the planets if situated in the 10th and 9th house help in the progress of the native. He attains some prestigious position.

One misconception which is prevalent is that if Saturn's main period is fourth from the period continuing at the time of birth then it may cause the native's death. He faces severe problems, wife or child may die suddenly, impoverishment may happen. Our experience is contrary to this. In my own birth chart Saturn's main period is fourth from the period at the time of birth but I have achieved the best results during this period only in my life so far.

Saturn is supposed to be bad for those with Leo or Cancer lagna, because in both these situations, being lord of the seventh, it is a potential "markesh". In my opinion for these lagnas, if Saturn forms auspicious yogas then it is beneficial only.

In the following couplet Sage Garga has clearly expressed his views regarding Saturn :

तुला कोदण्ड मीनानं लग्नं संस्थेऽपि चेत शनि ।
करोति करोति भूपतेर्जन्म महापुष्यां नु भावत ।।

that is, Saturn if in Libra, Pisces or Sagittarius ascendant, makes the native like a king.

Skandha Hora says :

इत्यासि घरो पापेषु लक्ष्मीप्रदः ।

In the above mentioned lagnas Saturn gives wealth, luxury and prosperity.

If Saturn is in its own sign Aquarius or Capricorn then it gives enough wealth, but being in a Jupiter sign, it overwhelms with immeasurable wealth, worthy progeny and a good wife. It also confers headship of some city or village. This is obvious from the Shloka given below :

स्वन्तः प्रत्ययितो नरेन्द्र भवने सत्पुत्रजायाधनो,
जीव क्षेत्रज्ञ तेऽर्कजः पुरवल ग्रामाग्रनेताथबा ।।

In the 4th and 5th house Saturn is inauspicious. Aspected by Jupiter Saturn loses some of its evilness. If Saturn is in the 7th house, the wife of the a native is dark complexioned but trustworthy and faithful. If Saturn is afflicted by evil effects then only it indicates dark complextion otherwise in Sagittarius, Pisces and Libra Saturn, if in the 7th house, the spouse is not dark complexioned.

For Cancer and Leo ascendant, Saturn in the 7th is injurious. For Scorpio ascendant, Saturn being lord of the 3rd or 4th is beneficial. If in the 11th of 3rd house it causes very good "Dhanyoga" (special money position). For Capricorn lagna Saturn is better than for Aquarius lagna. In Saravali, Kalyan Varma has stated :

शूरो विक्तसमृद्धौ नगराधिपतिर्यशस्वी च।
शनिं जीवयोः प्रधानः श्रेणि सभाग्रामसंघमाः।।

Combination of Saturn and Jupiter makes the native brave and courageous. He begets enough wealth and heads some village or town. In another shloka it has been stated that if Saturn is situated in the sign of Jupiter and is aspected by it, then the native becomes a king or commander of an army.

Saturn is also a planet causing renunciation. It possesses unlimited patience, tolerance and diligence. An ability to control all sensual powers and a capacity for concentration, loyalty and devotion are also present in Saturn – if it influences the 9th house.

Saturn makes one a king if it is well fortified. Saturn is a planet of renunciation and can make one a kingly Sanyasi like Vivekanand or the native may become the founder of the new religion or a perceptor of Dharma or so if well posited and is unafflicted in the 10th house. Saturn of the 10th house raises the native to the unaspected topmost position in the respective field or indicated by all other planets in the birth chart and navamsa occupied by concerning planets indicating field of work and means of livelihood. We have discussed the horoscopes of founder of different religions such as Guru Nanak, Gautam Buddha, Prophet Mohammad, Guru Govind Singh, Swami Vivekanand etc. who were blessed by the fortunate position of Saturn in the 10th house and that too without any blemish. Industrialist of worldwide fame also had well fortified Saturn in 10th house. Many leaders and ministers like Jag Jivan Ram, Sushma Swaraj, Shyama Prasad Mookerjee, etc. were born with good disposition of planets in addition to the placement of Saturn in the 1th house. Many of the best writers and authors like Premchand, H.G. Wells were also born with Saturn in the 10th house. A few top film artist, directors like Hrishikesh Mukherjee etc Many Prime Ministers and Presidents like Gyani Zail Singh, Gulzari Lal Nanda, Chandra Shekhar were born when Saturn owned the 10th house from their ascendant and aspected the 10th house along with the aspect of Jupiter over the 10th house.

These are the persons who are said to be ruled by Saturn in one or the other way as explained by us in this chapter. Mrs. Indira Gandhi, Mr. A.K. Chaturvedi, Gopal Das Neeraj, Mr. Ashok Srivastava, Amitabh Bachchan, and world renowned industialists achived the highest success in their respective fields due to glorious disposition of well fortified Saturn. World renowned scientist Albert Einstein rose to dizzy heights due to his exceptional research on theory of relativity due to placement of Saturn in 10th house in Pisces along with most important and prominent Raj Yogas. Saturn in the 10th house causes enormous rise and steep downfall which takes place in a miserable and pathatic way. In case of affliction by the killer planets like Mars like Libra and Taurus ascendant or due to conjunction with malefic and lord of trika houses. Saturn in 10th produces nagative results if weak afflicted or owns 6th, 8th or 12th house, or aspected by lords of these houses. Saturn's association with malefic Mars, Rahu or Ketu does not promote the native and in case of his elevation it brings a heavy watershed, many fighters and warriors like Adolf Hitler, Napoleon Bonaparte, suffered miserable end of their life due to afflicted Saturn in their 10th house. In the birth chart of Sheikh Mujiburrahman, Benazir Bhutto, Abraham Lincoln, the 10th house Saturn was afflicted by Mars. Therefore they suffered the brutal assassination. However American President Woodrow Wilson, Richard Nixon also had bad and undesirable end when they were forced to resign from the highest position and presidentship. It is not out of place to mention that it is not only 10th house placed Saturn which made these personalities great. But there is much powerful Raja Yoga present in the birth chart. Saturn is the strongest too in these charts that acted and assisted in making them a king or equal to a king in their respective field of work. So, after this long study of Saturn's influence on 10th house there remains no doubt in appreciating Saturn that Saturn is a king maker.

9.9 Conclusion

In line with the objective of this study to enlighten the readers on the nature of Saturn in an holistic manner we provided readers with a multi-dimensional analysis. A number of shlokas or verses about the shape and nature of Saturn by Varaha Mihir, Mantreshwar, Kalyan Varma, Vaidyanath and Punjraj have been cited to conjure up the picture of a Saturn-dominated individual. Similarly views of many present day astrologers both Indian and Western have been discussed to offer a clear idea on Saturn's origin and range of its influence.

We have delineated Saturn's placement in the twelve houses in details with a view to underlining the effects caused each such placement. Along side the views of classical astrologers like Mahesh, Vaidyanath, Gopal Ratnakar, Jeevanath etc., the views of western astrologer Allen Leo have been discussed in details. We found it noteworthy that individual differences arise due to signs, influence of aspect and strength and also that a detailed analysis of Saturn's placement in the twelve houses is the basic ground work that can unravel the innermost secrets of a personality.

We presented Saturn in twelve signs and aspects to highlight how the enigmatic Saturn renders multifarious results when placed in various signs and Rashis. Future cannot be properly ascertained if the effects of signs and Rashis is not adequately understood.

Saturn is the king maker par excellence. To elaborate this central theme we gave salient features of it and illustrated them by means of a score of examples both from India and other parts of the world. They range from medieval Indian saints like Namdeo, Tukaram to ancient greatman like Gautam Buddha to present day Babu Jag Jivan Ram, Kalraj Mishra, Mrs. Sushma Swaraj etc. to western personalities like H.G. Wells, Charlie Chaplin, let alone the great lyricist Gopal Das Neeraj. These are just a few examples. All these horoscopes suggest that the impact of Saturn is not as simple and straight as it is popularly thought about. Due to glorious disposition of well-fortified Saturn a number of great persons achieved great height in their specific pursuits.

We sincerely hope that our readers will be the wiser by shedding their simplistic notions about the nature of Saturn and in its place adopt an holistic view which adequately harbours the king-maker role of Saturn. And in its king-maker role is included the role of a true spiritual leader also.

●

10 Saturn in the 10th House: Fall From Power

It is believed that the placement of a powerful and unafflicted Saturn in the 10th house makes one extremely successful with regard to professional aspect. In other words Saturn in the 10th house makes one a king or somewhat like a king. But, finally one suffers steep downfall. This is a matter of experience, exercise and research. A native with Saturn in the 10th (from *janma lagna* or *Chandra lagna*) may have sudden elevation and depression in life and residence in foreign countries, and in his later life he is liable to become an ascetic; Saturn raises the native from the sphere of birth or surroundings and gives him name, fame and glory. It is said that Saturn invariably causes downfall after raising a man to dizzy heights unless it is in own sign or sign of exaltation. Saturn's position in the 10th house (from *lagna* or the moon) is enough to raise the native. It is generally accepted that Saturn's position in the 10th brings a native to the pinnacle of his chosen course of life and drops him steeply down, never to rise again. It is usually believed that the going up to the top of the ladder and falling off from there vertically is not averted whatever be the amount of strength of the 10th lord or Jupiterian aspect on Saturn. A native with Saturn in the 10th has extraordinary perseverance to reach his goal. Such natives will not be in a hurry and have enough patience to achieve the goal. Any amount of obstacles will not change their mind. "Presence of Saturn or its aspect to the 10th house either from *lagna* or the Moon has great bearing in the influence one achieves amongst the masses" observed by Prof. B.V.Raman in his *Notable Horoscopes*. Before proceeding further let us study the results of the Saturn in the 10th house. Various classicals like Bhrigu Sutra, Brahat

Hora Parashar, Saravali, Phaldeepika and Jataka Parijaat etc. have specified the prominent role of Saturn, if it is posited in the 10th house in any birth-chart. These results of Saturn are mentioned hereunder. With Saturn in the 10th in the horoscope of the native, his prosperity and career rise after the age of 36.

BHRIGU

पंचविंशतिवर्षे गंगास्नायी अतिलुब्धः पित्तशरीरी ।। 44 ।।
पापयुते कर्मविघ्नकरः शुभयुते कर्मसिद्धिः ।। 45 ।।

Saturn in the 10th house gives holy dip at the age of 25. It gives bilious temperament. It makes one very greedy. If it is combined with malefics, it may cause professional debacles, but if it is combined with benefics, it may give professional success.

VASHISHTHA

बहुकुकर्मरतं कुपुत्रं दौर्मनस्यं ।

It makes one indulge in nefarious activities. It gives evil mind and unworthy sons.

PARASAR

दशमे धनलाभं सुखं जयं ।
माने च मीने यदि वार्कपुत्रः सन्यासयोगं प्रवदन्ति तस्य ।।

Saturn in the 10th makes one rich, happy and victorious. Saturn in Pisces, however, makes one a Sanyasi.

GARGA

भवेत् वृन्दपुरग्रामपतिर्या दण्डनायकः ।
प्राज्ञः शूरो धनी मन्त्री नरः कर्मस्थिते शनौ ।

सेवार्जितधनः क्रूरः कृपणः शत्रुघातकः।
जंघारोगीनी नीच शत्रु राशिस्थे कर्मणे शनौ।।

Saturn in the 10th makes one a lord of town or villages. It makes one a Magistrate or a Judge. It makes one prudent, Valorous, rich or a minister. If it is debilitated or in inimical sign, one may earn his livelihood through services. It may make one cruel hearted and miser. It may make one subdue one's enemies. It may make one suffer from some illness in one's thighs.

GUNAKAR

सुखशौर्यभाकू खे शनिः।

Saturn in 10th makes one happy and valorous.

VARAHAMIHIRA

सुखशौर्यभाकू खे शनिः अर्कवत्।

Saturn in 10th like the Sun in the 10th gives happiness and courage.

KALYAN VERMA

धनवान् प्राज्ञः शूरौ मन्त्री वा दंडनायको वापि।
दशमस्थे रविनयेवृन्दपुरग्रामनेता च।।

Saturn in the 10th makes one wealthy, wise, brave, a minister or a commander. Such a native may be a public leader or a leader of town or villages.

BRIHAD YAVAN JATAKA

राज्ञः प्रधानमतिनीतियुतं विनीतं
संग्राम चन्दनपुरादयाधिकारयुक्तम्।

कुर्यान्नरं   सुखवरं   द्रविणेन
पूर्णमिषूरणे हितरणेस्तनुजः करोति ।।

Saturn in the 10ᵗʰ house makes one a minister or a secretary to the government. It may make one a policy-maker or a diplomat or a statesman. It may make one an expert in warfare, humble and polite, honoured as a V.I.P. or as head of town, village or some area, happy and rich.

JAYA DEVA

प्राज्ञः प्रधानमतिमान्ससभयो विनीतो
ग्रामाधिकारसहितः सघनोडम्बरस्थे ।

(Jataka Chandrika of Jayadeva)

Saturn in the 10ᵗʰ makes one scholarly, fortunate, polite, ruler and wealthy.

VAIDYA NATH

मन्दे यदा दशमगे दण्डकर्ता मानी धनी निजकुल
प्रभवृच   शूरः ।।   विवासः ।

(Jataka Parijatah)

Saturn in the 10ᵗʰ makes one wealthy honourable, brave, ruler magistrate or judge and a lamp to the family. It may also bestow Sanyasi.

MANTRESHWAR

मंत्री वा नृपतिः धनी कृषि परः शूरः ग्रसिद्धोम्बरे ।।

(Phala Deepika)

Saturn in the 10ᵗʰ house makes one a king or a minister. It makes one wealthy, brave and agriculturist.

DHUNDHI RAJ

राज्ञः प्रधानमतिनीतियुतंविनीतं सद्ग्रामवृन्दपरभेदनकाधिकारम् ।
कुर्यान्निरं सुचतुरं द्रविणेन पूर्ण मेषूरणेहितरणेस्तनुजः स्थितृचेत् ।।

Saturn in the 10th house from Lagna makes one endowed with intellect and advising capability of a minister. Such a native, though humble and polite, may rule over villages, towns and people by his diplomatic skill. He is very clever and rich.

KASHI NATH

कर्मभावे   सूर्यपुत्रेकुकर्मा   धनवर्जितः ।
दयासत्यगुणौर्हीनश्चंचलोऽपि भवेत् सदा ।।

Saturn in the 10th house makes one an evil doer, bereft of wealth, piety, truth and virtues. Such a native may be fickle-minded.

JAGESHWAR

शनौ कर्मणो   पितृघाती नरःस्यात् परं मातृकष्टं कथं ।
देहसौख्यं कुतः स्याद् ध्रुवं दुष्टंकर्मा भवेन्नीचवृत्तिः ।।

One with Saturn in the 10th house is detrimental and trouble some for his parents. Such a native is bereft of physical comforts, conveyances and friends. He may have low livelihood. He may be an evil doer too.

NARAYAN BHATT

अजातस्य   माता   पिता बाहुरेव
वृथा सर्वतो दुष्टकूर्माधिपत्यात् ।
शनैरघते कर्मणः शर्म मन्दो जयो विग्रहे
जीविकां ना तु यस्य ।।

शनौ व्योमगे विन्दते कि च माता सुखं
शैश वं दृष्यते किन्तु पित्रा ।
निधिः स्थापितो वा पिता वा कृषिश्च
प्रणश्येत ध्रुवं वृश्यतो ।।

CHAMATKAR CHINTAMANI

Natives with Saturn in the 10th house may lose their parents in childhood. They get comforts slowly. They win the battle. When in power, they do evil things unnecessarily their ancestral property, agriculture, lands etc. are ruined due to some temporal or unforeseen causes.

ARYA GRANTHA

शनैश्चरे कर्मग्रहे स्थितेऽपि महाधनी भृत्यजनानुररक्तः ।
प्राप्तप्रवासे नृपसद्मवासी न शत्रुवर्गाद् भयमेति मानी ।।

Saturn in the 10th house makes one very rich. Such natives take interest in servants. They live in palaces while abroad, they are fearless and respectable.

HARI VANSHA

बुद्धियुक्तं पूर्णवित्त मनुष्यं ग्रामधीशराजमान्यं करोति ।
स्वोच्च्स्थो वा स्वारूपस्थो विशेषात्
शैषस्थश्चेद् वैरिभीत्यं शनिश्च ।

Saturn in exaltation or own sign in the 10th house makes one wise, intelligent, rich, lord of the village or a state officials. In other signs Saturn causes fear from enemies.

KHETA KAUTUKAM

शाहमकाने जोहलश्चेषुदशाफते च मानवोशाहः।
अथवा भवेनूमुशीरः खुशखुल्कः सुकृतीगनी नेही।।

A native with Saturn in the 10th house may be a king or a minister if he is also running Dasa of Saturn. He is good natured. He performs good deeds. He is wealthy and a very dear person.

SHAMBHU HORA PRAKASHA

Punja Raja in his Shambhu Hora Prakasha says :

शनैश्चरः कर्मणि चन्द्रतन्वोर्विहीनवृत्तिं कुरुते सखेदम्।
काश्र्यं   शरीरे   धनधान्यहीनं   चिन्ता
विवादं   नितरां   कुशीलम्।।

(Chapter 6, S.H.R./212)

One with Saturn in the 10th from the Moon or the Ascendant will be in base professions. He will be saddened, physically emaciated and be bereft of wealth and grains. Worries, disputes and bad disposition may also result from this position of Saturn.

It further says that Saturn in the 10th house may give wealth through servants in its Dasa. We feel, it should also include Service or promotion in service in Dasa of such Saturn.

JYOTISHARNAVA NAVANITAM

पुरग्रमाग्रशिरेवमंत्र वा दंडनायकः।
खेशनौ पापदृष्टे शत्रुद्वेषसुघातकः।।

Jupiter or Saturn in the 10th house may bless one with lordship of a city or a village or may make one a Judicial Officer. With Saturn in the 10th house in aspect to malefic, the native may ruin or seriously injured his adversaries or he may eliminate his enemies.

MANASAGARI

शनैश्चरे   कर्मगृहस्थितेऽपि महाधनी   भृत्यजनानुरक्तः ।
प्राप्तप्रवासे नृपसदयवासी न शत्रुवर्गाद्भयमेति मानी ।।

Saturn in the 10th house makes one very rich and devoted to his servants and subordinates. Such a native gets government patronage abroad. He does not fear enemies.

Having all these in mind, now we will go through some horoscopes of heads of states who had Saturn in the 10th which we will try to find out how far the above results are true.

Many politicians and Head of State or Country, has Saturn in the 10th house. A few of them like Sheikh Mujibur Rehman, Adolf Hitler, Nepolean Bonaparte, Abraham Lincoln, Wilson Nixon and many other suffered the downfall or the tragic end of their life by assassination or so. Saturn if well fortified, *Yogakaraka* and strong gives enormous rise, if posited in the 10th house, but it does bring downfall which is a strong and common belief among as scholars of astrology.

However, we have gone through all such research works made by many recognised scholars and astrologers. These works and researches had been placed in "The Astrological Magazine" of Bangalore edited by Dr. B.V.Raman from time to time. However, very humbly we do not share the same opinion after a thorough and wide examination of the horoscopes of top ranking officers, ministers, capitalists, writers, scholars, industrialists and bureaucrats, who were having well fortified and strong Saturn in their 10th house. But they had never gone through the downfall. We have examined a number of such horoscopes and have keenly observed that the reason of downfall is not the placement of Saturn in the 10ᵗʰ house. There are various other strong astrological reasons that explain sudden downfall, imprisonment, destruction, death, assassination and loss of power, etc. We will try to examine the cases of downfall in the birth charts of a few VIPs who suffered downfall or sudden death, with Saturn in the 10ᵗʰ house.

If one reaches at the top, what happens thereafter. He will either stay there for some time or he will start moving down. Why only Saturn should be held responsible for the downfall of the individual. Let us look at a few cases of Saturn's placement in the 10ᵗʰ house from a different angle. We are trying to illustrate that Saturn in the 10ᵗʰ house gives a rise to dizzy heights but is not responsible for the downfall, if there is at all so. In fact the downfall, death or destruction takes place due to various other reasons of the particular birth chart. There are always ups and downs in the career due to unfavourable *dasa bhukti* and adverse planetary transits. There are elevations of individuals to the top most position even without Saturn's placement in the 10ᵗʰ house. Similarly, there are many cases of dethronement, destruction, assassination and downfall in various ways in which Saturn had nothing to do with the 10ᵗʰ house. Therefore, Saturn should not be held invariably responsible for the downfall etc., if it occupies the 10ᵗʰ house in a birth chart.

To begin with, we take up the horoscopes of a few very important Heads of State, Emperors, ministers, who reached at the top and also suffered steep downfall after attaining the highest position of their career. In all these cases there was severe affliction of Saturn or that of the lord of the 10ᵗʰ house in one way or the other. And that should be held responsible for the downfall. We will also try to illustrate other types of examples of Saturn in the 10th house which never resulted in any kind of downfall or destruction of the native. Let us place our view point as under:

Sheikh Mujibur Rehman

Illustration : 10.1   Horoscope No.: 56

Date of birth : 17.03.1920   Time of birth : 22:38:00 hrs

Place of birth : Faridpur   Lat 28:12 N Long 79:32 E

Ayanamsa   : 22:44:47   Sidereal Time : 10:06:00

Pln	Degree	Rasi	Nakshatra	Pad
Asc	0:43:02	Sco	Vishakha	4
Sun	4:04:13	Pis	U Bhadrapad	1
Mon	0:01:31	Aqu	Dhanishtha	3
Mar (R)	16:18:38	Lib	Swati	3
Mer (R/C)	8:55:10	Pis	U Bhadrapad	2
Jup (R)	15:49:59	Can	Pushya	4
Ven	6:06:30	Aqu	Dhanishtha	4
Sat (R)	14:05:53	Leo	P Phalguni	1
Rah (R)	24:07:14	Lib	Vishakha	2
Ket (R)	24:07:14	Ari	Bharani	4

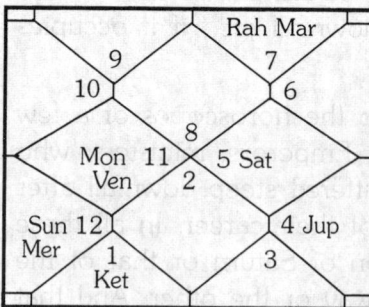

Lagna Chart   **Navamsa Chart**

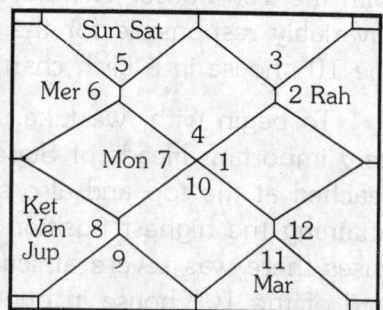

Balance of Vimshottari Dasa of **Mar 3Y 5M 25D**

The horoscope belongs to the first Prime Minister of Bangladesh, Sheikh Mujibur Rehman, who was popularly known as Bangabandhu (brother of the nation) by the people of Bangladesh. He came to power in February 1972 after being released from a Pakistani prison. By this time he was running under Saturn dasa Rahu bhukti. Saturn, *Vargottama* in the 10th from *lagna*. He ushered in the second revolution and on the 25th of January, 1975, he became the President of Bangladesh with sweeping majority. But in a pre dawn coup on 15-8-75 his chest was sprayed with bullets and his family (except two daughters away from the country) including his relatives, was destroyed. Sheikh Mujibur Rehman was born in Scorpio ascendant with Saturn in the 10th house. Saturn is retrograde in Leo corresponding with Poorva Phalguni constellation ruled by Venus. In fact, 4th lord Saturn, the 9th lord Moon and 7th lord Venus have mutual aspect on each other. Saturn is extremely powerful in the 10th house and obtains 1.57 *shadbala*. The 10th lord the Sun is posited in the 5th house giving rise to *Kendra trikona raja yoga*, in Pisces and receives the aspect of exalted Jupiter. Thus, the 10th house is under the influence of Saturn, Jupiter, Venus and 9th lord Moon which made Sheikh Mujibur Rehman, the President of Bangladesh. Mars is *Atmakaraka* planet in this horoscope and obtains *navamsa* of Saturn; Whereas, Saturn obtains *vargottama navamsa* in Leo, and the Sun obtains own *navamsa* in Leo. Jupiter and Venus obtain the *navamsa* of Mars which provided him a strong, impressive and influential personality with an intense feeling of patriotism. Opposition of Saturn and Mars in *navamsa* chart identical to Leo and Aquarius signs resulted into his assassination when he was in power.

We see that Sheikh Mujibur Rehman who fought for the freedom of Bangladesh, got ultimate success and became

President finally. Prominent role of the Saturn and Jupiter with regard to the 10th house is quite prominent in his horoscope.

It is a very strong belief that Saturn in the 10th makes one to reach dizzy heights and there is always a downfall or untimely and unnatural death at the critical juncture, when the native wants to enjoy his outstanding success and prosperity. Here again Saturn occupies the 10th house, Sheikh Mujibur Rehman was assassinated in the sub period of Jupiter and in the major period of Saturn. In fact, Saturn's placement in inimical sign and inimical *navamsa* Leo cannot be appreciated for a long lasting Presidentship. In fact Saturn is heavily afflicted due to its conjunction with the Sun in Leo *navamsa* and that too under the mutual aspect with ascendant lord Mars identical with Aquarius sign in the 8th house in *navamsa*. Thus, Saturn's affliction resulted into his assassination. He was murdered because the 3rd lord Saturn aspects the ascendant lord Mars in *rasi* chart and *navamsa* chart both. Moreover, Rahu and Mars are associated with each other in the 12th house and lend their unfavourable aspect over the 6th house in *rasi* chart. Jupiter is *Maraka* for Scorpio ascendant and that too falls in Saturn's constellation *Pushya*. Jupiter and Saturn are in *dwidwadash* position therefore, both became *maraka* for Sheikh Mujibur Rehman and his assassination resulted in the sub period of Jupiter in the major period of Saturn.

Napoleon Bonaparte

Illustration : 10.2   *Horoscope No.: 57*

Date of birth : 15.08.1769   Time of birth : 10:40:00 hrs
Place of birth :   Lat 41:55 N Long 08:40 E
Ayanamsa   : 20:38:45   Sidereal Time : 8:16:17

Pln	Degree	Rasi	Nakshatra	Pad
Asc	5:59:00	Lib	Chitra	4
Sun	2:05:05	Leo	Magha	1
Mon	7:51:15	Cap	Uttarasadha	4
Mar	21:23:36	Leo	P Phalguni	3
Mer	15:27:30	Can	Pushya	4
Jup	24:22:09	Lib	Visakha	2
Ven	16:21:46	Gem	Ardra	3
Sat	5:15:27	Can	Pushya	1
Rah (R)	1:36:11	Sag	Moola	1
Ket (R)	1:36:11	Gem	Mrigshira	3

Lagna Chart

```
           8              6
 Rah 9            Jup        5  Mar
                   7            Sun
      Mon 10    4  Sat
               1   Mer
     11                   3  Ven
        12           2       Ket
```

Navamsa Chart

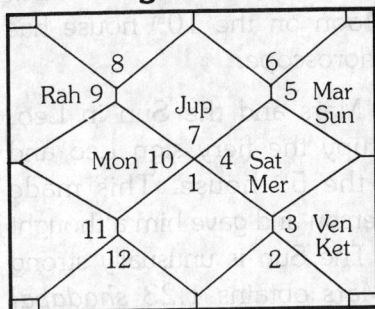

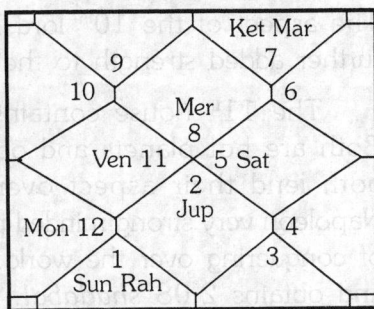

```
                        Ket Mar
          9                      7
 10                Mer        6
                    8
        Ven 11   5  Sat
                 2
     Mon 12      Jup        4
          1                3
       Sun Rah
```

Balance of Vimshottari Dasa of **Sun**   **0Y 11M 17D**

Napoleon Bonaparte was strong and arrogant Emperor of France. From the position of an ordinary soldier he rose to the throne. Although he acquired full powers, he crowned himself as the Emperor of France only on 2-12-1804, when he was running Rahu Dasa Mars Bhukti. After nine years as the undisputed Emperor of France, Napoleon lost a battle for the first time in his life. It was the Battle of Leipzig which started on 16th October 1813. Defeated Napoleon was removed to Elba Islands as prisoner on 6-4-1814. Yet he was able to escape from there and seize power for hundred days in the year 1815 before his final banishment to St. Helena Islands. After his return from Elba, the battle of Waterloo was started.

Napoleon was born in Libra ascendant with Saturn in the 10th house identical with Cancer. Jupiter occupies the Libra ascendant and it is shifted in the 2nd house from where it aspects *yogakaraka* Saturn placed in the 10th house and *bhagyadhipati* Mercury. In fact, the combination of Saturn and Mercury in the 10th house is exceptionally powerful for all professional prosperity and progress. Saturn and Mercury, both lords of triangles, and Jupiter aspect over these planets certainly enhanced the strength of the 10th house. Here Mercury and Jupiter are karmic control planets and these occupy the 10th house and the ascendant. The aspect of the 10th lord Moon on the 10th house has further added strength to the horoscope.

The 11th house contains Mars and the Sun in Leo. Both are hot planets and occupy the fiery sign Leo and both lend their aspect over the 5th house. This made Napoleon very strong minded person and gave him a thought of conquering over the world. The Sun is unusually strong and obtains 2.08 *shadabal*. Mars obtains 1.23 *shadabal* and Jupiter is *Atmakaraka* and it falls in its own constellation *vishakha*. Venus obtains 1.26 *shadabal* and Saturn obtains 1.04 *shadabal* and falls in its own constellation *Pushya*. All planets except Rahu and Jupiter are posited in the 6th, 7th and 8th house from Moon and 9th, 10th and 11th house from the ascendant. This has formed a kind of *Adhi Yoga*, *Dharmakarmadhipati Yoga*, *Vasumati Yoga*, *Kahal Yoga*, *Kendra Trikona Raja Yoga*, *Gaja Kesari Yoga* and *Vinimay Parivartan Yoga* between Moon and Saturn. The Sun is a planet of fame and prosperity. It is well placed in the 11th house in own sign and obtains *navamsa* of exaltation. This resulted in grand success of Napoleon Bonaparte.

The downfall and death took place when he was running under the major period of Jupiter which is a killer for Libra ascendant as it owns the 3rd and 6th house. Jupiter is shifted in the 2nd house and that has added much strength in its *marakatwa*. However, Jupiter obtains Taurus *navamsa* which is *mrityuaamsa yukta*.

Now let us see the reason of the downfall of Napoleon. There is mutual exchange between Saturn and Moon which is the most undesirable affliction of Saturn. Saturn and Moon do not only have mutual exchange of signs but they have a mutual aspect on each other as well. Ascendant lord Venus occupies the 9th house in friendly sign Gemini and it is quite strong in *shadabala* but Venus falls over the axis of Rahu and Ketu. The Saturn placed in the 10th house is hemmed between malefics like Ketu and Mars, similarly the 9th lord Mercury is also heavily afflicted because it is hemmed between Mars and Ketu giving rise to *Papa Kartari yoga* as well as the 9th lord Mercury occupies inimical sign Cancer and is under mutual aspect with its enemy Moon. Thus Saturn and Mercury, who occupy the 10th house have been afflicted by the aspect of inimical Moon and these are also hemmed between malefic *viz.*, Ketu and Mars. Apart from this combination 10th lord Moon, 9th lord Mercury, *yoga Karaka* Saturn, the 10th house and the 5th house are afflicted in various ways and that caused unnatural and untimely death of Napoleon. Affliction of Moon, Mercury and the 5th house made Napoleon highly ambitious to the extent of insanity desirous of wining the entire world.

These are the findings of a majority of the astrologers that Saturn if well placed in the 10th house raises the subject to the dizzy heights and causes steep downfall when the native reaches at the top. However, we have our own opinion and research observations about Saturn's placement in the 10th house.

Adolf Hitler

Illustration : 10.3

Horoscope No.: 58

Date of birth : 20.04.1889

Time of birth : 18:30:00 hrs

Place of birth :

Lat 48:00 N Long 13:00 E

Ayanamsa   : 22:18:22

Sidereal Time : 8:26:00

Pln	Degree	Rasi	Nakshatra	Pad
Asc	4:27:18	Lib	Chitra	4
Sun	8:30:00	Ari	Aswini	3
Mon	14:19:39	Sag	Purvasadha	1
Mar (C)	24:04:25	Ari	Bharani	4
Mer (C)	3:21:37	Ari	Aswini	2
Jup	15:56:18	Sag	Purvasadha	1
Ven (R)	24:23:15	Ari	Bharani	4
Sat	21:09:11	Can	Aslesa	2
Rah (R)	22:44:50	Gem	Punarvasu	1
Ket (R)	22:44:50	Sag	Purvasadha	3

Lagna Chart

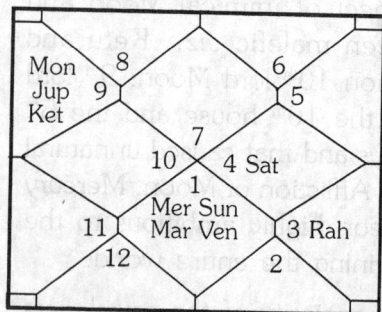

Navamsa Chart

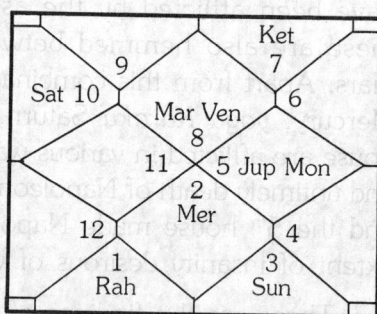

Balance of Vimshottari Dasa of **Ven 18Y 6M 3D**

It is the horoscope Adolf Hitler who has been recognised, appreciated and known for the 10th house Saturn. He was born in Libra ascendant with strong Saturn in the 10th house. In fact, Saturn is posited in Cancer corresponding with *Ashlesha* constellation. Saturn obtains own *navamsa* Capricorn. It happens to be a *yogakaraka* for Libra ascendant and if so well placed in 10th house can make one equal to a king provided Jupiter has a concern with the professional aspect of the native. It was not only Saturn in the 10th in Cancer with 1.52 *shadabala* which made Hitler equal to a king. Lord of the 10th house Moon is conjoined with 3rd and 6th lord Jupiter and aspects the 9th house. Mars and the *lagna* lord Venus occupy the 7th house in association with 11th lord the Sun in the sign of exaltation and *swakshetriya* Mars. Thus, Mars and Saturn both have mutual aspect over each other. This is a very rare combination of the conjunction of exalted Sun and *swakshetriya* Mars in 7th house, under malefic aspect of Saturn and Jupiter.

This birth chart signifies that Hitler was extremely fortunate person because Karmic Control planets Jupiter and Mercury are placed in triangular position from each other. The Sun is exalted, Mars occupies its own sign in *Kendra* giving rise to *Ruchhaka Yoga*. Jupiter falls in own sign Sagittarius in association with 10th lord Moon with Ketu. Venus is *Atmakaraka* planet in this birth chart and obtains *navamsa* of Mars in association with Mars. Venus and Mars are also associated in rasi chart under the aspect of Jupiter. This is a strong indication of being the Chief Of Army. 10th lord Moon obtains Sun's *navamsa* i.e. Moon is *Labhansha Yukta*. Saturn and Mars obtain own *navamsa*. The Sun, the Mars, Venus and Saturn are exceptionally strong planets in this birth chart. However, we intend to say that Saturn's placement in 10th house as a *Yogakaraka* is King Maker combination provided it is strong, unafflicted and the 10th house, its lord is supported by Jupiter. Thus, Saturn can make one a King or equal to a King if Jupiter plays a prominent role with regard to the professional aspect of the native.

Saturn in the 10th house made Hitler a King, but mutual aspect of killer Mars with Saturn made him a tyrant. Saturn is afflicted due to mutual aspect with Mars. The 10th lord Moon is afflicted due to association with Ketu. The ascendant is aspected by malefic Mars and the Sun, which created an intense desire to win the world, deep in his heart and mind. Exalted Rahu in the 9th house has enhanced the fortune. The 10th lord Moon is eclipsed by Rahu and Ketu. The Sun though exalted but has become a killer as it is posited in the 7th house with 7th lord Mars and is aspected by its bitterest enemy Saturn. The Sun obtains *navamsa* of Mercury identical with Ketu's constellation *Ashwini*. The sub period of the Sun in the major period of Rahu brought Hitler's disaster and he committed suicide on 30th April of 1945. In fact, here Saturn of the 10th house is afflicted in various ways which resulted in his untimely and unnatural end. If Saturn of the 10th house is well associated and aspected by benefics, the downfall does not take place. This is our firm belief after examination of hundreds of birth charts having Saturn in the 10th house.

Benazir Bhutto

Illustration : 10.4   Horoscope No.: 59

Date of birth : 21.06.1953   Time of birth : 19:43:00 hrs
Place of birth : Karachi   Lat 24:53 N Long 67:00 E
Ayanamsa   : 23:12:39   Sidereal Time : 13:08:59

Pln	Degree	Rasi	Nakshatra	Pad
Asc	12:01:14	Sag	Moola	4
Sun	6:41:52	Gem	Ardra	1
Mon	0:01:22	Lib	Chitra	3

Mar (C)	11:45:37	Gem	Ardra	2
Mer	1:14:20	Can	Punarvasu	4
Jup	16:47:36	Tau	Rohini	3
Ven	21:00:30	Ari	Bharar.i	3
Sat (R)	27:20:40	Vir	Chitra	2
Rah (R)	10:32:31	Cap	Sravna	1
Ket (R)	10:32:31	Can	Pushya	3

Lagna Chart

```
          Rah
      10          8
   11                7  Mon
          9
      12  \  6 Sat
          3
       Sun Mar
   Ven 1              5
      2            4
      Jup        Ket Mer
```

Navamsa Chart

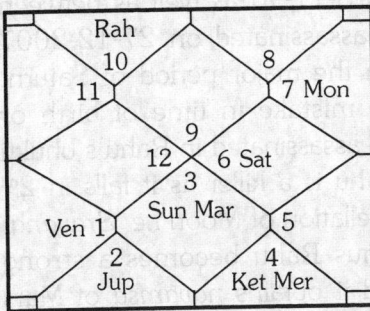

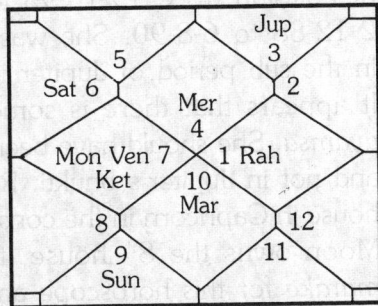

```
                      Jup
              5        3
   Sat 6                   2
              Mer
               4
   Mon Ven 7      1 Rah
      Ket       10
               Mar
          8           12
          9        11
          Sun
```

Balance of Vimshottari Dasa of **Mar 3Y 5M 26D**

Benazir Bhutto was the Prime Minister of Pakistan. She was the daughter of Ex-Prime Minister Zufikar Ali Bhutto who ruled Pakistan for quite a long time. Benazir Bhutto was assassinated by her rivals just before the general elections in Pakistan. Her opponents were confident of her roaring victory. Therefore, she was shot in her car when she was leaving after she addressed a large number of people. She was assassinated on 27-12-2007 when she was passing in the sub period of Jupiter in the major period of Saturn.

She was born in Sagittarius ascendant with Saturn in the 10th house in Virgo. Saturn is quite a strong planet in this horoscope as it obtains 1.32 *shadabala* and it is

Atmakaraka as well. Saturn is posited in the 10th house in Virgo corresponding with *Chitta* constellation ruled by Mars. Saturn obtains *vargottoma navamsa* and it is retrograde as well.

One certainly reaches to the top most position of his/ her field if Saturn occupies the 10th house in association or aspect by benefic Jupiter. In this chart, ascendant lord Jupiter aspects the 10th house and Saturn. This planetary configuration raised her to the position of the Prime Minister of Pakistan twice 19-10-93 to 5-11-96 as well as between 2-12-88 to 6-8-90. She was assassinated on 27-12-2007 in the sub period of Jupiter in the major period of Saturn. It appears that there is some mistake in time of birth or *ayamsa*. She should have been assassinated in Rahu's bhukti and not in Jupiter's bhukti. Rahu is a killer as it falls in 2nd house in Capricorn in the constellation of Moon i.e. *Sravana*. Moon owns the 8th house, thus Rahu becomes a strong *maraka* for this horoscope and it obtains *navamsa* of Mars as well. Thus Benazir Bhutto was assassinated during Saturn Rahu period i.e. in the same *dasa bhukti* in which Mrs. Indira Gandhi was assassinated. Mrs. Gandhi was killed during the sub period of Rahu in the major period of Saturn. In this horoscope Saturn and Rahu both are *markesh*.

Saturn of the 10th house raised Mrs.Benazir Bhutto to the top position but mutual aspect between Mars and Saturn largely afflicted Saturn. The 10th lord and the lord of *lagna* were also afflicted as explained above therefore she suffered the downfall and untimely as well as unnatural death.

Abraham Lincoln

Illustration : 10.5   Horoscope No.: 60

Date of birth : 12.02.1809   Time of birth : 07:32:00 hrs
Place of birth : Hardin   Lat 36:45 N Long 88:17 E
Ayanamsa   : 21:11:43   Sidereal Time : 17:07:34

Pln	Degree	Rasi	Nakshatra	Pad
Asc	17:58:37	Aqu	Satabhisha	4
Sun	2:18:01	Aqu	Dhanistha	3
Mon	6:49:44	Cap	Uttarasadha	3
Mar	4:18:30	Lib	Chitra	4
Mer	19:09:59	Aqu	Satabhisha	4
Jup	0:53:56	Pis	P Bhadrapad	4
Ven	16:18:31	Pis	U Bhadrapad	4
Sat	11:56:56	Sco	Anuradha	3
Rah (R)	15:04:53	Lib	Swati	3
Ket (R)	15:04:53	Ari	Bharani	1

Lagna Chart

```
        Jup Ven          Mon
          12              10
    Ket 1                      9
           Sun Mer
              11
            2     8 Sat
              3
                         7 Mar
        4                   Rah
          5          6
```

Navamsa Chart

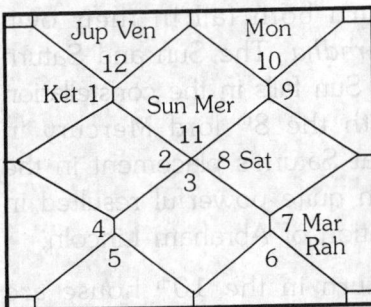

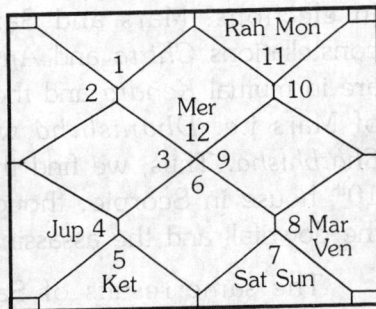

```
                    Rah Mon
                      11
        1                    10
    2           Mer
                 12
          3      9
             6
      Jup 4                8 Mar
          5           7     Ven
        Ket       Sat Sun
```

Balance of Vimshottari Dasa of **Sun   1Y 7M 25D**

The horoscope belongs to Abraham Lincoln, the first
American President who was assassinated. He was born in

a log cabin. He worked as a surveyor, legislator, county lawyer, Member of Congress and finally became the president of the United States at the age of 52. During Rahu and Jupiter *Dasa* he had a series of defeats for various posts. In 1838 he was defeated in speaker's contest, in 1840 lost the Congress election, in 1843 again lost the congress election, in 1846 elected to the congress, in 1855 lost the Senate election, 1856 lost the vice president contest, in 1858 again lost the Senate election, and at last was elected as President in November in 1860. He was born in Aquarius ascendant with Saturn in the 10th house in Scorpio. The Saturn obtains *navamsa* of exaltation and that is *bhagyansha yukta* as well. The Saturn in the 10th house raised Abraham Lincoln to the post of President of USA. However, he was assassinated on 14-4-1865 in Saturn *dasha* Sun's *bhukti*, both are killers. The aspect of Jupiter on the 10th house and Saturn was of great help in the elevation of Abraham Lincoln to the position of the President. Mars and Saturn both aspect the 12th house and 6th lord Moon that is the reason of his assassination. The 10th lord Mars falls over the axis of nodes that is the reason of problems and failures with regard to number of defeats in elections. Mars and Saturn both fall in their own constellations *Chitta* and *Anuradha*. The Sun and Saturn are in mutual *Kendra* and the Sun falls in the constellation of Mars i.e. *Dhanishtha* with the 8th lord Mercury in *Shatbhisha*. Thus, we find that Saturn's placement in the 10th house in Scorpio, though quite powerful resulted in the downfall and the assassination of Abraham Lincoln.

The same results of Saturn in the 10th house are observed by the scholars of astrology with Benazir Bhutto, Sheikh Mujibur Rehman, Richard Nixon, Napolean Bonaparte, Rajeev Gandhi, etc.

Woodrow Wilson

Illustration : 10.6   Horoscope No.: 61

Date of birth : 28.12.1856   Time of birth : 00:48:00 hrs
Place of birth : Virginia beach Lat 36:51 N Long 75:58 E
Ayanamsa   : 21:51:34   Sidereal Time : 7:11:41

Pln	Degree	Rasi	Nakshatra	Pad
Asc	22:51:43	Vir	Hasta	4
Sun	14:54:04	Sag	Purvasadha	1
Mon (C)	25:28:52	Sag	Purvasadha	4
Mar	24:25:40	Cap	Dhanistha	1
Mer (C)	25:17:07	Sag	Purvasadha	4
Jup	9:20:17	Pis	U Bhadrapad	2
Ven	24:01:25	Cap	Dhanistha	1
Sat (R)	19:13:28	Gem	Ardra	4
Rah (R)	19:17:26	Pis	Revati	1
Ket (R)	18:17:26	Vir	Hasta	3

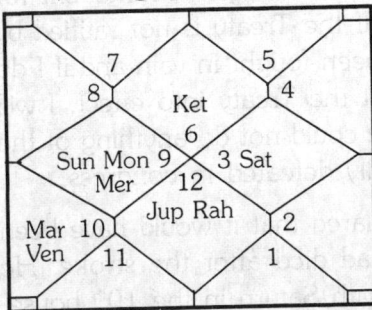

Lagna Chart   Navamsa Chart

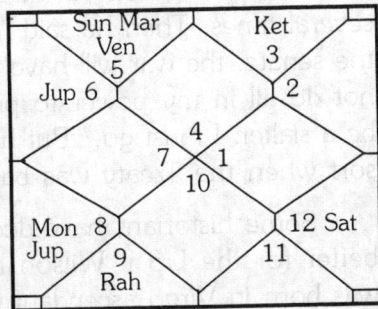

Balance of Vimshottari Dasa of **Ven 1Y 9M 10D**

The horoscope is of Woodrow Wilson, the First World War President of the USA. He was the 28th President to come to power in November 1912 elections. By this time he was running under Jupiter *dasa* Mars *bhukti*. He was elected for the second term in 1916 when he was running under the sub period of Saturn in the major period of Saturn. But in contrast to other leaders Wilson was removed from power till he completed his second term in November 1920. But he had two setbacks during the latter part of his second term. Firstly, on 2-10-1919 he had a severe heart stroke and a rumour swept New York that the President was dead. For six weeks, after President Wilson suffered the incapacitating stroke, his wife Edith Bolling Wilson ran the United States, and sustained her husband with her love and courage.

Due to this stroke, during the last year of his term, Wilson remained a crippled President. Secondly, the fight for the Treaty and the League of Nations went badly against the President. There came the last day that Congress would be in session- March 19, 1920. Wilson's intransigence had infuriated his enemies in the senate; and on that day the Treaty, and the dream for which Edith and Woodrow Wilson had sacrificed so much, went down in final crushing defeat. The President gazed out at the Washington Monument for several times. Then he said: "If the Treaty is not ratified by the senate, the war will have been fought in vain and if I do not do all in my power to put the Treaty into effect, I will be a slaker. I must go." But he could not do anything of the sort when the Treaty was badly defeated in congress.

Some historians have declared that it would have been better for the US if Wilson had died after the stroke. He was born in Virgo ascendant with Saturn in the 10th house. Saturn is aspected by 12th lord the Sun, the 11th lord Moon and the ascendant lord Mercury. Thus the opposition of the Sun and Moon with Saturn and their mutual aspect between them caused the downfall and defamation at the end of his career. He also suffered a massive heart attack before the end of his 2nd term. Finally, he received unmanageable criticism for support of the Treaty. Aspect of Mars and Saturn on the 12th house and Saturn's placement in *Aridra* constellation in the 10th house is extremely adverse.

Richard Nixon

Illustration : 10.7   *Horoscope No.: 62*

Date of birth : 09.01.1913   Time of birth : 21:43:00 hrs
Place of birth : California   Lat 35:07 N Long 117:59E
Ayanamsa   : 22:38:31   Sidereal Time : 5:07:38

Pln	Degree	Rasi	Nakshatra	Pad
Asc	26:26:02	Leo	P Phalguni	4
Sun	26:45:55	Sag	Uttarasadha	1
Mon	27:32:36	Cap	Dhanishtha	2
Mar	7:06:37	Sag	Moola	3
Mer	7:22:44	Sag	Moola	3
Jup	9:01:47	Sag	Moola	3
Ven	10:51:00	Aqu	Satabhisha	2
Sat (R)	4:50:32	Tau	Krittika	3
Rah (R)	13:40:09	Pis	U Bhadrapad	4
Ket (R)	13:40:09	Vir	Hasta	2

Lagna Chart

Navamsa Chart

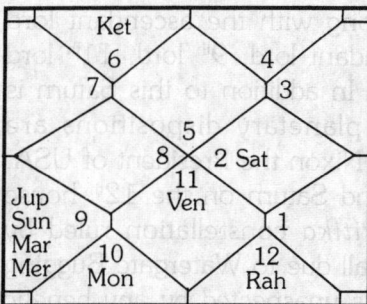

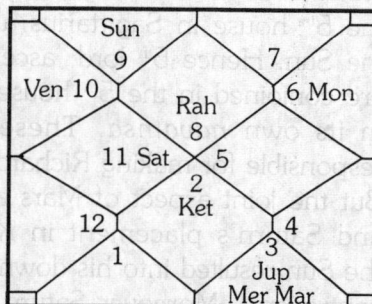

Balance of Vimshottari Dasa of **Mars 4Y 9M 14D**

The horoscope belongs to Richard Milhouse Nixon, the first President to resign his office in the 200 years old American history. There has been always something of the born loser about Richard Nixon. Save for his satellite days in the Eisenhower sun, he had never known the roman triumphs of an easy campaign in all his long political life. He was the 37th President of USA in November 1968 elections when he was running Jupiter *bhukti* in Saturn *dasa* and was re elected for the second term in 1972 with thumping majority when he was passing through Mercury *bhukti* in Mercury *dasa*. During Ketu *bhukti* in Mercury *Dasa* the Watergate scandal started to give him headache. During a news conference on 22-6-1972 he said that White House had no involvement whatsoever in the Watergate Bugging and again on 5-10-1972 he denied that he knew anything about the break in, but as soon as Venus *bhukti* started on 17-4-1973 he announced that he came to know of new serious charges.

His clinging to power reached a staggering climax, and with the active impeachment movement he voluntarily stepped down on 8-8-74, exactly six years after accepting the Republican nomination for presidential elections on 8-8-68. He was born in Leo ascendant with Saturn in the 10th house identical to Taurus. There is a mutual exchange between 7th lord Saturn and the 10th lord Venus. The 4th and the 9th lord Mars is conjoined with 5th lord Jupiter in the 5th house in Sagittarius along with the ascendant lord the Sun. Hence 5th lord, ascendant lord, 9th lord, 11th lord are conjoined in the 5th house. In addition to this Saturn is in its own *navamsa*. These planetary dispositions are responsible for making Richard Nixon the President of USA. But the joint aspect of Mars and Saturn on the 12th house and Saturn's placement in *Kritika* constellation ruled by the Sun resulted into his downfall due to Watergate Bugging controversy. Moreover Saturn is unaspected by any benefic planet.

We have dealt so many cases where Saturn in the 10ᵗʰ house raised the native to the dizzy heights as much as the Prime Minister, President and Heads of State. But there had been a steep downfall whenever Saturn was afflicted either in *Rasi* chart or in *navamsa* or it was posited in the constellation of the Sun, Mars, Rahu or Ketu etc. Joint aspect of Saturn and Mars, or Saturn and the Sun over each other, or on the 12ᵗʰ house also created problems and destruction, defeat, demotion, etc.

If Saturn was unafflicted it never resulted in downfall though it elevated the native to the unexpected heights, name, fame and honour. For example, let us illustrate the horoscope of Rahul Gandhi, Vallabh Bhai Patel, Einstein, etc who had unafflicted Saturn in the 10ᵗʰ house.

Vallabh Bhai Patel

Illustration : 10.8   *Horoscope No.: 63*
Date of birth : 11.10.1875   Time of birth : 18:45:00 hrs
Place of birth : Nadiad   Lat 22:42 N Long 72:55 E
Ayanamsa   : 22:07:17   Sidereal Time : 20:03:59

Pln	Degree	Rasi	Nakshatra	Pad
Asc	17:35:57	Ari	Bharani	2
Sun	25:43:09	Vir	Chitra	1
Mon	11:24:10	Aqu	Satabhisha	2
Mar	29:52:18	Sag	Uttarasadha	1
Mer	20:18:56	Lib	Vishakha	1
Jup	14:42:25	Lib	Swati	3
Ven (C)	0:31:37	Lib	Chitra	3
Sat (R)	27:25:27	Cap	Dhanistha	2

| Rah | 16:23:43 | Pis | U Bhadrapad | 4 |
| Ket (C) | 16:23:43 | Vir | Hasta | 2 |

Lagna Chart

```
          |  Rah  |
    2     |  12   |
  3       |         11  Mon
          |    1    |
      4  X  10 Sat
      7
    5     | Ven Mer  |  9 Mar
    6     |   Jup    |
          |    8     |
   Sun Ket
```

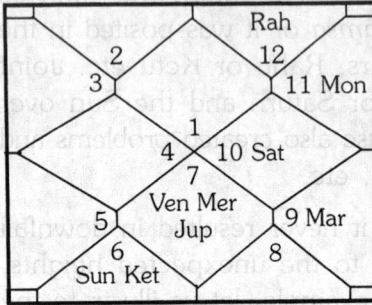

Navamsa Chart

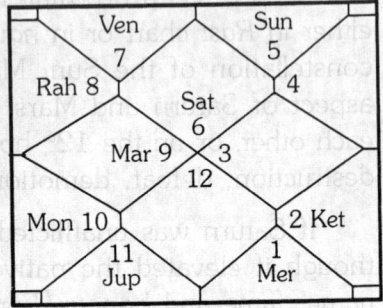

```
       | Ven  |  Sun  |
       |  7   |   5   |
 Rah 8 |        |        4
       |  Sat   |
       |   6    |
 Mar 9 X   3
       |   12   |
Mon 10 |        |  2 Ket
  11   |        |   1
  Jup  |        |  Mer
```

Balance of Vimshottari Dasa of **Rah   11Y 7M 8D**

Vallabh Bhai Patel was a political and social leader of India who played a major role in the country's struggle for independence and guided its integration into a united, independent nation. He was called "Iron Man of India" in India and across the world, he was often addressed as Sardar, which means *Chief* in many languages of India.

Raised in the countryside of Gujarat in Gurjar community and largely self-educated, Vallabh Bhai Patel was employed in successful practice as a lawyer when he was first inspired by the work and philosophy of Mahatma Gandhi. Patel subsequently organised the peasants of Kheda, Borsad, and Bardoli in Gujarat in non-violent civil disobedience against the oppressive policies imposed by the British Raj; in this role, he became one of the most influential leaders in Gujarat. He rose to the leadership of the Indian National Congress and was at the forefront of the freedom movement and political events, organising the party for elections in 1934 and 1937, and promoting the Quit India Movement.

As the first Home Minister and Deputy Prime Minister

of India, Patel organised relief for refugees in Punjab and Delhi, and led efforts to restore peace across the nation. Patel took charge of the task to forge a united India from the 565 semi-autonomous princely states and British-era colonial provinces. Using frank diplomacy backed with the option (and the use) of military action, Patel's leadership enabled the accession of almost every princely state. Hailed as the Iron Man of India, he is also remembered as the "Patron Saint" of India's civil servants for establishing modern all-India services. Patel was also one of the earliest proponents of property rights and free enterprise in India.

Vallabh Bhai Patel was born in Aries ascendant with Saturn in the 10ᵗʰ house of its own. Saturn has given rise to *Shasha Mahapurusha raja yoga, Anshavtaar Yoga, Malavya Mahapurusha Raja Yoga, Chaamar yoga, Raja Lakshan Yoga,*etc. are present in this birth chart which raised Sardar Vallabh Bhai Patel to the position of the first Deputy Prime Minister of India. In this horoscope Mars, Saturn, the Sun and Ketu aspects the 10ᵗʰ house but there is no downfall due to very strong Saturn in the 10ᵗʰ house. Moreover, all the three benefics in the 7ᵗʰ house give rise to *Lagnaadhi Yoga.* Sardar Vallabh Bhai Patel suffered a mysterious end of his life due to some kind of setback.

Martin Luther King Jr.

Illustration : 10.9   Horoscope No.: 64

Date of birth : 15.01.1929   Time of birth : 11:21:00 hrs
Place of birth : Atlanta   Lat 33:44 N Long 84:23 E
Ayanamsa   : 22:51:44   Sidereal Time : 18:21:59

Pln	Degree	Rasi	Nakshatra	Pad
Asc	15:33:19	Pis	U Bhadrapad	4
Sun	2:12:06	Cap	Uttarasadha	2

Mon	25:49:28	Aqu	P Bhadrapad	2
Mar (R)	29:02:45	Tau	Mrigshira	2
Mer	18:47:23	Cap	Sravna	3
Jup	8:18:22	Ari	Aswini	3
Ven	17:36:44	Aqu	Satabhisha	4
Sat	2:28:57	Sag	Moola	1
Rah (R)	5:48:29	Tau	Krittika	3
Ket (R)	5:48:29	Sco	Anuradha	1

Lagna Chart

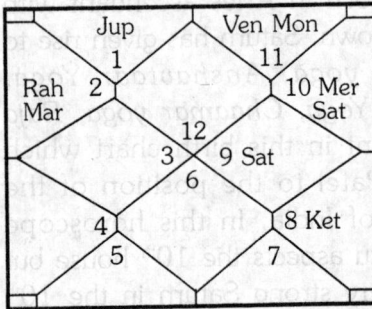

Navamsa Chart

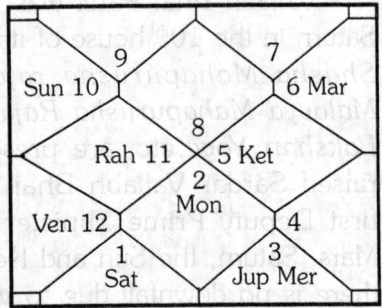

Balance of Vimshottari Dasa of **Jup 9Y 0M 3D**

Martin Luther King Jr. was an American clergyman, activist and prominent leader in the African American civil rights movement. His main legacy was to secure progress on civil rights in the United States, and he has become a human rights icon: King is recognized as a martyr by two Christian churches. A Baptist Minister, King became a civil rights activist early in his career. He led the 1955 Montgomery Bus Boycott and helped found the Southern Chritian Leadership Conference in 1957, serving as its first president. King's efforts led to the 1963 March on Washington, where King delivered his "I have a Dream" speech. there, he raised public consciousness of the civil rights movement and established himself as one of the greatest orators in U.S. history.

In 1964, King became the youngest person to receive the Nobel Peace Prize for his work to end racial segregation and racial discrimination through civil disobedience and other non-violent means. By the time of his death in 1968, he had refocused his efforts on ending poverty and the Vietnam War, both from a religious perspective. King was assassinated on April 4, 1968, in Memphis, Tennessee. He was posthumously awarded the Presidential Medal of Freedom in 1977 and Congressional Gold Medal in 2004; Martin Luther King, Jr. Day was established as a U.S. National Holiday in 1986.

He was born in Pisces ascendant with Saturn in the 10th house which is well aspected by the ascendant and the 10th lord Jupiter. It has been repeatedly said that Saturn in the 10th house if aspected by Jupiter or Venus or associated with any of these planets, promotes the matter of the 10th house to a large extent. Here the 10th lord Jupiter aspects the 10th house and Saturn as well. The position of the Saturn in the 10th house resulted in his winning of the Nobel Prize as discussed above. He became one of the best orators of the United States. Here killer Mars aspects Saturn and the 10th house which resulted in his assassination on 4th April 1968. Saturn falls in the constellation of Ketu, *Moola* and obtains the *navamsa* of Mars. Unfortunately Saturn is aspected by Mars in *Rasi* chart as well as *navamsa* chart. The present example of the affliction of Saturn by Mars in the 10th house has further confirmed that there is a downfall or, untimely or unnatural death if Saturn occupies the 10th house and is aspected by or associated with malefic like Mars.

Rajiv Gandhi

Illustration : 10.10   *Horoscope No.: 65*

Date of birth : 20.08.1944   Time of birth : 08:50:00 hrs
Place of birth : Bombay   Lat 18:58 N Long 72:50 E
Ayanamsa   : 23:04:46   Sidereal Time : 6:04:42

Pln	Degree	Rasi	Nakshatra	Pad
Asc	8:02:14	Vir	U Phalguni	4
Sun	3:53:25	Leo	Magha	2
Mon	17:57:45	Leo	P Phalguni	2
Mar	1:14:33	Vir	U Phalguni	2
Mer	28:35:49	Leo	U Phalguni	1
Jup (C)	12:13:06	Leo	Magha	4
Ven	18:44:29	Leo	P Phalguni	2
Sat	14:13:35	Gem	Ardra	3
Rah (R)	4:25:27	Can	Pushya	1
Ket (R)	4:25:27	Cap	Uttarasadha	3

Lagna Chart

	Ven Jup Mer Mon Sun		
7	5		
8		4 Rah	
	Mar 6		
9	3 Sat		
12			
Ket 10		2	
11	1		

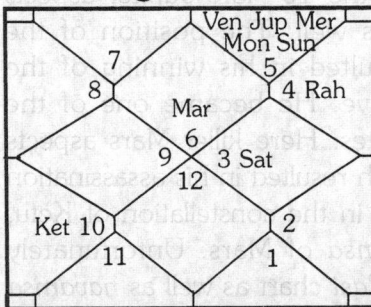

Navamsa Chart

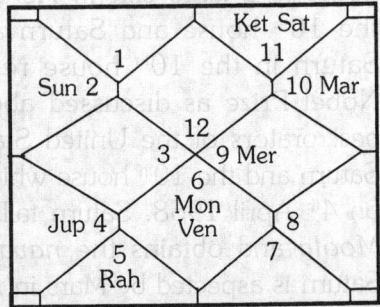

		Ket Sat	
1		11	
Sun 2		10 Mar	
	12		
3	9 Mer		
	6		
Jup 4	Mon Ven	8	
5 Rah		7	

Balance of Vimshottari Dasa of **Ven   13Y 0M 20D**

Rajiv Gandhi was born in the Virgo ascendant with Saturn in the 10th house. Five planets Jupiter, Venus, Moon, the Sun and Mercury occupy the 12th house. 8th lord Mars falls in the ascendant corresponding with inimical sign Virgo. Mars aspects the 8th house and owns it as well. Mars obtains

Saturn's *navamsa* which resulted into his brutal assassination. Saturn's placement in the 10th house in *Aridra* constellation raised him to the position of the Prime Minister. However, Saturn is devoid of any benefic aspect. Therefore, the downfall and assassination took place during the major period of Rahu. Rahu falls in Saturn's constellation Pushya.

The horoscopes of Hitler, Libra ascendant with Saturn in the 10th aspected by Mars from the 7th (Aries) and of Napoleon Bonaparte, Libra ascendant with Saturn in the 10th and Moon in the 4th, of Sheikh Mujibur Rehman of Bangla Desh, born in Scorpio ascendant with Saturn in the 10th in retrogression, are cited by the misleading theory of downfall due to Saturn in the 10th. Lately, Benazir Bhutto was assassinated during the major period of Saturn due to mutual aspect between Mars and Saturn, and placement of 10th lord in the 8th in inimical sign over the axis of nodes. Thus, it has been observed that Napoleon Bonaparte, Adolf Hitler, Sheikh Mujibur Rehman and Benazir Bhutto who all reached to the cliff due to placement of Saturn in the 10th house, suffered the steep downfall, death or assassination due to serious affliction of the 10th lord, along with Saturn or that of the ascendant lord by malefic or *trika* houses.

The famous scientist Albert Einstein was born in Gemini with Saturn in the 10th. It may be seen that Einstein's horoscope shows Mercury, Venus and Saturn in Pisces, with Jupiter in the 9th in Aquarius. Saturn in the said chart is associated with exalted Venus, a mighty and brilliant benefic for Gemini when it is in the 10th in Pisces and with Jupiter, having further exchanged their houses. There are two powerful *yogas*: 1. *Dharmakarmadhipati Yoga* (normally its difficult for Aries and Gemini ascendants) and 2. *Ishtabala yoga* formed due to the 1st, the 5th and the 9th lords in the 10th. There is no question of any 'fall' for the Nobel Laureate, Einstein who propounded the Theory of

Relativity and the Photoelectric Effect.

So, it is crystal clear that it may be incorrect to generalise and assert that Saturn in the 10th invariably causes a rise to dizzy heights followed by a steep fall. It has been observed that in hundreds of horoscopes by us that Saturn of the 10 house has not caused any downfall to the native. We are in close contact with a multi millionaire born in Libra ascendant with Saturn in 10th house corresponding with Cancer and having a mutual exchange with 10th lord Moon. The native is among top 10 richest persons of India. He has never seen downfall till date when he is more than 63 years of age. Similarly, a very ordinary union leader became a multi millionaire by virtue of the placement of Saturn in the 10th house. Jamna Lal bajaj, Swami Vivekanand, R.N.Goenka, Rahul Gandhi, Albert Einstein, etc., had Saturn in the 10th house and they did not bear the brunt of downfall. There are always ups and downs in the career irrespective of the position of Saturn in the horoscope.

Saturn in its own or exaltation house in the 10th as also as the lord of *lagna* in the 10th may not be adverse and, as lord of ascendant in the 10th especially for Capricorn ascendant it may not be evil. And, Saturn with or aspected by good Venus or good Jupiter will not cause any 'fall'. For, *Saaravali* says: if Jupiter and Saturn join, one is able, has plenty of wealth, and becomes famous as the Cheif of a city or town or of a guild. And, when Saturn is in a house or Jupiter (Sagittarius or Pisces) and is well aspected by Jupiter, the native becomes a chief ruler or a commander (of an army or police force). Causing downfall is not the privilege of Saturn in the 10th. Lord of the 6th or the 8th in the 10th or lord of the 10th in the 6th, the 8th or the 12th, unredeemed by Jupiter's aspect are also found to cause a fall.

11 The Sun–Saturn Relationship Regarding Marriage

The relationship between the Sun and Saturn is the most peculiar one in influencing a native in various ways. This needs a comprehensive research and examination. We intend to deal with one of the very important aspects of the relationship i.e. the Conjunction of the Sun and Saturn. We consider Saturn as the bitterest enemy of the Sun. Their character and significations are just the opposite. While Saturn represents west, the Sun represents east. The Saturn is cold and dard whereas the Sun is hot and bright. The Sun gets exalted in Aries where Saturn gets debilitated there only. The Sun gets debilitated in Libra, where the Saturn enjoys exaltation. The Sun represents life, power, prosperity, expansion, discipline and values of recognition and merits, whereas Saturn portends death, miseries, adversities, sorrows, sickness and their chronic persistence, losses, depressions, rejections, delay, deformation, debts and various kinds of reversal, humiliation, cheating and troubles. Saturn gets combust within 9^0 of the Sun. In Hindu Astrology conjuction means that the planets concerned are placed in the same sign within 30^0 of the arch. The Sun and Saturn are absolutely opposite in nature. Marriage of persons born in Leo or Aquarius is strictly prohibited with the natives born in Aquarius and Leo respectively. It is just because the lords of their respective Moon signs will be the Sun and Saturn, their thinking, nature and disposition will be just opposite to each other, resulting into severe marital disharmony giving rise to discord, murder, suicide so on and so forth.

We would like to discuss certain important aspects about the Sun and Saturn before touching upon our main subject.

The Sun is the most important planet and its strength must be judged properly. A strong and well placed Sun is a great asset to any horoscope. The Sun gives good results to the persons born in Scorpio, Sagittarius, Leo and Taurus. The Sun gives good results in the 3rd, 6th, 10th and the 11th houses. For Pisces the ascendant Sun shows magnificent results in the 6th house in Leo. For Capricorn, the Sun should be regarded as good in the 8th house too. The Sun results into prosperity and richness except to the natives of Aries, Cancer, Libra and Capricorn as the 11th is the obstructing (*Badhak*) house for moving signs. For Libra ascendant, the Sun does not give prominence and prosperity even if placed in own sign. The Sun always bestows the native with a prosperous and brilliant career, if posited in the 10th house, even if it owns 8th place. An unafflicted Sun in the 11th house provides a great strength to any horoscope.

The combination of the Sun and Venus is adverse as they are inimical. It is bad, similar to the combination of Moon and Venus. The Sun and Mercury, if placed together in the lagna or the 4th house cause Rajyoga for Sagittarius and Taurus ascendant in particular. The conjunction of the Sun and Mercury in Gemini or Virgo gives auspicious results. It is a fortunate combination in the lagna, inspite of the ownership of the 12th house for the Virgo ascendant. The combination of the Sun and Jupiter is also very encouraging and makes the native successful, sincere, prosperous, truthful, dutiful and popular but the Jupiter should not be combust.

The combination of the Sun and Moon should not be regarded as good as it happens almost on the new Moon day when Moon is very weak. This yoga is named as Kooho Yoga which is a malefic yoga. The Sun and Moon's conjunction is good only if it falls in the 3rd or 11th house or if associated or aspected by benefics like Jupiter and Venus. The Sun and Mars, if conjoined make one impulsive, hot tempered, hasty and aggressive. The combination is regarded as the best in the 10th house where both the planets are very strong. At times one is very arrogant also and acts like a dictator. However, by the aspect of Jupiter over the Sun-Mars combination, the native earns much fame and wealth. He becomes a commander or king and possesses gift of the gab. He is outspoken, aggressive, frank and becomes a terror to his enemies. Conjunction of Sun and Rahu is very bad, while with Ketu it is not so harmful. A strong and well placed Sun provides one a strong body free from ailments. This also gives a good position in the Government.

The combination of the Sun and Saturn is very bad. The opposition of these two planets is also adverse. This is a malefic combination and does not give stability in Govt. position or headship of the department. The Sun is the father of Saturn. *Chhaya* is the name of the mother of Saturn who was a maid servant. Due to unbearable hot rays of the Sun, Saturn became black and ugly as soon as he was conceived. Saturn became enemy of his father Sun as soon as he came to learn about the real cause of his ugly and dark appearance. Therefore, Saturn behaves like an enemy with the Sun though the Sun is not inimical towards his son Saturn.

This combination is also bad for marriage. It may delay or deny marriage if found at the sensitive points of marriage. We have already dealt with this matter elsewhere in the book we will especially focus on the relationship of the father and the son.

The conjunction of the Sun and Saturn is most mysterious. It creates inimical results in the lives of both father and son. If a person harasses, cheats, deceives, humiliates, beats, kills or troubles him in one way or the other, the other person becomes an enemy to the first one. The other person is not able to take his revenge with the first one due to various reasons. In that case both of them will be born as father and son in the next birth. This is most affectionate, loving and respectful relationship. Now, the fortune of the other one will be so managed that he may take the revenge from the first one. So, either the father will suffer badly immediately after the birth of his son or the son will never be able to prosper and the father will derive all the benefits of his good fortune. In that case the prosperity of father will be multiplied after the birth of his son.

Thus, the conjunction of the Sun and Saturn is very adverse for the prosperity of either the father or the son. This combination of the Sun and Saturn bring innumerable miseries leading to poverty, unemployment, sorrow, debts, humiliation, prosecution, imprisonment, insinuations, hunger and even death to either the father or the son. If the father suffers, prosperity of the son is definite. The success of the father may be predicted if the sufferings and miseries are indicated to the son. In fact it should be clear that the father and the son who are having the combination of the Sun and Saturn were enemies in their previous birth. One was weaker than the other who therefore failed to take his revenge. Therefore, to manage that old revenge the nature gave them birth under the most sensitive and closest relationship of father and son.

We now enumerate hereunder a few probabilities of how can this combination of the Sun and Saturn harm the father.

1. The father may die untimely within 10 years of the birth of the son. The death of father may also take place during the pregnancy of such a child.

2. The father may be suspended or he may have to seek compulsory or forced retirement.

3. The father may suffer serious mental tension, torture and frustation.

4. The father may suffer serious losses in business. He may even have to stop the business and may not find a way to re-establish himself due to regular failures and losses.

5. False charges may be levelled against the father. He may suffer loss of dignity and prestige. He may be involved in long and complicated litigation.

6. Loss of wealth due to theft, deceit or misplaced confidence, may take place. Inherited property and wealth may be lost. Self earned an accumulated wealth may also vanish. There may be serious losses or bankruptcy due to speculation of any kind.

7. The father may suffer frm insanity and poor health. He may even commit suicide or poison may be given to him.

8. Gradual downfall of prestige, honour and recognition, reduction in income and work will be common feature. The father may have to borrow money and articles from persons whom he hated. He may have to wander here and there aimlessly.

9. The faher may lose his glory or position after the birth of his son. There may be other kinds of disgrace and miseries to father due to one reason or the other.

In case the father remains free from such miseries and adversities of life, the son will have to undergo various adversitities as given below. It means that the element of enemity of the father is more than that of his son. Therefore, the nature managed their birth in the relation of father and son, so that he may take his revenge by becoming his father. In that case the native who has the combination of the Sun and Saturn present in his own horoscope will suffer himself. Who will suffer, the father or son? This can be known by the careful examination of the horoscope.

1. The native may die during his childhood.

2. He may run away from his home. As a result, he will remain devoid of love and affection of his father.

3. The native may be adopted by someone.

4. He suffers from any complicated disease.

5. The son does not get due success in business or service inspite of hard work and sincerity.

6. The native may suffer mentally. He may be mentally unsound or otherwise may suffer from epilepsy.

7. He does not get due importance in the family. The father may not treat him properly. He may be regarded as stupid though he receives due honour and importance in social circle.

8. He fails to earn properly so long as father is alive.

9. Many times, the father earns and the son spends. When the son earns, father sits idle. Both the son and father do not earn simultaneously.

10. Whenever the son suffers, the father progresses and when father suffers, the son prospers.

In certain cases having the combination of the Sun and Saturn, it has been observed that an individual prospered like anything after the birth of his son and the son suffered miseries, losses, reversals and various setbacks like imprisonment, income-tax or sales tax raids, poverty and regular failures in all his undertakings repeatedly. The son prospered only after the death of his father. In fact the progress and prosperity of father will begin only after taking the full revenge. The father may derive good luck from the fortune of his son or the son may do so from that of his father.

If a powerful placement of the combination of the Sun and Saturn is present in any nativity, the native will derive good luck from his father and son both. In such a case father of the native will suffer greatly after the birth of the native. As soon as the birth of son of the native takes place, the native will enjoy good luck and the son will start suffering. This happens with the persons having the conjunction of the Sun and Saturn in a favourable position like the 10th and 11th house with a strong lagna and the 9th house.

In certain cases where lagna and the 9th house are weak and the combination is placed in adverse position, the native will suffer from his birth to death. The father of the native will enjoy good luck in early life of the native whereas after birth of the son of the native, the son will enjoy good luck and the native will suffer.

The most astonishing factor of this unique and undesirable combination of the Sun and Saturn is that the date of the death of the father becomes the date of rise of fortune of the native. In many cases it has been found that the son, who could not progress inspite of the best efforts, prospered soon after the death of his father.

In this chapter, son means and includes daughter also. If similar combination is present in the horoscope of a girl, the same results will happen. There will be great difficulty in her marriage or in the marital happiness. She may not be benefited by the good association of her father and may face various miseries. The same combination may result in her unworthy children.

She may not receive real happiness from her progeny or otherwise they will not be properly settled or suitably married. They will always be a source of tension or frustations due to one reason or the other. It has been noted in a number of horoscopes that the opposition or conjunction of the Sun with Saturn has played a very negative role in the marriage of the native provided that touches the sensitive houses of marriage or otherwise there may be delay, separation or miseries. If Venus, the 7th house or its lord or even the lagna are under the adverse influence or Papakartari Yoga formed by the Sun and Saturn, problems in marriage are bound to surface.

In Hora Sara, it is mentioned that the conjunction of the Sun and Saturn gives good result in the 2nd, 6th and 9th houses as the native will be famous and happy. In all other houses, this combination is most undesirable. Different results will be experienced in various Bhavas. The sign in which the combination of the Sun and Saturn takes place also plays a vital role. In what follows we illustrate our observations with the help of natal charts.

Illustration : 11.1   *Horoscope No.: 66*

Date of birth : 25.08.1950   Time of birth : 21:48:00 hrs
Place of birth : Lucknow   Lat 26:50 N Long 80:54 E
Ayanamsa   : 23:10:04   Sidereal Time : 19:55:02

Pln	Degree	Rasi	Nakshatra	Pad
Asc	15:25:01	Ari	Bharani	1
Sun	8:42:58	Leo	Magha	3
Mon	14:30:33	Cap	Sravna	2
Mar	16:05:48	Lib	Swati	3
Mer	5:32:37	Vir	U Phalguni	3
Jup (R)	9:23:53	Aqu	Satabhisha	1
Ven	17:54:59	Can	Aslesa	1
Sat	26:51:53	Leo	U Phalguni	1
Rah (R)	5:24:59	Pis	U Bhadrapad	1
Ket (R)	5:24:59	Vir	U Phalguni	3

Lagna Chart

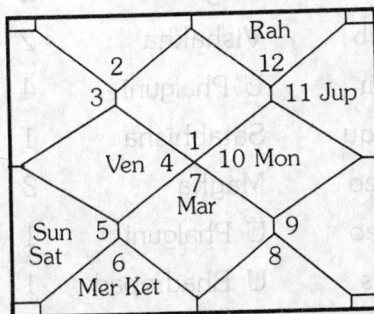

Navamsa Chart

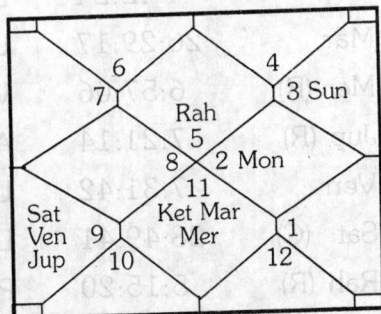

Balance of Vimshottari Dasa of **Moon 6Y 7M 12D**

The Sun joins the 5th house in conjunction with the 10th and 11th lord Saturn. The Sun is at 8° 42' while Saturn is at 26° 51'. Therefore, Saturn is not combust. The combination of Saturn and the Sun is being aspected by retrograde Jupiter. As we explained above, this combination is adverse which seriously harms the native or his father. The female was born on 25.8.1950 and she lost her father on 14.11.1958 when she was about 8 years of age. Poison was given to her father due to certain enemity which started soon after the birth of this female. The total Shadabal of the Sun is 7.54 Rupas and that of Saturn 5.85 Rupas. The native has been blessed with a son only.

Illustration : 11.2

Horoscope No.: 67

Date of birth : 10.09.1950   Time of birth : 20:41:00 hrs
Place of birth : Sagar   Lat 22:38 N Long 75:40 E
Ayanamsa   : 23:10:06   Sidereal Time : 19:30:00

Pln	Degree	Rasi	Nakshatra	Pad
Asc	6:08:19	Ari	Aswini	2
Sun	24:09:52	Leo	P Phalguni	4
Mon	4:42:24	Leo	Magha	2
Mar	26:29:17	Lib	Vishakha	2
Mer (R)	6:57:06	Vir	U Phalguni	4
Jup (R)	7:21:14	Aqu	Satabhisha	1
Ven	7:31:42	Leo	Magha	3
Sat (C)	28:49:41	Leo	U Phalguni	1
Rah (R)	5:15:20	Pis	U Bhadrapad	1
Ket (R/C)	5:15:20	Vir	U Phalguni	3

Lagna Chart

```
              Rah
       2      12
     3            11 Jup
          1
        4  X 10
          7
          Mar
Sat           
Sun  5        9
Mon      6    8
Ven    Mer Ket
```

Navamsa Chart

```
     Ven
      3        1
     4        12 Mer
       Mon Mar
          2
    Rah 5 X 11 Ket
          8
          Sun
      6        10
      7       9
          Sat Jup
```

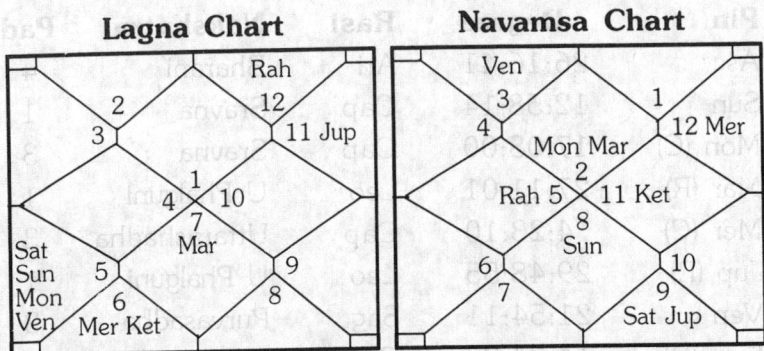

Balance of Vimshottari Dasa of **Ket 4Y 6M 10D**

In this case the position is almost similar to the previous case. The Sun and Saturn are conjoined in the 5th house in association with 2nd and 7th lord Venus and 7th lord Moon. This combination of Sun and Saturn in adverse for the native and fortunate for his father because the Sun obtains 1.77 Shadabal and Saturn obtain 1.15 Shadabal. He had a love marriage. The father of the native is a famous politician and has always won elections, though the native, could never win an election so far. The father is a great enemy of the native. The level of enemity cannot be described on paper. The father of the native went to jail, suffered heavy humiliation and defamation and fought more than a dozen cases in the court of law. The native suffered due to litigation and other inimical acts of his father. He is fighting against a serious charge of killing his wife under article 302 and has remained in central jail of H.P. for a long time.

Illustration : 11.3   *Horoscope No.: 68*

Date of birth : 26.01.1933   Time of birth : 12:27:00 hrs
Place of birth : Ghaziabad   Lat 28:40 N Long 77:26 E
Ayanamsa   : 22:55:27   Sidereal Time : 20:27:12

Pln	Degree	Rasi	Nakshatra	Pad
Asc	26:16:41	Ari	Bharani	4
Sun	12:58:14	Cap	Sravna	1
Mon (C)	17:08:00	Cap	Sravna	3
Mar (R)	27:11:01	Leo	U Phalguni	1
Mer (C)	4:23:10	Cap	Uttarashadha	3
Jup (R)	29:48:55	Leo	U Phalguni	1
Ven	21:54:11	Sag	Purvasadha	3
Sat (D)	14:04:27	Cap	Sravna	2
Rah (R)	15:05:59	Aqu	Satabhisha	3
Ket (R)	15:05:59	Leo	P Phalguni	1

Lagna Chart

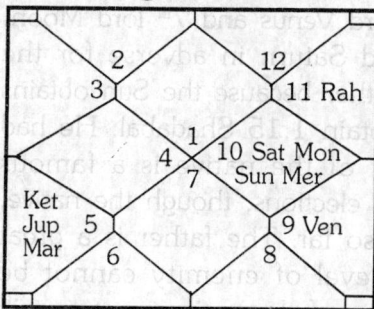

Navamsa Chart

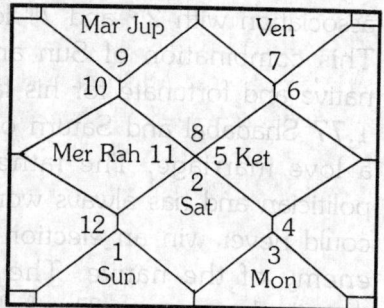

Balance of Vimshottari Dasa of **Moon 4Y 7M 24D**

The native was born in Aries ascendant. The 10th lord Saturn conjoins with the 5th lord Sun in the 10th house itself. Moon and Mercury are also associated in the 10th house with the Sun and Saturn. The native had been blessed with one son and four daughters. This is a very powerful horoscope and the native in a peculiar example of the combination of the Sun and Saturn. The father of the native was a very ordinary person. The business of his father started running in loss soon after the birth of the native and father expired some days later after facing acute poverty and misery. Thereafter the native took the business in his own hands. In the meantime he was blessed with a son. At that time the native had only three thousand rupees with him. Soon after the birth of the son, the native set up a factory and started earning good profits. The native had a number of factories, mills, cold storages etc. and had assets worth rupees 500 crores.

Here we can see that the native derived good luck only after the death of his father and achieved great heights and immense wealth only after the birth of his son. It means that the son of the native was also his enemy in the previous birth. The nature and planets managed the revenge in such a way as the stronger enemy became the son and weaker rival of the prior birth became the father. In this birth father took away all the good luck of his son. This is the reason that whatever business was given to the son by investing crores of rupees, started running in loss. A famous biscuit factory and cold storage, run by the son of the native accumulated loss so long as the native was alive. It proves the accuracy of observation that the rise of the son took place with leaps and bounds immediately after the death of the native.

Illustration : 11.4   *Horoscope No.: 69*

Date of birth : 27.04.1940   Time of birth : 11:47:00 hrs
Place of birth : Dholpur   Lat 26:43 N Long 77:53 E
Ayanamsa   : 23:01:29   Sidereal Time : 01:48:52

Pln	Degree	Rasi	Nakshatra	Pad
Asc	11:51:16	Can	Pushya	3
Sun	13:48:30	Ari	Bharani	1
Mon	19:50:07	Sag	Purvasadha	2
Mar	23:44:48	Tau	Mrigshira	1
Mer	20:45:40	Pis	Revati	2
Jup	2:30:22	Ari	Aswini	1

Ven	29:02:36	Tau	Mrigshira	2
Sat (D)	11:40:21	Ari	Aswini	4
Rah (R)	26:51:03	Vir	Chitra	2
Ket (R)	26:51:03	Pis	Revati	4

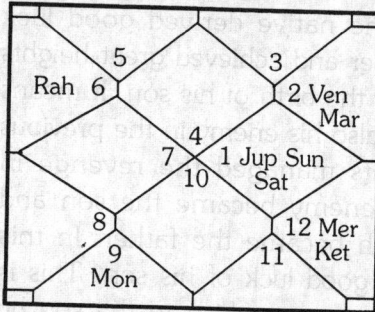

Lagna Chart   **Navamsa Chart**

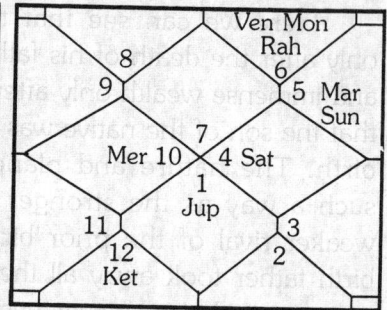

Balance of Vimshottari Dasa of **Venus 10Y 2M 29D**

In the present case, the native was a learned Engineer and was born in Cancer ascendant. The Sun, Saturn and Jupiter are placed together in the 10th house. Whenever Saturn and Jupiter are associated, the malefic tendency of Saturn gets heavily reduced and Jupiter's goodness gets minimised. Saturn here also obtains *Neecha Bhanga*. The native was a rich, smart, healthy, popular and very successful officer. He had been blessed with a son and two daughters. All were married and daughters are extremely happy and prosperous. The son was a Mechanical Engineer but had not yet been properly settled. So far, the son of the native joined and left as many as dozens of industries. He failed to adjust himself properly inspite of his best efforts. In fact the son and father were not in good terms. There were differences between them over various matters. The son's own horoscope is quite powerful but he is still suffering as the revenge of the previous birth is not yet complete which is being taken by his enemy of the prior birth who had become the father in this birth, as bestowed upon them by the nature. The intensity of the revenge had been reduced due to association of Jupiter. However, the native died due to blood cancer (leukemia). The rise of the son took place soon after the demise of the native.

Illustration : 11.5　　　　　*Horoscope No.: 70*

Date of birth : 07.03.1965　　Time of birth : 13:44:00 hrs
Place of birth : Lucknow　　　Lat 26:50 N Long 80:54 E
Ayanamsa　: 23:21:57　　　　Sidereal Time : 0:36:58

Pln	Degree	Rasi	Nakshatra	Pad
Asc	26:05:15	Gem	Punarvasu	2
Sun	23:11:09	Aqu	P Bhadrapad	1
Mon	10:10:34	Ari	Aswini	4
Mar (R)	26:13:11	Leo	P Phalguni	4
Mer (C)	3:18:28	Pis	P Bhadrapad	4
Jup	27:36:25	Ari	Krittika	1
Ven (C)	14:08:08	Aqu	Satabhisha	3
Sat (C)	15:18:51	Aqu	Satabhisha	3
Rah (R)	25:02:43	Tau	Mrigshira	1
Ket (R)	25:02:43	Sco	Jyestha	3

Lagna Chart　　　　　　**Navamsa Chart**

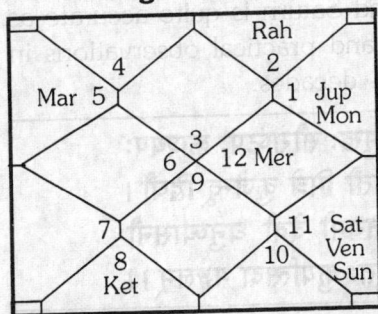

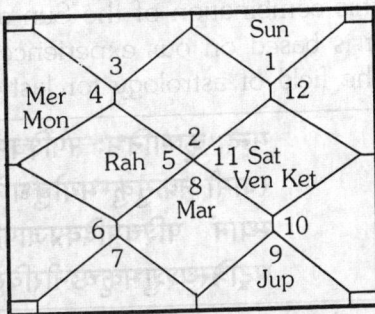

Balance of Vimshottari Dasa of **Ketu 1Y 7M 27D**

This is the horoscope of a very handsome native whose father was trapped in a false case when he was six months old. He sought voluntary retirement when the native was young. There is a serious difference of views between the native and his father. In fact, the father suffered a regular downfall after the birth of the native. The lord of the 6th and 11th house Mars is posited in the 3rd house and the Sun, Saturn and Venus jointly occupy 9th house. In this horoscope, there is a very clear indication of sufferings to the father after the birth of the native. The native's elder brother was murdered on 4.11.1992. Placement of Mars in the 3rd house, opposite to the Sun and Saturn is responsible for such a great misery.

We have illustrated a few cases above. Hundreds of cases can be illustrated, where the combination of the Sun and Saturn has heavily harmed either the son or the father. Miseries may come in different ways, upto the extent of death of either of them, depending upon the position occupied by the Sun and Saturn and their strength. Different kinds of result are realised in individual houses. The intensity of malefic nature of this combination may be reduced by the influence of Jupiter and can be aggravated by Mars and nodes. We have confined ourselves only upto the general effects of the combination of the Sun and Saturn on the relationship of the father and son. The malefic nature of this combination of the Sun and Saturn is quite accurate as it is based on our experience and practical observations in the field of astrology for last 4 decades.

मन्दः कृष्णनिभः सपश्चिममुखः सौराष्ट्रपः काश्यपः
स्वामी नक्रसुकुम्भयोर्बुधसितौ मित्रे कुजेन्दू द्विषौ ।
स्थानं पश्चिमदिक्प्रजापतियमौ देवौ धनुष्यासनौ
षट्त्रिस्थश्शुभकृच्छनीरविसुतः कुर्यात्सदा मङ्गलम् ।।

12 Misogamous Role of the Sun and Saturn

When the Sun and Saturn both work against Marriage

The question, whether marriage would only be delayed or it will not take place at all is of paramount importance.

Prior to its answer, it may be seen that certain combinations mentioned in the classics, in reference to denial of marriage, generally cause only a delay. Under such circumstances, it becomes quite difficult to judge whether the native will be married at all. The following is an account of two placements of Sun that cause absolute denial of marriage.

The Sun and Saturn are the greatest enemies of each other though the Sun is Saturn's father. Their dislike for each other is very severe, quite unlike the relationship between the Sun and Venus or Saturn and Mars. It is said in mythology that when Saturn was conceived, Sun's wife was severely burnt due to the proximity of the Sun and she went away to live in a cooler place. Later on, the son Saturn wanted to know who was his father, responsible for his ugliness. She told him the truth. Saturn swore eternal enimity with his father the Sun.

Saturn and the Sun are exactly opposite in nature, the former is cold while the later is hot. The former represents the west while the Sun is associated with the east. Sun is exalted in Aries where Saturn is debilitated. Sun is debilitated at 10^0 of Libra while Saturn is exalted at that longitude. Sun's Mooltrikona sign is Leo at 1^0 20' (i.e. in his own sign) while that of Saturn is diametrically opposite at 1°20' of Aquarius. Both do not tolerate each other at all. None of them allows the other to interfere in its reign. *Sun, when aspected by or conjoined with Saturn, will become the greatest malefic and will damage the pertaining house. Similarly, if both aspect each other, both houses will be spoilt.*

Here we are concerned with the role of the Sun and Saturn in denying marriage absolutely. If the 7th house or lagna comes under the influence of the Sun and Saturn, marriage cannot take place. Even, if Venus or lord of the 7th is influenced by these two planets, the marriage will never take place.

Some examples of affliction of the Sun and Saturn are given below for consideration :

Combination-1

If the Sun and Saturn are associated in the 7th house, there is no possibility of marriage. If the longitudes of Sun and Saturn are the same or very close to each other, marriage is ruled out provided the 7th lord is also weak or afflicted.

Illustration : 12.1   Horoscope No.: 71

Date of birth : 16.08.1949   Time of birth : 20:00:00 hrs
Place of birth : Lucknow   Lat 26:50 N Long 80:54 E
Ayanamsa   : 23:09:07   Sidereal Time : 17:32:12

Pln	Degree	Rasi	Nakshatra	Pad
Asc	27:10:17	Aqu	P Bhadrapad	3
Sun	0:12:53	Leo	Magha	1
Mon	26:16:55	Ari	Bharani	4
Mar	22:59:50	Gem	Punarvasu	1
Mer	19:09:55	Leo	P Phalguni	2

Jup (R)	0:53:01	Cap	Uttarasadha	2
Ven	2:08:13	Vir	U Phalguni	2
Sat (C)	14:18:42	Leo	P Phalguni	1
Rah	25:01:00	Pis	Revati	3
Ket	25:01:00	Vir	Chitra	1

Lagna Chart

```
        Rah        Jup
         12         10
  Mon 1              9
           11
         2   8
           5
         Sat Sun
  Mar 3   Mer      7
      4            6
             Ket Ven
```

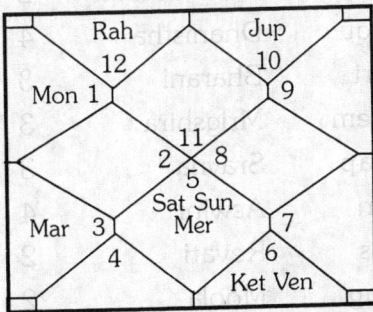

Navamsa Chart

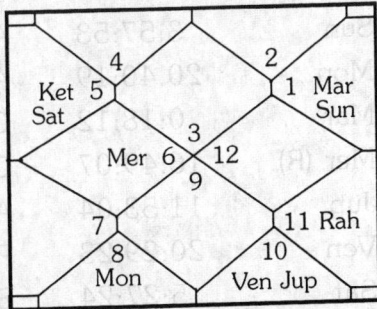

```
          4         2
  Ket 5          1 Mar
  Sat       3     Sun
  Mer 6   12
           9
    7            11 Rah
    8            10
   Mon        Ven Jup
```

Balance of Vimshottari Dasa of **Venus   0Y 6M 28D**

This is the horoscope of an Engineer who has not been married so far and is determined not to marry.

The combination of Saturn and the Sun in the 7th house can be noted which has deprived the native of marriage though Saturn owns lagna and the Sun rules 7th house. Thus, presence of Sun and Saturn in the 7th house does not permit marriage. The 7th lord Sun falls in barren sign Leo along with the ascendant lord vargottam Saturn with the association of the 8th lord Mercury.

Combination-2

If the lagna is hemmed in between Saturn and the Sun *i.e.* the Sun is posited in the 2nd house and Saturn when the 12th. Only under this position of Papakartari Yoga the Sun gets further afflicted due to Saturn's aspect on it.

Illustration : 12.2   Horoscope No.: 72

Date of birth : 16.02.1929   Time of birth : 05:10:00 hrs
Place of birth : Bareilly   Lat 28:20 N Long 79:24 E
Ayanamsa   : 22:51:48   Sidereal Time : 14:39:33

Pln	Degree	Rasi	Nakshatra	Pad
Asc	3:06:26	Cap	Uttarasadha	2
Sun	3:57:53	Aqu	Dhanistha	4
Mon	20:40:19	Ari	Bharani	3
Mar	0:18:12	Gem	Mrigshira	3
Mer (R)	16:49:07	Cap	Sravna	3
Jup	11:53:04	Ari	Aswini	4
Ven	20:29:23	Pis	Revati	2
Sat	5:27:24	Sag	Moola	2
Rah (R)	2:52:30	Tau	Krittika	2
Ket (R)	2:52:30	Sco	Visakha	4

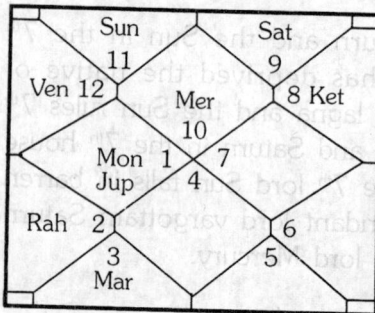

Lagna Chart   **Navamsa Chart**

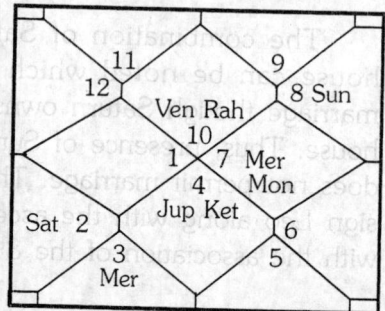

Balance of Vimshottari Dasa of **Venus 8Y 11M 27D**

This lady is a school teacher who remained unmarried.
She had four younger sisters. Her father retired when she
attained youth. There was great scarcity of money in the

family. She decided to serve and earn money to lead a prosperous life. She managed to get her sisters married off decently.

In her horoscope, the lagna is hemmed in between Saturn and the Sun. This Papakartari Yoga did not permit her to marry. The Sun received the aspect of Saturn while there is mutual aspect between Saturn and Mars. Both jointly aspect the 9th house. Thus, it is the most dreaded Papakartari Yoga. Therefore, if the lagna is hemmed in between the Sun and Saturn, marriage will not take place.

Combination-3

If the 7th house is hemmed in between Saturn and the Sun *i.e.* Saturn occupies 6th house and Sun joins 8th, there will be no conjugal happiness.

Illustration: 12.3   *Horoscope No.: 73*

Date of birth : 02.09.1944   Time of birth : 17:20:00 hrs
Place of birth : Lucknow   Lat 26:50 N Long 80:54 E
Ayanamsa   : 23:04:48   Sidereal Time : 14:59:28

Pln	Degree	Rasi	Nakshatra	Pad
Asc	9:05:45	Cap	Uttarasadha	4
Sun	16:44:42	Leo	P Phalguni	2
Mon	11:04:45	Aqu	Satabhisha	2
Mar	9:46:34	Vir	U Phalguni	4
Mer (R/C)	25:20:55	Leo	P Phalguni	4
Jup (D)	15:06:16	Leo	P Phalguni	1
Ven	05:09:05	Vir	U Phalguni	3
Sat	15:26:53	Gem	Ardra	3
Rah (R)	3:57:00	Cap	Pushya	1
Ket (R)	3:57:00	Can	Uttarasadha	3

Lagna Chart

```
        Mon
     11          9
  12        Ket    8
            10
        1  7
         4
        Rah
     2            6  Mar
      3          5   Ven
     Sat     Jup Mer
               Sun
```

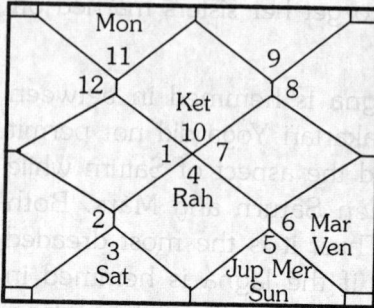

Navamsa Chart

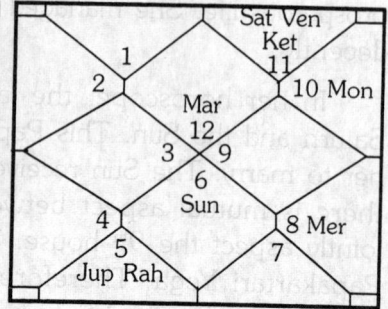

```
                  Sat Ven
              1     Ket
         2          11
                 Mar   10  Mon
                 12
             3  9
              6
         4   Sun      8  Mer
          5          7
       Jup Rah
```

Balance of Vimshottari Dasa of **Rahu 12Y 0M 15D**

The individual belongs to a very high status family and is highly placed. Here Saturn occupies the 6th house while the Sun is posited in the 8th house. Saturn is aspecting the Sun which kept the native devoid of marital happiness. The native, in fact, got married at 34 years of age, but on the very first night, there arose a misunderstanding between them and they took divorce. The Sun and Saturn both fall in barren sign Gemini and Leo respectively. Here Moon occupies Saturn's sign Aquarius and is aspected by Mars and the Sun from the 8th house. The native has a conjunction of Mars and Venus in barren sign Virgo. Mars and Saturn both aspect the 12th house as well. These all are negative factors for marital happiness.

Combination-4

If Saturn occupies the 7th house and Sun joins the ascendant, there will be absolute denial of marriage. In this position there will be mutual aspect between Saturn and Sun.

Illustration : 12.4   *Horoscope No.: 74*

Date of birth : 29.07.1933   Time of birth : 05:57:00 hrs
Place of birth : Bhopal   Lat 23:17 N Long 77:28 E
Ayanamsa   : 22:55:54   Sidereal Time : 2:01:42

Pln	Degree	Rasi	Nakshatra	Pad
Asc	13:28:25	Can	Pushya	4
Sun	12:29:52	Can	Pushya	3
Mon	27:26:27	Vir	Chitra	2
Mar	19:35:04	Vir	Hasta	3
Mer (R/D)	14:57:13	Can	Pushya	4
Jup	28:28:03	Leo	U Phalguni	1
Ven	8:40:15	Leo	Magha	3
Sat (R)	20:41:22	Cap	Sravna	4
Rah	5:52:44	Aqu	Dhanistha	4
Ket	5:52:44	Leo	Magha	2

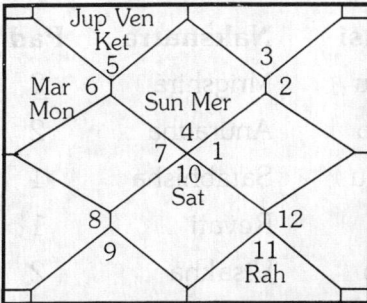

Lagna Chart   **Navamsa Chart**

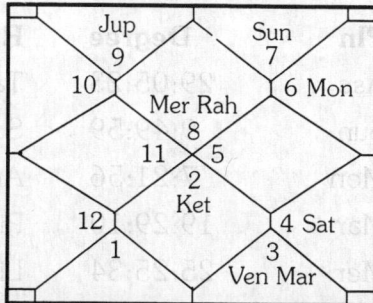

Balance of Vimshottari Dasa of **Mars 4Y 10M 3D**

This is the horoscope of a lady doctor who remains a spinster. She has sacrificed her life for serving mankind.

In the birth chart, the above combination is present. Saturn rules and also occupies the 7th house while Sun is present in the lagna. Thus, both Sun and Saturn are aspecting each other, denying marriage forever. Sun obtains the navamsa of debilitation life as Saturn obtains Moon's navamsa, which has multipued the evil effects of Saturn and the Sun for denial of marriage. Jupiter, Venus, Mars, Moon and Ketu occupy barren signs which is an important factor for denial of marriage.

Combination-5

If Saturn occupies lagna and Sun is posited in the 7th house (*i.e.* just in the reverse position as given in the previous combination) it will keep the native unmarried unless the 7th house is very strongly disposed or is also occupied by the strong benefics.

Illustration : 12.5   *Horoscope No.: 75*

Date of birth : 25.11.1941   Time of birth : 18:25:00 hrs
Place of birth : Allahabad   Lat 25:27 N Long 81:50 E
Ayanamsa   : 23:02:39   Sidereal Time : 22:38:38

Pln	Degree	Rasi	Nakshatra	Pad
Asc	29:05:23	Tau	Mrigshira	2
Sun	9:49:59	Sco	Anuradha	2
Mon	7:21:56	Aqu	Satabhisha	1
Mar	19:29:10	Pis	Revati	1
Mer	25:25:34	Lib	Visakha	2
Jup (R)	25:05:45	Tau	Mrigshira	1
Ven	27:00:20	Sag	Uttarasadha	1
Sat (R)	1:23:28	Tau	Krittika	2
Rah (R)	26:28:02	Leo	P Phalguni	4
Ket (R)	26:28:02	Aqu	P Bhadrapad	2

Lagna Chart   **Navamsa Chart**

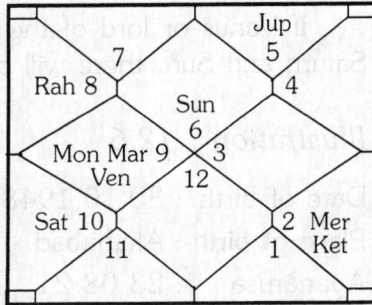

```
         Lagna Chart
    ┌──────────────────────┐
    │   3        /  1       │
    │ 4    \  /      12 Mar │
    │    Jup Sat           │
    │        2            │
    │  Rah 5 ╳ 11 Ket     │
    │        8    Mon      │
    │      Sun            │
    │  6        /  10      │
    │   7          9       │
    │  Mer        Ven      │
    └──────────────────────┘
```

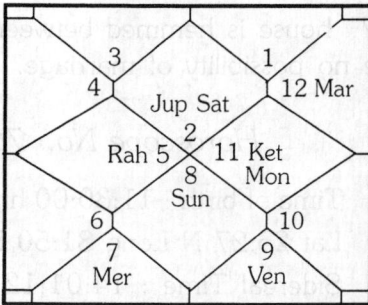

```
        Navamsa Chart
    ┌──────────────────────┐
    │          Jup         │
    │    7        5        │
    │ Rah 8        \   4   │
    │         Sun          │
    │          6           │
    │  Mon Mar 9 ╳ 3       │
    │    Ven      12       │
    │  Sat 10        2 Mer │
    │     11      1  Ket   │
    └──────────────────────┘
```

Balance of Vimshottari Dasa of **Rahu 17Y 0M 20D**

This is the horoscope of a metallurgical engineer working in the U.S.A. for almost 4 decades. The native has decided to remain a bachelor throughout life.

The Sun is tenanted in the 7th house in this birth chart and Saturn is positioned in the ascendant. Sun and Saturn both lend their aspect on each other which has resulted in denial of marriage. Here, Saturn also aspects Moon, which further ensures this by adding force for prevention of marriage. It may be noted if the ascendant Sun and Moon are under the influence of Saturn marriage is denied or delayed. Here Saturn is retrograde and falls in Sun's constellation Krittika which denies marriage completely.

A Note : If Moon is also aspected by Saturn, the possibility of denial of marriage increases. Further, if Venus also comes under the influence of Saturn by conjunction or aspect, or due to placement in the constellation of Saturn, there remains no possibility of marriage at all, even if the 7th house is well-disposed. This applies to all the combinations given, herein.

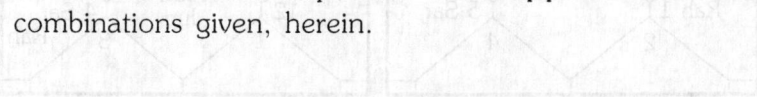

Combination-6

If Venus or lord of the 7ᵗʰ house is hemmed between Saturn and Sun, there will be no possibility of marriage.

Illustration : 12.6   *Horoscope No.: 76*

Date of birth : 30.10.1948   Time of birth : 11:30:00 hrs
Place of birth : Allahabad   Lat 25:27 N Long 81:50 E
Ayanamsa   : 23:08:21   Sidereal Time : 14:01:12

Pln	Degree	Rasi	Nakshatra	Pad
Asc	24:26:14	Sag	Purvasadha	4
Sun	13:35:09	Lib	Swati	3
Mon	16:28:14	Vir	Hasta	2
Mar	16:15:41	Sco	Anuradha	4
Mer	26:46:28	Vir	Chitra	2
Jup	3:41:48	Sag	Moola	2
Ven	4:26:32	Vir	U Phalguni	3
Sat	11:03:10	Leo	Magha	4
Rah	11:53:18	Ari	Aswini	4
Ket (D)	11:53:18	Lib	Swati	2

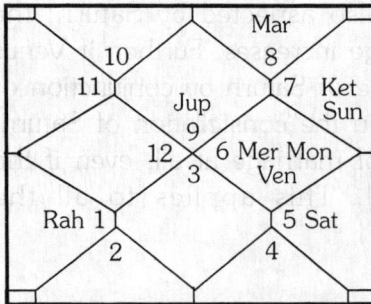

Lagna Chart	**Navamsa Chart**

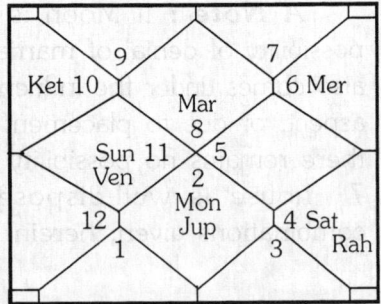

Balance of Vimshottari Dasa of **Moon 5Y 1M 23D**

In this horoscope, the lord of 7th Mercury is conjoined with 6th lord Venus and 8th lord Moon in barren sign Virgo in the 10th house. All the three planets are hemmed in between Saturn and the Sun. Where Sun is aspected by Saturn's closely. The 2nd lord Saturn obtains the navamsa of Moon and the Sun obtains Saturn's navamsa which is a strong negative factor for marriage. The native is a top engineer of telecommunications in U.S.A. and belongs to a royal family of Allahabad.

Combination-7

If the Sun and Saturn are under mutual aspect in such a way that Saturn aspects 7th house or the ascendant, the possibility of marriage will be very remote.

Illustration: 12.7   *Horoscope No.: 77*

Date of birth : 01.09.1935   Time of birth : 11:30:00 hrs
Place of birth : Delhi   Lat 28:39 N Long 77:13 E
Ayanamsa   : 22:57:47   Sidereal Time : 9:46:45

Pln	Degree	Rasi	Nakshatra	Pad
Asc	26:14:32	Lib	Vishakha	2
Sun	14:54:39	Leo	P Phalguni	1
Mon	19:50:51	Vir	Hasta	3
Mar	26:58:40	Lib	Vishakha	3
Mer	3:43:28	Vir	U Phalguni	3
Jup	24:10:51	Lib	Vishakha	2
Ven (R)	25:57:405	Leo	P Phalguni	4
Sat (R)	13:47:26	Aqu	Satabhisha	3
Rah (R)	27:58:29	Sag	Uttarasadha	1
Ket (R)	27:58:29	Gem	Punarvasu	3

Lagna Chart

```
        Mer Mon
    8        6
Rah 9           5  Ven
    Mar Jup         Sun
       7
      10   4
        1
  Sat 11        3  Ket
    12        2
```

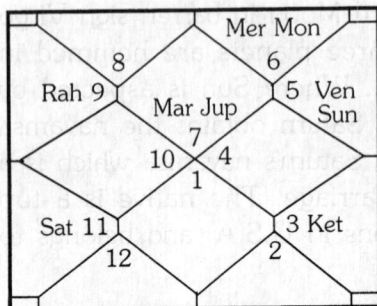

Navamsa Chart

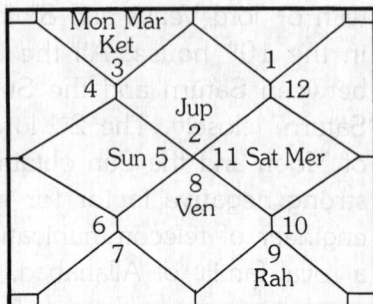

```
    Mon Mar
      Ket
       3        1
   4      Jup      12
          2
   Sun 5      11 Sat Mer
          8
         Ven
     6         10
       7        9
               Rah
```

Balance of Vimshottari Dasa of **Mon   2Y 7M 11D**

The individual was a Professor of Physics in Lucknow and has suffered greatly on account of some miscreants throwing acid on him to prevent his marriage with a particular girl. In this horoscope, there are many important combinations for denial of marriage. The main one being the mutual aspect between Saturn and the Sun in such a way that Saturn also aspects the 7th house, which denies the marriage.

The conjunction of Jupiter and Mars in the lagna is also adverse in the above case. Mars, Saturn and Jupiter lend their aspect over the 7th house and retrograde Saturn aspects the 2nd house, the Sun and the ascendant lord Venus. Longitude of the Sun and Saturn are almost the same.

Combination-8

Should the Sun be placed in the 7th house and Saturn aspect it, either from the 5th or the 10th house, there will be no performance of marriage provided the 7th house is also weak or the lord thereof is ill-disposed.

Illustration : 12.8 Horoscope No.: 78

Date of birth : 13.10.1946 Time of birth : 17:38:00 hrs
Place of birth : Lucknow Lat 26:50 N Long 80:54 E
Ayanamsa : 23:06:31 Sidereal Time : 18:57:25

Pln	Degree	Rasi	Nakshatra	Pad
Asc	26:43:07	Pis	Revati	4
Sun	26:26:28	Vir	Chitra	1
Mon	2:19:54	Tau	Krittika	2
Mar	19:45:39	Lib	Swati	4
Mer	15:10:07	Lib	Swati	3
Jup	10:41:09	Lib	Swati	2
Ven	5:35:19	Sco	Anuradha	1
Sat	14:27:44	Can	Pushya	4
Rah (R)	19:46:57	Tau	Rohini	3
Ket (R)	19:46:57	Sco	Jyestha	1

Lagna Chart

Rah 2 Mon — 1	11 / 10
12 3 9 6 Sun	
Sat 4 5	8 Ven Ket
	7 Jup Mer Mar

Navamsa Chart

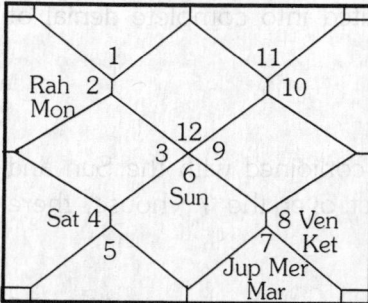

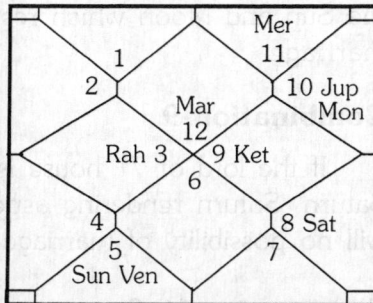

1	Mer 11 / 10 Jup Mon
2	Mar 12
Rah 3	9 Ket 6
4 5 Sun Ven	8 Sat 7

Balance of Vimshottari Dasa of **Sun 3Y 5M 12D**

The native has completed 64 years of age and still remains unmarried. Here, the Sun joins the 7ᵗʰ house and Saturn aspects it from the 5ᵗʰ house causing great damage. The lord of the 7ᵗʰ house, Mercury, is posited in the 8ᵗʰ house which reinforce the marriage denial. *Moreover the combination of Mercury, Mars and Jupiter is very harmful for marital happiness.*

There are many other factors which also must be taken into consideration. The possibility of denial of marriage gets stronger if the 7th or the 2nd house is totally afflicted.

If retrograde planets are in the 2nd or 7th house or they aspect these houses, their lords or Venus, in addition to the above combinations, the possibility for denial of marriage gets strengthened.

In case of Saturn and the Sun's affliction, if Saturn is retrograde, there will be enhanced influence for the denial of marriage. In case both the luminaries come under the influence of Saturn, and Venus occupies the constellation of Saturn in addition to the above combination, this comprises the strongest indication for denial of marriage. Here Saturn is posited in Moon's sign Cancer and Moon obtains Saturn's navamsa Capricorn. Moreover, in navamsa chart malefic Saturn has an aspect over both the luminaries the Sun and Moon which resulted into complete denial of marriage.

Combination-9

If the lord of 7th house is conjoined with the Sun and Saturn, Saturn rendering aspect over the 7th house, there will no possibility of marriage.

Illustration : 12.9   Horoscope No.: 79
Date of birth : 15.10.1951   Time of birth : 11:54:00 hrs
Place of birth : Lucknow   Lat 26:50 N Long 80:54 E
Ayanamsa   : 23:11:06   Sidereal Time : 13:19:31

Pln	Degree	Rasi	Nakshatra	Pad
Asc	13:31:47	Sag	Purvasadha	1
Sun	27:54:20	Vir	Chitra	2
Mon	0:42:28	Ari	Aswini	1
Mar	13:05:44	Leo	Magha	4
Mer (D)	29:04:35	Vir	Chitra	2
Jup (R)	14:21:57	Pis	U Bhadrapad	4
Ven	15:49:08	Leo	P Phalguni	1
Sat (C)	14:14:00	Vir	Hasta	2
Rah (R)	16:05:32	Aqu	Satabhisha	3
Ket (R)	16:05:32	Leo	P Phalguni	1

Lagna Chart

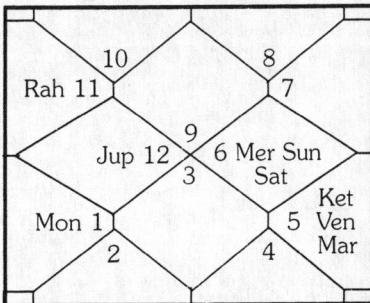

Navamsa Chart

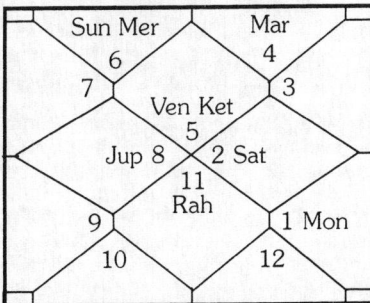

Balance of Vimshottari Dasa of **Ketu   6Y 7M 16D**

The individual is a famous medical practitioner. He is a bachelor as yet and has decided not to marry throughout his life. Lord of the 7th house Mercury conjoins with the Sun and Saturn in barren sign Virgo and Saturn lends its aspect over the 7th house. This combination of the lord of the 7th Mercury with Saturn and the Sun made the native a life long bachelor inspite of the benefic aspect of Jupiter. Venus in Leo also causes problems, delay or denial in marriage especially if associated with Moon. Here Venus, Moon and Ketu fall in barren sign Leo, in addition to the placement of Sun, Saturn and Mercury in barren sign Virgo. This denied the marriage forever.

In fact, Gemini, Leo and Virgo are the barren signs, if the 7th or 2nd lord occupy barren signs in addition to Mars and Venus, marriage gets miserably delayed or denied as the case may be. If the Sun and Saturn are conjoined closely with regard to the concerning houses or *papakartari yoga* is formed by the Sun and Saturn around the concerning planet or house the marriage does not take place.

We may, therefore, conclude that if the 7th lord occupies the 7th, and Saturn's influence gets reduced by the conjunction or aspect of Jupiter, the Sun and Saturn will create obstruction only but do not deny the marriage.

13 Saturn Jupiter Nexus : An Exposition

The correct judgement of the horoscope needs a deep understanding of the planetary relationships. At times it is so tough to interpret the intricate relationship of planets, that the judgements go wrong. We believe that application of the fundamental rules of Astrology must be based on keen practical observation. Whatever has been said by our sages in the classics appears to be corret in different positions of planets for different lagnas. This is the reason that the results differ for the similar position of planets, as maintained by various writers. Some of the astrologers hold that Jupiter in the 5th gives mostly daughters while others hold the view that this position gives more sons while still a few say that there will be no son at all. All this is correct if properly applied and tested e.g. Jupiter in watery signs gives mostly daughters, in fiery signs results into male births and gives very bad results for Capricorn ascendant and so on.

Moon and Mars are supposed to be friends but Mars is debilitated in Moon's sign Cancer, while Moon is debilitated in Mars sign Scorpio. Jupiter and Mars are vary good friends but Jupiter is debilitated in Capricorn where Mars is exalted and Mars is debilitated in Cancer where Jupiter is exalted. Mars and Saturn are inimical but Mars is exalted in Saturn's sign Capricorn, whereas Saturn gets debilitated in Mars sign Aries. Suppose Moon is exalted in the 7th house, what results should be expected. Moon is inimical to Venus. Will it give inimical results in Taurus due to ownership of Venus or will it give the results of exaltation as Moon is exalted there? We find that mostly Moon in Taurus in the 7th house, though *Bhagyaadhipati* too, gives inimical results. In the 4ᵗʰ house exalted Moon shows tensions with mother. Jupiter is inimical to Venus but Venus is exalted in the sign of Jupiter, Pisces. Saturn is exalted in friend's sign Libra and debilitated in enemies sign Aries, which appears justified but why does not Mars do so? Mars is exalted in Saturn's sign while debilitated in friends sign Cancer. Such type of planetary relationship and behaviour is beyond our comprehension. What we can say is that both are the different aspects and should not be mixed together. Further, significance should be attached to their position of exaltation and debilitation, alongwith the acceptance of their friendly or inimical behaviour with each other.

In our opinion it is always safer not to consider the exaltation or debilitation of planets at all. This is our bitter experience which needs a serious debate.

Here, we are concerned only with the relationship between Jupiter and Saturn. Jupiter is debilitated in Saturn's sign Capricorn and does not give auspicious results here. On the other hand, Jupiter's placement in Aquarius *i.e.* other sign of Saturn is very baneful. It has been described as very good in Saravali.

Case No. 1

In early 1987, a person dealing in medicines came to us. He was born in Libra ascendant with Saturn in the lagna, and Jupiter and Saturn were in opposition to each other. We had earlier experienced that whenever Jupiter and Saturn are opposite to each other, they exchange their character. On the basis of this experience, we told the native that your wife should have very ordinary complexion, she must have a sort of pain in body like rheumatic pain or arthiritis. Saturn's position in Libra in ascendant should make your wife attractive and beautiful. We also told the

Illustration : 13.1   *Horoscope No.: 80*

Date of birth : 30.11.1952   Time of birth : 05:00:00 hrs
Place of birth : Karnal   Lat 29:41 N Long 76:59 E
Ayanamsa   : 23:12:08   Sidereal Time : 9:13:04

Pln	Degree	Rasi	Nakshatra	Pad
Asc	18:30:04	Lib	Swati	4
Sun	14:30:35	Sco	Anuradha	4
Mon	25:21:54	Ari	Bharani	4
Mar	13:00:53	Cap	Sravna	1
Mer (R/D)	15:37:09	Sco	Anuradha	4
Jup (R)	19:56:53	Ari	Bharani	2
Ven	23:53:05	Sag	Purvasadha	4
Sat	0:26:36	Lib	Chitra	3
Rah (R)	21:42:27	Cap	Sravna	4
Ket (R)	21:42:27	Can	Aslesa	2

Lagna Chart

```
       Sun Mer
         8
              6
Ven 9        5
        Sat
         7
Mar Rah 10   4 Ket
         1
    Mon Jup
  11          3
    12      2
```

Navamsa Chart

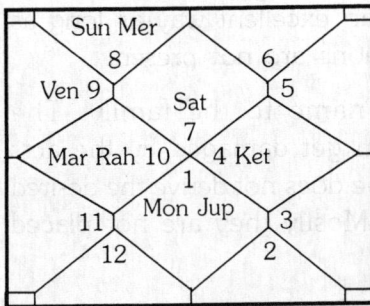

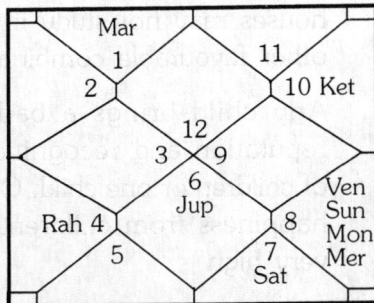

```
     Mar
      1       11
   2         10 Ket
        12
    3    9
         6       Ven
   Rah 4 Jup   8 Sun
              Mon
    5      7   Mer
         Sat
```

Balance of Vimshottari Dasa of **Venus 1Y 11M 13D**

native that he will join various other females. Jupiter's placement has given a handsome physique, delightful manners, kind heartedness, sincerity, influential behaviour, generosity etc. Thus Jupiter's influence as described for Jupiter's position in Lagna could be noticed in the native.

This incident reinforced our earlier conviction that Jupiter and Saturn if placed opposite to each other change their characteristics.

Whatever we found in our experience about the relationship between Jupiter and Saturn, we mention here in this chapter.

1. Whenever Jupiter and Saturn are placed together, the Saturn will soak the results of Jupiter and Jupiter will soak the results of Saturn *i.e.* Saturn will be improved while Jupiter will be spoiled.

2. If Jupiter and Saturn are conjoined with regard to the 5th house, there will either be no male child or male children will not survive.

3. This is not a good combination for high education. One having this combination in the Lagna and other houses may not study in an excellent way as long as other favourable combinations are not present.

4. Any child brings a bad name to the family. The reputation and recognition get damaged by the acts of children or one child. One does not derive the desired happiness from children. Mostly they are not placed very high.

5. They do not have much wealth as the Karaka of money gets spoiled owing to conjunction with Saturn. This Yoga should be regarded for hand to mouth living as far as financial affaris are concerned.

6. The conjunction of Jupiter and Saturn in the 10th house

makes one a Lawyer, Advocate, Magistrate, Judge or a Law Profressional. It will be particularly so if these planets own the 6th house.

7. Jupiter and Saturn's influence on the 5th house may cause liver troubles, jaundice, cirrhosis of liver or a sluggish liver. It may also cause gall-bladder stone. This is very prominently indicated when Mars also influence this combination.

8. If Jupiter and Saturn are retrograde, the results will not be adverse *i.e.* the combination will not produce much of inauspicious results. It will promote Jupiter's influence.

9. If this combination takes place in any of the saturnine sign or in the exaltation sign of Saturn *i.e.* Libra, evils of Saturn will be automatically removed.

10. This combination will produce excellent rather best results in the 4th house. The opposition of Jupiter and Saturn will also be very favourable. The native will be blessed with good children, movable and immovable property. It is good for profession, education, recognition, etc.

11. In case of opposition of Jupiter and Saturn, if any planet falls in own sign the stronger results of that planet will be experienced and the results of another planet will become feeble.

12. Jupiter and Saturn in the Lagna and 7th house do exchange their qualities but if any of these planets occupy own sign, the results of the other will be absorved to a great extent. We have found that such persons are not very happy and successful as long as other strong indications are not present. This is mostly applicable on Jupiter and Saturn's opposition in respect

of the lagna and the 7th house. This gives one wife only.

13. Conjunction of Jupiter and Saturn in the lagna is equally bad for proper settlement in life. This may cause physical disability, provided other factors are also present.

14. This Yoga should be treated as 'Daridra' Yoga and this results so in most of the cases. But the things will be better if the combination takes place in Jupiter or Saturnine signs.

15. Combination of Jupiter and Saturn is not so bad in fiery signs as it is in earthy sign. There are so many other factors which must be considered.

No combination can give the same results in all possible positions or for each ascendant. A combination may be auspicious for another ascendant. Dr. B.V. Raman explains in his various articles how the results of Yoga could be applied in a horoscope. Care must be taken for this Yoga as well. The application of the findings should not be made verbatim. This is a very valuable yoga for accuracy in the judgement of the horoscope.

According to a school of thought the combination of Jupiter and Saturn is auspicious for Aries, Leo and Sagittarius ascendant, if these planets join ascendant or the 5th house. For Taurus ascendant, it is not bad if it falls in the 8th i.e. Sagittarius. For Virgo ascendant, it is good if conjunction occurs in the 4th, 5th, 9th or 12th house. For Capricorn ascendant it is good in the 2nd house; for Gemini ascendant it is good in the 11th and 3rd house. For Aquarius ascendant, the combination is auspicious in the 2nd, 7th and 12th house, while bad for all other houses. For Libra ascendant this combination does not give good results in any of the house.

Jupiter stands for good and open actions while Saturn acts for low and hidden things. Jupiter represents prosperity, wealth and children etc. whereas Saturn indicates adversities, poverty, sadness, depression etc. Mixed results should be expected when both these planets conjoin.

In the first house Jupiter and Saturn make one cruel, indolent and lazy. Such a native does not get much happiness and comforts.

If these two planets conjoin in the 4th house, good results are produced. The native will be wealthy and famous, will have good friends and relatives. He will have land and property.

The combination cannot be appreciated in the 7th house. The native will lose money on account of any woman. He will be addicted to vices. He will be anxious to get his father's wealth and will not be good looking.

In the 10th house, the conjunction of Jupiter and Saturn is praiseworthy. The native will have means of conveyances and cattle. He achieves a high position and favours from the ruler.

In Chapter 31, Shlokas 79, 80, 81 and 82 of Saravali, Kalyan Verma describes the Yoga of Jupiter and Saturn for all positions of Kendra.

In Chapter 25 Shloka No. 24 the author of Hora Sara has mentioned that the combination of Jupiter and Saturn in the 3rd, 6th, 10th and 11th houses is auspicious and in all other houses it is bad. In the 8th Chapter of Jatak Parijata, there are almost similar views for this combination. Garga Rishi describes the combination of Juipter and Saturn for all the 12 houses.

There are some books that maintain that the combination of Jupiter and Saturn as bad and others have described it as good. There is much difference in their views. Let us see the effect of this combination in the life of natives.

Case No. 2

This is the horoscope of a lady who was a very good dancer and had defeated Gopi Krishna in her college days. She got married with a doctor and is blessed with two daughters. Combination of Jupiter and Saturn may be noted in the 5th house in Aries. Here Jupiter owns lagna and the 4th house and the position of Jupiter in the 5th must be encouraging due to relationship between angles and triangle. But Saturn's conjunction with Jupiter has damaged the combination to a great extent.

Illustration : 13.2   Horoscope No.: 81

Date of birth : 16.03.1941   Time of birth : 01:15:00 hrs
Place of birth : Lucknow   Lat 26:50 N Long 80:54 E
Ayanamsa   : 23:02:09   Sidereal Time : 12:40:40

Pln	Degree	Rasi	Nakshatra	Pad
Asc	4:40:29	Sag	Moola	2
Sun	1:48:09	Pis	P Bhadrapad	4
Mon	4:17:22	Lib	Chitra	4
Mar	24:45:01	Sag	Purvasadha	4
Mer	6:40:21	Aqu	Satabhisha	1
Jup	20:54:20	Ari	Bharani	3
Ven (C)	23:00:47	Aqu	P Bhadrapad	1
Sat	18:29:45	Ari	Bharani	2
Rah	8:39:10	Vir	U Phalguni	4
Ket (C)	8:39:10	Pis	U Bhadrapad	2

Lagna Chart   Navamsa Chart

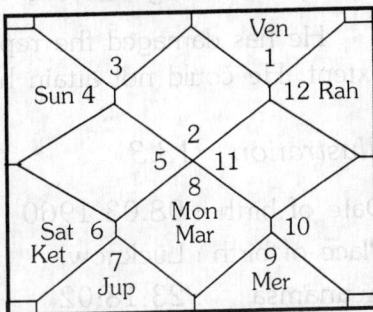

Lagna Chart	Navamsa Chart

Lagna Chart:
- 10
- 8
- Ven 11, Mer
- 7 Mon
- Mar 9
- Sun 12 Ket, 6 Rah, 3
- Jup 1 Sat, 2
- 5
- 4

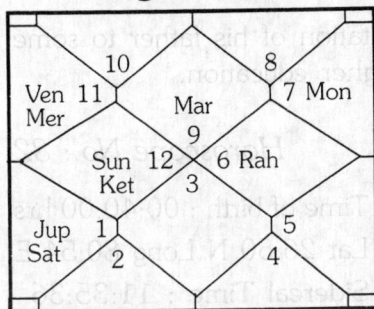

Navamsa Chart:
- Ven
- 3
- 1
- Sun 4
- 12 Rah
- 2
- 5, 11
- 8 Mon Mar
- Sat 6 Ket
- 7 Jup
- 10
- 9 Mer

Balance of Vimshottari Dasa of **Mars**   **1Y 2M 29D**

The following are the results which she faced as a result of this combination. There have been only female children. The lady and her husband are very fair and good looking but the case is just reverse with her daughters. The elder daughter brought a kind of defamation to her parents when she got pregnant before her marriage.

Jupiter and Saturn's conjunction is responsible for such type of children. This is not a good combination for wealth also, it it has anything to do with the houses concerned. Here Saturn owns 2nd and aspects the 11th house. Her husband had a very good private medical practive before her marriage but the income gradually went down. The combination may cause liver problems. She suffered from liver troubles more then once and certain problems of sluggish liver are still there.

Case No. 3

The native is the son of a highly reputed and rich person. All his family members are highly placed except him. Saturn's conjunction with Jupiter in the 2nd house can be noted. Here Saturn owns the 3rd and 4th house while Jupiter owns 2nd and the 5th house. The native has no money. He has to depend on others even for a few rupees.

He is just roaming here and there in search of a job.

He has damaged the reputation of his father to some extent. He could not attain higher education.

Illustration : 13.3   *Horoscope No.: 82*

Date of birth : 08.03.1960   Time of birth : 00:40:00 hrs
Place of birth : Lucknow   Lat 26:50 N Long 80:54 E
Ayanamsa   : 23:18:02   Sidereal Time : 11:35:36

Pln	Degree	Rasi	Nakshatra	Pad
Asc	19:58:34	Sco	Jyestha	1
Sun	23:55:54	Aqu	P Bhadrapad	2
Mon	19:24:15	Gem	Ardra	4
Mar	17:06:24	Cap	Sravna	3
Mer (R/C)	29:49:49	Aqu	P Bhadrapad	3
Jup	7:30:47	Sag	Moola	3
Ven	26:30:15	Cap	Dhanistha	1
Sat	23:06:07	Sag	Purvasadha	3
Rah (R)	1:17:35	Vir	U Phalguni	2
Ket (R/C)	1:17:35	Pis	P Bhadrapad	4

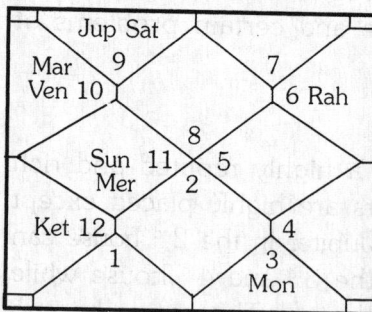

Lagna Chart   **Navamsa Chart**

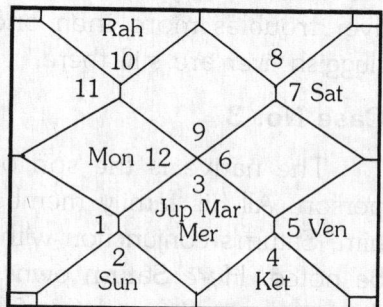

Balance of Vimshottari Dasa of **Rahu   0Y 9M 19D**

Case No. 4

The horoscope pertains to a native who has established many factories out of his own efforts and has established himself as an 'A' class businessman.

Combination of Jupiter and Saturn may be noted in the 4th house. Both are retrograde in Capricorn. Here Jupiter is giving the result of exaltation, since retrograde planets in the sign of debilitation behave like exalted planets. The native is only a graduate and possesses a new car, big house and all other modern comforts of life. He has one daughter at present and owns many factories of manufacturing various articles. So here we find that the combination of Jupiter and Saturn gives very good results in Capricorn and in the 4th house.

Illustration : 13.4   *Horoscope No.: 83*

Date of birth : 30.08.1961   Time of birth : 09:45:00 hrs
Place of birth : Lucknow   Lat 26:50 N Long 80:54 E
Ayanamsa   : 23:19:08   Sidereal Time : 8:11:05

Pln	Degree	Rasi	Nakshatra	Pad
Asc	5:46:39	Lib	Chitra	4
Sun	13:13:56	Leo	Magha	4
Mon	8:47:27	Ari	Aswini	3
Mar	15:05:43	Vir	Hasta	2
Mer	27:15:22	Leo	U Phalguni	1
Jup (R)	4:57:09	Cap	Uttarasadha	3
Ven	7:21:56	Can	Pushya	2
Sat (R)	0:34:07	Cap	Uttarasadha	2
Rah (R/C)	3:56:23	Leo	Magha	2
Ket (R)	3:56:23	Aqu	Dhanistha	4

Lagna Chart

```
              Mar
     8       6  Sun
  9            5 Mer
        7        Rah
   Jup 10   4 Ven
   Sat    1
        Mon
 Ket 11        3
      12     2
```

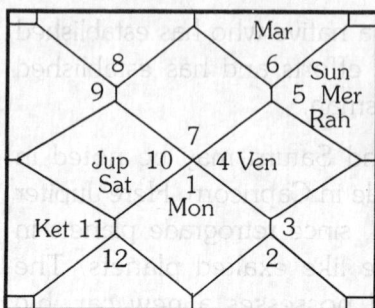

Navamsa Chart

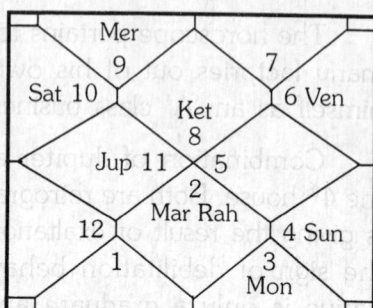

```
       Mer
        9        7
 Sat 10          6 Ven
           Ket
            8
   Jup 11    5
            2
 12     Mar Rah  4 Sun
   1         3
          Mon
```

Balance of Vimshottari Dasa of **Ket   2Y 4M 18D**

Case No. 5

The native is a highly educated and very intelligent person. The combination of Jupiter and Saturn can be noted in the second house. Here Jupiter is the Lord of Lagna and the 4th house and occupies 2nd house *i.e.* Capricorn, in retrogation. As said earlier, debilitated Jupiter in retrogration gives the results of exaltation, the native has a good financial position. We don't see if this combination has harmed any native when Jupiter is retrograde.

Illustration : 13.5   *Horoscope No.: 84*

Date of birth : 06.08.1961   Time of birth : 16:00:00 hrs
Place of birth : Fatehpur   Lat 27:10 N Long 87:12 E
Ayanamsa   : 23:19:05   Sidereal Time : 13:17:42

Pln	Degree	Rasi	Nakshatra	Pad
Asc	12:47:23	Sag	Moola	4
Sun	20:23:26	Can	Aslesa	2
Mon	25:12:19	Tau	Mrigshira	1

Mar	0:00:52	Vir	U Phalguni	2
Mer (C)	11:27:35	Can	Pushya	3
Jup (R)	7:23:26	Cap	Uttarasadha	4
Ven	9:50:48	Gem	Ardra	1
Sat (R)	1:55:47	Cap	Uttarasadha	2
Rah (R/C)	3:57:19	Leo	Magha	2
Ket (R)	3:57:19	Aqu	Dhanistha	4

Lagna Chart   **Navamsa Chart**

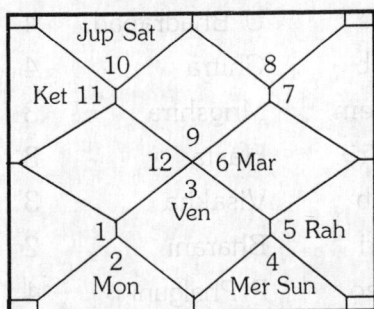

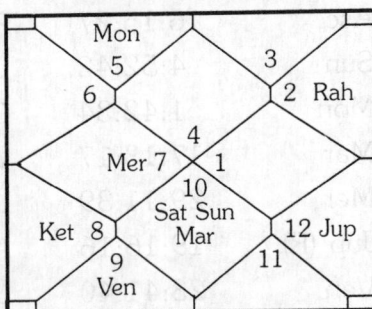

Balance of Vimshottari Dasa of **Mars   6Y 0M 6D**

Case No. 6

The native is an Executive Engineer in P.W.D. having two daughters and a son. The children are very smart, beautiful and throughout first divisioners. The son is doing M.Tech. The native also possess own house, various movable and immovable properties. The conjunction of Jupiter and Saturn falls in the 2nd house. Both these planets are retrograde in Aries. Retrograde planets in debilitation act as exalted planets. So Saturn and Jupiter are quite favourable here for wealth, profession, education ad children.

Thus in all the three cases as cited above, we see that if Saturn and Jupiter are retrograde and conjoin with each, there will not be any inauspicious effect of this conjunction. On the other hand it will produce good results.

Illustration : 13.6   *Horoscope No.: 85*

Date of birth : 21.10.1940   Time of birth : 16:46:00 hrs
Place of birth : Muzaffarnagar Lat 29:28 N Long 77:42 E
Ayanamsa : 23:01:50   Sidereal Time : 18:25:48

Pln	Degree	Rasi	Nakshatra	Pad
Asc	16:15:27	Pis	U Bhadrapad	4
Sun	4:52:42	Lib	Chitra	4
Mon	1:42:34	Gem	Mrigshira	3
Mar	17:13:17	Vir	Hasta	3
Mer	29:11:39	Lib	Visakha	3
Jup (R)	19:16:16	Ari	Bharani	2
Ven	23:41:40	Leo	P Phalguni	4
Sat (R)	19:20:11	Ari	Bharani	2
Rah (R)	17:58:22	Vir	Hasta	3
Ket (R)	17:58:22	Pis	Revati	1

Lagna Chart   Navamsa Chart

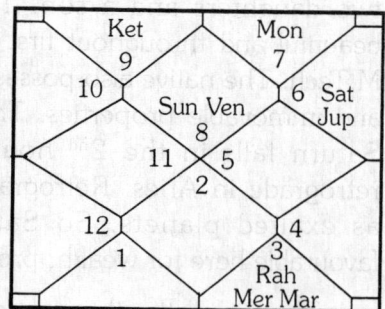

Lagna Chart:
- 1: Jup Sat
- 2
- 11
- 10
- 12: Ket
- 3: Mon
- 9
- 6
- Mar Rah
- 4
- 8
- 5: Ven
- 7: Mer Sun

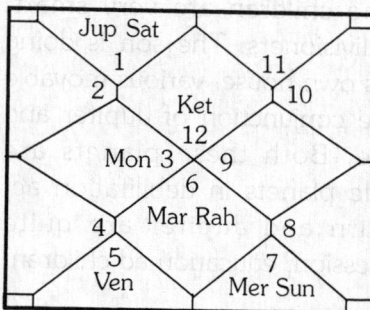

Navamsa Chart:
- 9: Ket
- 7: Mon
- 10
- 8: Sun Ven
- 6: Sat Jup
- 11
- 5
- 2
- 12
- 1
- 4
- 3: Rah Mer Mar

Balance of Vimshottari Dasa of **Mars 2Y 7M 7D**

Case No. 7

As explained earlier Jupiter and Saturn's conjunction or opposition in respect of the 4th house is auspicious. In the present case of Virgo native, Jupiter and Saturn are conjoined in the 4th house. The Sun and Venus occupy the 10th house. The native is an IAS and is quite a happy person from all angles. What are the combinations which have made him an IAS, for this my article "Planets and Administrative Career" published in January, 1989 issue of Astrological Magazine may be referred, if so desired.

Illustration : 13.7   *Horoscope No.: 86*

Date of birth : 06.07.1960   Time of birth : 10:55:00 hrs
Place of birth : Lucknow   Lat 26:50 N Long 80:54 E
Ayanamsa   : 23:18:16   Sidereal Time : 5:45:23

Pln	Degree	Rasi	Nakshatra	Pad
Asc	3:25:54	Vir	U Phalguni	3
Sun	20:49:45	Gem	Punarvasu	1
Mon	13:54:37	Sco	Anuradha	4
Mar	18:07:01	Ari	Bharani	2
Mer (R)	6:39:43	Can	Pushya	1
Jup (R)	3:25:39	Sag	Moola	2
Ven (C)	24:33:38	Gem	Punarvasu	2
Sat (R)	21:53:59	Sag	Purvasadha	3
Rah (R)	24:26:44	Leo	P Phalguni	4
Ket (R)	24:26:44	Aqu	P Bhadrapad	2

Lagna Chart

```
            Rah
      7      5
Mon 8            4 Mer
         6
   Jup  9    3 Ven
   Sat    12    Sun
   10            2
      11      1
      Ket    Mar
```

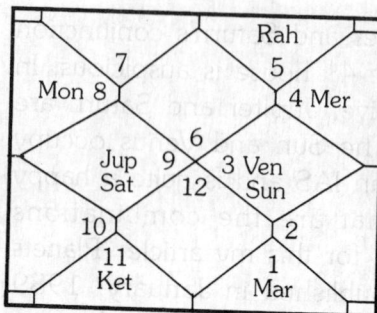

Navamsa Chart

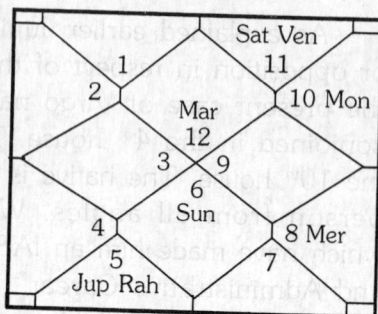

```
               Sat Ven
      1     11
   2            10 Mon
         Mar
          12
      3      9
         6
      4   Sun    8 Mer
      5      7
    Jup Rah
```

Balance of Vimshottari Dasa of **Sat 3Y 11M 4D**

Case No. 8

Here Jupiter and Saturn are placed in the 11th house in Sagittarius. Jupiter is occupying 11th house as an owner of the 2nd in association with the lagna lord Saturn. The lord of 10th Mars is also involved in mutual aspect with Jupiter and Saturn, so the native must have been a rich person as per the rules of astrology. But the fact is just reverse. He has suffered losses in all business and every business. He is doing nothing now. The education of the native is also very less and life is quite unhappy.

Illustration : 13.8   *Horoscope No.: 87*

Date of birth : 16.09.1960   Time of birth : 05:53:00 hrs
Place of birth : Hapur   Lat 28:43 N Long 77:47 E
Ayanamsa   : 23:18:25   Sidereal Time : 5:13:58

Pln	Degree	Rasi	Nakshatra	Pad
Asc	26:33:57	Leo	P Phalguni	4
Sun	29:49:34	Leo	U Phalguni	1
Mon	3:30:28	Can	Pushya	1

Mar	3:58:28	Gem	Mrigshira	4
Mer (C)	12:57:57	Vir	Hasta	1
Jup	1:32:03	Sag	Moola	1
Ven	22:55:54	Vir	Hasta	4
Sat (S)	18:30:49	Sag	Purvasadha	2
Rah (C)	22:16:52	Leo	P Phalguni	3
Ket	22:16:52	Aqu	P Bhadrapad	1

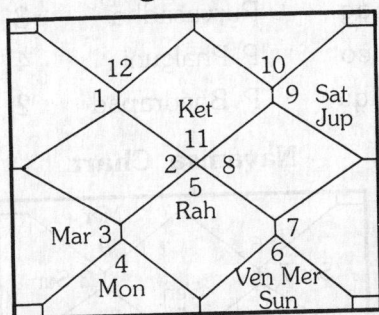

Lagna Chart   Navamsa Chart

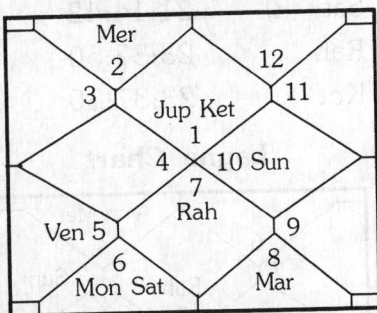

Balance of Vimshottari Dasa of **Sat 10Y 2M 27D**

Case No. 9

This native expired on 15.10.1982 at an age of 22 due to serious liver trouble. Jupiter and Saturn's conjunction in the 5th house in Sagittarius may be noted which is responsible for the death of the native. The aspect of the Sun over Saturn added fuel to the fire.

Illustration : 13.9   *Horoscope No.: 88*

Date of birth : 15.07.1960   Time of birth : 09:00:00 hrs
Place of birth : Etah   Lat 27:33 N Long 78:39 E
Ayanamsa   : 23:18:18   Sidereal Time : 4:16:34

Pln	Degree	Rasi	Nakshatra	Pad
Asc	13:48:24	Leo	P Phalguni	1
Sun	29:19:55	Gem	Punarvasu	3
Mon	23:18:17	Pis	Revati	2
Mar	24:23:42	Ari	Bharani	4
Mer (R/C)	2:22:39	Can	Punarvasu	4
Jup (R)	2:26:58	Sag	Moola	1
Ven (C)	5:31:52	Can	Pushya	1
Sat (R)	21:14:42	Sag	Purvasadha	3
Rah	23:37:50	Leo	P Phalguni	4
Ket	23:37:50	Aqu	P Bhadrapad	2

Lagna Chart

```
            Ven Mer
      6        4
   7        3 Sun
      Rah
       5
    8    2
     11
     Ket
 Jup  9      1 Mar
 Sat    10
          12
          Mon
```

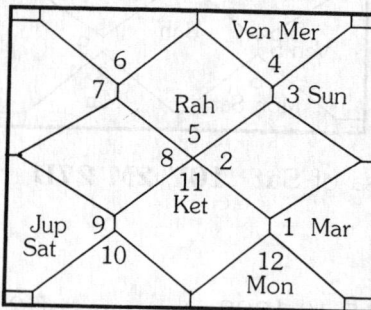

Navamsa Chart

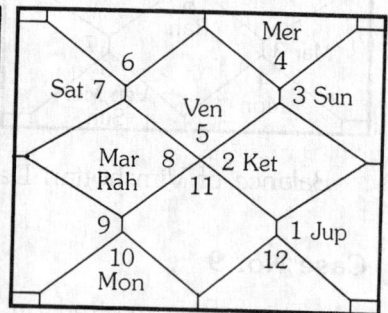

```
             Mer
      6        4
 Sat 7      3 Sun
       Ven
        5
 Mar  8   2 Ket
 Rah    11
   9        1 Jup
      10
      Mon
```

Balance of Vimshottari Dasa of **Mer 8Y 6M 13D**

Case No. 10

The combination of Jupiter and Saturn is there in the 5th house in Sagittarius *i.e.* in the same position as in Case No. 9 above. Mars occupies the 11th house and has an aspect over Jupiter and Saturn which is most damaging for liver troubles. The native also suffered Jaundice, Liver, abcess and various other liver troubles.

Illustration : 13.10   *Horoscope No.: 89*

Date of birth : 26.09.1960   Time of birth : 04:45:00 hrs
Place of birth : Lucknow   Lat 26:50 N Long 80:54 E
Ayanamsa   : 23:18:25   Sidereal Time : 4:57:40

Pln	Degree	Rasi	Nakshatra	Pad
Asc	22:47:16	Leo	P Phalguni	3
Sun	9:33:43	Vir	U Phalguni	4
Mon	12:14:18	Sco	Anuradha	3
Mar	9:06:55	Gem	Ardra	1
Mer	28:28:28	Vir	Chitra	2
Jup	2:27:27	Sag	Moola	1
Ven	5:09:33	Lib	Chitra	4
Sat	18:35:46	Sag	Purvasadha	2
Rah (R)	22:09:14	Leo	P Phalguni	3
Ket (R)	22:09:14	Aqu	P Bhadrapad	1

Lagna Chart   **Navamsa Chart**

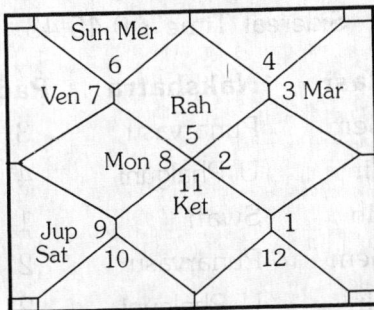

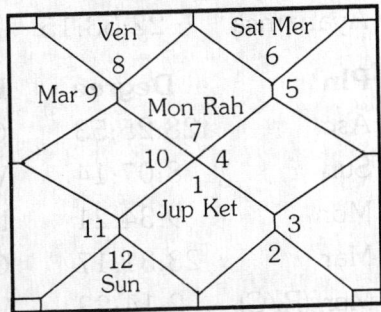

Balance of Vimshottari Dasa of **Sat 6Y 3M 21D**

The purpose of both of these illustrations is only to show that Jupiter Saturn combination in the 5th house causes liver troubles, stones in gall-bladder and other trouble in digestive system.

Now we will illustrate a few cases where Jupiter and Saturn are 7th from each other *i.e.* opposite to each other.

Case No. 11

In this horoscope Mars and Jupiter occupy Gemini lagna while Saturn joins the 7th house in Sagittarius.

Saravali describes that Jupiter in lagna gives an attractive appearance to the native. The native lives long and possesses energy. He will act after judging the consequences, will be learned, courageous and great (Ch. 30, Shloka 50).

Bhrigu Sutram mentions (Ch. 5, Shloka 1 to 6) that Jupiter in lagna in own sign makes one a good speaker, well versed in Shastras, he will be happy, learned and

Illustration : 13.11   *Horoscope No.: 90*

Date of birth : 25.09.1930   Time of birth : 00:48:00 hrs
Place of birth : Etawah   Lat 26:46 N Long 79:02 E
Ayanamsa   : 22:53:15   Sidereal Time : 0:45:43

Pln	Degree	Rasi	Nakshatra	Pad
Asc	28:25:53	Gem	Punarvasu	3
Sun	8:07:14	Vir	U Phalguni	4
Mon	9:34:21	Lib	Swati	1
Mar	23:31:17	Gem	Punarvasu	2
Mer (R/C)	2:14:23	Vir	U Phalguni	2
Jup	24:36:04	Gem	Punarvasu	2
Ven	23:50:29	Lib	Visakha	2
Sat	12:32:59	Sag	Moola	4
Rah	0:53:00	Ari	Aswini	1
Ket	0:53:00	Lib	Chitra	3

Lagna Chart   Navamsa Chart

Lagna Chart	**Navamsa Chart**

Lagna Chart:
```
        4              2
    5        Mar Jup       1 Rah
               3
      Sun  6  ✕  12
      Mer     9
            Sat
 Ket   7              11
Ven        8       10
Mon
```

Navamsa Chart:
```
        Sat        Jup Mar
        4           Ven 2
    5                    1 Rah
               3
         6  ✕  12 Sun
               9
            Mon
 Ket 7              11
          8         10
                    Mer
```

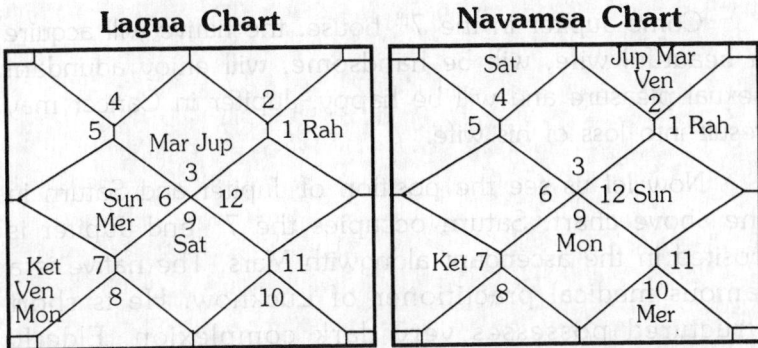

Balance of Vimshottari Dasa of **Rahu**   **14Y 0M 28D**

enjoy long life. If the Jupiter in lagna is placed in any inimical sign, or in debilitation, the native will indulge in sinful deeds. He will be childless, full of false vanity, will forsake near relatives and well wishers, like travelling and will be inimical towards others and miserable.

Phaldeepika says that Jupiter in lagna will give a delighted appearance. He will perform religious acts, will live long, be fearless and will have children.

Now let us see the results of Saturn in the 7th house. Saravali says in Shloka of Ch. 30 that the native will possess a weak body, lose his wife, be bereft of wealth, will present himself ugly and will do mean acts. Bhrigu Sutram (Ch. 7, Shloka 31 to 30) adds that the native will have a lean bodied wife, will be afflicted in body and will indulge in prostitution. He will be having sorrowful intimacy with many women.

To prove the above findings, the results as described for Saturn in lagna and Jupiter in the 7th house should also be understood. Saturn in ascendant makes one dirty, poor, ugly in appearance, miserable, suffer from many diseases, sinful, miserable etc., but in exaltation or own sign it makes the native equal to a king.

Come Jupiter in the 7th house, the native will acquire a beautiful wife, will be handsome, will enjoy adundant sexual pleasure and will be happy. Jupiter in Cancer may result into loss of his wife.

Now let us see the position of Jupiter and Saturn in the above chart. Saturn occupies the 7th and Jupiter is posited in the ascendant alongwith Mars. The native is a famous medical practitioner of Lucknow. He is short structured possesses very dark complexion. Elderly appearance and other qualities of Saturn in ascendant are present in him, whereas his wife is extremely fair in complexion, very charming in appearance and behaviour. She comes from a royal family. She is a famous TV actress. Married life is just tolerable, inclined towards unhappiness.

Here Saturn is giving the result as if it is placed in lagna, whereas Jupiter's influence is of the 7th house instead of the ascendant. Thus Jupiter and Saturn appear to have exchanged their roles here in this horoscope. Let us see another chart for the confirmation of the findings.

Case No. 12

The native is a professor in Engineering College. He possesses property, a house of his own and plots of land along with various movable properties. He has been blessed with two beautiful male children and enjoys a very high reputation in society and among relatives. Jupiter and Saturn's opposition can be noted in the 10th and the 4th house. Here Jupiter and Saturn do not appear to exchange their results as the Jupiter in Pisces has made the native a teacher. Saturn in the 4th house in Virgo had caused lungs trouble in his boyhood. Saturn in Virgo with the 5th lord Venus created inclination of the native towards engineering. Saturn is the lord of the 8th house and its placement in the 4th house will cause ches trouble, illness to mother, gains

through legacy and a complicated mind. Such a native hardly reveals his thought and planning to any one. The native possesses these qualities. The mother of the native expired due to Cancer in 1989.

Illustration : 13.12   Horoscope No.: 91

Date of birth : 06.11.1951   Time of birth : 19:59:00 hrs
Place of birth : Farrukhabad   Lat 27:23 N Long 79:35 E
Ayanamsa   : 23:11:09   Sidereal Time : 22:47:19

Pln	Degree	Rasi	Nakshatra	Pad
Asc	2:00:06	Gem	Mrigshira	3
Sun	20:11:03	Lib	Visakha	1
Mon	24:13:08	Cap	Dhanistha	1
Mar	26:31:00	Leo	P Phalguni	4
Mer	4:25:51	Sco	Anuradha	1
Jup (R)	12:00:22	Pis	U Bhadrapad	3
Ven	3:46:04	Vir	U Phalguni	3
Sat	16:50:06	Vir	Hasta	3
Rah (R)	14:10:36	Aqu	Satabhisha	3
Ket (R)	14:10:36	Leo	P Phalguni	1

Lagna Chart   **Navamsa Chart**

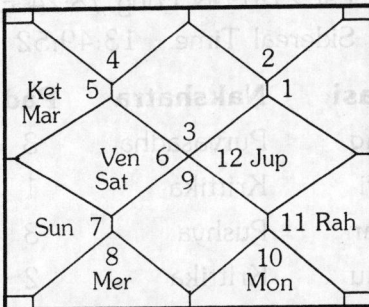

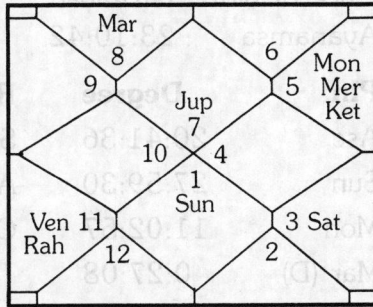

Balance of Vimshottari Dasa of **Mars 6Y 6M 12D**

Case No. 13

The native is an engineer. He is good looking, posseses movable and immovable property, has three children (two sons and one daughter). The financial position is also sound. As regards the horoscope, the native was born in the Sagittarius ascendant.

Jupiter falls in the 4th house in Pisces and Saturn is in opposition to Jupiter in the 10th house. The native's Jupiter is stronger so its result will be more prominent. The native is very good natured, well behaved, kind hearted and God fearing person. Jupiter in the 4th house has bestowed upon him much and profitable landed property. Saturn in Virgo in the 10th has made the native an engineer.

If we compare this and the previous case, we find that Jupiter is there in Pisces and Saturn in Virgo in both the cases. In previous case, Jupiter occupied the 10th house so the native is a teacher while in the present one, Saturn is there in the 10th so the native is an engineer. Jupiter is stronger as it is in own sign, therefore, Jupiter's result is prominent in both the cases.

Illustration : 13.13   *Horoscope No.: 92*

Date of birth : 12.05.1951   Time of birth : 22:47:36 hrs
Place of birth : Firozabad   Lat 27:09 N Long 78:24 E
Ayanamsa   : 23:10:42   Sidereal Time : 13:49:52

Pln	Degree	Rasi	Nakshatra	Pad
Asc	20:41:36	Sag	Purvasadha	3
Sun	27:59:30	Ari	Krittika	1
Mon	11:02:57	Can	Pushya	3
Mar (D)	0:27:08	Tau	Krittika	2
Mer	5:51:39	Ari	Aswini	2

Jup	11:20:11	Pis	U Bhadrapad	3
Ven	8:42:12	Gem	Ardra	1
Sat (R)	2:35:21	Vir	U Phalguni	2
Rah (R)	23:31:04	Aqu	P Bhadrapad	2
Ket (R)	23:31:04	Leo	P Phalguni	4

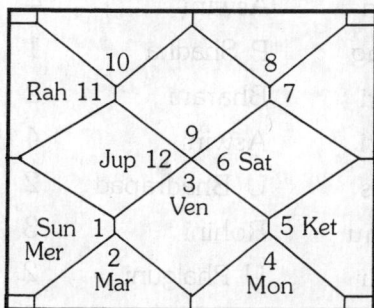

Lagna Chart **Navamsa Chart**

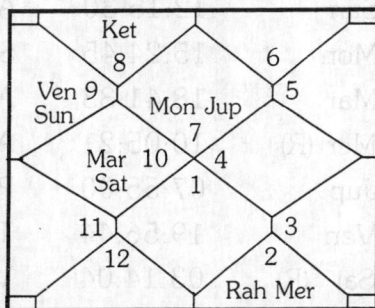

Balance of Vimshottari Dasa of **Sat 8Y 0M 1D**

Case No. 14

The native is born in Virgo with Saturn in lagna and Jupiter in the 7th house. The wife of the native regularly is sick. She is an Air Hostess. She suffers from windy diseases, pains in the body, stomach troubles. As far as the native's physique and personality are concerned, he is like that of Jupiter in the lagna. He is very tall, extremely handsome and smart, very generous and kind hearted. So here again we find that Jupiter and Saturn have exchanged their character when placed opposite to each other.

The native changed many vocations including film-making but he remained an unsuccessful person. Still he is unsettled. He has one daughter.

Illustration : 13.14   *Horoscope No.: 93*

Date of birth : 26.04.1951   Time of birth : 17:00:00 hrs
Place of birth : Patna   Lat 25:37 N Long 85:12 E
Ayanamsa   : 23:10:36   Sidereal Time : 07:25:25

Pln	Degree	Rasi	Nakshatra	Pad
Asc	26:01:44	Vir	Chitra	1
Sun	12:15:30	Ari	Aswini	4
Mon	15:24:45	Sag	P Shadha	1
Mar	18:41:33	Ari	Bharani	2
Mer (R)	10:05:21	Ari	Aswini	4
Jup	07:55:00	Pis	U Bhadrapad	2
Ven	19:56:44	Tau	Rohini	3
Sat (R)	03:14:04	Vir	U Phalguni	2
Rah (R)	24:58:11	Aqu	P Bhadrapad	2
Ket (R)	24:58:11	Leo	P Phalguni	4

Lagna Chart

```
           Ket
      7      5
   8      Sat    4
           6
     Mon 9    3
          12
          Jup
   10          2 Ven
     11        1
     Rah     Sun
           Mer Mar
```

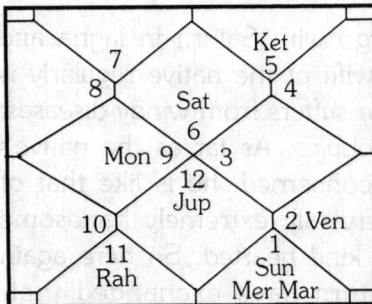

Navamsa Chart

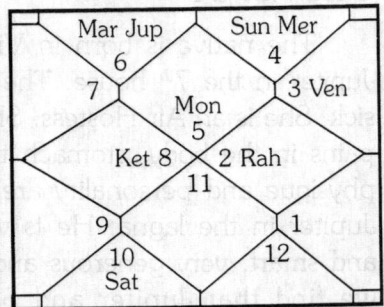

```
    Mar Jup    Sun Mer
       6          4
    7     Mon      3 Ven
           5
    Ket 8      2 Rah
          11
    9              1
      10        12
      Sat
```

Balance of Vimshottari Dasa of **Ven 16Y 10M 18D**

Here, we would like to repeat again that as Jupiter is there in own sign Pisces, Jupiter's result will also be experienced for the 7ᵗʰ house, and as such the wife is quite good looking, noble and earning. Jupiter has absorbed

Saturn's nature also, which has caused secret, chronic diseases that are difficult to diagnose. Saturn's influence over Jupiter delayed the marriage which took place in the 30ᵗʰ year. However, Jupiter's great influence is present in her husband. He is a very handsome and attractive person. He is noble, sober and honest in general. No influence of Saturn's is present in her husband, except that Jupiter and Saturn have not made the native successful in his life. Practically he is an unsuccessful person who took to various jobs and business but could not be successful in any of his undertakings.

The opposition of Jupiter and Saturn has not made the native successful in respect of job and wealth.

In Case No. 1, Jupiter and Saturn are in opposition in respect to the Lagna and the 7ᵗʰ house. The native is not a successful person. He had many ups and downs in career. His failures are much more than successes. In Case No. 10, we cannot call him a successful person in his private medical practice. In Case No. 11, frustations are there in respect of children and in Case No. 15, which follows there is a great dissatisfaction in respect of the job and wealth.

We have many more such horoscopes where Saturn and Jupiter's opposition is present in respect to the ascendant and the life is settled mostly under a fear.

Case No. 15

The native is an engineer in P.W.D. and is a frustated person. He faced a lot of troubles in life. There had mostly been a downward trend. He has two daughters and three sons. Even after completing 32 and 30 years of age, the daughters could not get married yet. The sons are a cause of great humiliation, disturbance and conflicts in home. Financially the native's position is below par and he is dependent on his sons. Jupiter is posited in Gemini in lagna while Saturn is the 7th. Wife's nature and appearance is that of Jupiter and native's personality is that of Saturn. There is only such position because both Jupiter and Saturn have exchanged their nature. Jupiter and Saturn's opposition in respect to lagna should not be regarded as good. We have found that such a native is not a happy person as far as his professional settlement is concerned. There are many downs in life and he remains unsettled for a very long time. His earnings are not smooth—children are not placed in high walks of life and they are often a cause of worry. As far as physical characteristics are concerned, Saturn and Jupiter exchange their properties. Mostly it is exactly so when the Lagna and 7th house is involved in their tenancy.

Illustration : 13.15   *Horoscope No.: 94*

Date of birth : 01.12.1930   Time of birth : 06:42:00 hrs
Place of birth : Bulandshahar   Lat 28:30 N Long 77:49 E
Ayanamsa   : 22:53:24   Sidereal Time : 10:59:58

Pln	Degree	Rasi	Nakshatra	Pad
Asc	11:57:18	Sco	Anuradha	3
Sun	15:14:05	Sco	Anuradha	4
Mon	15:43:16	Pis	U Bhadrapad	4
Mar	22:03:12	Can	Aslesa	2
Mer (C)	28:22:15	Sco	Jyestha	4
Jup (R)	26:45:30	Gem	Punarvasu	3
Ven (R)	2:10:51	Sco	Visakha	4
Sat	17:17:45	Sag	Purvasadha	2
Rah	29:55:44	Pis	Revati	4
Ket	29:55:44	Vir	Chitra	2

Lagna Chart

```
          Sat
           9
  10    Sun Mer      7
        Ven        6 Ket
         8
       11    5
         2
 Mon 12           4  Mar
 Rah    1        3
              Jup
```

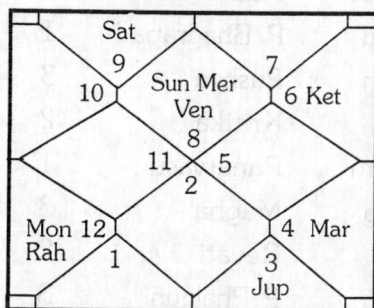

Navamsa Chart

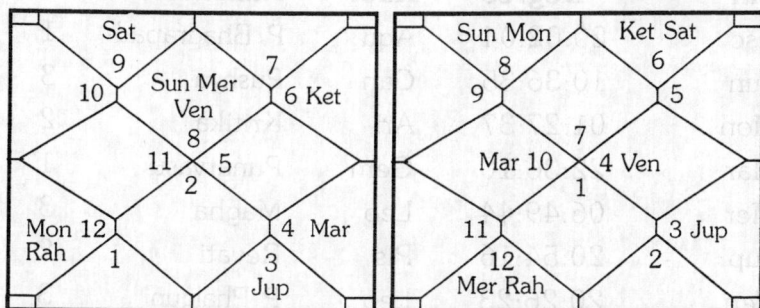

```
     Sun Mon      Ket Sat
         8           6
      9             5
                7
      Mar 10      4 Ven
         1
      11           3 Jup
         12      2
      Mer Rah
```

Balance of Vimshottari Dasa of **Sat 1Y 4M 5D**

Case No. 16

The native is born in Aquarius. Here Jupiter falls in the 2nd house in Pisces and Saturn in the 8th in Virgo. The native is the son of an engineer but he himself is a Driver. Jupiter in the 2nd house should have given him a good, happy and peaceful family life. But it did not happen so. The native got married thrice. He troubled his family so much that police had to interfere seriously. Financially the native is below par though Jupiter in the second house as 11th lord must have made the native quite a rich person. He has three daughters from his present wife and is frustrated on this account also. One son, aged 20 is there from his earlier wife, is like a bitter enemy for him. So exchange of character of Jupiter and Saturn may be seen here.

Illustration : 13.16   *Horoscope No.: 95*

Date of birth : 27.07.1951   Time of birth : 20:55:00 hrs
Place of birth : Faizabad   Lat 26:46 N Long 82:08 E
Ayanamsa   : 23:10:48   Sidereal Time : 17:11:30

Pln	Degree	Rasi	Nakshatra	Pad
Asc	20:02:04	Aqu	P Bhadrapad	1
Sun	10:36:35	Can	Pushya	3
Mon	01:27:37	Ari	Kritika	2
Mar	22:36:10	Gem	Punarvasu	1
Mer	06:49:44	Leo	Magha	3
Jup	20:54:16	Pis	Revati	2
Ven	20:26:23	Leo	P Phalguni	3
Sat	05:10:04	Vir	U Phalguni	3
Rah (R)	17:05:05	Aqu	Satabhisha	4
Ket (R)	17:05:05	Leo	P Phalguni	2

Lagna Chart

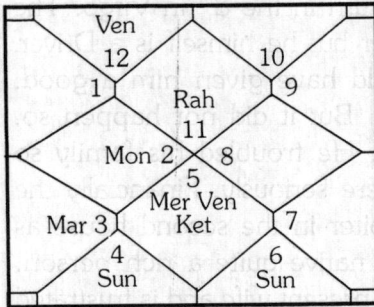

Navamsa Chart

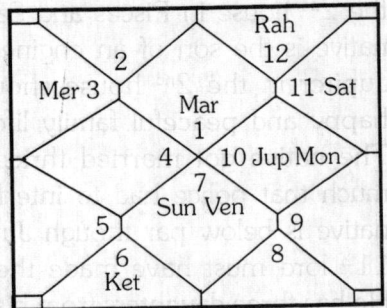

Balance of Vimshottari Dasa of **Sun 3Y 10M 4D**

Case No. 17

The native was born in Gemini ascendant with Jupiter in the 11th and Saturn in the 5th in the sign of exaltation. The native is a clerk in the bank and is a very truth loving person. Saturn in the 5th would have made him a liar, cunning, very clever etc., as Saturn owns the 8th house but it is just reverse in this case. The native has been blessed with daughters only.

Illustration : 13.17   *Horoscope No.: 96*
Date of birth : 17.12.1952   Time of birth : 19:15:00 hrs
Place of birth : Lucknow   Lat 26:50 N Long 80:54 E
Ayanamsa   : 23:12:11   Sidereal Time : 0:53:06

Pln	Degree	Rasi	Nakshatra	Pad
Asc	29:44:15	Gem	Punarvasu	3
Sun	2:23:00	Sag	Moola	1
Mon (C)	8:51:29	Sag	Moola	3
Mar	26:31:13	Cap	Dhanistha	1
Mer	10:57:18	Sco	Anuradha	3
Jup (R)	18:22:37	Ari	Bharani	2
Ven	14:51:38	Cap	Sravna	2
Sat	2:01:18	Lib	Chitra	3
Rah (R)	20:04:36	Cap	Sravna	4
Ket (R)	20:04:36	Can	Aslesa	2

Lagna Chart   **Navamsa Chart**

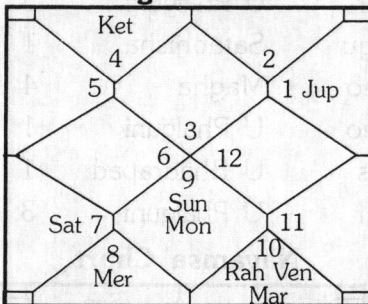

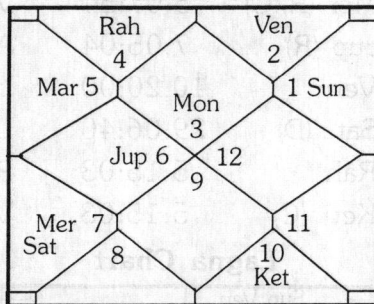

Balance of Vimshottari Dasa of **Ket 2Y 4M 5D**

Case No. 18

This is the horoscope of an ENT Surgeon, who is a very handsome and smart person. He has an extremely beautiful wife and two charming daughters. Now look at Saturn's position in the second house in Leo. That should not have given him such a magnetic face, magnetic speech and captivating eyes which he has with Jupiter's position in the 8th in opposition to Saturn. Jupiter in the 8th house and Saturn in the second have exchanged their results. Jupiter causes the effects of the second house in Leo. Saturn in the 8ᵗʰ house has resulted in a serious accident between his Maruti Car and a Truck during the Saturn's sub-period in Jupiter, when Mars was transiting in Leo. The accident took place on 12ᵗʰ August, 1989.

Illustration : 13.18   *Horoscope No.: 97*

Date of birth : 13.09.1950   Time of birth : 03:10:00 hrs
Place of birth : Bijnor   Lat 29:22 N Long 78:09 E
Ayanamsa   : 23:10:06   Sidereal Time : 2:17:53

Pln	Degree	Rasi	Nakshatra	Pad
Asc	18:51:47	Can	Aslesa	1
Sun	26:22:26	Leo	P Phalguni	4
Mon (C)	6:21:06	Vir	U Phalguni	3
Mar	28:00:27	Lib	Visakha	3
Mer (R/C)	5:07:54	Vir	U Phalguni	3
Jup (R)	7:05:04	Aqu	Satabhisha	1
Ven	10:20:00	Leo	Magha	4
Sat (D)	29:06:40	Leo	U Phalguni	1
Rah	5:15:03	Pis	U Bhadrapad	1
Ket (C)	5:15:03	Vir	U Phalguni	3

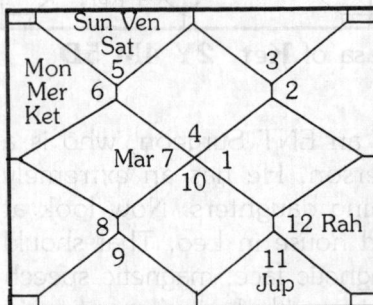

Lagna Chart   **Navamsa Chart**

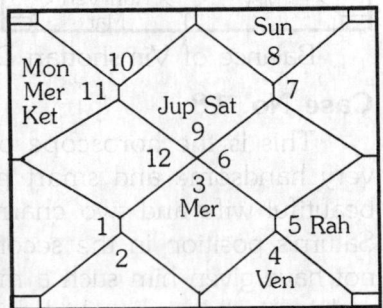

Balance of Vimshottari Dasa of **Sun 1Y 7M 21D**

14 Birth in the Sun's Dasa: Elevation in Saturn's Dasa

Saturn's *mahadasa* gives the best results such as promotions, progress, popularity, power and prosperity, expansion, extension and elevation if the birth takes place during the *mahadasa* of the Sun. This has been experienced and observed by us. We will try to prove the findings regarding this research through various examples given below.

After a thorough analysis of the horoscopes of some of the great, inspirational and leading figures, we noticed that those natives who were born in the Sun's *dasa* reached to the height during the *dasa* of Saturn. Therefore, we collected horoscopes of the natives born in Sun's constellation to verify our research. We collected as many as 100 horoscopes of such natives to check the authenticity of our research. After analysing those birth charts we found that all these natives reached to the zenith position during Saturn's *dasa*.

Prior to the horoscopic discussion of the charts, its very important to understand the relationship between the Sun's constellation and Saturn's *dasa*. When a native is born in the *dasa* of the Sun which means the native has a balance *dasa* of the Sun at birth, it means that the native is born in one of the constellations ruled by the Sun viz., *Kritika, Uttara Phalguni* and *Uttarashadha*. The native will have Saturn's *dasa* as his 6th *dasa* of the *Vimshottari Dasa* system. The 6th *dasa* is also known as the *Kshema dasa*, and is very favourable.

Secondly, the stars belonging to the Sun are distributed in six signs of the zodiac. The 3rd constellation *Kritika* has its 1st quarter in Aries and the other three quarters in Taurus; the 12th constellation *Uttaraphalguni* has its first quarter in Sagittarius and the other three quarters in Capricorn. Therefore the earthy signs Taurus, Virgo and Capricorn, predominate while the fiery signs, Aries, Leo and Sagittarius play a minor role. Saturn is a benefic for earthy signs. Saturn is a *Yogakaraka* for Taurus ascendant, a benefic for Venus and the *lagna* lord for Capricorn. When the native reaches his 30th or 32nd years, the *Chandra lagna* (the Moon sign at birth) begins to dominate. When *Chandra Lagna* is more powerful than the ascendant, this becomes more effective. Therefore, as 9 out 10 quarters fall in Taurus, Virgo and Capricorn and Saturn is a benefic for them, it may be argued that it gives good results. If so, what about the other three quarters? For Aries, Leo and Sagittarius, Saturn is a malefic. But without taking into account, Saturn gives beneficial results to all these six Moon signs when the Sun *dasa* operates at birth. Here it must be noted that Saturn as a natural malefic which favours *Upachaya* and gives results when Saturn happens to be the lord of the 6th *dasa*.

Thirdly, there are six sets of 6th *dasa* combinations like the Sun-Saturn excluding Rahu and Ketu (the nodes reflect the *dasa* of the sign lords). They are (1) the Sun and Saturn, (2) Jupiter and the Sun, (3) Mercury and Mars, (4) the Moon and Mercury, (5) Saturn and Moon, (6) Venus and Jupiter. Among these six sets of combinations, the Sun Saturn combination is a purely malefic combination (both the Sun and Saturn are natural malefics). There is another factor: these two planets are natural enemies as also father and son. Therefore, some understanding between them is inevitable.

Fourthly, when a Sun *dasa* native reaches Saturn *dasa*, the native must be at least 51 years old. This is an old age when the native will have all faculties of mind fully developed. The experience gathered by him during the Moon, Mars, Rahu and Jupiter *dasas* enables him to lead a sensible life during Saturn *dasa*. Especially, Rahu *dasas*, which is not available for other four combinations (except the Moon Mercury) is highly significant. Rahu *dasa* is the only *dasa* which will give a native all types of experiences, good and bad in his life.

Now we would like to discuss our point with the help of a few birth charts:

Case : Jyoti Basu

Illustration : 14.1   *Horoscope No.: 98*

Date of birth : 08.07.1914   Time of birth : 10:50:00 hrs
Place of birth : ....   Lat 23:43 N Long 90:26 E
Ayanamsa   : 22:39:54   Sidereal Time : 5:59:37

Pln	Degree	Rasi	Nakshatra	Pad
Asc	7:14:49	Vir	U Phalguni	4
Sun	22:30:46	Gem	Punarvasu	1
Mon	0:26:51	Cap	Uttarasadha	2
Mar	14:23:46	Leo	P. Phalguni	1
Mer (R)	5:31:56	Can	Pushya	1
Jup (R)	28:30:20	Cap	Dhanistha	2
Ven	28:41:15	Can	Aslesa	4
Sat	2:11:22	Gem	Mrigshira	3
Rah (R)	14:17:57	Aqu	Satabhisha	3
Ket (R)	14:17:57	Leo	P. Phalguni	1

Lagna Chart

```
        Ket Mar
    7       5
  8           4 Ven
        6        Mer
    9     3 Sat Sun
      12
Mon 10        2
Jup    11    1
    Rah
```

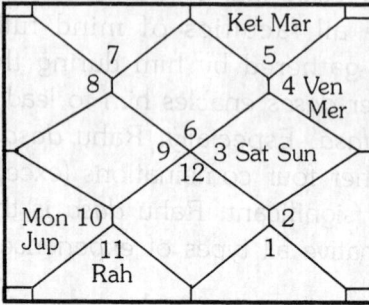

Navamsa Chart

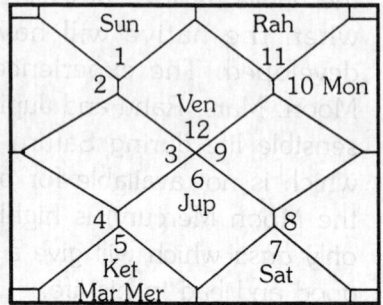

```
    Sun       Rah
    1          11
  2              10 Mon
        Ven
         12
      3 × 9
         6
    4   Jup    8
    5          7
   Ket        Sat
  Mar Mer
```

Balance of Vimshottari Dasa of **Sun   4Y 3M 17D**

Jyoti Basu or 'Jyotirindra Basu' was an Indian politician belonging to the Communist Party of India (Marxist) from West Bengal, India. He served as the Chief Minister of West Bengal from 1977 to 2000, making him the longest-serving Chief Minister of any Indian state. He was a member of the CPI(M) Politburo from the time of the party's founding in 1964 until 2008. From 2008 until his death in 2010 he remained a permanent invitee to the central committee of the party. On his death, he was the last founding Politburo member of the Communist Party of India (Marxist). He was born in *Uttarashada* conatellation and Capricorn Moon sign. Thus, the birth of this great man took place in the major period of the Sun. He was born in Virgo ascendant with 5th and 6th lord Saturn placed in the 10th house with 12th lord the Sun. Saturn is also exlated in the navamsa chart. The Sun is the strongest planet in the horoscope having 2.15 *Shadabala* and Saturn is the weakest planet having 0.98 *Shadabala*. The Sun is the *Atma Karaka* planet as well and is exalted in the *navamsa* chart. The lords of all the quadrants i.e. Mercury and Jupiter are *samsaptak* from each other. 11th house of the native is well disposed as the 2nd and 9th lord Venus is conjoined with the ascendant and 10th lord Mercury. Along with this Venus is also exalted in the *navamsa* chart. Saturn's major period started on 20.09.1969 to 20.09.88. His major breakthrough in the career came in the years 1967 and 1969 when he was elected as the Deputy Chief Minister of West Bengal. But in 1970, he narrowly escaped an assassination attempt at the Patna railway station by the Anand Margis. Though CPI(M) became the single largest party in the assembly elections in 1971, the party was refused the chance to form a ministry and Presidents' Rule was imposed in West Bengal. Saturn is the 6th lord and is placed in the constellation of Mars. Mars is the 3rd and 8th lord and is placed in the 12th house over the axis of nodes. So quite humbly we infer that Saturn contains the *Maraka* influence of Mars. After the sweeping victory of the Left Front in 1977, Jyoti Basu became the Chief Minister of the Left Front government, a position he held continuously for more than 23 years, a record in the country (From June 21, 1977, to November 6, 2000, Basu served as the Chief Minister of West Bengal for the Left Front government). Under his leadership, the Left Front government embarked on land reforms on a scale unprecedented in the country; it instituted a panchayati raj system which was radical for its times, which gave the poor peasants and small farmers a say in running the panchayati institutions. So it can be firmly said that since Saturn's major period Sri Jyoti Basu never looked back and advanced like a king, sweeping anyone who came in his way and enjoyed his life like an honoured king. Thus, the birth in Sun's *dasa* brings enormous popularity, prosperity and success during the major period of Saturn.

Case: Balasaheb Thakrey

Illustration : 14.2   *Horoscope No.: 99*

Date of birth : 23.01.1927   Time of birth : 07:00:00 hrs
Place of birth : Poona   Lat 18:34 N Long 73:58 E
Ayanamsa   : 22:50:02   Sidereal Time : 14:31:28

Pln	Degree	Rasi	Nakshatra	Pad
Asc	5:42:42	Cap	Uttarasadha	3
Sun	9:12:46	Cap	Uttarasadha	4
Mon	6:11:55	Vir	U Phalguni	3
Mar	23:03:58	Ari	Bharani	3
Mer (C)	5:31:29	Cap	Uttarasadha	3
Jup	8:11:23	Aqu	Satabhisha	1
Ven	24:10:56	Cap	Dhanistha	1
Sat	12:29:34	Sco	Anuradha	3
Rah (R)	14:02:08	Gem	Ardra	3
Ket (R)	14:02:08	Sag	Purvasadha	1

Lagna Chart

	Jup 11	Ket 9	
12	Sun Mer Ven 10	8 Sat	
Mar 1	7 4		6 Mon
2	3 Rah	5	

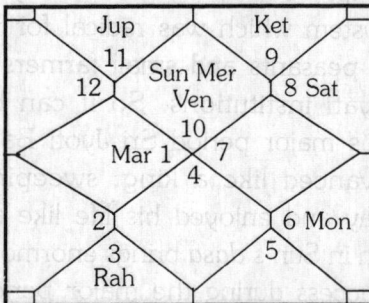

Navamsa Chart

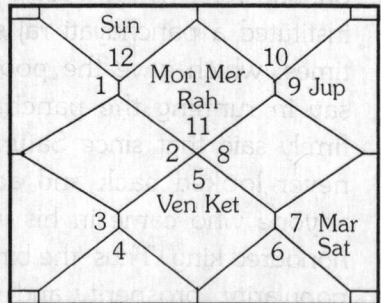

	Sun 12	10	
1	Mon Mer Rah 11	9 Jup	
2	8 5 Ven Ket		7 Mar Sat
3	4	6	

Balance of Vimshottari Dasa of **Sun   1Y 8M 16D**

Bal Keshav Thackeray, popularly known as *Balasaheb* Thackeray, is the founder and chief of the Shiv Sena, a

Hindu nationalist, Marathi ethnocentric and populist party active mainly in the western Indian state of Maharashtra.

Balasaheb Thackeray started his career as a cartoonist in the *Free Press Journal* in Mumbai in the 1950s. His cartoons were also published in the Sunday edition of *The Times of India*. In 1960, he launched a cartoon weekly *Marmik* with his brother. He used it to campaign against the growing influence of non-Marathi people in Mumbai targeting Gujaratis and South Indian labourers.

He formed Shiv Sena on 19 June 1966 with the intent of fighting for the rights of the natives of the state of Maharashtra (called Maharashtrians). The early objective of Shiv Sena was to ensure job security for Maharashtrians against immigrants from southern India, Gujaratis and Marwaris.

Politically, Sena was anti-communist, and wrested control of major trade unions in Mumbai from the Communist Party of India and demanded protection money from mainly Gujarati and marwari business leaders. It later allied itself with the Bharatiya Janata Party (BJP). The BJP-Shiv Sena combine won the 1995 Maharashtra State Assembly elections and came to power. During the tenure of the government from 1995 to 1999, Thackeray was nicknamed "remote control" since he played a major role in government policies and decisions from behind the scenes.

Thackeray has claimed that Shiv Sena has helped the *Marathi manoos* (the Marathi commoner) in Mumbai, especially in the public sector. Opposition leftist parties allege that Shiv Sena has done little to solve the problem of unemployment facing a large proportion of Maharashtrian youth during its tenure, in contradiction to its ideological foundation of 'sons of the soil. He is born in the *Uttara Shadha* constellation and Virgo Moon sign i.e. in the major period of the Sun. He is born in the Capricorn ascendant with the 5th lord Venus and the 9th lord Mercury conjoined in the ascendant along with the 8th lord the Sun. So the lords of the trines are conjoined in the ascendant giving rise to *Maharaja Yoga.* Ascendant and 2nd lord Saturn is placed in the 11th house and is aspect by Mars. Saturn is exalted in the *navamsa* chart and is conjoined with Mars in the *navamsa* chart. Saturn is quite strong in this chart as it obtains 1.3 *shadabala.* Saturn's major period started from 09.10.79 to 09.10.98. So it can be said that the rise of Balasaheb Thakrey was during the major period of Saturn.

Case : Ram Vilas Paswan

Illustration : 14.3   *Horoscope No.: 100*

Date of birth : 05.07.1946   Time of birth : 12:00:00 hrs
Place of birth : Madhubani   Lat 26:27 N Long 85:08 E
Ayanamsa   : 22:06:19   Sidereal Time : 7:01:10

Pln	Degree	Rasi	Nakshatra	Pad
Asc	20:34:51	Vir	Hasta	4
Sun	19:31:24	Gem	Ardra	4
Mon	8:33:21	Vir	U Phalguni	4
Mar	15:29:36	Leo	P Phalguni	1
Mer	15:34:42	Can	Pushya	4
Jup	24:57:54	Vir	Chitra	1
Ven	26:58:54	Can	Aslesa	4
Sat (C)	3:14:44	Can	Punarvasu	4
Rah (R)	27:30:48	Tau	Mrigshira	2
Ket (R)	27:30:48	Sco	Jyestha	4

Lagna Chart

```
                    Mar
         7           5        Mer
                             4 Ven
  Ket 8                         Sat
            Mon Jup
               6
          9    3 Sun
             12
    10                    2 Rah
      11            1
```

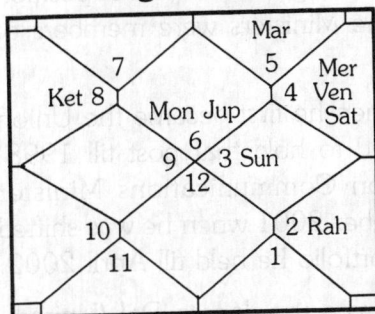

Navamsa Chart

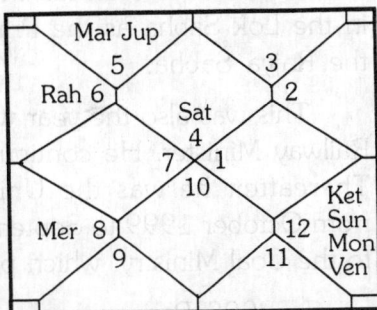

```
         Mar Jup
            5              3
  Rah 6                      2
                  Sat
                   4
                 7   1
                  10
  Mer 8                     12  Ket
           9          11        Sun
                                Mon
                                Ven
```

Balance of Vimshottari Dasa of **Sun   0Y 7M 24D**

Ram Vilas Paswan is the president of the Lok Janshakti Party, political party.

Paswan was elected to the Bihar state assembly in 1969 as a member of the Samyukta Socialist Party (*"United Socialist Party"*). In 1974, as an ardent follower of Raj Narain and Jayaprakash Narayan, Paswan became the general secretary of the Lok Dal. He was personally close to the prominent leaders of anti-emergency like Raj Narain, Karpuri Thakur and Satyendra Narayan Sinha.

In 1975, when emergency was proclaimed in India, he was arrested and spent the entire period in jail.

In 1977, when released, he became a member of the Janata Party and won election to Parliament for the first time on its ticket. He was re-elected to the 7th Lok Sabha in 1980.

In 1983, he established the Dalit Sena, an organization for Dalit emancipation and welfare.

Paswan was re-elected to the 9th Lok Sabha in 1989 and was appointed Union Minister of Labour and Welfare in the Vishwanath Pratap Singh government. He has been a member of Lok Sabha since then to date (as of 2009).

In 1996 he even led the ruling alliance or Proposition in the Lok Sabha as the Prime Ministers were members of the Rajya Sabha.

This was also the year when he first became the Union Railway Minister. He continued to hold that post till 1998. Thereafter, he was the Union Communications Minister from October 1999 to September 2001 when he was shifted to the Coal Ministry, which portfolio he held till April 2002.

In 2000 Paswan broke from the Janata Dal (United), to form the Lok Janshakti Party (LJP). Following the 2004 Lok Sabha elections, Paswan joined the United Progressive Alliance government and was made the Union Minister in Ministry of Chemicals and Fertilizers and Ministry of Steel.

In February 2005 Bihar State elections, Paswan's party LJP along with the Indian National Congress contested the election. The result was that no particular party or alliance could form a government by itself.

For the Indian general election, 2009 Paswan forged an alliance with Lalu Prasad Yadav and his Rashtriya Janata Dal, while dumping their erstwhile coalition partner and leader of the United Progressive Alliance, the Indian National Congress from the new alliance. The duo was later joined by Mulayam Singh's Samajwadi Party and were declared the Fourth Front. He lost the elections from Hajipur to the Janata Dal (United)'s Ram Sundar Das, a former Chief Minister of Bihar. His party the Lok Janshakti Party was not able to win any seats in the 15th Lok Sabha, while his coalition partner Yadav and his party too failed to perform well and were reduced to 4 seats.

He is born in *Uttara Phalguni* constellation ruled by the Sun i.e. the native is born in the major period of the Sun. He is born in Virgo ascendant with 11th lord Moon and, 4th and 7th lord Jupiter placed therein. 5th and 6th lord

Saturn is placed in the 11th house with 2nd and 9th lord Venus and, ascendant and 10th lord Mercury. Saturn is placed in *Puranvasu* constellation ruled by Jupiter. The Sun is the strongest planet in the birth chart acquiring 2.23 *shadabala*. In *Bhava* chart Saturn and the Sun are conjoined in the 10th house. So in *Bhava* chart, Moon, Jupiter, the Sun and Saturn are in quadrants. Venus is exalted in the *navamsa* chart. The major period of Saturn started on 27.02.1998 and will last till 27.02.2017 so it can be said that the major period of Saturn is quite beneficial for the native.

Case: Abraham Lincoln

Illustration : 14.4   *Horoscope No.: 101*

Date of birth : 12.02.1809   Time of birth : 07:32:00 hrs
Place of birth : Hardin   Lat 36:45 N Long 88:17 E
Ayanamsa   : 21:11:43   Sidereal Time : 17:07:34

Pln	Degree	Rasi	Nakshatra	Pad
Asc	17:58:37	Aqu	Satabhisha	4
Sun	2:18:01	Aqu	Dhanistha	3
Mon	6:19:44	Cap	Uttarasadha	3
Mar	4:18:30	Lib	Chitra	4
Mer	19:09:59	Aqu	Satabhisha	4
Jup	0:53:56	Pis	P Bhadrapad	4
Ven	16:18:31	Pis	U Bhadrapad	4
Sat	11:56:56	Sco	Anuradha	3
Rah (R)	15:04:53	Lib	Swati	3
Ket (R)	15:04:53	Ari	Bharani	1

Lagna Chart

```
       Jup Ven        Mon
          12           10
   Ket 1              9
          Sun Mer
             11
            2    8 Sat
             5
        3              7   Mar
        4              6   Rah
```

Navamsa Chart

```
                    Rah Mon
            1          11
      2                10
            Mer
             12
          3    9
             6
   Jup  4              8   Mar
        5              7   Ven
       Ket         Sat Sun
```

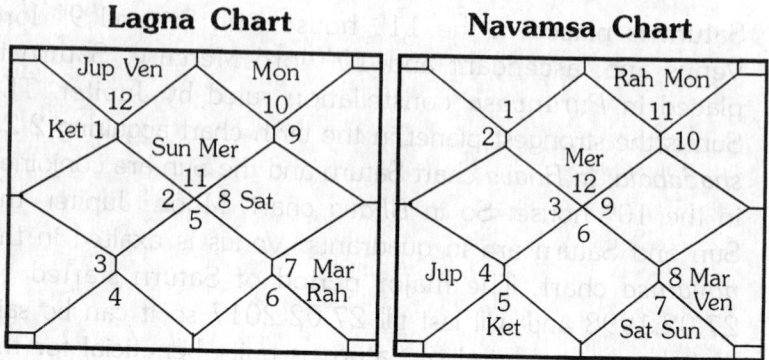

Balance of Vimshottari Dasa of **Sun   4Y 3M 17D**

Abraham Lincoln served as the 16th President of the United States from March 1861 until his assassination in April 1865. He successfully led his country through its greatest internal crisis, the American Civil War, preserving the Union and ending slavery. Before his election in 1860 as the first Republican president, Lincoln had been a country lawyer, an Illinois state legislator, a member of the United States House of Representatives, and twice an unsuccessful candidate for election to the U.S. Senate. As an outspoken opponent of the expansion of slavery in the United States, Lincoln won the Republican Party nomination in 1860 and was elected president later that year. His tenure in office was occupied primarily with the defeat of the secessionist Confederate States of America in the American Civil War. He introduced measures that resulted in the abolition of slavery, issuing his Emancipation Proclamation in 1863 and promoting the passage of the Thirteenth Amendment to the Constitution. Six days after the large-scale surrender of Confederate forces under General Robert E. Lee, Lincoln became the first American president to be assassinated.

Lincoln had closely supervised the victorious war effort, especially the selection of top generals, including Ulysses

S. Grant. Historians have concluded that he handled the factions of the Republican Party well, bringing leaders of each faction into his cabinet and forcing them to cooperate. Lincoln successfully defused the *Trent* affair, a war scare with Britain late in 1861. Under his leadership, the Union took control of the border slave states at the start of the war. Additionally, he managed his own reelection in the 1864 presidential election.

Copperheads and other opponents of the war criticized Lincoln for refusing to compromise on the slavery issue. Conversely, the Radical Republicans, an abolitionist faction of the Republican Party, criticized him for moving too slowly in abolishing slavery. Even with these opponents, Lincoln successfully rallied public opinion through his rhetoric and speeches; his Gettysburg Address (1863) became an iconic symbol of the nation's duty. At the close of the war, Lincoln held a moderate view of Reconstruction, seeking to speedily reunite the nation through a policy of generous reconciliation. Lincoln has consistently been ranked by scholars as one of the greatest of all U.S. Presidents.

Abraham Lincoln was born in *Uttarashadha* constellation ruled by the Sun. He was born in Aquarius ascendant with 7th lord the Sun and, 5th and 8th lord mercury placed therein. Venus is *yogakaraka* for Aquarius ascendant, being the lord of 4th and 9th house, is placed in the 2nd house in the sign of exaltation with *swakshetriya* Jupiter. Ascendant and 12th lord Saturn is placed in the 10th house in the sign of Mars, Scorpio and is not aspected by any planet. Saturn is exalted in the *navamsa* chart. Jupiter is also exalted in *navamsa* chart and Mars occupies own sign. Mercury and the Sun are debilitated in the *navamsa* chart. Saturn occupies its own constellation *Anuradha*, Mars occupies its own constellation *Chittra* as well as Jupiter also occupies its own constellation *Poorva Bhadrapada*.

Case: Indira Gandhi

Illustration : 14.5   *Horoscope No.: 102*

Date of birth : 19.11.1917   Time of birth : 23:33:00 hrs
Place of birth : Allahabad   Lat 25:27 N Long 81:50 E
Ayanamsa   : 22:42:52   Sidereal Time : 3:23:05

Pln	Degree	Rasi	Nakshatra	Pad
Asc	2:11:30	Leo	Magha	1
Sun	4:08:25	Sco	Anuradha	1
Mon	5:47:35	Cap	Uttarasadha	3
Mar	16:22:57	Leo	P Phalguni	1
Mer (C)	13:15:08	Sco	Anuradha	3
Jup (R)	15:00:00	Tau	Rohini	2
Ven	21:01:17	Sag	Purvasadha	3
Sat	21:47:15	Can	Aslesa	2
Rah	9:18:39	Sag	Moola	3
Ket	9:18:39	Gem	Ardra	1

Lagna Chart

		Sat 4	
6 7			3 Ket
Sun Mer 8	Mar 5 11	2 Jup	
Ven 9 Rah 10	Mon	12	1

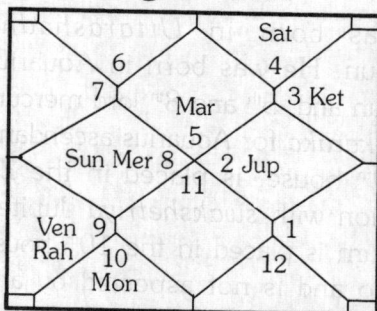

Navamsa Chart

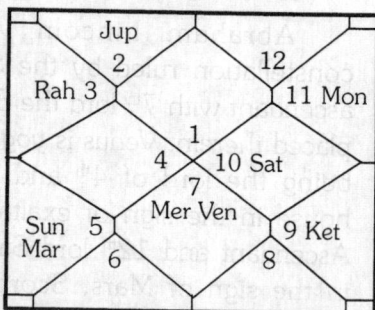

	Jup 2		12
Rah 3		1	11 Mon
	4 7	10 Sat	
Sun Mar 5	Mer Ven 6		9 Ket 8

Balance of Vimshottari Dasa of **Sun 1Y 10M 21D**

Mrs. Indira Gandhi was born in Capricorn Moon sign corresponding with *Uttara Shadha* constellation. There was a balance of the Sun's dasa at birth for 1 year 10 months and 20 days. She entered in the major period of Saturn on 10.10.1970. Major period of Saturn operated over her till her last breath i.e. 30.10.1984. It is needless to say that the major period of Saturn was the best period of Mrs. Indira Gandhi. She had a roaring and historical victory during the general elections of 1980. She became the Prime Minister of India from 1966 till 1977 for three consecutive terms and was re-elected as the Prime Minister of India in 1980 for the fourth term. Thus, Saturn's major period popular all over the globe for her hard, tough and unpopular decisions for the progressive advancement of the nation in all respects. She got roaring victory in the historical war with Pakistan in the year 1971 when Bangladesh was formed. Many such actions and decisions made her name immortal not only for India but it has also made an immortal mark in the history of the globe. She sacrificed her life for the nation due to her bold actions on 31.10.1984 during the sub period of Rahu in the major period of Saturn. Saturn and Rahu are in *khadashtaka* position and are killers. Thus, Mrs. Indira Gandhi who was born in sun's dasa enjoyed Saturn's dasa as the best period of her life.

Case : George Washington

Illustration : 14.6   *Horoscope No.: 103*

Date of birth : 22.02.1732   Time of birth : 10:00:00 hrs
Place of birth : San Francisco   Lat 37:46 N Long 122:25E
Ayanamsa   : 20:07:23   Sidereal Time : 19:57:49

Pln	Degree	Rasi	Nakshatra	Pad
Asc	24:58:25	Ari	Bharani	4
Sun	13:19:05	Aqu	Satabhisha	2
Mon	28:31:58	Sag	Uttarasadha	1
Mar	3:09:34	Sco	Vishakha	4

Mer	16:32:14	Cap	Sravna	2
Jup (R)	18:29:01	Vir	Hasta	3
Ven	9:26:22	Pis	U Bhadrapad	2
Sat	12:35:05	Pis	U Bhadrapad	3
Rah (R)	6:47:10	Sag	Moola	3
Ket (R)	6:47:10	Gem	Ardra	1

Lagna Chart

```
        Sat Ven
   2      12
Ket 3        11 Sun
        1
    4  10 Mer
    7
  5         9 Mon
  6       8  Rah
  Jup     Mar
```

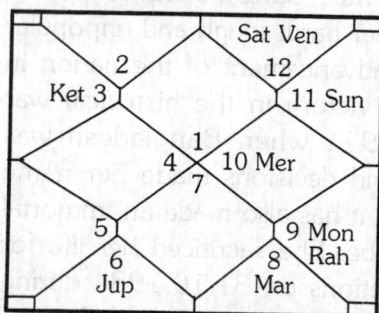

Navamsa Chart

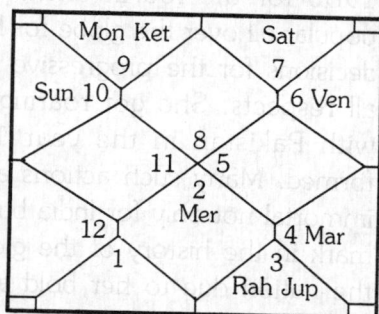

```
  Mon Ket      Sat
    9           7
Sun 10        6 Ven
         8
     11   5
          2
          Mer
   12          4 Mar
   1        3
          Rah Jup
```

Balance of Vimshottari Dasa of **Sun 5Y 1M 28D**

George Washington served as the first President of the United States from 1789 to 1797 and as the commander of the Continental Army in the American Revolutionary War from 1775 to 1783. Because of his significant role in the revolution and in the formation of the United States, he is often revered by Americans as the "Father of Our Country".

The Continental Congress appointed Washington commander-in-chief of the American revolutionary forces in 1775. The following year, he forced the British out of Boston, lost New York City, and crossed the Delaware River in New Jersey, defeating the surprised enemy units later that year. Because of his strategy, Revolutionary forces captured the two main British combat armies at Saratoga and Yorktown. Negotiating with Congress, the colonial states, and French allies, he held together a tenuous army and a fragile nation amid the threats of disintegration and failure. Following the end of the war in 1783, King George III asked what Washington would do next and was told of rumors that he would return to his farm; this prompted the king to state, "If he does that, he will be the greatest man in the world." Washington did return to private life and retired to his plantation at Mount Vernon.

He presided over the Philadelphia Convention that drafted the United States Constitution in 1787, because of general dissatisfaction with the Articles of Confederation. Washington became President of the United States in 1789 and established many of the customs and usages of the new government's executive department. He sought to create a nation capable of surviving in a world torn asunder by war between Britain and France. His unilateral Proclamation of Neutrality of 1793 provided a basis for avoiding any involvement in foreign conflicts. He supported plans to build a strong central government by funding the national debt, implementing an effective tax system, and creating a national bank. Washington avoided the temptation of war and a decade of peace with Britain began with the Jay Treaty in 1795; he used his prestige to get it ratified over intense opposition from the Jeffersonians. Although never officially joining the Federalist Party, he supported its programs and was its inspirational leader. Washington's farewell address was a primer on republican virtue and a stern warning against partisanship, sectionalism, and involvement in foreign wars. He was awarded the first Congressional Gold Medal in 1776.

Washington died in 1799. Henry Lee, delivering the funeral oration, declared Washington "first in war, first in peace, and first in the hearts of his countrymen". Historical scholars consistently rank him as one of the greatest United States presidents.

George Washington was born in Taurus ascendant *Uttarashadha* constellation, and was elected the first President of the United States of America unanimously on February 4th, 1789. His Saturn *Dasa* commenced on 26.4.1788. Therefore his elevation as the President took place during Saturn *dasa* Saturn *bhukti* in his 57th year. His Saturn is in the 11th house in Pisces with exalted Venus and aspected by Jupiter from the 5th.

From our analysis we can observe following facts:

1. For a native who is born in any of the constellations of the Sun, Saturn can occupy any sign in any ascendant, and without taking this into account, the native will reach to the zenith.

2. It is interesting to note that the rise takes place during the sub-periods of Saturn itself, Mercury or Venus. The sub periods of Venus, Saturn and Mercury come in order in raising the natives. It can be easily observed that Saturn gives the rise during the sub periods of its intimate friends, namely Venus and Mercury.

3. Where the native reaches the zenith during Jupiter *dasa*, Saturn helps the native to maintain the position during its own *dasa* or part of its *dasa*.

●

नीलाम्बरः शूलधरः किरीटी गृध्रस्थितस्त्रासकरो धनुष्मान् ।
चतुर्भुज सूर्यसुतः प्रशान्तः सदाऽस्तु मह्यं वरदोऽल्पगामी ।।

"The blue attired, carrying bow and lance, wearing a respondent crown, mounted on the vulture, four armed, terror-evoking, calm and slow moving mighty son of the Sun may always grant me my boons."

Bibliography

Acharya Mukund Daivagya "Jaatak Bhushanam", Ranjan Publications, New Delhi, 1993

Acharya Neeraj, "Vriddh Yavanjatakam", Ranjan Publications, New Delhi, 1994.

Balbhadra Mishra, "Hora Ratnam", Motilal Banarasi Dass Publishers Pvt. Ltd., Delhi, 1979.

Balmukund Pandeyen, "Phalit Prakash", Babu Baijnath Book Seller, Kashi

Bepin Bihari, "Astrological Biographies", Motilal Banarasi Dass Publishers Pvt. Ltd., Delhi.

Bepin Bihari, "The Timing of Events", Motilal Banarasi Dass Publishers Pvt. Ltd., Delhi.

Bhaskaracharya, "Bhav Deepika", Ranjan Publications, New Delhi

Bitthal Dixit, Muhurta Kalpdruma", Ranjan Publications, New Delhi, 2005.

Bhojraj Dwivedi, "Jyotish Yog Sahastri", Motilal Banarasi Dass Publishers Pvt. Ltd., Delhi, 2003.

B.S. Gupta, "Astrological Insights and Experiments", Divya Gyan Kendra, Kurukshetra, 1981.

B.S. Gupta, "Stars and Human Destiny", Sagar Publications, New Delhi

B.V. Raman (Dr.), "A Catechism of Astrology", Raman Publications, Bangalore, 1991.

B.V. Raman (Dr.), "Three Hundred Important Combinations", Motilal Banarasi Dass Publishers Pvt. Ltd., Delhi, 1991.

B.V. Raman (Dr.), "How to Judge A Horoscope (2 Parts)", Motilal Banarasi Dass Publishers Pvt. Ltd., Delhi, 1995.

B.V. Raman (DR.), "Grah Aur Bhavbal (Translation- Om Prakash Palival)", Motilal Banarasi Dass Publishers Pvt. Ltd., Delhi, 1999.

B.V. Raman (Dr.), "Jaatak Nirnaya", Motilal Banarasi Dass Publishers Pvt. Ltd., Delhi, 1995.

B.V. Raman (Dr.), "Notable Horoscopes", Motilal Banarasi Dass Publishers Pvt. Ltd., Delhi, 1995.

B.V. Raman (Dr.), "Hindu Predictive Astrology", IBH Prakashana, Bengaluru. 2009.

Chandra Dutt Pant, "Lagna Chandra Prakash", Motilal Banarasi Dass Publishers Pvt. Ltd., Delhi, 2004.

Col. A.K. Gour, "Professions (Inclination, Fructification and Career Profile)", Alpha Publication, Delhi, 2002.

462   *Bibliography*

Daya Shanker, Sharing With Parashar", The Times of Astrolgy, Nishkam Peeth Prakashan, 2005.

Devi Dutt Joshi, "Sugam Jyotish", Motilal Banarasi Dass Publishers Pvt. Ltd., Delhi, 1922.

Devaki Nandan Singh, "Jyotish Ratnakar", Motilal Banarasi Dass Publishers Pvt. Ltd., Delhi, 1983.

Dennis M. Harness David Frawley, "The Nakshatras", Motilal Banarasi Dass Publishers Pvt. Ltd., Delhi.

Dhundhiraj, "Jataka Bharanam", Ranjan Publications, New Delhi

Gauri Shanker Kapoor (Dr.), "Jatak Satyacharya", Ranjan Publications, New Delhi, 2003.

Gayatri Devi Vasudev, "Astrology and the Hoax of Scientific Temper", Motilal Banarasi Dass Publishers Pvt. Ltd., Delhi.

Girija Shankar Shastri (Dr.), "Bharatiya Kundali Vimarsh", Jyotish Karmkand Evam Adhyatm Shodh Sansthan, Allahabad.

Gopesh Kumar Ojha, "Triphala (Jyotisha)", Motilal Banarasi Dass Publishers Pvt. Ltd., Delhi, 1971.

Gopesh Kumar Ojha & Ashutosh Ojha, "The Solar Return or Varshaphal", Motilal Banarasi Dass Publishers Pvt. Ltd., Delhi, 1975.

Gopesh Kumar Ojha, "Sugam Jyotish "Praveshika, Motilal Banarasi Dass Publishers Pvt. Ltd., Delhi, 2002.

Gopesh Kumar Ojha & Ashutosh Ojha, "Aspects in Vedic Astrology", Motilal Banarasi Dass Publishers Pvt. Ltd., Delhi.

Gopesh Kumar Ojha & Ashutosh Ojha, "Astrology and You", Motilal Banarasi Dass Publishers Pvt. Ltd., Delhi, 2002.

Govind Shastri, "Jyotisha Rahasya", Sadhana Pocket Books, Delhi.

G.S. Agarwal, "Practical Vedic Astrology", Sagar Publications, New Delhi.

Harishankar Pathak (Dr.), "Dasaphal Darpan", Chowkhamba Surbharti Prakashan, Varanasi, 2007.

H.N. Katve, "Bhava Vichaar", Nagpur Prakashan, 1970.

H.N. Katave, "Griha Vichaar (Surya, Chandra, Mangal, Buddha, Guru, Shukra, Shani & Rahu-Ketu Griha Vichaar)", Nagpur Prakashan, 1975.

H.N. Katve, "Bhavesh Vichaar", Nagpur Prakashan, 1983.

H.N. Katve, "Dev Rahasya", Nagpur Prakashan, 1983.

Jagjeevan Dass Gupta, "Jyotish Rahasya", Motilal Banarasi Dass Publishers Pvt. Ltd., Delhi, 1985.

Jagjeevan Dass Gupta, "Dasaphal Vichaar", Motilal Banarasi Dass Publishers Pvt. Ltd., Delhi, 2008.

Jagannath Bhasin, "Phalit Sutra", Nav Bharat Printing Press, Delhi, 1974.

Jeevnath, "Bhaav Kutuhalam" (Ed.- Dr. Hari Shankar Pathak), Chowkhamba Surbharti Prakashan, Varanasi, 2004.

Jeevnath Ojha, "Bhava Prakash", Ranjan Publications, New Delhi

Kadalangudi Natesa Shastri, "Jataka Dwadasa Bhava Phala or Hindu Astrological Results", Kadalangudi Publications, Madras.

Kalyan Verma, "Saravali", Ranjan Publications, New Delhi, 1998

Kalidas, "Purva Kalamrita", Ranjan Publications, New Delhi, 1999.

Kalidas, "Uttar Kalamrit", Alpha Publication, Delhi, 2008.

Kalidas, "Jyotirvida Bharanam", Motilal Banarasi Dass Publishers Pvt. Ltd., Delhi, 2011.

Kailash Nath Upadhyay, "Janmang Phal Vichaar", Motilal Banarasi Dass Publishers Pvt. Ltd., Delhi.

Kailash Nath Upadhyay, "Jeevan Phal Darpan", Motilal Banarasi Dass Publishers Pvt. Ltd., Delhi.

Kevalanand Joshi, "Aap Aur Aapki Rashi", Motilal Banarasi Dass Publishers Pvt. Ltd., Delhi, 2000.

Khankhana, "Khetkautukam", Ranjan Publications, New Delhi, 2000.

Krishan Kumar, "Secrets of Varga", Alpha Publications, Delhi, 2002.

Krishna Kumar, "Shadvarg Phalam", Alpha Publications, Delhi, 2003.

Krishna Kumar, "Aajivika Vichaar (Jyotish ke Jharokha Se)", Alpha Publications, Delhi, 2004.

Krishna Kumar, "Bhavphal Vichaar", Alpha Publications, Delhi, 2010.

K.N. Rao, "Advanced Techniques of Astrological Predictions", Bhartiya Prachya Evam Sanatan Vigyan Sansthan, New Delhi.

K.K. Pathak, "Astrology of Professions (Principles and Practices—2 Parts)", Alpha Publications (Publishers), Delhi, 2007.

K. Subramaniam, "K.P. Krishman's Profession", Krishnan & Co., Chennai.

K.C. Saxena, "Venus in Astrology", Sagar Publications, New Delhi.

K.N. Rao, "Ups and Downs in Career", S. Kumar & Associates, Lucknow.

L.R. Choudhary, "Mars and Astrology", Sagar Publications, New Delhi.

L.R. Choudhry, "Transit of Planets", Sagar Publications, New Delhi.

— "Maan Sagari", Sagar Publications, New Delhi, 1954.

Maharishi Parashar, "Brihat Parashar Horoshashtra", Ranjan Publications, New Delhi, 2008.

Maharishi Bhatt Narayan, "Chamatkar Chintamani" (Ed.- Braj Bihari Lal Sharma), Motilal Banarasi Dass Publishers Pvt. Ltd., Delhi, 1981.

Mantreshwar, "Phala Deepika", Motilal Banarasi Dass Publishers Pvt. Ltd., Delhi, 1981.

Mahan Vir Yuli, "Predictive Astrology and Financial Prosperity", Gyan Sagar Publications, Delhi.

Mahendra Nath Kedar, "Bhava Nirnaya, Dasa Evam Gochar Dwara Samay Nirdharan", Bhartiya Prachya & Sanatan Vigyan Sansthan, New Delhi, *Samvat* 2059.

Mahendra Nath Kedar & Shankar Nath Kapoor, "Vivah ka Samay", Bhartiya Prachya Evam Sanatan Vigyan Sansthan, New Delhi, 2012.

M.N. Kedar, "Nine Planets & Twelve Bhavas their Effect on Human Life", Bhartiya Prachya Evam Sanatan Vigyan Sansthan, New Delhi, 2000.

Mukund Ballabh Mishra, "Shadvarga Phal Prakash", Motilal Banarasi Dass Publishers Pvt. Ltd., Delhi.

Mukund Daivagya, "Prasava Chintamani", Ranjan Publications, New Delhi, 1984.

Mukund Daivagya, "Bhava Manjari", Ranjan Publications, New Delhi, 2008.

M.S. Mehta, "Planets and Travel Abroad", Sagar Publications, New Delhi.

M.R. Bhatt, "Fundamentals of Astrology", Motilal Banarasi Dass Publishers Pvt. Ltd., Delhi.

M. Ramkrishna Bhatt (Prof.) (Translator), "Brihat Samhita (English)", Motilal Banarasi Dass Publishers Pvt. Ltd., Delhi

Nemichandra Jyotishacharya (Dr.), "Bhadrabahu Samhita", Bhartiya Gyanpeeth, New Delhi, 2009.

Nemichandra Shastri (Dr.), "Bhartiya Jyotish", Bhartiya Gyanpeeth, New Delhi, 2002.

Nimai Banerjee (Dr.), "Scaling Human Lives", Maa Parameswari Publications, Cuttack, 2001.

N.N. Saha, "Vocational Guidance Through Astrology", Fate & Destiny Publications, Jalandhar.

O.P. Verma, "Secrets of Vimshottari Dasa", Ranjan Publications, New Delhi, 1996.

O.P. Verma, "Profession Through Astrology", Ranjan Publications, New Delhi, 1994.

Pavan Chandoliya, "Jyotish Ke Anubhoot Rahasya", Motilal Banarasi Dass Publishers Pvt. Ltd., Delhi.

Padumnai Chomadri, "Jaatak Deshmarg", Motilal Banarasi Dass Publishers Pvt. Ltd., Delhi, 1992.

Peter West Jologan, "How to Judge a Nativity", Sagar Publications, New Delhi

Pt. Ramyal Ojha, "Phalit Vikas", Ranjan Publications, New Delhi.

Pt. Umashanker Dubey, "Saral Jyotish Gyan", Jagannath Publishing House, Kanpur, 1993.

Pt. Maheedhar Sharma," Shambhu Horaprakash", Khemraj Srikrishna Dass, 1998.

Pt. Mukund Ballabh Mishra, "Phalit Martand", Motilal Banarasi Dass Publishers Pvt. Ltd., Delhi, 1968

Pt. Mahadev Pathak, "Jatak Tatvam", Ranjan Publications, New Delhi, 1988.

Pt. Ramswaroop Sharma, "Jyotisha Sarva Sangrah", Jawahar Book Depot, Meerut, *Samvat* 2052.

Pt. Suryakant Siddhanti, "Brihajjyotissar", Thakur Prasad, Varanasi, 1978.

Pt. Laxmikant Kanyal, "Jyotitatva Prakash", Motilal Banarasi Dass Publishers Pvt. Ltd., Delhi, 2004.

Pt. Sohan Lal Vyas, "Muhurta Parijat", Chowkhambha Vidya Bhawan, 2006.

Prem Kumar Sharma, "The Stars and Your Profession", Rupa & Co., New Delhi.

Prithu Yasho, "Shatpanchashika", Ranjan Publications, New Delhi, 2007.

Prithu Yasho, "Horasaar", Ranjan Publications, New Delhi, 1982.

P.V.R. Rayudu, How to Match Horoscopes for Marriage", Motilal Banarasi Dass Publishers Pvt. Ltd., Delhi.

P.V.R. Rayudu, "How to Read a Horoscope", Motilal Banarasi Dass Publishers Pvt. Ltd., Delhi.

Ramanujacharya, "Bhavarth Ratnakar", U.B.S. Publishers' Distributors Ltd. , 2005.

Ram Dayalu, "Sanket Nidhi", Ranjan Publications, New Delhi, 2003.

R. Santhanam, "Essentials of Astrology", Sagar Publications, New Delhi

R. Santhanam, "Jyotisharnava Navanitam", R. Santhanam Associates, New Delhi.

Rawal Harishankar Surisunu Ganapati, "Muhurta Ganapati", Motilal Banarasi Dass Publishers Pvt. Ltd., Jawahar Nagar, Delhi, 1988.

R.G. Rao, "Profession from the Position of Planets", Sagar Publications, New Delhi, 1995.

Sage Bhrigu, "Bhrigu Sutram" (Ed.-Dr. Gauri Shanker Kapoor), Ranjan Publications, New Delhi, 1981.

Satyacharya, "Satya Jatakam", Ranjan Publications, New Delhi, 2003.

Shankar Adawal (Dr.), "Your Profession (Ups and Downs with Remedial Measures)", Sagar Publications, New Delhi, 2006.

Shailendra Sharma, "Vitta Evam Vratti Prabandh", Mukund Prakashan, Jaipur.

Shailendra Sharma, "Sitaron Ke Sitare", Mukund Prakashan, Jaipur, 1999.

Sri Ganesh Kavi, "Jatakalankar", Ranjan Publications, New Delhi, 1992.

Sriram Daivagya, "Muhurta Chintamani", Chowkhambha Vidya Bhawan, 1972.

Suresh Chandra Mishra, "Jyotisha Sarvasva", Ranjan Publications, New Delhi, 2014.

S.G. Khot, "Jyotish Aur Parivar Niyojan", Motilal Banarasi Dass Publishers Pvt. Ltd., Delhi, 2000.

S.G. Khot, "Laghu Parashari Siddhant", Motilal Banarasi Dass Publishers Pvt. Ltd., Delhi.

S.G. Khot, "Vividh Yoga Chandra Prakash", Motilal Banarasi Dass Publishers Pvt. Ltd., Delhi.

S.P. Walia, "Astrological Guidance to Occupations", D.B. Taraporevala Sons & Co. Pvt. Ltd., Bombay, 1983.

S.S. Chatterjee, "Fortune and Finance", Alpha Publications, Delhi, 2002.

Sukhdev Chaturvedi, "Jyotish Shastra Mein Rog Vichaar", Motilal Banarasi Dass Publishers Pvt. Ltd., Delhi, 1984.

Sumeet Chugh, "Determining Profession and Ups & Downs in Career", Sagar Publications, New Delhi.

Sunita Jha, "Yoga Pushpanjali", Alpha Publications, Delhi, 2003.

— "The Prediction Book of Astrology", Gaurav Publishing House, New Delhi.

Uday Kant Misra (Dr.) & Col. A.K. Gour, "Introduction of Astrology", Alpha Publications, Delhi, 2007.

U.S. Pullippani (Dr.), "Gochar Phal Deepika", Alpha Publications (Publishers), Delhi, 2002.

Vaidyanath, "Jatak Parijat" (Ed.- Dr. Suresh Chandra Mishra), Ranjan Publications, New Delhi, 1979

Varahmihir, "Daivagya Vallabha", Ranjan Publications, New Delhi, 1983.

Varahmihir, "Laghu Jatakam", Chowkhamba Surbharti Prakashan, Varanasi, 1989.

Varahmihir, "Brihajjatakam", Motilal Banarasi Dass Publishers Pvt. Ltd., Delhi, 1994.

Venkatesh Sharma, "Sarvarth Chintamani", Chowkhamba Surbharti Prakashan, Varanasi, 2010

V.K. Chaudhary (Prof.), "Systems Approach for Interpreting Horoscopes", Sagar Publications, New Delhi, 2002.

V.K. Choudhry & K. Rajesh Choudhry, "How to Avert Professional Setbacks", Sagar Publications, New Delhi, 2011.

V.K. Choudhary (Prof.), "Self Learning Course In Astrology", Sagar Publications, New Delhi. 2014.

V. Raghuraman, "Vedic Nadi Astrology & Career", Sterling Publications Pvt. Ltd., Delhi.

Books written by
Mrs. Mridula Trivedi & T.P. Trivedi